The Modern Girl's Guide to Life,

Revised Edition

The Modern Girl's Guide to Life,

Revised Edition

More Modern. More Tips. More Fun!

Jane Buckingham

WILLIAM MORROW

An Imprint of HarperCollins*Publishers*

Also by Jane Buckingham:

The Modern Girl's Guide to Sticky Situations
What's Next; The Experts' Guide
What's Next: Predictions from 50 of America's Most Compelling People
The Modern Girl's Guide to Motherhood
The Modern Girl's Guide to Life

HarperCollins books may be purchased for educational, business, or sales promotional use. For information please e-mail the Special Markets Department at SPsales@harpercollins.com.

An Avon Books Trade Paperback Edition was published in 2004.

FIRST WILLIAM MORROW TRADE PAPERBACK EDITION

Book design by Judith Stagnitto Abbate / Abbate Design
Illustrations on page 54 by Russ Maschmeyer

The Library of Congress has cataloged the original edition as follows:

Buckingham, Jane.
    The modern girl's guide to life / Jane Buckingham.— 1st ed.
      p. cm.
    ISBN 0-06-073416-7 (alk. paper)
    1. Young women—Conduct of life. 2. Young women—Life skills guides.
    3. Self-perception in women. I. Title.
    HQ1229.82 2004
    646.7'0084'22—dc22   2004046892

ISBN 978-0-06-236296-4

15 16 17 18 19 DIX/RRD 10 9 8 7 6 5 4 3 2 1

To Marcus:

Because every Modern Girl should be
lucky enough to have one

Contents

Acknowledgments

Every Modern Girl needs a little help from her friends, and this girl required more than most:

First, to those who have loved Modern Girl since she was "born" and have asked for more and stayed loyal to her and me: I can't tell you how much that means. I thank you so much for loving her as much as I do.

Riann Smith is so much of the heart, soul, and body of this book (and boy, what a body). If you loved this book, much of it is her spirit that you are loving. To say I couldn't have done it without her is a huge understatement.

Emma Stevens Smith, Kristin Jones, and Jessica Blumenthal made updating this book as much fun as a weekend at the beach, literally. I couldn't have done this, or practically anything else in my life, without them. I wish I could have them as my sisters; I feel very lucky to call them my friends.

Liz Gray, Romi Lassally, and Renee Lee gave me ideas, edits, and so much support and helped me keep the trains rolling—and occasionally put them back on the tracks.

Kaye Kramer believed there was still more Modern Girl to come.

Turns out she was right. Thank you for always being such a supportive friend.

Kara Zauberman managed to decipher my scribbles and inserts. She's no editor—she's psychic. Thank you.

Kristin Bennett knows how to find information better than any detective or government agency. There are tips and tricks she found that make this book a hundred times stronger than it would have been without her. I can never thank her enough for her devotion and time.

Jen Furmaniak is a Modern Girl to her soul. She doesn't need to read about this stuff—she lives it. Her edits, intolerance of vagueness, and wry sense of humor made every chapter stronger.

Joni Evans took up where my mother left off. I wouldn't dare ask her how to darn a sock, but her guidance, support, wisdom, and love mean more than a million book advances ever could. To call her an agent sounds cliché. To call her a mom would piss her off. So we'll leave it at fairy godmother.

Andi McNicol showed me how to convince a generation of pre-pared women that my generation needed a book like this. Without a proposal there would have been no book. Without Andi, there would have been no proposal. She continues to endlessly support me and my ideas. We've grown in this business. I've gotten older, she's gotten wiser.

Thank you, Justin Ongert and Richard Weitz, for getting me and Modern Girl back on the air. Oh, don't stress. I'm patient.

Cassie Jones has stuck with me for years. And I am eternally grateful for her loyalty to me and to Modern Girl.

She was more than an editor; she was a mini—Martha Stewart, coming up with facts, tips, and insights I would never have thought of.

Kary McHoul believed in Modern Girl when everyone else thought I was nuts. Without her, Modern Girl may have never seen the light of day.

Rebecca McQuigg not only found great tips but helped me find time to write the darn thing.

Julie and Mark Rowen are the Modern Couple one would love to be—with a perfect son, Luke, to match. And Karen and Ben Sherwood are inspirations in so many ways.

Kate White showed me that you can hold down a full-time job, raise two wonderful kids, and write books on the side. I still don't know how she does it.

To Mindy, Mark, Melanie, Dianne, and everyone else at Style and E! who helped bring *The Modern Girl* to life, thanks for believing in it the way you did.

My close friends Debbie Hutman, Clare Ramsey, Barbara Coulon, Melissa Thomas, Dana Oliver, Andrea Brokaw, Amanda Freeman, and Danyelle Freeman helped keep me honest and sane, and each provided nuggets I was amazed to learn.

Linda and Mitch Hart offer the kind of love and support every child dreams of. I'm so lucky to have found them. I only hope they didn't read the chapter on sex!

Dad, Beth, and Paul, unfortunately I still can't cook. . . . Thanks for tolerating endless Chinese food.

My mother-in-law, Jo, and sister-in-law, Pippa, helped me without making me feel inadequate. Pretty amazing. I'm lucky to have them in my life.

My brother, Michael, supports me in everything I do, everything I forget to do, and for just being me. Could a Modern Girl ask for more?

My children, Jack and Lilia, make being a modern mom far more important than being a Modern Girl. I love you. You were so little when this book came out. And ten years later I couldn't be more proud of who you've become.

Marcus. I could fill a book with acknowledgments to you. For love, for support, for being my everything—and for always forgiving (or not noticing) my incompetence. I love you even more today than I did ten years ago.

And to my mom, how I wish you could be here. I love you.

Introduction

All right, this is hard to admit, but I know very little. Well, that's not exactly true. I know a lot about finding a good job, getting ahead in business, and dealing with corporate politics. I've started and sold one successful company and someday may start another. I can tell you the designer must-have boots for the season—and which knockoffs look exactly the same. But I won't watch Nigella Lawson, Katie Brown, or any other kitchen maven because they terrify me, and I live in fear that my mother-in-law will recognize my complete failings as a wife and mother and encourage my fabulous husband to dump me for someone who majored in home ec. I dread the day my son asks me whether all families eat out of Chinese food containers three nights a week. So no matter how many promotions I get, no matter how adorable the family photos, no matter how witty my cocktail conversation, I will always feel like a failure.

And I'm not the only one. This new dirty little secret pervades women in their twenties and thirties. While my generation was being bred to be superwomen and shoot up the corporate ladder, no one bothered to teach us how to clean the ladder, fix the broken rungs, or look presentable when we reached the top. I blame my mother. Now, mind you, she couldn't have been a better mother. She gave me confidence, an education, ambition, and unconditional love. She just refused to teach me how to iron ("Iron? That's what held women back!" she would say), or make a bed properly, or stock a pantry, or pick out a decent bra that fit.

Yet ironically, we motivated women of the new millennium are finding that while we know how to bring home the bacon, we don't have the slightest clue how to fry it up in a pan. And while I'm certainly not saying we want to backslide into the domestic misery of the fifties, there is a renewed emphasis on niceties like arranging flowers, creating a welcoming guest room, or having at least one recipe we can impress a date with. That's not even counting the triumphs we've achieved. We can buy our own jewelry (if only we knew how to not get ripped off), art (ditto), and insurance (but what does a gal *really* need?), and we're supposed to know how to change a tire (but isn't that what AAA's for?).

We're not trying to be June Cleaver. We're just trying to get by.

So enter *The Modern Girl's Guide to Life*. It's everything busy women need to know in one place. It gives answers to the questions you're too embarrassed to ask and most reference books assume you already know (yup, it takes three minutes to soft-boil an egg, eight to hard-boil). It's information that can help you feel more refined, more in charge, more together. It's learning the basics—and just a bit beyond. It's giving you the shortcuts without making you feel as if you cheated (like putting a few drops of Clorox in a vase to help those flowers last longer, since no one really changes the water every other day). It's dispelling the myths that we need to abolish. (Did you know that you are not supposed to send a thank-you note if you've thanked the giver in person? Thank-you notes, according to Miss Manners, are meant to acknowledge gifts that have not been acknowledged . . . not waste time and countless forests.)

The Modern Girl's Guide to Life will let you cheat without getting caught—or even feel like you're cheating. It's about helping you juggle the demands placed on a Modern Girl gracefully, easily, and perhaps even confidently. It's knowing what to do whether you're entertaining, interviewing for a job, or trying to use a power drill. It's a combination of research from experts, advice from friends, tried-and-true secrets handed down through families, and even a few things I knew on my own. It's living for dummies and living the best life you deserve. If nothing else, it will teach me how to be the Modern Girl I (and my mother) always hoped I might be.

CHAPTER 1

The Only Thing You Should Ever Fake . . . Being a Domestic Goddess

I'll admit it: The words *domestic goddess* give me a panic attack. Maybe it's because I consider myself a twenty-first-century career chick who's better at making spreadsheets than folding bedsheets. Or maybe it's because the idea of spending eight gazillion hours of my (nonexistent) free time fashioning swan-shaped soufflés and embroidered his-and-hers laundry bags just doesn't sound like a party to me.

The problem is I want to revive the traditions that made me feel at home as a little girl. I want my mother-in-law to know that her son isn't living one step up from a hostel, my children to realize that dinner doesn't have to come from a delivery boy, and my houseguests to enjoy staying with me, rather than balking: "No, really, Jane! We'll just stay at a hotel!" But the more I try to make my house the perfect example of domestic goddestry, the more befuddled I become.

Meanwhile, so many of my friends seem ridiculously "together" on the home front. Take my friend Brooke, for example. Every time I walk into her home, there are tuberose Diptyque candles burning, fresh flowers in clean glass vases in every room, and freshly folded towels in her bathroom . . . rolled in a basket, just like the B&Bs do it.

The second I sink into her (vacuumed) couch, she always offers me something freshly baked or freshly squeezed from her kitchen. Her pantry, medicine cabinets, and closets are perfectly organized (I snooped, sue me). And she doesn't just go into Martha mode when she knows company's coming over—her abode has looked equally abundant when I've dropped by unexpectedly. On top of that, she holds down a demanding nine-to-seven job at a law firm. I admit, all of that je ne sais quoi she had for chic living started making me feel resentful . . . and increasingly horrified to invite her and her husband to my own messy digs. That is until the night I got it out of her over cocktails: She has a housekeeper. Twice a week. Who cooks. Everything.

So there you have it. Not all domestic goddesses are quite as savvy as they seem. It's fairly reassuring, no? Sure, some women are more naturally adept at keeping house than others (surely Brooke surpasses me). But what I've recently learned is that being a modern (aka "mock") domestic goddess isn't about doing it all: it's about taking shortcuts to give the impression of having it all. And all you need to do is get a little more organized, learn some kitchen basics, and cut a few corners here and there. Not only will these tips and tricks streamline your life, you'll probably feel just a tad more in control of your day-to-day. Because while a girl's identity doesn't revolve around playing little miss homemaker anymore (thank God!), knowing that you *can* do a flawless load of laundry, whip up a fabulous dish fast, keep your palace in order, nip a vino stain in the bud, and play hostess like a pro will give you confidence that you've got your *entire* act together (and will impress everyone, especially you). Here's your crash course in domestic goddestry.

Welcome to the Scariest Room in a Modern Girl's House . . . the Kitchen!

Let's face it: Our purses often contain more items than our fridges do. And when we do go to the kitchen to make a meal, our grub tends to fall within the four basic Modern Girl food groups: booze, baby carrots, microwave popcorn, and leftover takeout. Now, there's a legit reason for it all—we're just too busy to cook up something elaborate. But if you know what to stock up on beforehand, and can get it all in one time-saving trip to the market, you may find yourself more inspired to let your inner chef come out to play.

Things You Need in Your Kitchen

No need to outfit the room like Williams-Sonoma or a five-star restaurant, but certain props and utensils will make a difference:

You Really Should Have

- Blender (skip the dicer-slicer—blenders can do most things)
- Dish rack
- Manual can opener
- Microwave
- Toaster oven (comes in handy if you need to cook two things at once at different temps)
- Timer (but many ovens and microwaves have them built in)
- Coffeemaker
- French press

Preparing/Cooking

- Cheese grater
- Chopping board*
- Cookie sheet[†]
- Colander[‡]
- Garlic press
- Kitchen shears
- Knives[§]
  - 6-inch chef's knife (and ideally also a 4-inch pantry knife and an 8-inch knife, but it depends on how violent you get)
  - Serrated bread knife
- Measuring spoons
- Meat tenderizer

*MG TIP: New information suggests that wood is better than plastic. Evidently the wood itself contains properties that help to kill bacteria. However, the one downside of wood is that you can't toss it in the dishwasher, so be sure to hand-wash thoroughly.

[†] MG TIP: A Silpat goes over your cookie sheet and truly keeps everything from sticking. Buy one at Amazon.

[‡] MG TIP: Skip the strainer—it's more important to have the big one.

[§] MG TIP: Don't put your knives in the dishwasher—it dulls them.

*MG TIP: Plastic mixing bowls are easier to lift and pour, but if you're short on cash, buy decent ceramic ones that can double as serving dishes.

†MG TIP: I prefer GreenPans, made with a ceramic-based nonstick material that is supposed to be more environmentally friendly than traditional non-stick. A good friend swears by stainless-steel pans that have hollow handles, which also don't get very hot. Try Target for good deals.

‡MG TIP: I also recommend getting a cast-iron skillet (the older the better) for high-heat cooking. Cooking juices and grease sink in, adding flavor to whatever you cook next. If you're lucky enough to swipe your grandma's, you're golden. If you get a new one, cook something greasy like bacon or ham to help give it a head start. And don't even think of washing it; simply wipe it down with paper towels after use.

MG TIP: Every Modern Girl should also have a Dutch oven or a Crock-Pot handy. Cooking with them is almost impossible to mess up—just throw in all the ingredients in the morning and you'll have a meal waiting for you by the time you get home.

- Glass measuring cup for liquid measurement
- Measuring cups for dry ingredients (but you *can* live without these)
- Microwave-safe dish
- Mixing bowls (1, 3, and 5 quarts)*
- Muffin pan
- Pastry brush
- Pots and pans†
  - Small saucepan (1½ quarts)
  - Large saucepan (3 quarts)
  - Large stockpot (8 quarts)
  - Large roasting pan
  - 9 × 9-inch baking pan
  - Cast-iron skillet‡
- Rubber spatula
- Stirring spoons—one metal *and* one wood
- Slotted spoon
- Tongs
- Vegetable peeler
- Wire whisk

Serving

- Bottle opener
- Corkscrew
- Salad tongs
- Serving fork and spoon
- 2 large bowls (for pasta, soup, or salad)—ideally with lids
- 2 small bowls (for side dishes and condiments)
- Large tray (for serving meats or chicken)
- Soup ladle
- Salt and pepper mill

MG TIP: Plating your meal (putting everything on the plate before you bring it out) is a great way to avoid needing a lot of serving pieces and it also allows you to control portions (so everyone gets enough) and presentation!

Storing

- Wine stoppers
- Plastic wrap, wax paper, aluminum foil, and plastic storage bags
- Assorted glass storage containers*

Extra Credit to Have Around

- Kitchen scale
- Vegetable brush
- Lemon zester
- Citrus reamer or hand juicer
- Meat thermometer

*MG TIP: Go with glass storage containers instead of plastic. They ultimately cost less since they last longer and are better for the environment. Just remember to stick with one brand so you don't wind up with tops that don't fit bottoms, missing lids, and frustration.

MEASUREMENTS

No, we don't mean bust and height. These are all of those measurements you think don't matter, but actually do.

1 pinch = just under ⅛ teaspoon (dry)
1 dash = 3 drops and just under ⅛ teaspoon (liquid)
3 teaspoons = 1 tablespoon = ½ fluid ounce
2 tablespoons = 1 fluid ounce = ⅛ cup
4 tablespoons = 2 fluid ounces = ¼ cup
16 tablespoons = 1 cup = ½ pint = 8 fluid ounces
2 cups = 1 pint = 16 fluid ounces
4 cups = 2 pints = 1 quart = 32 fluid ounces
8 cups = 4 pints = ½ gallon = 64 fluid ounces
4 quarts = 1 gallon = 128 fluid ounces

How to Stock a Pantry

First things first: Keep your pantry cool—foods will keep longer and stay fresher. Ideally, it should be away from the stove and refrigerator motor. Store everything in airtight containers—plastic tubs are easiest—to prevent spillage and keep out bugs. Here's what you'll need:

MG TIP: Canned foods, salsa, maple and chocolate syrups, mustard, ketchup, tomato paste and sauce, pickles, olives, red pepper flakes, and chili powder should be refrigerated after opening. Pure honey and pure maple syrup, however, should *not* be refrigerated.

Baking powder
Baking soda (and no, they're not the same thing)
Canned soups/beans/chili
Canned veggies
Canned whole tomatoes
Chicken stock or bouillon cubes
Chips, crackers, cookies, popcorn
Chocolate chips
Cornmeal
Dried beans, peas, lentils
Dried fruits
Dry soup mixes
Extracts: vanilla, lemon, almond
Flour
Herbs and spices (basil, chili powder, chives, cinnamon, cumin, mint, nutmeg, oregano, paprika, parsley, red pepper flakes, rosemary, summer savory, tarragon, thyme)
Hot chocolate mix
Nonstick cooking spray
Nuts (except pine nuts, which should be refrigerated)
Olive oil
Pancake mix
Pasta
Pepper/peppercorns
Rice
Salt
Sugar (white granulated, brown, *and* powdered)
Syrups: maple, honey, chocolate
Tea
Tomato paste and sauce
Worcestershire sauce

MG TIP: Every Modern Girl should have Wondra flour (comes in a 13.5-ounce shaker made by Gold Medal) in her cupboard. Just a few shakes and your sauce thickens up pronto.

Cooking 101

What's a kitchen full of items if you don't know how to put them to delicious use? Here's a cooking terms cheat sheet to get you started:

Bake: Cooking in the oven by dry heat. For meats, it's called roasting.

Baste: To moisten food during cooking with pan drippings, water, or sauces in the oven.

Blanch: To cook food quickly in boiling water on the stove, then take if off the stove and cool with an ice bath.

Braise: To brown in a small amount of hot fat on the stove, then add a small amount of liquid and cook slowly, covered tightly, on the stove or in the oven.

Broil: To cook by direct heat from above, usually in the broiler.

Brown: To cook meat on the stove at a high temperature to brown the outside before baking or sautéing.

Caramelize: To melt sugar slowly over low heat on the stove until the sugar browns.

Marinate: To allow a food to stand in a liquid to soften or add flavor.

Pan-broil: To cook, uncovered, in a hot frying pan on the stove top, pouring off fat as it accumulates.

Poach: To cook in hot liquid on the stove top so that food holds its shape (often done to fruit, eggs, or salmon).

Reduce: To cook a sauce until much of the liquid is evaporated.

Roast: See baking, above.

Sauté: To cook in a small amount of hot fat—such as butter or oil—on the stove.

Scallop: To bake a food, usually in a casserole with a sauce or other liquid.

Sear: To brown quickly over intense heat on the stove. The food will shrink but get fab flavor.

Simmer: To cook slowly in liquid over low heat on the stove. The surface of the liquid will show tiny bubbles.

Stew: To simmer slowly in a small amount of liquid for a long time, usually in the oven.

MG TIP: More and more studies are being released on what kinds of oils are healthy for cooking. Not all oils stand up to heat, and you want to make sure your oil doesn't oxidize (convert into trans fat!) when the temperature rises. Use coconut oil, avocado oil, or red palm oil for high heat, and extra-virgin olive oil, sesame seed oil, or peanut oil for low to medium heat.

Be a Modern Eco-Princess

Being eco-friendly and organic has come a long way since I first wrote this book. At the time, wearing Birkenstocks meant you spent your time hugging trees and chewing the bark, not carrying a cool FEED tote and wearing Stella McCartney. Somewhere along the way, we finally realized that we could actually look good, feel good, and do good all at the same time.

But since most of us are still unable to fork over our entire paycheck at Whole Foods, totally give up leather, and be fully eco-everything, here are a few of the musts for being an eco-princess.

First Rule of (Green) Thumb: Buying Organic

When it comes to organic, everyone talks about the dirty dozen, and they don't mean your ex-boyfriends. They mean the foods with the highest levels of pesticides. Here they are:

1. Peaches

2. Apples

3. Sweet bell peppers

4. Celery

5. Nectarines

6. Strawberries

7. Cherries

8. Pears

9. Grapes (imported)

10. Spinach

11. Lettuce

12. Potatoes

But should you really care? Well, *not* using pesticides means that we'll wind up with healthier soil, water, and wildlife. Good, right?

Plus, when we buy organic, we support small farmers, who typically earn a fairer price for organic produce versus factory farming. And even though the research is inconclusive on whether eating organic food is healthier for people, it seems pretty obvious that *not* eating pesticides (which kill things) is better than eating them. After all, USDA tests show that even after washing, most nonorganic produce contains residual pesticides. I mean, *yuck*.

And if you're thinking you're going to have to choose between a new pair of Louboutins and organic lettuce, don't worry. You don't have to go to the fancy food store these days to get organic. Many big grocery stores, like Ralphs, Vons, Kroger, Albertsons, Pavilions, and Winn-Dixie, carry organic lines that are just as good.

That said, sometimes a Modern Girl has to roll with a super-tight budget, so if you want to cut a few corners and not buy organic, opt for foods with the thickest skins. The "cleanest" fruits and veggies include:

1. Onions

2. Avocados

3. Sweet corn (frozen)

4. Pineapples

5. Mangoes

6. Asparagus

7. Sweet peas (frozen)

8. Kiwi

9. Bananas

10. Cabbage

11. Broccoli*

12. Papaya

---

*Typically broccoli doesn't retain that many pesticides because the crop faces fewer pest threats, meaning less spraying.

While we're getting healthy, you should probably know the superfoods you should try to eat as much of as possible. And while sadly Skittles are not on the list, there are plenty of things I actually like that are. I asked Pamela Salzman, natural foods cooking instructor and certified holistic health counselor, whom seemingly every celebrity and woman in L.A. is turning to for cooking classes and nutritional advice, for some thoughts. After all, she can make pretty much anything healthy taste so good it seems like it shouldn't be. Here's what she said.

According to Pamela, which superfoods are the most important is somewhat debatable, but hers would be:

- Cruciferous vegetables (broccoli, cauliflower, cabbage, bok choy, etc.)
- Blueberries
- Wild salmon
- Spinach
- Sweet potatoes
- Turmeric
- Oats
- Chia seeds
- Black beans, as well as kidney and pinto beans
- Free-range-chicken eggs

Besides the well-known superfoods, here are a few more foods she thinks we should definitely be eating:

Kale

A member of the cabbage family, kale is loaded with health-promoting sulfur compounds, and it has been found to have the highest antioxidant capacity of all fruits and vegetables. It's an amazing source of vitamins K, A, and C, as well as manganese, and a very good source of dietary fiber, calcium, iron, and potassium. All for very few calories! Supermarkets generally stock curly kale, the variety with the green ruffled leaves. Keep an eye out for other varieties, including the dark green cavolo nero (aka Tuscan kale), plum-red Redbor kale, and red Russian kale, which has purplish leaves and red veins. They can usually be used interchangeably. How to use kale:

- In a raw salad
- Sautéed with garlic and olive oil
- Roasted into crispy chips
- Stirred into soups or tomato sauce
- Juiced for a green drink

Pamela was also nice enough to let me have one of her coveted recipes.

Raw Kale Salad with Citrus Dressing

2 bunches black kale (aka Tuscan, lacinato, or dinosaur kale), 12 to 14 ounces,
    washed and dried
Optional add-ins: Toasted pine nuts or sunflower seeds, pomegranate seeds,
    dried cranberries, crumbled feta, chopped avocado, cooked quinoa

Dressing

2 teaspoons minced shallot
½ teaspoon fine sea salt
Freshly ground black pepper
2 tablespoons fresh lemon juice or unseasoned rice vinegar
2 tablespoons fresh orange juice
2 teaspoons 100% pure maple syrup
6 or 7 tablespoons unrefined, cold-pressed extra-virgin olive oil

Strip the kale leaves from the stems and compost or discard the stems. Finely shred the leaves with a sharp knife. Place in a serving bowl.

Prepare the dressing: Whisk all the ingredients in a small bowl until emulsified or place all dressing ingredients in a glass jar with a lid and shake until emulsified.

Add enough dressing to coat the kale lightly. Massage the dressing into the kale leaves with your hands to soften the leaves. Add your favorite salad fixings. Can be made a day or even two days ahead.

MG TIP: There's much more to olive oil than virgin and extra virgin. When using it as a dressing in a salad like my kale salad, it's important to have a quality bottle. Check out a specialty store; they'll have experts who can help you discover your new favorite flavor. I promise it's worth the splurge!

Coconut Oil

After suffering a bad rap for years because of its saturated fat content, coconut oil is now known to contain medium-chain fatty acids, which are used by your body quickly as energy, as opposed to being stored as fat. It contains lauric acid, also found in breast milk, which has been shown to improve digestion, strengthen the immune system, and protect against bacterial, viral, and fungal infections. Look for "unrefined" or "virgin." Raw coconut oil smells tropical, but once you cook with it, it just adds a subtle sweetness without imparting a coconut flavor. A bonus is that it has a high smoke point and can withstand higher-heat cooking. How to use it:

- Stovetop popcorn
- Cooking pancakes and French toast
- Chicken and vegetable curry
- Granola
- Baked goods
- Roasting vegetables like cauliflower and sweet potatoes
- As a skin moisturizer (just be sure to rub it in well, as I stained my favorite J.Crew shorts once)

Quinoa

Although used as a grain, quinoa (pronounced KEEN-wah) is a tiny, ancient seed native to South America that has a mild, nutty flavor and bouncy texture. It is gluten-free and super high in protein because it contains all the essential amino acids. Rinse the seeds well, because they are naturally coated with a bitter substance that protects them against birds and other predators. Quinoa cooks in fifteen minutes, after which time its telltale white thread curls from around the seed. How to use it:

- In place of less nutritious orzo or couscous
- Sprinkled in a salad
- As a breakfast cereal
- Added to pancake batter
- In a veggie burger

Avocado

It may surprise you that avocados are high in protein, enzymes, fiber, potassium, and vitamin E as well as healthy fats. The fats in avocados, like those in olives and nuts, are mostly monounsaturated fats—particularly oleic acid, the primary fat in olive oil. Avocados are rich and creamy and not just for guacamole! How to use them:

- Smooshed on top of toast with tomato and/or smoked salmon
- Blended into a smoothie
- On top of salad or an omelet
- In a sandwich or tacos
- Mashed up as baby food
- Stirred into salsa

Seaweed

Seaweed contains a tremendous concentration of minerals, far more than are contained in land vegetables. It's a great source of vitamin B, magnesium, iron, folate, and calcium. Several varieties contain high levels of iodine, which is essential in regulating the thyroid. Interesting fact: Seaweed contains all the minerals found in human blood, as the minerals in seawater are similar to those found in our blood, with nearly identical concentrations. Different varieties you may find in the grocery store are nori, kombu (kelp), arame, hijiki, and dulse. How to use it:

- Nori can be wrapped around sushi rice for sushi rolls, crumbled on top of salads or into soups, or roasted for a crispy snack.

- Kombu is great for soaking with dried beans to help improve their digestibility and alkalinity.

- Arame and hijiki are wonderful rehydrated and added to soups, noodles, and Asian-inspired salads.

- Dulse can be found in flakes to be used as a condiment sprinkled over soups, salads, and whole grains.

Thanks, Pamela. I feel healthier already!

Egg Basics for Brunch-Lovin' MGs

Now that studies have revealed eggs yolks have "good" cholesterol that could actually decrease the body's "bad" cholesterol levels, eggs have risen in popularity as a nutritious and affordable protein-rich staple. Don't be afraid to stock up; they're easy to hard-boil and eat on the go, not to mention they make a great breakfast, lunch, or dinner for an unexpected guest (omelets, anyone?). Here are the basics:

Picking Perfect Eggs

MG TIP: To tell whether an egg is fresh enough to eat, place it in a pan of cold water. If it lies on its side, it's fresh. If it tilts on an angle, it's about three or four days past being put in the carton. If the egg stands upright, it's about ten days old. If the egg floats to the top, it is old and should not be used.

Eggs that are simply marked "A" or "AA" or "B," but do not have the USDA grade shield, are not officially graded, and you risk getting lower quality. Avoid "B" grade eggs if you happen upon them, but for the most part you won't find them in a supermarket because of their relatively low quality. These days, lots of great options are available—look for ones that are organic, hormone-free, and free-range. Some even have omega fatty acids in them!

Sneak a peek at the shells by opening the carton—the best eggshells should be dull-looking, not shiny or bright. Store eggs in the carton on a shelf in the refrigerator to ensure freshness. Their shelf life is just under ten days.

Boiling Eggs

MG TIP: Stir the water while the eggs are boiling to help the yolks stay centered.

Place the eggs in one layer in a saucepan and fill the pan with cold water to about one inch above the eggs. Put the pan over medium heat and bring the water to a rolling boil (which means it can't be dissipated by stirring), then reduce the heat and simmer for fifteen minutes. (If the eggs came right out of the fridge, let 'em cook two minutes more.) Immediately plunge the cooked eggs into a bowl of ice water for two minutes to keep them from cooking further (and the yolks from turning an icky greenish color). Cool the eggs for twenty minutes on a paper towel. To peel, crack the egg gently on all sides, roll it between your hands to loosen the shell, and remove the egg from the shell. Boiled eggs left in the shell can be kept for up to one week in the fridge (don't peel them until you're ready to eat them).

Scrambling Eggs

Crack two eggs per person into a bowl. Tilt the bowl at a forty-five-degree angle and whisk the eggs with a fork or wire whisk by making little upward circles. If you want to cut down on calories, crack a whole egg into the bowl and add an egg white as your second egg. Add a bit of butter or nonstick cooking spray to your pan and bring to medium heat. Pour in the eggs, sprinkle in salt and pepper, and let set for one minute. Move a spatula around the edges of the egg, folding inward. When large pieces start to form, flip as much egg as you can with as few strokes as possible. Break up the eggs into smaller pieces (depending on your preference) with the flat tip of your spatula.

Poaching Eggs

Crack an egg into a small dish. Pour water four inches deep into a pan and bring it to a boil over medium heat. Stir the simmering water to make a swirl in it, and slip the egg right into the middle of the swirl. Turn the heat down a bit. It takes three to five minutes for the egg to cook, depending on how runny you like it. Remove the egg with a slotted spoon. Poach one or two eggs at a time.

Frying Eggs

Coat a skillet with butter or nonstick cooking spray and place it over medium heat. If you're using butter, wait until small bubbles form (otherwise, wait about five minutes). Add the eggs and season with salt and pepper. When the whites of the eggs are set and the edges look crinkly, add half a teaspoon of water per egg to the pan. This method is called steambasting and will help you to fry your eggs with a small amount of fat without drying them out. Cover the pan and cook until the eggs are done to your taste (about three to four minutes). To make them sunny-side up, just don't flip the eggs. For eggs over easy, give 'em a flip, wait thirty seconds, and transfer from the pan to your plate.

Cooking Vegetables Without Turning Them to Mush

Cooking veggies perfectly is an art, and the trick, I've learned, is being a little premature. It's like a hot first date: you want to pull out before things get too steamy and well, *you* turn to mush.

MG TIP: It's easier to slice a hard-boiled egg if the knife has been dipped in cold water first. Egg also cleans off utensils more easily with cold water than hot. This will keep your plates from retaining that eggy smell!

MG TIP: When beating egg whites, add a teaspoon of cold water and you'll almost double the quantity of egg. Water will also make regular scrambled eggs fluffier; milk will bind the yolks and make them heavier.

MG TIP: When poaching eggs, add a little white vinegar and salt to the water to help the eggs keep their shape. Or you can use PoachPods, one of my favorite inventions, for a no-fail poaching process.

MG TIP: If you have an extra egg yolk or two, don't throw them away if you plan to bake anything within the next few days. Put them in a bowl with a little water over them and cover with plastic wrap. They'll keep for up to three days in the fridge.

Asparagus (six spears per serving, to serve four)

Hold both ends of a spear and bend; it will naturally snap where it's supposed to. Discard the tough ends. If you are serving super-thick, tough asparagus, also peel the lower portion of the spear; it will be more tender. Lay the asparagus flat in a saucepan and add just enough water to cover. Turn the heat to medium and boil, uncovered, from four to seven minutes (depending on the thickness), or until the asparagus bends slightly. Remove and drain on a paper towel. Drizzle melted butter or fresh lemon juice over the warm asparagus. Or, serve them cold with your favorite vinaigrette. Personally, I recommend buying Newman's Own Vinaigrette dressing. Dressing isn't hard to make, but the bottled variety can be better and faster.

Broccoli (one and a half pounds, to serve four)

Cut off the florets and peel the stems so that the "trunks" look pale green. Boil, uncovered, two to four minutes, until tender but with a slight crunch. Remove immediately. For a finisher, sprinkle on three tablespoons fresh bread crumbs sautéed in one tablespoon butter, or toss in a hot sauté pan with one tablespoon olive oil and one large clove minced garlic.

Green Beans (one and a half pounds, to serve four)

Snap off the ends and peel the little strip that runs down the bean. Boil for five minutes or until just cooked through. Drain immediately and toss in a frying pan with one tablespoon butter, one teaspoon lemon juice, and ⅛ teaspoon seasonings, such as chopped fresh dill or seasoned salt, to taste.

Spinach (two pounds, to serve four)

I know this sounds like an amount that even Popeye would cringe at, but trust me, spinach cooks down to nothing—each serving will be only about three-quarters of a cup. Rinse the spinach in cold water in a colander set in the sink. Lift out and repeat until it's clean. Pull the stems from the leaves. Or, better yet, buy the prepackaged fresh spinach . . . the dirty work is done for you. But you should still give it a quick wash. Fill a large sauté pan with an inch or two of salted water, bring to a boil, and add spinach. Then cover and steam spinach for one to three minutes over medium heat. Remove the cover and stir the spinach with a spatula to make sure all the spinach cooks. But *don't* cook it until it's a pile of dark-green mush. Toss with two tablespoons olive oil and two cloves minced garlic. Remember: Spinach shrinks to at least a quarter of its size when cooked, so use frozen spinach if you're not willing to buy bunches and bunches. But frozen spinach tends to be much mushier, so consider yourself warned.

Fabulously Fresh Fruits (okay, it's not cooking, but buying fruit can be tricky!)

If cooking vegetables right is like passing basic chem, really knowing how to buy and store fruit is akin to a degree in quantum physics. But nothing says domestic goddess like offering a perfectly ripened apple or a succulent peach to a visitor, who will assume you're a better judge of produce than your local farmer's market.

Apples
Make sure they feel firm and smell sweet. Keep them in the fridge in an open plastic bag. Apples will spoil ten times faster when kept at room temperature. Me? I'm a Granny Smith fan. They tend to be firmer, shinier, and, I think, tastier.

Bananas
You may not want brown spots on your body, but you actually might like them on bananas. They're sweeter when spotted with brown. Never store them in the fridge—their skins will discolor, but they'll stay unripe underneath.

MG TIP: To speed-ripen green bananas, place them in a closed brown bag on the counter.

Cantaloupe
Find the blossom end and press. If it yields to gentle pressure and smells like sugar, it'll taste wonderfully sweet.

MG TIP: The blossom end of a cantaloupe is opposite the indentation where the stem once was.

Grapes
Make sure to pick 'em plump, with pliable stems. But don't wash them until you're ready to eat them. They'll last longer that way.

MG TIP: Unwashed grapes stored in sealed plastic at the back of your fridge will last two to three weeks.

Peaches

Depending on your taste, the best peaches can range from fairly firm to a little soft, so you'll have to squeeze them to decide. Either extreme won't be too peachy. Ripen peaches at room temp in a loosely closed paper bag.

MG TIP: Wash the raspberries and blueberries and lay them out on a paper towel until completely dry. Store them this way and they'll last a lot longer.

Raspberries and Blueberries

As these usually come in boxes you can't open, the best you can do is grab a box from the back, as grocers put the newest produce there. Turn the box over to make sure no berries have been squashed or become moldy.

MG TIP: Green tomatoes ripen in three to four days and are best if eaten one to two days after they are ripe.

Tomatoes

(Yes, tomatoes are actually a fruit.) They're at their best when they give slightly to gentle pressure. Store them at room temperature, stem side up and out of direct sunlight.

MG TIP: Though it seems like they would love your furry friends, most farmer's markets do not allow dogs (except for service dogs) due to health and safety laws.

MG TIP: Just because it's at the farmer's market doesn't mean it's organic. If buying organic is important to you, check for vendors' certification.

HOW TO SHOP A FARMER'S MARKET

Whether you're trying to eat healthier, support your local growers, or just save a few bucks, hitting a farmer's market is a great way to get out, have fun, and sometimes nab some great things. But like everything else, as they get more popular, the deals are getting a little harder to find, so before you go out, go armed with your *Modern Girl's Guide*.

Come ready to charm. Who doesn't like a compliment? Remember, these growers treat their products like their children! And hearing how their raspberries made the perfect tart or their mint added the perfect touch to your salad is sure to go straight to their heart. Better yet, show them a picture of something you made with their product!

continued

Though haggling isn't really recommended, vendors may offer you a deal, particularly when you are a repeat customer.

If flattery isn't your thing, at least be genuinely interested. Not only is it respectful, but you might learn a thing or two. However, remember that vendors are working, and if there is a big crowd, don't lock them into conversation and force them to lose a sale.

Leave the credit cards at home. Remember that these are often small businesses and the extra percentage that credit companies charge can take its toll. Pay in cash and bring small bills, as they often run out of change.

What have you got to offer? If you happen to be a great website designer, illustrator, even haircutter, consider offering to trade services. You may be able to get a year's worth of your fruits and veggies for something you can easily do on the side.

If you can go to the market with friends and buy more from a particular vendor, he may be more willing to give you a price break or more for your money. Plus, it's a fun activity to do with a group. If you're going alone, that doesn't mean you can't benefit from the group rate! Look for fruits and veggies you can use year-round that you might can or freeze for soups or smoothies.

Don't forget that your haul can get pretty heavy. Consider a rolling tote so you can whiz through the market with ease and not quit halfway through.

Cooking Red Meat Correctly

Many of us shy away from preparing red meat because of the high potential for food poisoning. But if you follow these tips, you shouldn't have a problem:

MG TIP: Don't forget you are what your food eats. Opt for beef, butter, and dairy products from grass-fed cows. I know it is pricier, but this is one place it is worth the splurge.

- Buy a top-grade cut from your butcher, like USDA Prime, USDA Choice, or USDA Select. Remember, when possible, opt for organic and grass-fed meat as well.

- Buy a meat thermometer and use it *every single time*. You're more likely to find E. coli in hamburger meat than steaks, so don't skimp on putting your thermometer into your burgers on the grill. They should read at least 160°F in the thickest part of the patty. For medium rare steaks, your thermometer should read 145° to 150°F. For medium steaks, your thermometer should read 155° to 160°F. For medium-well, your thermometer should read 165°F. For well done, your thermometer should read 170° to 180°F.

- Thoroughly clean any surfaces that fresh meats are prepared on.

- Fresh beef is cherry-red in color. The darker the beef, the longer the meat has been sitting around.

- Thaw meats as quickly as possible in the fridge, and then cook them immediately.

- Meats should be stored in the fridge no more than three days in their original wrapper.

- Never refreeze meats, especially luncheon meats and hot dogs. They spoil more easily.

The Simplest Steaks

MAKES 4

I suggest buying rib eyes; they're tender, delicious, and readily available. Simply place 4 steaks (5 ounces each) in a dish and rub them with olive oil. Sprinkle the steaks with salt and pepper and let stand at room temperature for 1 hour. Melt 2 tablespoons butter in a heavy skillet over medium-high heat (never cook meat on high; it will significantly decrease its nutritional value). Add the steaks to the skillet and sear on both sides, turning once. Continue cooking to your desired doneness, approximately 5 minutes per side for medium-rare.

The Simplest Burgers

Combine 1 pound ground beef, 1 egg (optional), ¼ teaspoon pepper, ⅛ teaspoon salt (optional), and 1 teaspoon Worcestershire sauce (optional) in a medium mixing bowl, using your hands. Form the meat mixture into four patties, each ¾ inch thick in the center and at the edges. Spray a skillet with nonstick cooking spray and heat it over medium-high heat. Add the patties and cook on both sides until they are medium to medium-well done (about 5 to 7 minutes per side for medium burgers). Remember to cook the burgers to at least 160° to protect against E. coli. The juices should run clear when you pierce the meat with a fork.

MAKES ABOUT 4

Taste Tips for Red Meat

- Always cut meat across the grain when possible; it will be easier to eat.

- If you scorch meat, put it in a towel. Cover the meat and let it stand for five minutes before scraping off the burned spots with a knife.

- When reheating meat, place the pieces in a casserole dish with lettuce leaves in between the slices to keep the meat tender.

- Store meat in its own cooking juices.

- Place meat in white vinegar and oil (one part vinegar to two parts oil) as a marinade. This will make it more tender, as will adding canned whole tomatoes to roasts when cooking. When marinating all foods, be sure to keep them in the fridge.

- To keep bacon from curling in the microwave, place four strips between paper towels. It should be cooked in three to five minutes.

- To keep meatballs from falling apart while cooking, place them in the fridge for twenty minutes before cooking.

- The best herbs to use with red meat: basil, thyme, marjoram, summer savory, and rosemary.

- Never press down on meat with a spatula while cooking. This pushes all the juices out and dries out the meat.

Chicken for Chickens

So many of us MGs count poultry as a main staple in our diet, yet we freak out at the thought of preparing it ourselves. Here are some basic safety tips before you get started:

- Never buy a chicken on Monday. It's likely you'll get one that's been sitting in the store over the weekend.

- To thaw anything from a frozen whole chicken to a breast, unwrap and place your frozen meat in a pan of cold water with at least a quarter cup of salt added. In order to keep the chicken immersed in the water (the chicken will eventually float to the top), you must cover your pan with a heavy lid. If you don't have a lid, thaw your chicken in a large bowl, cover with a portable cutting board, and weight it by placing a paperweight on top. (Just be sure to wash the cutting board and bowl thoroughly after use to protect against salmonella poisoning.) The flavor will be improved and the chicken will taste cleaner. Thawing time will vary depending on the cut of meat—about three to four hours for a whole chicken, and one hour for a breast. The chicken *must* be kept in the fridge while it thaws.

- After working with raw poultry, wash your hands, the utensils used, and the surface with hot soapy water before placing any other food on it. Poultry can be contaminated with a number of bacteria.

- Use separate cutting boards for vegetables and raw meat. If you don't have two, scrub the board with hot soapy water before chopping veggies.

- The USDA recommends inserting a meat thermometer into a whole chicken and eating it only after it's reached 180°F. Bone-in chicken parts should reach 180°F as well, and a breast should reach 170°F. Chicken should always be thoroughly cooked.

- Chicken will keep longer in the fridge if it is rewrapped in wax paper instead of the plastic wrap used at grocery stores.

- Fresh packaged poultry should be frozen or refrigerated and eaten within two days.

The Simplest Chicken Breast Recipe Ever

To tenderize the chicken, wash your hands, place plastic wrap over the boneless, skinless breast meat, and press down with your hands. The plastic wrap will provide a more stable surface for your hands than will a slippery chicken breast and will also lessen the chance of salmonella contamination. Sprinkle the breasts with ½ teaspoon salt and ¼ teaspoon pepper. In a nonstick skillet over medium heat, heat 1 tablespoon vegetable oil and 1 tablespoon butter. Add the chicken breasts and cook 4 minutes on each side. Insert a meat thermometer into the thickest part of the chicken breast. A chicken breast will be safely cooked at 170°F. If you don't have a meat thermometer (which I highly recommend purchasing), pierce the center of the breast with a knife, fork, or skewer. If the juices run clear, the breast should be done. If the juices run pink, it isn't done. Also, a skewer, knife, or fork will be easier to push in and draw out of the breast if it is cooked thoroughly. Add your favorite lemon-caper sauce or cut the chicken into chunks and add to a green salad or to a Caesar salad (page 29).

MG TIP: A lower cooking temperature over a longer period of time will produce a juicier chicken.

Microwave Chicken

Hey, sometimes a girl just feels low maintenance, and that's where the microwave comes in. Remove and discard the skin. In a shallow microwavable dish, arrange the chicken breasts with the meatier parts toward the outside of the dish. Brush the chicken with barbecue sauce if desired (I personally love Stubb's). Brush the chicken with 1 tablespoon melted butter or olive oil. Cover with wax paper and microwave. I recommend about 8 minutes for two breasts (rotating the dish halfway through if your microwave doesn't have a carousel), but be sure to keep a close watch. Cooking times will vary depending on the power of your microwave and the thickness of the breasts. Sprinkle the chicken breasts with ½ teaspoon salt and let them stand, covered, for 5 minutes before serving.

Oven-Roasted Chicken

Serve this chicken with rice and sautéed vegetables.

MAKES 4 SERVINGS

One 3½- to 4-pound roasting chicken (not a fryer)
1 tablespoon Dijon mustard
½ tablespoon herbes de Provence, crushed
Garlic salt
Pepper to taste

MG TIP: Try free-range chickens. They're fed natural grains and allowed to run free, unlike regular chickens, which are caged and pumped with growth hormones. On the package, look for the label "natural grain–fed."

Preheat the oven to 375°F. Remove the giblets package from the chicken. Rinse the chicken in cold water and dry it with paper towels. Rub the skin with the mustard and sprinkle it inside and out with the herbs, garlic salt, and pepper. Hook the wing tips under the back (as if you're folding them underneath its body) and place the chicken breast side up on a roasting rack in a shallow roasting pan. If you have an ovenproof meat thermometer, insert it now into one of the inner thighs, near the breast of the chicken but not touching the bone (otherwise you will want to insert an instant-read thermometer into the same place at the end of the cooking time). Roast about 1 hour or more, until the thigh feels tender when pierced with a fork. Check the thermometer or insert your instant-read meat thermometer. The internal temperature should read 180°F. Using poultry shears, cut the chicken into four pieces. This will give you two breast/wing combos and two thigh/leg combos. Throw the back away (the back has very little meat, and most Modern Girls choose to discard it). Arrange the chicken pieces on an ovenproof platter and return to the oven on low to keep warm.

Foolproof Vegan Quinoa

You know that quinoa is great for you, but did you know it's also one of the most versatile grains out there? This staple is wonderful alone, as a base, and even as a toasted garnish. Here's a simple recipe that works well in just about everything.

4 cloves garlic, chopped
1 teaspoon olive oil
1 cup rinsed quinoa
2 cups chicken stock (see note)
½ teaspoon sea salt

In a small saucepan, sauté garlic in olive oil for 1 minute. Add rinsed quinoa, salt, and chicken stock. Bring to a boil, then cover and reduce to a simmer. Cook for about 20 minutes. Let sit for 5 minutes and fluff with a fork. Note: Make it vegetarian-and-vegan-friendly by using vegetable stock.

Preparing Primo Pasta

Woman cannot live by eggs, veggies, and meat alone. Well, maybe she can . . . but when a deep-seated carb craving kicks in, pasta is pretty much the most easy, economical, satisfying dish you can imagine.

The trick to perfect pasta is cooking it al dente—until it is tender but still chewy. You're looking for it to be a little chewier than you may be used to. Why? Because the water (and the sauce you'll add) is so hot that the pasta will keep cooking even after you've turned off the stove.

MG TIP: You may have heard it's correct to rinse the pasta under cold water, but for the best flavor, don't! Pour it into a colander and give a few good shakes to get all the water out. Cooked pasta will keep refrigerated for up to twelve hours. After that its flavor may sour.

To serve six people, you'll need 1 pound of dried pasta and 5 to 6 quarts of water. Bring the water to a boil in a large pot (try to get one with a strainer insert). Add 1½ tablespoons salt. When the water reaches a rolling boil (remember, that means it can't be dissipated by stirring with a spoon), add the pasta. If the boil turns to nothing, cover the pot to crank up the heat. Cooking time varies with the pasta's shape, so check the package for specifics. The best way to know when the pasta is done is to try it yourself. By the way, that whole theory about throwing spaghetti against the wall doesn't work. If it sticks, it's not al dente anymore.

MG TIP: Nowadays you can even get brown rice and quinoa pasta at the market if you're on a gluten-free diet or have celiac disease. If you want to be super healthy, spaghetti squash also makes a great pasta alternative.

How to Make a Killer Cream Sauce

Technically, a sauce made with butter, flour, and milk is called a white sauce. It's more commonly called a cream sauce, regardless of whether it actually contains cream. It is used for creaming foods like vegetables, fish, and chicken and as a base for other sauces. Even if you are watching your weight, it is good to know how to make this basic component of many recipes.

In a small saucepan over low heat, melt 2 tablespoons butter. Add 1½ to 2 tablespoons flour and blend for 3 to 5 minutes, whisking constantly. Slowly stir in 1 cup milk *or* a combination of milk and light chicken stock *or* light chicken stock and cream. Bring the sauce to a simmer. You can add any of the following to the mix:

- Grated nutmeg
- 1 teaspoon lemon juice (fresh-squeezed is ideal, but bottled is fine)
- ½ teaspoon Worcestershire sauce
- 1 teaspoon sherry
- 2 tablespoons chopped parsley
- 2 tablespoons chopped chives

Whisk the simmering sauce until it is thickened and smooth.

Combine the cream sauce with your other ingredients just before it boils, so it doesn't become watery. An easy ratio to remember: Use about half as much sauce as vegetable, fish, or chicken.

MG TIP: If your sauce is too thick, slowly add a little more liquid (milk, water, or stock), whisking constantly until you get the right consistency.

MG TIP: If your sauce is too thin, cook it on low heat for a few minutes, stirring constantly, uncovered, until it thickens (this is called "reducing" or "cooking down"). If you get impatient, you can thicken the sauce with flour or cornstarch. (In a small bowl, place 1 tablespoon flour or cornstarch and 2 tablespoons cold water. With a fork, blend into a smooth paste. Add 4 tablespoons warm cream sauce and combine well. Pour the mixture into the original batch of sauce and whisk until smooth.) Cook over low heat, whisking constantly, until the sauce reaches the desired consistency.

Vegan Pesto

Who doesn't love a good pesto? The best part about this one is that it's delicious and dairy-free. Use it as a pasta sauce, sandwich spread, or dip.

2 cups basil leaves, packed
¾ cup toasted walnut halves
1 cup fresh mint leaves
1 to 2 cloves of garlic, peeled
½ cup extra-virgin olive oil
Salt and pepper
1 tablespoon lemon juice

Place basil, walnuts, mint leaves, and garlic in a food processor and pulse until coarsely ground. Drizzle in olive oil and add salt, pepper, and lemon juice to taste. Pulse until combined.

Cooking 102: Three Easy, Impressive Dishes for the Cooking Phobic

Every Modern Girl should have a few easy recipes up her sleeve. Note: I stress the word *e-a-s-y* here because like most women after a hard day at work the only word I'm thinking of is *takeout*. But come on, there are only so many times you can say, "Order Number Thirty-four, two Number Elevens, and a Number Fifty-eight with orange sauce . . . yes, that'll be on the credit card," over the phone. It gets a little pathetic when they know your order as soon as they hear your voice.

So on those nights when you're feeling a little more industrious than usual, remind yourself, "Hey, if Jane can cook this, I sure as hell can," and try out one of these three dishes. You'll be able to prepare each of them in less than an hour. And if you goof and make a wrong turn along the way like I often do, chances are it'll still taste good.

Easy Dish 1: Fettuccine Alfredo

Here, you're putting your pasta skills and your cream sauce skills to good use. This is a delicious comfort dish any guy will love. Hey, he may even love it so much, he'll volunteer to do the cooking honors next time.

10 ounces fettuccine noodles

6 tablespoons (3/4 stick) unsalted butter

1 cup heavy cream

1 3/4 cups grated Parmesan cheese

Sprinkling of ground nutmeg

2 tablespoons finely chopped chives

Pepper to taste

MG TIP: Lighten up your pasta by adding steamed or sautéed vegetables. You can't go wrong with broccoli, peas, or mushrooms—even sun-dried tomatoes are great in this.

Cook the pasta noodles according to the directions on page 26 and drain. Set aside. Melt the butter in a large sauté pan over low heat and add the noodles. Add the heavy cream and stir 1 to 2 minutes. Add the Parmesan, nutmeg, and half the chives and continue stirring until the cheese is melted. Sprinkle the rest of the chives on top and serve. Easy.

Easy Dish 2: Caesar Salad with Parmesan Crisps

This salad is super simple and always impresses. It serves four—or two very hungry people.

2 heads romaine lettuce

1 sourdough baguette (2 inches wide)

4 tablespoons extra-virgin olive oil or olive oil spray (for croutons)

Salt and pepper

Small block of Parmesan cheese

1 cup shredded Parmesan cheese

1/2 cup or more of Cardini's Caesar Dressing, to taste

MG TIP: Never cut lettuce with a metal knife; it makes it wilt and taste funny. Either tear it or cut with a special plastic lettuce knife. Also, you can tear up your salad and wrap it in clean, damp dish towels the night before, dump it into the salad bowl the next day, and have a wonderful salad without the mess.

Preheat the oven to 325°F. Pull the outer leaves off the heads of lettuce and discard. Wash the inner leaves and pat dry with a paper towel. Tear the leaves into bite-size pieces and place in a large bowl. Cut the baguette into 1/4-inch-thick diagonal slices. Brush both sides with olive oil, using 4 tablespoons total, or spray with olive oil spray.

MG TIP: To make this more of a main course, try adding some grilled chicken, shrimp, or even filet mignon to the top.

Sprinkle the slices with salt and pepper. Lay the slices on a cookie sheet and bake for 5 minutes. Sprinkle the slices with the 1 cup shredded Parmesan. Bake 10 minutes, or until the cheese is melted. Set aside.

Pour your desired amount of Cardini's dressing over the lettuce and set aside. Cut ten Parmesan slivers from the cheese block and toss with the salad. Transfer the salad to plates and garnish with the Parmesan crisps.

Easy Dish 3: Chicken Marsala

I love that this dish sounds so sophisticated, and yet it can all be made before a rerun of Friends *is over. Serve it with the Caesar Salad recipe above.*

4 boneless, skinless chicken breasts
1/4 cup all-purpose flour
1/2 teaspoon salt
1/4 teaspoon freshly ground black pepper
1 teaspoon dried basil
3 tablespoons olive oil
3 tablespoons butter
1 cup sliced fresh white mushrooms
2/3 cup dry Marsala wine

MG TIP: Invest in a meat tenderizer; there is really no good substitute.

With a meat tenderizer, pound the chicken between two sheets of plastic wrap to 1/2-inch thickness. Combine the flour, salt, pepper, and basil in a small bowl. Heat the oil and butter in a large nonstick skillet over medium-high heat. Dredge the chicken in the seasoned flour mixture and set the first two breasts in the pan. Cook 2 minutes on each side, until lightly browned. Remove and set aside, then brown the second set of breasts for 2 minutes on both sides. Remove chicken and sauté the mushrooms for 2 minutes. Place the 4 breasts that you've set aside back into the pan; add the Marsala wine, and stir. Cover and simmer for approximately 12 minutes or more, turning the breasts once at the 6-minute mark to ensure that all sides touch the bottom of the pan during cooking time. Check to see that the chicken is cooked through (no longer pink inside and the juices run clear). If you have a meat thermometer, each breast should register 170°F (because these are breasts and you've pounded the chicken so flat, they don't need to get hotter than this). Remember, breasts can be cooked safely at 170° while a *whole* chicken must be cooked to 180°.

Okay, well done. Now you have a few recipes for any emergency situation (and if you're daring, look for more extensive menus in chapter 2). But time to get out of the frying pan and into the dishwasher . . .

Cleaning Tips for Kitchen Slobs

And you thought *cooking* was the hard part. For every fabulous meal, there's a little scrub-'n'-scour aftermath involved. Here's how to deal so your kitchen doesn't look like a toxic wasteland:

Apply the Law of Immediate Damage Control

Spilled flour and milk on the floor while making your cream sauce, or left a trail of Marsala and mushrooms on the stove top? The longer you wait to clean it off, the more it'll stick, which will make it hard to chisel off later (not to mention the fact that spills attract insects, ants, roaches, and bacteria).

Wash as You Go

Once you're done using something, rinse it and put it in the dishwasher. Sounds a little OCD, I know, but you're keeping the area clear for additional cooking and saving yourself time. If you don't have a dishwasher, at least rinse the pots and pans and stack them to the side. A good rinse at the time will save you a lot of scrubbing later.

Stash a "Product Bucket" Under Your Kitchen Sink

Half the time when I actually want to clean something, I realize my cleaning products are in a gazillion different places. It's easier to group them all in a bucket or other plastic container under the sink in your kitchen, and another in your bathroom (more on that later). A bucket can do double duty to hold the water and soap when you mop the floor.

Cleaning Products You'll Need

MG TIP: Run out of cleaning spray and have guests coming over pronto? Make your own household cleanser with 1/4 cup white vinegar, 1/2 teaspoon liquid soap, and 2 cups of water. Pour the mixture into a spray bottle and spritz away.

- An all-purpose spray with antibacterial ingredients, like Formula 409
- Windex (for windows, glass coffee tables, and mirrors)
- Pledge or Old English (to clean polished wood surfaces—an all-purpose cleaner will leave 'em looking dull)
- Pine-Sol or Mr. Clean (to clean tile or linoleum floors)
- Murphy's Oil Soap (to clean wood floors . . . other cleaners will strip it)
- A sponge mop
- Oven-cleaning spray
- Clorox bleach
- Rubber gloves
- Sponges
- Dishwashing detergent

Eco-Cleaning

There's a lot of controversy over the ingredients in cleaning solutions these days and some people smarter than me certainly make a very good case for going eco when you are cleaning. It's a little too late for me to change horses midstream, but here are some of the reasons why you might want to consider doing it:

- 7 to 15 percent of the population is allergic to traditional cleaning products.
- If you look at many cleaning products, the word *poison*, *danger*, or *caution* is on them. Scary, right?

So while you may not want to trade in all of your cleaning favorites, I suggest at least sampling some of the more eco-friendly products out there, as they often do just as good a job as some of the more traditional ones without some of the worry. My favorites come from the Honest Company. They make fantastic products for home, bath and body, and health and wellness, and the *best* baby products out there.

The Perks of Being White Vinegar

It may be a bit smelly, but white vinegar is truly one of the most amazing household products you can buy. In addition to being cheap, gentle, and eco-friendly, the stuff will disinfect, deodorize, and de-gunkify just about everything you can think of. Here are some of my favorite ways to use this flexible fixer:

- Mix white vinegar with baking powder for an all-natural cleaning paste that does the tough jobs, whether it's a smelly garbage disposal or a seriously dirty bathroom.

- For a quick fruit fly fix, set out a small dish of white vinegar with some smashed fruit and cover with plastic wrap. Make tiny holes in the plastic; that way, when the flies crawl into the trap, they can't easily escape.

- Remove water condensation marks on wood by rubbing in equal parts vinegar and vegetable oil with the grain. And then go buy some coasters!

- Get rid of deodorant discoloration by spraying white vinegar onto the spots before you wash. (It's also great for many other clothing stains and won't harm your fabrics.)

- Perk up your wilted veggies by soaking them in cold water and a little bit of white vinegar.

- Add a cup of white vinegar to your wash to instantly fluff up new sheets and towels.

- White vinegar even fixes beauty problems! Use vinegar and baking soda as an all-natural hair mask to soften strands and improve shine. Here's the trick:

    - Mix 1 part baking soda with 3 parts water. Apply the baking soda and water mixture to dry or wet hair by starting at the roots and working to the ends. Let it sit for 1 to 3 minutes, then rinse with warm water. After washing and rinsing with the baking soda mixture, you'll want to apply a vinegar rinse. Mix 1 part white or apple cider vinegar with 4 parts water. To minimize the vinegar smell, you can add essential oils (I like to use lavender or peppermint). I keep it in a spray bottle in the shower and that way it doesn't get in my eyes. If you can bear it, after about 30 seconds, do a cold water rinse and voilà—shinier, healthier hair!

Soak Stubborn Pans the Right Way

Sometimes stains get so stubborn even scrubbing them immediately doesn't cut it. A little trick is to boil your pans clean. Put them back on the burner with hot water up to the level of the stains and add a few drops of dish soap. Bring them to a boil, turn off the heat, and leave them until after dinner. Put them in the sink, add a little soap, and scrub with a wire sponge. The crud should come off.

Keep Your Fridge and Your Food Fresh

MG TIP: Don't store easily perishable items like milk in the refrigerator door (the warmest place in your fridge). Instead, store condiments and nonfood products (such as film or suntan lotion) in the door.

MG TIP: Leave eggs in their container, not the fridge egg bins, where they'll spoil faster. Also, the carton has the expiration day printed on it.

You may be saying to yourself, "Wait, it looks pretty clean, doesn't it?" But the truth is, invisible germs from spills, molds, and old foods can contaminate your fridge and the fresh foods you stock it with. Plus, odors can ruin foods as well. So every two days, go through your fridge and throw out any fruits or veggies that have rotted (one spoiled item will rot the whole bunch). Chuck all leftovers that are more than three days old.

Also get in the habit of washing your fridge once a month. Put all perishable items onto one shelf and move all other items to your countertop. Remove drawers and shelves and wash them in hot, soapy water. Next, unplug your fridge (not with wet hands!). Wash all the walls and surfaces with hot sudsy water and wipe them down with a dry cloth. If you have any mold in your fridge, add chlorine bleach to your water-soap combo (3/4 cup of bleach to every gallon of H_2O). It'll both clean and deodorize your fridge.

Manage Your Arctic Freezer

Most modern freezers that are labeled frost-free don't need to be defrosted. Here's how to defrost a freezer that needs it—when ice builds up to a quarter to a half inch thick.

- Turn the freezer off (the switch may be inside the fridge).

- Put all food from the freezer into an ice chest or cooler with bags of ice.

- Remove the ice in the freezer compartment by putting a bowl of hot water in the freezer and closing the door, then checking for melting ice after an hour. Repeat until the ice is gone.

- Pick up the ice pieces with a dishcloth as the ice melts (grabbing it bare-handed could cause it to stick to your skin) and drop it into the sink.

- Once the freezer is cleared of ice, use a sponge or a dishcloth and a bowl of warm water (no soap!) to thoroughly wipe out the inside of the freezer.

- Turn the freezer back on, close the door, and let it run for ten to fifteen minutes before returning the food to it.

MG TIP: Don't take your bad mood out on your freezer and chip at it with an ice pick; it can puncture the lining of your freezer. And tempting as it sounds, don't use your hair dryer to melt the ice. Electrically shocking yourself isn't worth it.

MG TIP: Clean out your ice bin every month or so. Mold can grow even in there!

Cleaning Other Parts of Your House in a Flash

Let's face it: There's nothing really *fun* about keeping your kitchen—or the rest of your pad—in order. But the more efficient you are about it, the more free time you'll have to do the other things in life that you *do* love. (And you'll be less likely to have an anxiety attack when guests mysteriously drop by.) So stop procrastinating! Here are a few tips and tricks to get you started:

Clean in Small Bursts

Are you a crash-cleaner, waiting until the last possible minute when you have one thong left or the dishes have piled up so high you can barely turn on the faucet? Then you wind up spending hours—or even an entire weekend—playing catch-up? I'm totally with you. But what I eventually realized is that cleaning is like exercising—you'll get the best results if you do a little bit of it a few times per week. I like to make deals with myself that I won't go to bed with clothes on the floor or dirty dishes in the sink. Even if I just rinse them and put them in the dishwasher, I've still cleared a visible space in my kitchen. If you're a morning person, do a mini-cleanup before you have your first cup of coffee. Soon it will become a habit.

Group Things Together

A mess is always easier to attack when you divide things into piles. For example: newspapers/books/bills; purses/shoes; dirty clothes/towels/blankets. Start with the smallest pile first so that you don't get overwhelmed.

Have Blind Ambition

Put your hand in an old sock, spritz some all-purpose cleaner on it, and go over the slats of the blinds with your thumb and forefinger.

Be a Sucker

The most satisfying way to get rid of dirt is vacuuming both hardwood and carpet—and it saves you from having to wash your floors as often. Go through every room of the house, and include the furniture cushions. In a rush and can't do everything? Go for the corners of the room—that's where dust bunnies like to hide.

Get Fakeout Polish

Wood polish like Old English instantly makes beat-up tables look like new, and putting it on will remove dust at the same time.

MG TIP: Make sure you change the head or adjust the setting (depending on the model) of your vacuum cleaner before switching from hard surfaces to carpeting. Using an oscillating brush on hardwood floors just scatters the dirt around, and using a hardwood attachment on carpet is way too much work.

MG TIP: Don't forget to change your vacuum bag when it gets full. If it's too clogged up, it won't suck up the dust. It's also not a bad idea to get your vacuum serviced every year for optimal performance.

MG TIP: Turns out your sponge could be the dirtiest thing in your house, storing bacteria from everywhere. Wash it in the dishwasher or microwave it for sixty seconds every night. Too lazy? Splurge for a new sponge pack every few weeks.

No time for cleaning? Just this once, if guests are coming over, spritz a lemon-scented cleaner (lightly) in each room. Just the scent of a cleaner might make your guests think you spent hours scrubbing.

Easy Clothes-Cleaning Tips for Super-Busy Chicks

No matter how careful you are in the kitchen (not to mention other rooms of the house), sooner or later you're going to have to do laundry. And nothing says domestic goddess like knowing how to take primo care of your clothes. Why bother having your home look great if you're wearing a blazer with a missing button, or you have Pinot Noir eternally dribbled down your cocktail dress? It's not about spending loads of time being anal about laundering your wardrobe (not much fun in that), but rather, learning some of the basics that will save you time, money, and the humiliation of walking around with an outfit that screams, "I shop in the sale bin."

Washing and Drying for Dummies

Some of the biggest mistakes you can make with clothes don't happen while you're wearing them, but when you're trying to clean them. I've been known to dye an entire load of white towels periwinkle . . . and to turn my favorite beautiful silky bra into something so shredded, it looked like I'd bought it at an S&M parlor. On both counts, my mistake happened because I was impatient. I threw the white towels in with new navy ones (Who needs two loads? I lamely thought) and threw my lacy black bra in the washing machine—on *hot*—without a lingerie bag. My lesson? Taking a little more time up front saves more time and grief in the end. Now I have it down to a science:

MG TIP: If you are buying a washing machine, consider a top-loader with no agitator. Some experts say front-loaders can trap mold in the door, and agitators can do just that: agitate your clothes.

Separate

Rule number one: You have to keep the darks away from the lights. Period. There's no way around this. I usually do three batches: one of whites, one of lights, and one of darks. Lights can be anything from pinks to light grays—things that won't bleed into each other if you wash them in warm or cool.

MG TIP: When you're washing a brightly colored item (like bright red or denim) for the first time, wash it by itself, or in cold with the darks. Otherwise, the fresh dyes on the material may bleed.

Lingerie Bag It

If you're *so* not a fan of hand-washing your underwear—bras, hose, and camisoles—(which really is the best tactic, by the way), invest in a zip-up mesh bag that can safely hold your personal items while you wash them with the rest of your load. It acts as a buffer between the delicate fabrics and the inside of the washing machine.

Use the Right Temps

MG TIP: If you're doing several loads of laundry, wash the items that take longest to dry first (comforters, towels, denims).

Choose the hottest wash temperature the fabrics can stand without shrinking, fading, or getting damaged. The hotter the wash, the better the soap will clean the fabric. But it will also cause more fading, bleeding, and shrinking. Whites and pastels should be washed in hot (unless they're delicate, in which case warm). Colors and sturdy darks should be washed in warm. Delicates and darks that bleed should be washed in cool. (But don't wash delicates and bleeding darks together; run two separate loads.)

Pick the Perfect Cycle

MG TIP: Have problems with pilling (rough little pieces of fabric coming up on your clothes)? Turn your garments inside out before you wash. Also, use a little more water than you normally do so clothes can move more freely instead of rubbing against the side of the machine.

Your clothes will come out a lot better and fresher if you know which way to turn the dial. Although washers vary, here's a basic guide:

* *Regular:* This cycle is accompanied by a hot wash and a cold rinse. It's for heavily soiled items and sturdy cottons and linens—towels, T-shirts, jeans. But it's not great on everything; this vigorous wash can wear down more delicate clothes over time.

* *Permanent Press:* This cycle uses a shorter agitation period and shorter spin cycle than the regular cycle. It's great for synthetic fibers (besides the ones listed under "delicate cycle"). It's paired with a warm cycle and cool rinse plus a final cold rinse to protect the colors.

MG TIP: Fabric softener does make your clothes feel softer; but use it only every two or three washes so that it doesn't leave an oily residue on your clothes. (If you do get oily residue, wash your clothes again with detergent only and let them soak on the "soak" cycle. Then put on the rinse cycle twice.)

* *Delicate:* This cycle has the shortest agitation time, slowest spin cycle, and coolest temperatures to keep your fabrics from falling apart. Use DC for machine-washable silk and wool, viscose rayon, acrylic, and acetate, lace, and sheer and loosely knitted fabrics. Cooler temperatures are often best.

Fill Before You Dump

Fill the machine with water and add the detergent before you pile in your clothes. If you put in the clothes first and then fill the machine with water and detergent, it will distribute unevenly and you may get blue spots on clothes where the detergent sat too long. If you're adding bleach, also do so in the filling stage.

If you are using detergent pods, add them to the washer before adding clothes and water; otherwise they may not dissolve properly. Also make you sure you keep them out of reach of children and pets. If using a front-loader, the pod must be placed directly in the drum, not the dispensing drawer.

Pretreat

Wait, stop! Before you even think of putting your threads into the washing machine, use a stain remover like Shout or Spray 'n Wash on your soiled clothes. They'll help release stains while you're laundering your clothes. You can pretreat items as you're sorting them and going through pockets. That way, the stain remover will have a few minutes to absorb into the fabric before you toss it in the washer. It really doesn't need to sit on it longer than that; it'll just dry out. And never stain-treat anything overnight, because it could bleach the fabric. Before applying your pretreat, first test it on an out-of-sight place on your shirt, like the inside back seam, to make sure it doesn't damage the fabric or color.

MG TIP: If the stain is still there after you've laundered the item, re-treat it and wash it again. Just make sure you don't put it in the dryer until you see the stain is gone—heat from the dryer will set stains.

MG TIP: There are a few kinds of stains (such as lipstick) that get *spread* by water—so you have to sponge them with a "dry spotter" like Carbona and K2r. These contain a nonwater-based solvent that lifts the stain out without setting it. K2r can be found at hardware stores, such as ACE Hardware and True Value. To find a retailer that carries Carbona, go to www.carbona.com.

THE SMART CHICK'S STAIN CHART

One of the most stressful things is when you spill something on an item you care about—whether it's clothes, carpet, or couch—and you're stuck in limbo wondering what the heck is the right thing to get it out. Hot water? Cold water? Prayer? Here are the most common stains and how to remove them, courtesy of the *Stainbuster's Bible,* written by stain-fighting expert Don Aslett. I recommend picking up the book for even more useful info.

• **Beer:** Blot up all you can, and sponge the spot with a mild white vinegar and water solution (always 1 part vinegar to 4 parts water). Rinse with lukewarm water and apply digestant paste such as Biz, Wisk, or Era Plus. (Digestants contain enzymes that "eat" protein stains; never use them on wool or silk.) Let it sit for 30 minutes, then rinse with warm water. If it's a dry-cleanable item, you're better off taking it to the pros.

• **Blood:** Keep the stain wet. Blot out fresh blood, then soak in cold salty water or rinse out under the cold-water tap, then do a cold-water wash. For dry-cleanables, carpets, and mattresses, sponge cold water onto the spot. (A friend of mine swears by putting salt on the carpet plus cold soda water.)

• **Chocolate:** Scrape and blot as much as you can without grinding it into the fabric even more. Apply absorbent (cornstarch or talcum powder) to soak up as much of the grease as possible, wait 15 minutes, then scrape off, then sponge the stain with a dry spotter until no more chocolate comes off. Then soak it in digestant—unless it's silk or wool—and launder it in warm water.

• **Coffee/Tea:** Blot with a clean cloth, and sponge with cool water. Apply pretreat and launder in warm water—air dry. If it's a dry-cleanable item, sponge with a wet spotter (a mixture of detergent, solvents, and chemicals; buy it at the drugstore) and a few drops of vinegar, then flush with cool water and pat dry. Just make sure not to use ammonia or heat—that will set a coffee stain.

• **Fruit Juices:** If the fabric is durable (colorfast cotton or linen) turn the item over and pour a quart boiling water through the stain from a height of two to three feet. If the fabric won't tolerate boiling water, rub it with a fresh-cut lemon or lemon juice, rinse with water, and air-dry.

continued

- **Grass:** Sponge with alcohol (test it first). If the stain's still there, soak it in digestant for twenty minutes, then launder in warm water with as strong a bleach as the fabric can take.

- **Gum:** If the gum is soft, remove as much of it as you can, then freeze it with "gum freeze." It's an aerosol spray you can pick up at a janitorial supply store. Or, simply use an ice cube. Rub the dull edge of a butter knife over the cold gum so it breaks up in crumbs. (Got it in your hair, too? Try peanut butter . . . then shampoo your hair.)

- **Ink/Ballpoint Pen:** Sponge with water, blot, spray it with cheap hair spray and blot it through a cloth. Do this until no more pen color is coming off. Then apply laundry pretreat and air-dry.

- **Ketchup/Barbecue Sauce:** Scrape off the stain, blot, and sponge with cool water. Put on pretreat (like Spray 'n Wash), rinse, and launder in warm water. Stain still there? Sponge it with a solution of white vinegar and water (1:4 ratio, remember), and rinse again. If it's a dry-clean item, sponge it with cool water and let it dry. Then sponge it with a dry spotter.

- **Lipstick/Makeup:** Blot with a dry spotter, and make sure to change your blotting cloth often so you won't spread the stain. Work in a little vegetable oil, mineral oil, or shortening, let it sit 15 minutes, and blot again with dry spotter. Sponge any remaining stain with wet spotter and a few drops of ammonia, then apply pretreat and launder in warm water. (Baby Wipes can also work wonders in a pinch.)

- **Liquor:** Use a wet spotter or an undiluted neutral detergent (like Ivory dish soap) along with a few drops of vinegar. Launder in warm water.

- **Lotion:** Apply laundry pretreat, then smear the spot with petroleum jelly and wash in hot water. But for delicate items like silk, take to a dry cleaners. For upholstery and carpet, apply dry spotter and blot until the stain is gone. Sponge with a neutral detergent solution and rinse.

- **Nail Polish:** Scrape as much as you can off. For acetate, rayon, silk, and wool, take it to a dry cleaner. For other fabrics, apply acetone or nonoily fingernail polish remover (in a test spot first). Flush with dry spotter and air dry.

- **Soy Sauce:** Blot up all you can and sponge with cool water, then a mild vinegar solution, plus pretreat, and launder in cool water.

continued

- **Vomit:** Modern Girls have their rough days . . . and sloppy party guests. Quickly scrape and blot up all you can, then flush the spot with water. If the item is washable, soak it in a solution of one quart warm water to one teaspoon neutral detergent and two tablespoons of ammonia. Scrape to loosen the stain if the fabric will tolerate it. Rinse with cool water. If the stain remains, soak it in digestant for 30 minutes to an hour, then launder in warm water. Dry-clean item? Let the pros handle it. If the vomit is on upholstery or carpet, sponge on water liberally and blot it back out with a bacteria/enzyme digester (it eliminates organic waste by eating it). Ask the salesperson at a pet or janitorial-supply store to find it for you. This also works on pet stains on your carpet. Just be advised: you can't use it on wool or silk.

- **Wine:** Blot first, then sponge with cool water. For sturdy fabrics, rub salt into the stain, and treat with the boiling water method you use for fruit juice stains, above. If the fabric can't take boiling water (whether it's dry-cleanable or not), sponge it with a wet spotter and a few drops of vinegar. Rinse with cool water. If the stain's still there, sponge with rubbing alcohol (if the fabric is acetate, dilute with equal parts water). Let it sit for 30 minutes without drying, then rinse with cool water. Another trick: Simply pour salt over the stain, grind it in a bit, and let it sit for a few hours. Then, treat with Stain Stick or Spray 'n Wash and wash normally. If it's a carpet spill, blot immediately and cover with a generous handful of salt. Let it sit overnight, then vacuum up the salt.

MG TIP: When in doubt, leave stain removal to the pros, and take your item to a good dry cleaner.

MG TIP: I'm a big fan of Shout Wipes and Tide to Go stain remover. These individual mini-wipes and stain stick can remove stains easily, and you can bring them anywhere. But always remember to test a spot before you use them.

To Bleach or Not to Bleach . . . That Is the Question

Bleach can be a very effective stain remover for whites, but you can't use it on colors. Instead, go with a detergent that simply has "Color-Safe Bleaching Action." You also can't use bleach on the following fabrics: silk, wool, Spandex, permanent press, or anything treated with flame-retardant resins. If you *are* working with a bleachable material, remember the following:

- Always pretest diluted chlorine bleach before using it on a part of the garment that isn't easily visible.

- Check the labels on your clothes—some whites cannot be bleached.

- Never mix bleach with another cleaning chemical, like ammonia. It can have toxic effects.

- Always dilute bleach—with four parts water for sturdy fabrics; eight parts water for delicate ones.

- Rinse right after you bleach an item.

- Bleach the entire garment, rather than just the spot, so you'll avoid a color change.

- Keep your eyes and hands well protected. Bleach is harmful to the skin and can even cause blindness.

How to Save a Mint on Dry Cleaning

I used to dry-clean my whole closet because I was too scared (and lazy) to do otherwise. But here's a little trick I learned: Just look at the tags on your garments. If it says DRY CLEAN ONLY, go ahead and send it off to the pros. But if the label simply says DRY CLEAN, you can go ahead and hand-wash the item—yep, most cashmere, silk, silk blends, rayon, and linens can be hand-washed.

To wash, fill your sink or tub with cool water and a capful of Woolite. Let the item soak, and rinse thoroughly in warm water. Tops should hang dry; sweaters should be laid flat to dry. Once I realized that most of the sweaters in my closet could be hand-washed, I started saving money, and my sweaters started feeling softer because they were sans chemicals. Also, washing gets rid of smoke and other odors better than dry-cleaning can.

MG TIP: If your DRY CLEAN ONLY garment is not dirty, but just a little bit smelly and wrinkled, refresh it with a few sprays of Febreze and your favorite brand of wrinkle spray.

Ironing . . . Instant Botox for Clothes

I know, I know—just the word *iron* sounds hopelessly time-intensive. But you can get more wears out of your clothes (i.e., less time washing and hauling things to the dry cleaners) if you learn how to iron efficiently.

MG TIP: Begin ironing with those items that are to be ironed at the lowest temperatures and end with the ones that need the hottest settings.

Finding the Right Board

Make sure your board is at the correct height—level with your hips so you're not slouching. Adjust it so that whether you're sitting or standing, you can place your palms on the board without bending your knees.

Temperature-Setting Tips

Use the right temperature setting by checking the labels first for the manufacturer's suggestions. Here are a few rules to go by: For man-made fabrics (such as acetate and acrylic) use the coolest setting suggested. For silk and wool, use a warm setting. Iron cotton and linen on a hot setting.

Ironing Order

MG TIP: Ironing works best on slightly damp clothes—if they're too dry you'll scorch and yellow your garments. Keep a spray bottle or damp bottle at hand for spot dampening.

1. First iron all parts that have a double thickness—ties, bows, collars, sleeves, pockets, and so on. They will wrinkle less quickly than larger, thinner areas like shirt backs (which you should save for last).

2. Iron outward in a slow up-and-down pattern on major areas, pressing harder on the forward motion than the return one. Do not move in circles—that will stretch the fabric. And don't press too hard. The heat and steam should do all the work.

MG TIP: Never iron over buttons, zippers, or snaps—move around them instead with the nose of the iron. For delicate buttons, try using a spoon to protect them and iron the surrounding area.

3. Move backward on shirts. For button-down shirts, iron the reverse side of the button row first, because it will give it a smoother line. Iron the wrong side of a shirt collar first (the backside) and then the front for less wrinkling. For pockets and cuffs, do the wrong side first.

Mastering Pleats

Love having perfect pleats, but can't manage making them? To iron a pant leg or skirt with pleats, pin them in place first (you can pin them to the ironing board cover with stickpins). Holding the pleats taut against the iron pressure, move in long strokes, from waist to hem. If this seems really overwhelming, take your garment to the dry cleaner.

Shine-Free Finish

Avoid shiny spots on your delicate clothes by placing a clean towel (or pressing cloth, which can be found at drugstores) over your clothes. If shine develops, wipe lightly with a damp cloth.

Tricky Fabric Fixes

For silks, rayons, velvets, and corduroys, iron these fabrics inside out. For ruffles and gathers, hang the garment up and use a vertical burst of steam from your iron (or a hand steamer). If the clothing is lined, turn it inside out and iron the lining first.

The Steaming Sensation

You can also cut professional cleaning costs by steaming items that are wrinkled but not dirty. Supposedly a third of the items that wind up at the dry cleaner could do with just a simple steam. A steamer is gentler than an iron and even sanitizes your clothes. I recommend a stand-up steamer; these usually range from $25 to $150. Regardless, it is a worthwhile investment and will save you tenfold in dry cleaning.

MG TIP: When left with no other option, your flat-iron can also double as a clothes iron. But make sure to test it out on something first to ensure there is no hair product residue left on the iron.

Solving Button-Popping Nightmares

For a good three months, I walked around with the southernmost black button missing on one of my skirts because I was too daunted to stitch on a button. Hell, I even *stapled* the skirt together at one point. But it's really not hard—and you certainly don't need a sewing machine to do minor button surgery.

MG TIP: If you lose a jeans button, try Adjust-a-Button, available on Amazon. It is also great when you lose or gain weight but don't want to sacrifice your favorite pair of denim.

Pick the Right Thread

As a general rule, use strong thread that is slightly darker than the fabric you'll be stitching on, as thread appears a little lighter off the spool. Use thinner thread on flimsy fabrics and super-thick threads on denims. Remember: the thicker the cloth, the thicker the thread. Also keep in mind you need a stronger needle for stronger fabrics.

MG TIP: Once you thread your needle, decide if you want your thread to be double thick or not. I usually like to double the thread when sewing on buttons so it's stronger. Just knot both loose ends together.

For a Four-Hole or Two-Hole Button

Close the buttons above and below the missing button area on the garment so you have a clean line to work with. Anchor the thread to the right side of the material with some little stitches—yank on it a little to make sure it's in place. Now place your button where you want it to go. Insert the needle into one hole of the button from the *wrong* side. Then insert the needle into the other hole on the button's right

MG TIP: Never work with a line of thread that's longer than the length of your arm.

MG TIP: When you notice a button is coming loose, reinforce it by stitching over it with thread before it falls off.

MG TIP: Never, ever throw out the extra buttons that come with clothes. I like to keep them in a small velvet box in my cupboard, so I'll always have a spare. If you're really committed, sew the extra buttons into the bottom hem of your outfit as soon as you get it; that way they'll always be on hand.

MG TIP: Can't find a matching button? If you're missing a button on a shirt or dress where it shows and you can't find a button that matches, take one from the bottom edge and put it in the place everyone will see. Then find a close match to put in the less prominent place.

side, passing it through to the wrong side of the garment. Repeat five times, making sure never to sew over the edge of a button (a dead giveaway that you're a novice). When the button is on tight, draw the needle through to the wrong side of the garment, and secure with several tiny stitches, one on top of the other. Cut the thread and you're done. Also, never pull the thread too tight. You need the button to have a little give to ensure it will fasten correctly.

Hemming Pants Like a Pro (without even sewing)

Okay, this is the kind of trick I love, because truthfully, I'll probably never be great at hemming pants (nor do I want to spend the time stitching). All you need are a pair of scissors, fusion tape (find at any notions or mega-supply store), and an iron. Let's say you want to update those pegged pants from the eighties to cute, summery capris, or your calf-length skirt into a mini. Simply cut the material to the length you want (always err on the long side). The beauty of this trick is that you don't even have to cut perfectly straight, because you'll be folding it over. Next, apply your fusion tape on the underside of the garment, fold over to make a neat crease, and iron over it on warm to seal. Let it cool, and iron once again. Your hemline will stay in place, even in the washing machine. But avoid sheer fabrics like chiffon or silk—while the fusion tape may not show through, it might look a little bulky. Better to bring those to the tailor.

Organizing 101

I always thought the reason my house looked messy was that it was too small. But then I moved into a bigger house and, um, had the same problem. The truth is, most of us have knickknacks lying around that can easily be consolidated . . . which equals instant clean.

Cut the Clutter

- Eight picture frames threatening to take over your nightstand or bookshelf? Transfer all your pics into a sleek multiphoto frame that hangs on your wall (find them at Pottery Barn). And though photos have sentimental value on a fridge, taped to mirrors, or tacked to bulletin boards, they can instantly weigh down a room. Put as many photos as you can into albums or clearly marked shoe boxes.

- If you're a magazine fiend like I am and find them piling up everywhere, consider subscribing to their digital issues and making Pinterest boards with your favorite articles and images.

Digital Clutter

Just because it's online doesn't mean it doesn't pile up. In fact, if you're drowning in digital clutter, you are not alone. Here are some ways to manage feeling overwhelmed online:

- Just have too many e-mails to get motivated? Start fresh by labeling one folder "My Past Life" and shove everything in there. Begin your reformed ways with every e-mail after that. Read and respond. Never open an e-mail more than once.

- Create folders for e-mails, but no more than ten. Each folder should be action based—for example, "Responding," "Pending," "Reading," and "Follow Up."

MG TIP: Can't let go of your daily dose of subscription e-mails? Consider starting an account just for newsletter e-mails.

- Pick a target number of e-mails that you want left in your inbox and try to get down to that by the end of the workday.

- Visit a site like www.unrollme.com, which will help you unsubscribe from unwanted junk e-mails.

Streamline Your Bills

MG TIP: To really reduce bill clutter, go to your primary bank's website and register to have all your bills paid online. You'll also save on postage.

MG TIP: Tired of receiving eight million credit card solicitations and junk mail every day? You can put yourself on a do-not-receive list by going to www.dmaconsumers.org.

MG TIP: Identity theft is becoming one of the fastest-growing crimes in the United States. Do yourself a favor and invest in a paper shredder (about $40 at Staples stores). Anything that has an account number, your address, or any other personal information on it should be shredded before it's chucked.

Believe it or not, bills and bank statements can be the biggest clutter items of all. If you're not ready to take it all online just yet, here's how to keep those bills from piling up into mini–Mount Everests on your kitchen counter, coffee table, or nightstand:

- Buy a rectangular basket with two slots, and make one your "in" box (to-be-opened mail) and the other your "out" box (bills to pay, mail to send). Junk everything else immediately.

- For items you want to keep for safety/record purposes, buy accordion files to keep in a designated cabinet. Label each file accordingly, like Visa statements, Rent receipts, Bank Card Info, Tax Returns, and so on. Slip papers into their designated file as soon as you walk through the front door with your mail. It's a little work up front, but you'll instantly feel more organized and in control.

Organizing Your Closet

I'm what you'd call an SWGI (Slob With Good Intentions). As soon as I moved into my current house, I vowed to keep my closet neat. Two months later, new purchases accumulated, and I stopped worrying about what went where, much less hanging things up. It got to the point where I needed a SWAT team to locate my favorite black cashmere sweater. I figured I'd lost it, so I bought another one. Then, when I finally cleaned out my closet top to bottom, there it was, scrunched up in a little ball inside another sweater. Oops. The moral of the story is, if you systematize your stuff, getting dressed each morning will be a whole lot easier.

Take Out "Iffy Items"

It's much better to have a sparse closet of must-have items than a packed-to-the-gills mishmash of random outfits you haven't worn since Bush was in office. Whether it's those skinny jeans from college you're still waiting to fit into or a trendy impulse buy you hated the second you brought it home, ditching clothes that take up dead space is a must. Don't let yourself get nostalgic—if you loved the way it looked on you that much, you would've worn it already. So fill up a trash bag with clothes you haven't donned in at least a year to give to Goodwill, a women's shelter, or the Salvation Army. Perk: You can often get a tax write-off and free pickup service.

MG TIP: If you've got some designer digs you can't bear to donate, try reselling them on eBay or the Real Real, or even taking them to a local thrift/consignment store. You may not break even, but you could at least get a few extra bucks.

Group

Arranging your clothes by pants, skirts, coats, and tops can help you put an outfit together in a matter of milliseconds. Subdivide tops into blouses, button-downs, tanks, and evening stunners, placing your work-wear within easiest reach and your nighttime items farthest away. Split up your suit jackets and matching suit pants into their proper categories—you'll broaden your style options.

Don't Get Bent Out of Shape

Mommy Dearest was right: Wire hangers are a big no-no. They usually come from the dry cleaners (because they're cheapest) and stretch your clothes out of shape and leave little indents—especially on silk items. They can also rust and stain clothes. Opt for wooden or plastic ones instead to improve the life span of your clothes.

MG TIP: If you must go wire, at least get paper-covered ones.

MG TIP: Grab a few velvet hangers for your sweaters and cotton tees or dresses to avoid leaving stretch marks in the shoulders. They'll also prevent slipping and are super thin to maximize space. You can usually find them at Target, Bed Bath & Beyond, or the Container Store. (Or buy them in bulk on Amazon.)

Go Vertical

Maximize every inch of height you have in your closet. Buy hangers that go over the back of your closet door so you can hold belts, purses, and any other light items. For clothes, get multitiered hangers that can hold up to four skirts or pants in one. Have a suitcase that's just taking up space? Put it on your top shelf and fill it with items from the opposite season. For a more permanent solution, buy preassembled stackable shelves that can expand to fit your closet. Or build them yourself (stay tuned for how to use a power drill in chapter 6). Your local home improvement store will have all the materials—and may offer a DIY workshop so you can learn how to install them like a pro.

Stow Seasonal Items Away

MG TIP: Don't store your clothes in dry-cleaning bags; they can collect moisture and cause clothes to yellow.

MG TIP: Don't make containers airtight, as they won't allow air to circulate and may discolor the fabric.

MG TIP: Slip cedar blocks or shelf liners in with your clothes to keep moths at bay.

In winter, you're probably not touching any of your spring/summer clothes, and vice versa. Put all items that can be folded in plastic bins that can easily slide underneath your bed, or garment bags to hang in another closet. Clean them before you store them (and before you go to the store). Stains can attract bugs and dirt can act like sandpaper and create holes. Also, nothing is worse than planning to pull out your fabulous black-tie gown only to find that, unlike your date that night, the chicken sauce came home with you.

Have Enough Light to See, But Not More Than You Need

Like your jokes, your closet should be dark, dry, and clean. Your clothes will be much happier if your closet is darker. Artificial light can fade clothes as well as increase the temperature, which can invite mildew and moths (yuck).

Get a Shoe Tree

MG TIP: Want to keep your boots in shape but don't want to spring for pricey boot trees? Roll up an old copy of your favorite magazine and stick it in lengthwise to keep your boots in shape.

Just two pairs of shoes sprawled out on the floor already make a room look messy. And when you don't have a designated place to put them, it's hard to find the pair you want to wear when you're scrambling around in the morning. Invest in a shoe tree that sits at the base of your closet or that hangs vertically from your coat rod. Store your best shoes inside their boxes, and stash tissue paper in the toes to help keep their shape. If you're a Christian Louboutin fiend and need easy identification, snap a picture of each pair, print it out, and paste it to the top or side of the box.

Keeping Your Bedroom Blissful

When it comes to keeping house, there is no space more sacred than your bedroom. Considering that we spend a third of our lives in bed (and countless more hours doing naughty things there), it only makes sense that you pick the best possible boudoir items and know how to maintain them.

Choosing and Caring for Your Mattress

When looking for a mattress, try to find a combination of support *and* comfort. The right mattress will provide support for all points of your body, but won't be so firm that it can't mold to the body's natural curve. Keep in mind that support isn't everything; several studies suggest that comfort matters more than support when it comes to a good night's sleep, so try to find a balance. Thicker, heavier mattresses with a higher number of coils tend to be higher quality, offering more support, comfort, and longevity.

MG TIP: Don't underestimate the importance of a good box spring. It acts as a shock absorber and will add years on to the comfort life of your mattress.

MG TIP: Buy a plush mattress pad instead of a "featherbed." The latter is too warm to sleep on in the summer, must be professionally cleaned, and doesn't protect against dust mites or stains.

Pillow tops are a good choice for comfort mongers (as long as the body of the mattress is thick and firm and provides enough internal support). However, some people complain that pillow tops tend to be more flimsy and don't last as long as regular mattresses. Ultimately it comes down to a matter of taste. If you do choose a pillow top, be sure to buy sheets large enough and deep enough for the mattress; you will most likely need sheets with a nine- to thirteen-inch pocket to accommodate the added height.

For every mattress, turn, turn, turn. A good mattress will conform to your body's natural contours, but it can't do that if you sleep on one side of the mattress for too long. You should turn your mattress once every two to three weeks for the first three months of use. After that once every three to four months will do the trick.

Picking Out the Perfect Pillow

- Choose a firm pillow if you sleep on your side because you want your head to stay in alignment with your spine. But if you sleep on your stomach, choose a softer pillow. Why? A firm one holds your head and neck up too high, causing you to arch your back out of whack.

- If you have allergies, buy a hypoallergenic pillow cover with a zipper and slip your regular pillowcase over it, or choose a fiberfill pillow instead. Also vacuum under the bed once a week; allergens love to hide there.

- Change your pillowcases once or twice a week. Pillowcases collect a lot of dirt and grease. In fact, cleaner cases may help lead to clearer skin.

- Goose-down pillows should be replaced every five to ten years; synthetic pillows every two years.

What Kind of Sheets Should You Buy?

The next time you're in the sheet section, here are three key things to keep in mind: *thread count, fiber,* and *finish:*

MG TIP: Fold your fitted sheets with finesse with the simple steps illustrated on page 54.

- Choose a 200- to 300+-thread count (this is the total number of threads woven per square inch). The higher the thread count, the bigger the price tag. But you also want to look at the ply. Single ply tends to be softer, as two ply is made from yarns that are twisted together. Don't be deceived by a high thread count on a two-ply sheet: a single-ply 200-count sheet will be about the same softness as a two-ply 400-count sheet.

MG TIP: If there's cat or dog hair on your bedspread, throw it in the dryer and it'll come right off.

- Make sure the fiber is silk or cotton (preferably Egyptian cotton). Egyptian cotton is the softest and most durable. Skip polyester blends and satin sheets—they don't breathe well, which means you'll be sweaty.

MG TIP: To keep sheets organized and handy, put a complete sheet set inside one of the pillowcases. Then stick a safety pin with a label on top, noting the size of the set.

- A sateen finish will give your sheets a silky smooth quality. For a crisper sheet, choose a combed all-cotton percale with a thread count of 250.

- Change your sheets every week and duvet covers every two weeks.

How to Make a Hotel-Heavenly Bed

Now that you have all of your sleeping essentials, it's time to make them look as luxurious as possible. What I love most about staying at hotels is how amazing it feels to sink into their freshly made beds. Here are a few secrets from the hotel pros on how to make one up yourself:

- Create room for your feet: Lay your top sheet flat over your bottom sheet. At the foot of the bed, pull it back over itself eight inches so it creates a pocketlike fold. Then tuck the sheet in at the edges. This "foot fold" creates space for your feet.

- For optimum airy coolness, let the sides of the sheets hang down on their own.

- Give your bed a "turned-down" look by folding your duvet or comforter over twelve inches.

- For a supersoft feel, dust talcum powder over white cotton sheets.

- Notice how in posh hotels, beds look plush but never fussy? Two clean-lined, oversize rectangular shams in neutral or all white look fresher than five frilly colored ones.

> **MG TIP:** Make your bed right before or after your morning shower. Once your bed looks neat, your room will look 75 percent cleaner. Plus, at the end of your long workday, you'll love slipping under freshly smoothed covers and sheets.

How to Fold a Fitted Sheet

1.

Hold the sheet with your hands inside two of the pockets on one of the short ends.

2.

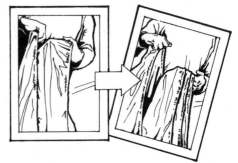

Fold the corner in your right hand over the corner in your left hand and continue with the other two corners until all four corners are tucked in.

3.

Lay the sheet on a table or the bed and tuck in all the edges.

4.

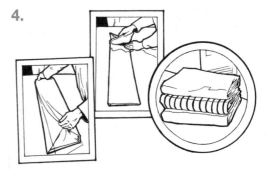

Fold the sheet neatly until it is the desired size.

WHIP YOUR GUEST ROOM INTO B&B SHAPE FOR WEEKEND GUESTS

Just as important as making your own bedroom livable is setting up the perfect guest room. I'd love to say that I plan weeks in advance whenever I have friends or family coming to stay for the weekend, but the truth is, I'm often pulling late nights in the office all week and find myself scrambling to get everything in order come Thursday evening. While my schedule will probably never let up, I've learned a few last-minute tricks to make my guests feel comfortable:

- *Push the bed away from the wall* so your guests don't have to climb over each other to get in and out of it.

- *Set the room temperature* between 68°F and 70°F and show your guests where the thermostat is so that they can adjust it to their liking.

- *Fix a squeaky metal bed frame* by spraying WD-40 on all the places where metal hits metal (you don't want to hear them having sex, do you?). For a wooden frame, sprinkle baby powder into the joints, and then work it into the cracks with a toothbrush.

- *Put an alarm clock in their room* as well as a night-light so they have a clear path to the bathroom.

- *Keep a blanket and bath towels* folded near the bed. That way they won't be hunting around for them (or using yours).

- *Make up an amenities basket* of aspirin or Tylenol, toothpaste, shampoo, disposable razors, lotion, bottled water, and Walker's shortbread cookies or nuts for them to snack on.

- *Leave a duplicate of your house key* on their dresser so they can come and go as they please.

- *Light vanilla-scented candles* to give the room a welcoming vibe.

- *Hide your sex toys!*

Zen and the Art of Bathroom Maintenance

I know, keeping your bathroom in order isn't half as much fun as maintaining your bedroom. In fact, it sounds about as sexy as getting a root canal. But if you establish a schedule for yourself and do a quick scrub here and there (rather than leaving it all for one sad, grime-filled Saturday) it'll be a lot easier. Oh, and once you're done, it's required that you reward yourself with a long bubble bath and a glass of Chardonnay.

Mold, Mildew, and Soap Scum: Three Uninvited Guests

Your first step in making your bathroom look great is getting rid of the grime. (Blue cheese is yummy, but not when it looks like there are traces of it in your shower and tub.) To prevent this from happening:

Buy These Products
- Toilet bowl cleaner
- Windex (for bathroom windows, shower doors, and mirrors)
- A mildew-removing spray cleaner (like Lysol Basin Tub & Tile Cleaner)
- Comet (to scrub stubborn bathtub stains)
- A toilet brush
- A tub brush
- All-purpose spray with antibacterial ingredients (like Formula 409)
- Clorox premoistened wipes
- You can also consider eco-friendly versions like the ones from The Honest Company

Do a Daily Wipe-Down
Spritz an antibacterial cleanser on the walls and corners of your bathtub, shower curtain, sink tops, toilet, and faucets and wipe down with a paper towel (sponges harbor bacteria). Do this for two minutes a day and you're golden. Also, keep Clorox premoistened wipes under your

sink to do quick cleanups like face powder residue and hairspray buildup. Better yet, try using facial wipes before you go to bed on your face, and then give the sink a quick wipe with the cloth when you're done.

Okay, You Forgot to Do the Wipe-Down . . .

If serious soap-scum stains have built up, coat the surface with undiluted detergent and allow it to dry for several hours. Wet the same surface with a solution of liquid detergent and water. While the surface is still wet, sprinkle it with scouring powder; then scrub it with a stiff brush.

Bleach It

For nail polish, blood, coffee, tea, food, fruit juice, or lipstick stains in your bathroom, apply household bleach using plastic gloves. (Bleach also works wonders for stubborn toilet stains.) But *never* mix bleach with other cleaning products—especially any with ammonia in them. This mixture creates poisonous fumes.

Grime Between Your Tiles?

Just color the grout. Go to your local hardware store and ask for a simple grout colorant. It spreads right on with a toothbrush or Q-Tip, dries quickly, and does for your bathroom what Crest Whitestrips do for yellowed teeth.

Keeping the Rest of Your Bathroom Clean

- Spray the bathroom mirror with air freshener (it cleans and leaves a nice scent). Wipe with paper towels, or for fewer streaks, use newspaper.

- Use a toilet bowl cleaner or drop-in tablet and give the bowl a good scrubbing once a week. Rinse your toilet brush by sticking it in the clean toilet and flushing. Store it in a big plastic cup so as to avoid toilet water drips across the floor.

- Remove your shower curtain every month and give it a good scrub with a bristle brush and Comet. Wash it under the tub faucet. Still grimy? Your best bet is to trash it and replace it with a clear plastic

MG TIP: Don't stash your prescriptions and vitamins in the medicine cabinet, where it's humid. Rx's keep better in the fridge; vitamins keep better in a cool, dry place like your pantry or cupboard (refrigeration will speed deterioration of their two- to three-year shelf life).

one. Skip fabric curtains; they hold on to wetness, which leads to mildew. If you love decorative shower curtains, however, buy clear liners in bulk that can deal with all the water. They're cheap and can be replaced often.

- Make sure there's a plunger in the bathroom. Go for a stylish chrome one that sits in its own case.

- If you have a hair ball the size of Chewbacca in the tub drain, slip your hand inside a damp coffee filter to pull it out.

WHAT EVERY MODERN GIRL SHOULD KEEP IN HER MEDICINE CHEST

- Ace bandage and tape
- Antacid
- Antibiotic ointment
- Band-Aids
- Clear nail polish
- Dental floss
- Eye drops
- Hydrogen peroxide
- Ibuprofen
- Mini-scissors
- New toothbrush
- Over-the-counter cold meds (A.M. and P.M.)
- Over-the-counter cough syrup (check expiration date)
- Pepto-Bismol
- Petroleum jelly
- Rubbing alcohol
- Sunscreen
- Tweezers

MG TIP: We all know houseguests like to snoop in medicine cabinets (I'm guilty of it myself after a few too many drinks). Keep a small plastic container under your sink so at the last minute, you can toss in items you don't want anyone to see (think: mustache bleach).

Aggh! What's That Crawling Across the Floor?

There's nothing more disconcerting after stepping out of a nice hot shower or padding barefooted into your kitchen for a snack, only to see something large and multilegged scuttling across your floor. After you're done freaking out (which it totally warranted, by the way), here's how to get rid of the most common household pests:

Mice and Rats

- *Don't use rat poison on your own.* A pet could eat the poison (or the dead poisoned rat). If you fear you have a big rat problem and there's not just one scurrying around, call an exterminator to distribute the poison instead. Otherwise, follow these tips:

- *Meet Mr. Tupperware.* Mice and rats are born grazers and will go anywhere to nibble. Don't keep open packages of pasta, cereal, cookies, or chips in the cupboard and don't leave other food lying around.

- *Consider getting a cat or dog.* Your furry friends will play bodyguard and keep mice and rats at bay.

- *Buy a glue trap.* Glue traps are pieces of cardboard or wood that have a gooey glue coating. They work effectively and don't decapitate the pests' heads like snap traps often can. Use heavy gloves when removing the trap and putting it in your outside trash can.

- *Buy a catch and release trap.* If the idea of killing a mouse makes you squirm, buy one of these at your local hardware store. The mouse enters the baited trap and the little door closes behing it, trapping the mouse inside. The trap can then be moved to a new location and the mouse can be released unharmed.

MG TIP: Oftentimes cockroaches will come into your home hidden in boxes or shopping bags and you won't even realize it until you find them snooping around your kitchen. So don't freak if you find just one roach . . . investigate the issue before assuming it's a larger problem.

Cockroaches

The best solutions to keeping cockroaches away are not leaving food or damp spots around and fixing leaky plumbing (hence the big guys' name, "waterbugs"). But, hello—sometimes you can't control when these hideous creatures come, no matter if you keep zero food in your house and every room dry as a bone.

That's when you go with a professional exterminator who can use concentrated insecticide sprays and boric acid powder in clever places where roaches like to hide—places you may not have considered—and can plug up small holes with steel wool. But in the meantime, if you want to tackle them, you have a couple of options:

Roach Motels

I like using these best because you don't ever have to see the disgusting roach. Products such as Combat and Raid Max work as baits and can be put under your bathroom and kitchen sinks, as well as in cupboards. What they do is lure in roaches, which subsequently eat the poison, take it back to their extended families living in the walls—and are killed. Pick up the motel with a rubber glove, place it in areas pets and kids can't get to (under low couches, behind book shelves), and toss every three months. Since they're out of sight, put a reminder in your phone so that you know when it's time to get new ones.

Raid-Type Sprays

If the problem is localized in one small area (like your kitchen drawers or cupboards), you may want to use a spray that kills on contact. Just make sure to keep food, dishes, and utensils out of sight. Also cover your hands with rubber gloves when you spray, and try not to inhale. I made the mistake of not being careful of either and wound up getting so much spray on my right hand that it went numb for a few minutes. Not good.

Bug Bombs

If you still find that the critters are cropping up, use a more permanent solution: a bug bomb. Once you activate this kind of spray in your room (by holding down the button) it's time to get the hell out of the room or better yet, the house (to be super safe, wait twelve to twenty-four hours before reentering the room, but check the directions on your specific spray can). The bonus of these sprays is that they are designed to wipe out all the offending bugs you *can't* see in one fell swoop.

Nature-Bait 'Em
Greenpeace.org recommends this natural alternative: Try lightly greasing the inner neck of a milk bottle and putting a little stale beer or a raw potato in it. Roaches will get in and won't be able to get out. They may not live the best life, but they'll live.

Ants

Certainly not as disgusting as cockroaches or mice, ants are still a horror to deal with because they travel in such large numbers (talk about codependency!). Therefore, to nail them, you have to go to their source. Figure out what the ants are coming in the house for, and where their food source is. Is it sugar, cereal, or honey in the pantry? (They're especially drawn to sweet foods.) They may also be coming in from outside. Once you locate the spot, don't try to block it right away—it's easier to kill ants if they're undisturbed. You have a few options for your next step:

Use Ant Motels
Like the roach motels, they "trick" the ants into taking the powder back into the wall to share with their friends. Make sure not to spray insecticide around the motel. It will repel ants. And be patient; it may take a few weeks to kill them.

Poof on Some Boric Acid Powder
The powder works well when you can see exactly where the ant trail is. Put the dust directly on their path so they can't crawl around it.

Try a Natural Solution
Greenpeace.org recommends you locate the place of ant entry, squeeze a lemon onto it, and leave the peel. Ants are also believed to

retreat from lines of talcum powder, chalk, bonemeal, charcoal dust, and cayenne pepper.

Once you've killed the suckers, block their entry point with petroleum jelly, tape, or a caulking material. If this doesn't work or you simply don't want to deal, call an exterminator.

Hey, we never said being a domestic goddess was glamorous, but look at it this way: You can upgrade your title to domestic gladiator. And now that you've got that down, you can move on to entertaining . . .

CHAPTER 2

Your Cheat Sheet for Fabulous Entertaining (Because Who Has Time to Make Cutesy Canapés?)

I love to throw dinner parties. Not because I relish torturing myself over the stove, planning grocery lists days in advance, and polishing silver in my spare time. It has more to do with the fact that I'm tired of expensive evenings in places with bad service, attitude from waitresses whose thighs are the size of my biceps, and music so loud I can't talk to the people I'm with. I far prefer an intimate evening at home with a few chosen friends who I know I'll enjoy catching up with. The only problem? I'm a terrible hostess. But my Modern Girl secret is that none of my friends know. Let me tell you how I manage to pull it off. But first, you should truly understand just how bad I am.

The first time I met my future husband's father, I invited him and nine of my friends over to our new pad for dinner. I work full time and had barely unpacked the boxes in our new place. I'm a girl who knows my limitations, so at least I wasn't insane enough to cook. Instead, I bought things to make it *look* like I cooked.

As the guests assembled, I made sure they had enough mini-carrots and Carr's crackers to last and excused myself. Time to look busy in the kitchen (pretending you've cooked takes *a lot* of work—there's creatively dabbing flour on your cheek, messing up the kitchen, and ensuring no takeout containers are anywhere to be seen). I had preheated my fancy new oven, but when I went to pop in the baked pasta casserole, the oven wouldn't open. In fact, it wouldn't even turn off. I had turned it to self-clean. And after furiously searching for the manual, I discovered that I would have a better chance of getting into the vault at the Chase bank down the street than into my oven for the next two hours. I summoned my boyfriend and, after explaining the situation, begged him to not tell our guests. (I also needed him to help convince *me* that a completely cold meal wouldn't be suspicious.) We agreed to proceed as planned, to appear continental and have a refreshingly "chilled" meal (turns out cold pasta can be very tasty). No sooner had my boyfriend returned to the living room than I heard gales of laughter. I hoped someone had just told a joke. The truth was, the joke was on me.

In the end, no one cared. My guests had a wonderful time, my future father-in-law went to bed full and welcomed me into the family, and as an added bonus, I had a very clean oven.

The lesson learned? I vowed that never again would I feel quite so ill-equipped to be the hostess I've already convinced everyone I am. Read on for the best ways to "fake it."

Spur-of-the-Moment Entertaining Staples

I always wanted to be the type of woman who could easily handle unexpected guests dropping by after work or for a nightcap after a great night out. You know the gal I mean. She winds up pulling out truffles she picked up last week in Paris or mini–mushroom tarts from her dinner party the evening before. Neither my lifestyle nor my brain will get me there. If I found myself in Paris I'd be too busy scrounging for cheap Chanel to think of guests who haven't even been invited; and should I happen to have actually thrown a dinner party recently, I'd be too afraid to serve the leftovers for fear of food poisoning. And, of course, if I left it up to my natural pantry selection to pull me out of a bind, my only serving options would be Campbell's soup or Lucky Charms, and neither seems to set the right tone. Instead, I try to keep a well-planned, well-stocked pantry, just in case.

I've come up with a failproof list of ten things to have on hand, all designed to satisfy even the most ravenous of spur-of-the-moment guests. Virtually all of it can be bought at a grocery store—and keeps for months. Trust me, once you've pulled it out and entertained effortlessly after a full day at the office and a jam-packed yoga class, you'll be a believer and never run dry again.

1. *Carr's Table Water Crackers*—No matter what you put on them, Carr's somehow look classy enough to make it seem as though you entertain like a professional. Unlike Wheat Thins or Triscuits (which I happily indulge in late at night), Carr's add an elegance you'll need.

2. *Tapenade or marinated artichokes*—Sure, if I'm prepared I buy Brie and some snazzy pâté. But too often my purchase has gotten moldy in my fridge, and one friend barely escaped botulism when I simply ignored an expiration date (Come on, what's an extra two weeks anyway?). Tapenade looks gourmet, and since people aren't really sure whether they like it, you probably can get by with a small jar. Just make sure you also have toothpicks and cute cocktail napkins on hand. Modern Girls know that a harmless little artichoke can drop pellets of oil onto clothes, furniture, or worse yet, your new handbag. (Should this happen anyway, refer back to chapter 1 to help get it out.)

3. *Garlic-, Brie-, or jalapeño-stuffed olives*—Olives somehow say "cocktail hour" and "hors d'oeuvres" in one. They're the gourmet's answer to the bar nut. They can prove quite filling and can wind up either in martinis or on a little serving plate. And if you buy pitted ones, even olive skeptics will dive in.

4. *Nuts*—Go for candied walnuts, pecans, almonds, and cashews, as these look fanciest and can be served at virtually any occasion, from brunch time to cocktail hour.

5. *Bread sticks*—When in doubt, pull these out. I like the thin Italian ones that aren't too filling. Sure, they may be a bit phallic, but depending upon your guests this may not be the worst thing.

6. *Walkers Shortbread Cookies*—You have to hand it to the English. They make a crusty cookie seem like the height of refinement. They somehow convey to your guests that they're lucky, sometime you'll invite them to a proper dinner party when you've had more notice.

7. *Box of chocolates*—If you're like me, you'll have to store these on a high shelf and convince yourself they don't exist. Otherwise you'll wind up opening them hoping some visitor—*any* visitor—might pop by. Assuming you can resist, chocolates are perfect whether a guest shows up at 4 P.M. or 4 A.M.

8. *Bread/muffin mix*—If your evening visitor turns into a morning after, then nothing says prepared like fresh baked goods. Find a mix that requires neither eggs nor milk. Modern girls are gracious, but *not* dairy queens.

9. *Bottle of champagne*—If nothing else, get some champagne in the house—preferably a label that will wow them, but any will do. No matter what the time or the other accoutrements, champagne signals festivity and makes your guests feel you're happy to see them (even if you're annoyed because you seem to be blowing a fortune on champagne lately). On top of that, chances are your guests will leave a little too tipsy to realize you didn't feed them enough.

10. *French onion soup mix*—Okay, this falls in the realm of extra credit. I'll toss it in with plain yogurt, cream cheese, or sour cream that has yet to grow curd. Whipping up a dip is a super-easy way to satisfy guests when you have minimal prep time.

MG TIP: You can "speed-chill" wine or champagne in about twenty minutes by completely submerging the bottle in a bucket filled with half ice and half water. This will chill the bottle much faster than ice alone.

MG TIP: What good are crackers without spread or spread without crackers? The key to maintaining your last-minute entertaining ability is to replace any item you've used virtually the instant you've used it. Keep the empty box or container out of the garbage and to the side when you're done. That way you're more likely to remember to refill it tomorrow.

The Full-Blown Cocktail and Dinner Party

When I finally do get around to hosting a proper party, Carr's crackers and champagne alone won't cut it. And unfortunately for me, choosing a menu is akin to taking the SATs: No matter how much I try to prepare, I need to hope for luck. Recipe books seem to be written for another species. What's a "pinch"? What's "season to taste"? If I had so much confidence in my "taste" I wouldn't need a damn cookbook! What's worse is finally getting around to deciphering the cookbook code and slaving in the kitchen, only to find out no one can eat your concoction (despite its beautiful plating). How can anyone keep up with the ever-expanding list of restrictions? Gluten-free, vegan, sugar-free, soy-free, raw, probiotic, sustainable—it's never ending. So I've decided that Modern Girls don't need to experiment (in the kitchen anyway)—they just need to have a few surefire hits.

Fabulous Small Bites for Eight

I love this menu because it's fun, easy, and even looks a little exotic. Somewhere between a cocktail party and a dinner, it will impress your guests and fill them up more than the standard cocktail party fare of cheese and crackers. But there are other reasons that I depend on it to please a crowd:

MG TIP: Do your homework. Ask guests before setting your menu if they have any dietary restrictions. You can't cater to everyone, but this way you hopefully avoid watching guests dodge every piece of chicken in your stew.

- When you're inviting eight people or more and aren't a master chef, I find it's better to do a handful of little dishes that can be prepped in advance, rather than sweating over a grand masterpiece that may or may not flop, shrivel, or blow up in your oven.

- All the dishes can be made before the guests arrive and can be served at room temperature.

- Serving is simple. Everything is arranged on large rectangular or oval plates, set on the table, and passed from person to person so they can serve themselves. Translation: You aren't running back and forth from the kitchen eight times to arrange people's individual plates.

MG TIP: Small bites are sexy because you can eat many of them with your fingers, taste a lot of different flavors at one meal, and share with your fellow dinner guests.

• If one dish burns or I miss an all-important ingredient and it tastes like my shoe, I've got other dishes ready to go.

THE MENU

First Round:

Assorted gourmet olives and nuts, Asparagus Mushroom Tarts, Prosciutto and Melon

Second Round:

Mini-Meatballs with Cool Yogurt Sauce, Warm Figs with Goat Cheese, Grilled Garlic Shrimp

Dessert:

Easy Homemade Ice Cream

Drinks:

Prosecco, Rosemount Shiraz, and Robert Mondavi Fumé Blanc

THE TIMETABLE

Since you're working with a handful of dishes here, you'll need a timetable:

1 day before your party: Buy all ingredients.

3½ hours before: Prepare the tarts, make the meatball mixture and the yogurt sauce, and assemble the prosciutto and melon; refrigerate all.

2½ hours before: Hop in the shower, do your hair and makeup, and put on something comfortable (but not your party clothes . . . you don't want last-minute spills).

1½ hours before: Cook the meatballs; put on the top rack of oven set at 200°F.

1 hour before: Cover and transfer the meatballs to the microwave to keep warm, while using the oven to cook the tarts at 400°F in the oven. Reduce the heat to 200° degrees when you have finished. Put the meatballs back into the oven to keep warm.

30 minutes before: Grill the shrimp and slide onto an ovenproof dish into the warm oven.

15 minutes before: Slip into your party outfit and touch up your makeup and hair.

5 minutes before: Set out the olives and nuts, the assembled tarts . . . and *breathe*!

MG TIP: As soon as people walk through your door, offer them a glass of Prosecco (Italian sparkling wine). It looks and tastes like champagne but often gives you more bang for your buck.

Putting It All Together

Olives

You should already have these stocked (since they're one of the Modern Girl staples listed earlier). If not, go to your local gourmet grocery store and fill three plastic containers with assorted olives in different shapes and colors (Niçoise, Kalamata, spicy green . . .). Make sure one tub is spicy, but not all of them.

Nuts

Think almonds, pecans, cashews, and Brazil nuts. If you have time before your guests arrive, heat them on a cookie sheet for five to seven minutes at 300°F—they'll have a richer, toastier flavor.

Asparagus Mushroom Tarts

1 17.3-ounce package frozen puff pastry (typically 2 sheets), thawed

¼ cup (½ stick) unsalted butter

12 ounces fresh cremini mushrooms, chopped

2 teaspoons coarse kosher salt, divided

1½ teaspoons coarsely ground black pepper, divided

1 pound slender asparagus spears, trimmed, cut on diagonal into 1-inch pieces

1½ teaspoons chopped fresh thyme

1½ teaspoons finely grated lemon peel

½ cup crème fraîche

½ cup (packed) coarsely grated Gruyère cheese (about 2 ounces)

Fresh thyme sprigs (for garnish)

SERVES 8

The day before:

Roll out each pastry sheet on a floured work surface and cut into approximately 2-inch squares. Using a small knife, score a half-inch border (do not cut through pastry) inside the edges of each square and arrange on 2 rimmed baking sheets.

Melt butter in a large skillet over medium-high heat. Add mushrooms, sprinkle with 1 teaspoon salt and 1 teaspoon pepper, and sauté until tender and lightly browned, about 4 minutes. Transfer the mushrooms to a bowl and cool, about 15 minutes. Toss with asparagus, thyme, lemon peel, and remaining salt and pepper. Add crème fraîche and Gruyère. Cover and chill.

The day of:

Preheat the oven to 400°F. Mount filling atop squares, leaving a half-inch border. Bake 20 to 22 minutes, or until puffed and golden and filling is cooked through. Garnish with thyme sprigs and serve.

Prosciutto and Melon

1 cantaloupe
1/2 pound thinly sliced prosciutto

Slice the cantaloupe into U-shaped slices ¼ inch thick, removing the outer rind of the melon. Slice each piece again into a "half-U." Trim the excess fat from the outer edges of the prosciutto. Wrap one slice of prosciutto around each half slice of melon so that only the ends of the melon show. Arrange on a plate, cover with plastic wrap, and refrigerate. Just before serving, insert a toothpick into each slice—it will keep the prosciutto in place and make eating it easier for your guests.

Warm Figs with Goat Cheese

16 ripe figs (If you can, look for Black Mission figs, the smaller the better.
    Figs are in season in the summer and fall.)
4 ounces goat cheese
1 1/2 tablespoons balsamic vinegar
Fresh cracked pepper

Preheat the oven to 350°F. Cut the figs into four slices that are still connected (so they look like open flowers), making sure not to cut all the way to the bottom. Arrange the figs cut side up on a cookie sheet, spoon a little goat cheese inside each fig, and lightly brush the figs with vinegar. Bake for about 8 minutes. Top with a twist of cracked pepper. Transfer the figs to a platter just before serving. Your guests can simply pick them up and eat them with their hands (it takes about two bites), but have forks and knives on the table for daintier eaters who would prefer to cut the figs into small pieces.

Mini-Meatballs

1 pound ground beef (ideally lean, but it doesn't really matter)

1/2 pound lean ground pork

1/2 cup minced onion

3/4 cup dried bread crumbs

1 teaspoon dried parsley

2 teaspoons salt

1/8 teaspoon finely ground pepper

1 teaspoon Worcestershire sauce

1 egg

1/2 cup milk

1/4 cup canola oil

Place all the ingredients except the oil in a large mixing bowl. With clean hands, mix the ingredients thoroughly. Cover the bowl with plastic wrap, and refrigerate for 45 minutes to an hour to set. Form the mixture into about 16 meatballs the size of golf balls (or a little larger if you prefer, because they will shrink down when you cook them). Pour the canola oil into a large skillet over medium-high heat, preheating the oil for 3 to 4 minutes. To test that the oil is hot enough, place one "sample" meatball in the oil; if it sizzles, the oil is ready. Set half the meatballs in the pan with a slotted spoon and reduce the heat to medium. Cook for approximately 7 minutes, turning them occasionally, until they're browned on all sides. Test one by cutting through it—the inside should be a light pinkish brown. Repeat with the second batch of meatballs. To keep the first batch of meatballs warm while the rest are cooking, set them in an ovenproof dish in a warm oven set at about 200°F. Serve the meatballs with the Cool Yogurt Sauce (recipe follows).

Cool Yogurt Sauce

One 16-ounce container plain yogurt
1 tomato, diced
1 cucumber, chopped
1 scallion, finely chopped
1 tablespoon white vinegar
Paprika

Spoon the yogurt into a large mixing bowl and add the tomato, cucumber, and scallion (the white and light green parts). Mix in the white vinegar and top with two shakes of paprika. Do not mix in the paprika, or it will all turn pink! Cover and refrigerate.

Grilled Garlic Shrimp

2 tablespoons olive oil
2 cloves garlic, pressed or minced
1¹/₂ pounds raw jumbo shrimp, peeled and deveined
1 lemon
Salt and pepper

Heat the olive oil and garlic in an ovenproof skillet over medium-high heat. Add the shrimp and cook for 3 minutes, turning once halfway through. Squeeze the lemon over the shrimp and give the entire dish ten shakes of salt and four twists of pepper. Transfer the skillet directly into a 200°F oven to keep warm.

MG TIP: While I can get everything ready, I've never found the secret to getting it all hot at the same time. Sure, it would be great to have two ovens, but most of us don't live in a kitchen showroom. But you can get the same effect of having everything heated at once by covering your food with aluminum foil and not removing the food from its cookware until you are ready to serve. Once you've transferred your food to oven-safe serving platters, stick your plates in the oven for just a few minutes to warm them.

MG TIP: Ever wonder how to clean and devein shrimp? Hold the shrimp with the outside curve and tail away from you. With kitchen scissors, cut through the shell along the top of the shrimp to the tail. Peel back the shell and remove it, keeping the tail intact. Hold the peeled shrimp under running water. Make a shallow incision with a paring knife along the backside of the shrimp. Remove the "vein" (really the shrimp's digestive tract), a dark brown or occasionally green or orange membrane. Just scrape it out.

I know, shrimp deveining can be a bit gross. If you're like me (easily queasy in the kitchen), you may want to shop for shrimp that have already been cleaned and don't require deveining. You may even want to invest in a deveiner. You can get a manual deveiner for about $2.50 or an electric deveiner for $40 to $50 online.

Easy Homemade Ice Cream

SERVES 8

2 small, very ripe bananas
1 cup heavy cream
24 ounces frozen berries, divided
2 teaspoons vanilla extract
2 teaspoons rum

MG TIP: For a sweet twist your foodie friends will love, try incorporating fresh herbs such as mint, lavender, or basil into your ice cream. The fruit-and-herb combination is surprisingly refreshing and delicious!

Blend banana, cream, half the frozen berries, vanilla extract, and rum in a food processor on high for 1 minute. Add the other half of the berries and blend until smooth and creamy. If desired, add honey, agave, or sugar for extra sweetness. Freeze for two hours and serve.

Very Easy Vegan for Six

These days, it seems like most everyone has some sort of food allergy or dietary restriction, so it's always good to have an easy, delicious menu that will please just about everyone. This meal is vegetarian, vegan, *and* gluten-free, but it tastes so good you and your guests won't even notice!

THE GLUTEN-FREE MENU

Crudité Platter with Black Bean Hummus and Red Pepper Dip

Roasted Vegetables with Quinoa

Dessert:
Vegan Chilled Chocolate Pie

Drinks:
A good sauvignon blanc like Giesen Sauvignon Blanc 2012

Putting It All Together

Black Bean Hummus

1 cup cooked black beans
1 garlic clove, minced
2 tablespoons olive oil
1–2 tablespoons lemon juice
1 tablespoon white wine vinegar
Kosher salt
Freshly ground black pepper
½ avocado, sliced, to garnish (optional)

Blend all ingredients except avocado in a food processor until almost smooth. Let sit 15 minutes, then serve with sliced avocado on top.

Red Pepper Dip

6 large red bell peppers
1 cup (6 ounces) golden raisins, coarsely chopped
¼ cup plus 2 tablespoons extra-virgin olive oil
3 tablespoons salt-packed capers, rinsed well and drained
1½ teaspoons coarsely chopped fresh oregano
Coarse salt
Red wine vinegar

Roast peppers over a gas flame or under the broiler until charred all over. Transfer to a heatproof bowl and cover with plastic wrap. Let cool, then peel and seed. Pulse peppers in a food processor until finely chopped. Add raisins, oil, capers, and oregano and pulse to combine. I know I complain about nonspecific recipes, but as salt and vinegar are very taste specific I will tell you that I use about ½ teaspoon salt and about 1 tablespoon vinegar, but you may prefer to mix in more (or less) and serve with hummus and 3–5 assorted vegetables.

MG TIP: If you're low on serving bowls, serve the dip and hummus in large leaves of iceberg lettuce. It makes for a cute presentation, not to mention fewer dishes to clean.

MG TIP: Brush slices of baguette with olive oil and grill as an extra item to dip. You'll earn bonus points from your guests for sprinkling them with salt, pepper, and parsley.

MG TIP: If you have a gas stove, the easiest method for roasting peppers is right over the open flame. Turn your burner to the highest setting and rest your pepper directly on the flame. Rotate the pepper every minute or so until the skin is charred on all sides.

Quinoa with Roasted Vegetables

First, make the quinoa on page 25. While it's cooking, start your vegetables.

Roasted Vegetables

2 medium zucchini

1 red bell pepper

1 yellow or orange bell pepper

1 pound mushrooms

1 fennel bulb

1 small red onion

2 tablespoons good olive oil

1 tablespoon minced garlic (about 3 cloves)

1 teaspoon kosher salt

½ teaspoon freshly ground black pepper

1 tablespoon herbes de Provence

MG TIP: When cooking anything, make sure to provide some breathing room in your pan, dish, skillet—whatever. If you don't, the food will cook unevenly and won't taste as good. Trust me, nobody likes a soggy "roasted" vegetable.

MG TIP: You can add just about anything to quinoa and it tastes great! Swap seasonal vegetables and mix up the proteins for a healthy meal that's never boring.

Dice the vegetables and toss with olive oil and garlic in a bowl. Spread vegetables in one layer on two sheet pans. Sprinkle with salt and pepper and place herbes de Provence on top. Roast at 400°F for 15 minutes. Turn each piece and continue roasting for another 5 to 10 minutes until vegetables are crisp-tender. Sprinkle with extra salt, toss with quinoa, and serve.

Vegan Chilled Chocolate Pie

For the crust:

¼ cup coconut oil, plus a little extra to grease the pie dish

¾ cup raw almonds

3 tablespoons maple syrup

¼ teaspoon fine-grain sea salt

½ cup oat flour

1 cup rolled oats

For the filling:

1 (15-ounce) can full-fat coconut milk, chilled in fridge overnight
  (so the cream solidifies)
1 bag dark vegan chocolate or carob chips (about 340 grams)
Pinch of salt
1 teaspoon vanilla extract
Liquid sweetener (to taste)
1 cup fresh raspberries to garnish

MG Tip: Trader Joe's regular chocolate chips are already vegan!

For the crust: Preheat the oven to 350°F and lightly grease a 9-inch pie dish with a little coconut oil. Add almonds to food processor and process until fine, sandlike crumbs form. Add remaining crust ingredients and process until dough comes together and sticks. Press dough evenly over base of pie dish, starting from the middle and moving outward and upward (press hard!). Use a fork to poke 5 or 6 holes in the crust and bake for 10 to 13 minutes, until lightly golden. Remove and cool for 20 minutes.

For the filling: Carefully scoop out the solid white cream from the chilled coconut milk, discarding the water. Add chips and stir until combined. Heat over low-medium heat until just melted. Remove from heat and stir in salt, vanilla, and sweetener (if desired) until smooth.

Pour filling into crust and spread evenly. Place in the freezer for 2 hours or until firm throughout. Serve chilled with fresh berries on top.

Refreshing Spa Dinner with Grilled Dill Salmon for Six

What I like about this menu is that it seems fancy, but requires virtually no prep time, few utensils, and is pretty hard to mess up.

THE MENU

Garlic Bread

Orange and Jicama Salad

Grilled Dill-Mustard Salmon

Herb-Roasted Potatoes

Broccoli with Garlic and Parmesan Cheese

Dessert:
Fresh Raspberries and Cream

Drinks:
Serve with a crisp white wine like Nepenthe 2001 Sauvignon Blanc. If you prefer red, go with a light pinot noir that won't overpower, such as Kenwood Pinot Noir.

THE TIMETABLE

1 day before: Buy all ingredients.

3 or more hours before: Cut up salad ingredients; cover in separate containers in fridge. Prep broccoli.

2 hours before: Shower, do hair and makeup.

1 hour before: Make sour cream sauce for salmon; refrigerate, covered.

45 minutes before: Prepare and roast potatoes. Sauté broccoli.

20 minutes before: Assemble salad. Make garlic bread.

10 minutes before: Set salmon steaks on plate in your fridge for easy transfer to your broiler.

5 minutes before: Take a big sip of vino and slip into something sexy. Voilà.

Once guests have started on their salad course, transfer the salmon steaks to oven. They will take approximately 10 minutes to broil.

Putting It All Together

Garlic Bread

½ cup (1 stick) butter, melted
4 cloves garlic, minced or pressed
One 1-pound loaf unsliced French baguette, halved lengthwise
4 tablespoons freshly grated Parmesan cheese
Freshly ground black pepper
1 tablespoon dried parsley

Preheat the oven to 400°F. In a small bowl, combine the butter and garlic. Place the bread halves on a cookie sheet and brush the cut surfaces with the butter mixture. Sprinkle each piece of bread with 2 tablespoons of the Parmesan. Season with pepper and the parsley, and bake until golden brown, 10 to 12 minutes. Cut the bread into 1-inch-wide slices and serve.

Orange and Jicama Salad

1 pound jicama, peeled and cut or julienned into skinny sticks
6 navel oranges, segments cut free from their membranes
    (you know, that white stuff)
¾ small red onion, peeled and sliced into rings
½ cup minced fresh cilantro or watercress leaves
1½ tablespoons fresh lemon juice
1 teaspoon salt
3 tablespoons toasted pine nuts

MG TIP: To cut membranes from an orange, take a whole, unpeeled orange and with a sharp knife shear away the peel; go deep enough so that the knife takes off the membrane as well. Then separate into sections. Be sure to save the juice.

In a large bowl, combine all the ingredients except the pine nuts. You can make this salad 1 day in advance and refrigerate it. Sprinkle each serving with nuts before serving.

Broiled Salmon with Dill-Mustard Sauce

2 tablespoons chopped fresh dill (buy one bunch), plus
    fresh dill sprigs for garnish
4 tablespoons Dijon mustard
2 tablespoons honey
¾ cup mayonnaise
¼ cup sour cream
1 lemon cut into 6 wedges
Six 1-inch-thick salmon fillets (each about 6 ounces)
Nonstick cooking spray

MG TIP: This salmon recipe works just as well with skinless salmon. The cooking time should remain the same.

Preheat the broiler in your oven. In a small bowl, combine the chopped dill, mustard, and honey. Place 2 tablespoons of the mixture in a smaller dish and reserve the sauce for basting the salmon later. Mix the mayonnaise and sour cream with the remaining dill mixture. Cover and chill in the refrigerator until serving time.

Spray the skin side of the salmon with the nonstick cooking spray. Place the salmon, skin side up, in a broiler pan but *do not spread it with the mustard mixture!* I made this messy mistake once, but only once. Broil the salmon 4 to 6 inches from the heat for about 5 minutes. Then turn the fillets over, brush them with the dill-mustard-honey sauce, and broil for 5 more minutes. You'll know they're done when the fish flakes easily with a fork. Serve the salmon on plates with a dollop of the refrigerated sour cream and dill sauce and garnish with sprigs of fresh dill. Put a lemon wedge on each plate and serve.

MG TIP: For each inch thickness of fish you cook, figure it will take 10 minutes of cooking time.

Herb-Roasted Potatoes

2 tablespoons olive oil

1 pound red-skinned new potatoes; each cut in half, eyes removed

½ teaspoon dried thyme, crumbled

½ teaspoon dried marjoram, crumbled

Salt

Freshly ground black pepper

MG TIP: For a distinctly Mediterranean flavor, squeeze a little fresh lemon juice over the top of the potatoes 5 minutes before they're done.

Preheat the oven to 450°F. Brush a large heavy baking sheet with 1 tablespoon olive oil. Combine the potatoes, herbs, and remaining 1 tablespoon olive oil in a mixing bowl and toss well. Spread the seasoned potatoes over the prepared baking sheet. Sprinkle with salt and pepper. Roast for 30 minutes, or until the potatoes are golden brown, stirring once.

Broccoli with Garlic and Parmesan Cheese

2 tablespoons olive oil

2 tablespoons chopped garlic

2 teaspoons grated lemon peel

2 pounds broccoli (about 3 heads), stalks discarded and crowns cut into florets

½ cup water

½ cup grated Parmesan cheese (about 1½ ounces)

Salt

Freshly ground black pepper

In a large skillet over high heat, heat the oil. Add the garlic and lemon peel and stir for 30 seconds. Add the broccoli and toss to coat. Add the water. Cover the skillet and cook until the broccoli is crisp-tender and the water has cooked away, about 5 minutes. Add the Parmesan and toss to coat. Season with salt and pepper.

Fresh Raspberries and Cream

3 pints raspberries, rinsed and gently patted dry

One 8-ounce carton fresh heavy whipping cream (plus sugar to taste)

¼ cup Grand Marnier or other orange liqueur

6 Walkers Shortbread Cookies

Whip the cream until it forms soft peaks, adding sugar to taste. Refrigerate until ready to serve. Spoon the raspberries into six goblets and top each with two heavy dollops of the chilled cream. Give each serving a splash of Grand Marnier (ask guests beforehand if they'd like theirs nonalcoholic). Serve with the cookies.

Fabulous French Steak Frites for Four

I know. . . meat preparation is to a Modern Girl what ballet is to Mike Tyson: *tricky*. But I promise this one's easy and a crowd favorite; it has McDonald's fries, after all! Now, this doesn't mean I encourage devouring a daily Quarter Pounder with Cheese, but the occasional fast-food fry stop is permitted and your guests will be grateful for the indulgence. As for the meat, it's actually a lot easier than it looks. Just be sure to check ahead of time that your guests are carnivores. If all's a go, by dessert they'll be worshipping the ground you walk on.

THE MENU

Simple Mesclun Salad

Filet Mignon with Peppercorn Sauce

McDonald's Fries

Dessert:
Affogato

Drinks:
Serve with a full-bodied red wine,
such as Raymond 2000 Reserve Cabernet Sauvignon
or Matanzas Creek 2001 Syrah

THE TIMETABLE

The morning of: Buy all your ingredients except the fries.

2 hours before: Hop into the shower, do your hair and makeup, and put on comfy clothes. Meanwhile, send your "sous-chef" out to buy McDonald's fries, then transfer them to a cookie sheet and place in the oven at 200°F to keep "warm."

1 hour before: Wash salad greens and prepare the dressing.

40 minutes before: Open the red wine to let it breathe.

30 minutes before: Prepare the Peppercorn Sauce and set aside.

5 minutes before: Quickly slip into your party outfit. Dress and toss the salad just before serving.

After serving guests their salads, slip into the kitchen, remove the fries from the oven, and turn the temperature up to 425°F. Sear your steaks and then put them in the oven, and rejoin your guests. But be sure to check on your steaks after 5 minutes.

MG TIP: Don't drive yourself crazy trying to make everything from scratch. It's sometimes more cost-effective, and almost always more time-efficient, to leave a few things to the experts.

Putting It All Together

Simple Mesclun Salad

2 tablespoons red wine vinegar
1/4 teaspoon salt (kosher or sea)
6 to 8 tablespoons olive oil
3 small shallots, minced
1/2 cup loosely packed parsley leaves, finely chopped
Freshly ground black pepper
2 packages prewashed mixed fresh field greens
2 tomatoes, diced

In a small bowl, combine the vinegar and salt and stir until the salt is dissolved. Slowly pour in the oil, whisking to blend. Stir in the shallots, parsley, and several generous turns of the pepper mill. Place the lettuce in a large salad bowl and toss with the dressing and tomatoes just before serving.

Fries

This is my favorite part of the recipe: Send your "sous chef" (aka spouse, partner, or a willing admirer) out to Mickey D's to pick up three orders of large fries. Warn your sous chef that if even one is eaten (or if he or she dares inhale a burger before coming home), there will be no after-party booty. Keep the fries warm on a cookie sheet in the oven at 200°F. Cover and transfer them to the microwave to keep warm while you cook your steak, then stick them back into the oven you're cooking your steak in for the final 4 minutes. Skip the ketchup when serving—steak frites never includes it (the French and Belgians actually consider it an insult). Your guests can mop up their Peppercorn Sauce with the fries. Or serve a side of mayonnaise with herbs if you have compulsive dippers at the table.

Filet Mignon with Peppercorn Sauce

MG TIP: To get the best-quality meat, ask your local butcher for help. Typically, you're looking for the brightest-red pick possible. Bypass anything that is brown or grayish, and make sure the date says it's fresh.

Peppercorn Sauce

1 cup unsalted beef stock

1/2 cup brandy

1/2 cup whipping cream

2 tablespoons green peppercorns with their pickling juice
    (the liquid you see in the jar)

1 teaspoon cornstarch

1/2 cup (1 stick) butter, cut into pieces

For the steak:

Four 7-ounce center cuts of USDA choice filet mignon

2 teaspoons salt

1/2 teaspoon pepper

1 teaspoon canola oil

2 tablespoons butter

Since cooking the filets will take no time at all, you'll be making the Peppercorn Sauce first. To make the sauce, in a small saucepan over medium-high heat, combine the stock, brandy, and whipping cream and bring to a boil, whisking frequently. When you see the level of the sauce start to lower (this is called "reduction"), open your jar of green peppercorns and spoon 2 tablespoons of them into the pan, getting some of the pickling liquid in. Add the cornstarch and whisk for 2 minutes. Turn off the heat and, with a whisk, beat in the butter pieces until the sauce is smooth. Cover the sauce and set aside.

To make the filets, preheat the oven to 425°F and pat the steaks dry with paper towels. Rub with salt and pepper on both sides. In a large ovenproof skillet, warm the canola oil over high heat until almost smoking. Add the steaks (all four will fit, since filets are thick and small) and cook for just 1 minute on each side. Resist the urge to keep turning them over and poking them or pushing them into the pan. You want to sear the steaks so they're browned on the outside and juicy pink on the inside.

MG TIP: Do not cut the fat off the edges of the steak before you cook it. The fat will cook down and give the meat its flavor.

Pour off the excess oil from the pan and add the butter. Lower the heat to medium and sauté the steaks for 2 minutes. Place the pan in the preheated oven and cook for 4 to 8 minutes (times may vary depending on the oven) for medium-rare steaks. The steaks should be springy to the touch when squeezed from the sides. Just before you remove your steaks, reheat the peppercorn sauce over medium heat for a minute or two, whisking occasionally. Remove the steaks and transfer to plates. Pour your sauce over them, and voilà.

MG TIP: The best way to brown meat is to avoid nonstick pans. Teflon and other nonstick coatings were designed to avoid burning food—but they also hinder the browning process. A cast-iron oven-proof skillet works best for this recipe.

Affogato

2 cups strong, chilled coffee
1 pint vanilla gelato or ice cream (I'm partial to Häagen-Dazs)
4 Pirouette cookies (optional)

This Italian dessert is one of my favorites because it's not overly sweet or rich—a perfect finisher after filet mignon. Admittedly, Affogato is best prepared with espresso as opposed to coffee, but how many MGs have a high-tech cappuccino machine? I've found that coffee works well as a substitute, as long as it's super-strong, fresh, and top quality.

At the beginning of your dinner party, brew two cups of coffee and refrigerate for at least 45 minutes (you can also make Affogato with warm coffee, but I find that it melts too fast). At dessert time, set out four small tumblers, add two scoops of ice cream to each, then slowly pour just enough chilled coffee over the scoops to generously coat them. Stick a swirly Pirouette cookie in the ice cream. Serve immediately.

Easy Chicken Cordon Bleu and Baked Potatoes for Four

I like this menu because it seems impressive, but the Easy Chicken Cordon Bleu is literally one of the simplest recipes on the planet to make. My friend calls it her easy "gourmet" meal. I call it comfort food at its finest.

THE MENU

Easy Chicken Cordon Bleu

Baked Potatoes

Baby Green Salad

Hard rolls or sourdough bread
from a local bakery (or supermarket bakery in a pinch)

Dessert:
Berry Cream Pie

Drinks:
Serve with a California Chardonnay like McManis 2002
or Morgan Metallico 2002

THE TIMETABLE

This meal is so easy that you almost don't need a timetable, but the following is a basic outline.

1 day before the dinner: Buy all the ingredients.

3¹/₂ hours before: Set the table. Make the pie.

3 hours before: Hop into the shower, do your hair and makeup, put on comfy clothes.

2 hours before: Scrub the potatoes and wrap them in foil. Do the chicken prep.

1 hour and 30 minutes before: Preheat the oven to 350°F.

1 hour and 15 minutes before: Put the chicken and potatoes in the oven to bake (set the timer for 1 hour).

1 hour before: Wash the lettuce and put it in a salad bowl. Slice the fresh Parmesan and put aside, well wrapped.

45 minutes before: Refresh your makeup and hair.

15 minutes before: Check the chicken and potatoes and remove them if they're done. Keep the chicken covered and the potatoes wrapped in foil.

10 minutes before: Drizzle the salad with olive oil, vinegar, salt, and pepper and toss. Garnish with the fresh Parmesan slices.

5 minutes before: Quickly slip into your party outfit.

Easy Chicken Cordon Bleu

4 boneless, skinless chicken breasts
1/2 pound precooked sliced ham
1/2 pound sliced Swiss cheese
One 10 1/2-ounce can cream of mushroom soup
1 cup (8 ounces) sour cream

MG TIP: Whenever you're working with raw chicken, keep the chicken well away from any other ingredients and utensils to avoid salmonella poisoning; and be sure to wash everything the chicken touches (including your hands) with warm, soapy water.

MG TIP: To reduce the fat and calories by one third, use Campbell's 98% Fat-Free or Healthy Request Cream of Mushroom Soup and any brand of light sour cream.

MG TIP: Once again, I recommend investing in a meat thermometer. Chicken breasts should be 170°F in the thickest part when done.

Preheat the oven to 350°F. Lay the chicken breasts on a cutting board, cut off any excess fat, and lightly pound them with a meat tenderizer. Lay the chicken flat. On top of each chicken breast, lay one slice of precooked lean ham and one of Swiss cheese (enough to cover the breast). Roll up the chicken breast, starting at the narrowest end, wrapping in the cheese and ham in the process. Secure the rolled breast with a toothpick in the center. Transfer the rolled breasts to an ovenproof baking dish. In a small bowl, combine the cream of mushroom soup (don't balk, it's every wannabe gourmet cook's staple) with the sour cream. Mix thoroughly and pour over the chicken.

Cover the dish with foil and place it on the center oven rack (place the foil-wrapped potatoes—see below—on the rack surrounding the chicken). Bake for approximately 1 hour, or until the chicken is tender and no longer pink inside and the potatoes can be pierced easily with a fork.

Cover the chicken to keep it warm. Fill a gravy boat or saucer with any sauce that remains in the pan and serve it alongside the chicken and baked potatoes.

Baked Potatoes

MG TIP: If you prefer to use large baking potatoes, be sure to put them in a preheated oven a half hour before putting the chicken in, as the large potatoes will require more cooking time than your chicken dish.

4 to 6 small to medium baking potatoes, such as Russet or Idaho

Scrub the potatoes with a potato scrubber. An unused scouring dish sponge will work just as well. Rinse them thoroughly and towel dry. Wrap them in foil (shiny side out) and pierce each potato through the foil two to three times with a fork. Set them aside until the chicken prep is done. After you place the chicken dish in the oven, arrange the potatoes on the rack around it. To check the potatoes for doneness, pierce them with a fork. If you can insert and remove the fork easily, your potatoes should be done. You can also squeeze them to see if they're soft enough, but be sure to wear oven mitts.

> **MG TIP:** Mashed Potatoes with Chicken Broth
> If you are going to mash instead of bake, you can relieve some of the guilt by adding chicken broth instead of cream. And some may call this sacrilege, but you can even skimp a bit on the butter by adding extra herbs like parsley or chives to add flavor without calories.

Baby Green Salad

4 to 6 cups prepackaged, prewashed assorted baby greens

1/4 to 1/3 cup extra-virgin olive oil

1 1/2 to 2 tablespoons balsamic vinegar

Salt to taste

Freshly ground black pepper

6 very thin slices Parmesan cheese or other hard cheese for garnish (optional)

MG TIP: Use a vegetable peeler for very thin slices.

MG TIP: Invest in a salad spinner. You can buy one quite inexpensively anywhere from Target to Bed Bath & Beyond. You'll never have to dry washed lettuce by hand again.

Empty your greens into a large salad bowl and drizzle them with oil and vinegar. Salt and pepper your greens lightly, then toss and taste, adding more salt and pepper if desired. Garnish with the sliced Parmesan, and serve.

Berry Cream Pie

One 8-ounce package cream cheese

2 tablespoons milk

1/2 teaspoon vanilla extract

1 cup powdered sugar

One 8-ounce container of whipped topping, thawed (to thaw, leave out for 2 to
    3 hours at room temperature or overnight in the refrigerator)

One "ready to use" graham cracker pie crust

1 can cherry pie (or any favorite) filling/topping

Combine cream cheese, milk, and vanilla extract with a hand mixer on medium speed until smooth. Reduce mixer to low speed and gradually blend in powdered sugar. Add entire container of thawed whipped topping and blend thoroughly on medium speed. Pour mixture into graham cracker crust. Cover with plastic wrap and chill for 3 hours in the refrigerator. Top with a can of your favorite pie filling before serving.

A Sexy Aphrodisiac Supper for Two

Whomever you break out this menu for is one very lucky person. Artichokes, basil, lobster, and strawberries are all considered aphrodisiacs, and all these foods can be fed to each other using just your hands. Although this spread will look luxe, it's actually a snap to prepare—in fact, you can do some of it in the microwave. This menu is devoid of garlic, bloat-inducing breads, and side dishes for a reason: They all may get in the way of other amorous activities!

THE MENU

Artichokes with Basil-Lime Dipping Sauce

Lobster Tails with Butter

Dessert:
Chocolate-Dipped Strawberries

Drinks:
A rich, buttery Chardonnay, such as Byron Chardonnay, or Franciscan 2002 Chardonnay. Champagne works too.

THE TIMETABLE

One day before your private party: Buy all the ingredients except the lobster tails.

That morning: Buy the lobster tails and prepare the Chocolate-Dipped Strawberries.

3 hours before: Prepare the Basil-Lime Dipping Sauce, cover, and refrigerate. Trim the artichokes so that they're ready to go.

2 hours before: Shower, get fabulous, and chill the champagne or white wine.

1 hour before: Make the lobster sauce. Begin boiling water for artichokes.

45 minutes before: Drop the artichokes into boiling water. Prepare the lobster tails. When cooked, cover with foil and keep them warm in a 200°F oven.

20 minutes before: Speed-chill your champagne (page 66) if you forgot to do it earlier.

15 minutes before: Slip into your sexiest clothes and spritz perfume in naughty places. Touch up your makeup and hair.

5 minutes before: Pop a breath mint into your mouth and Al Green into your CD player . . .

Putting It All Together

Artichokes with Basil-Lime Dipping Sauce

MG TIP: Raw or cooked artichokes will keep up to a week in the refrigerator. Make sure to sprinkle them with water and place them in an airtight plastic bag.

2 artichokes (go for the firmest, heaviest ones you can find; spring is peak season for artichokes)

16 cups (4 quarts) water

1/4 cup lemon juice (optional)

1 1/2 tablespoons salt, plus more to taste

1 1/2 tablespoons olive oil (optional)

1/4 cup mayonnaise

Juice of 1/2 lime

A few basil leaves

Freshly ground black pepper

MG TIP: The heart of the artichoke is the tenderest part. After eating all the meat from the leaves, scoop the fuzzy center out (the choke—don't eat) with a spoon, leaving the firm base behind (the heart). Eat your heart out.

To rid the artichokes of thorns, cut off the top inch of the bud and trim off one-third of each leaf with a pair of kitchen scissors. Fill a large pot with the water, lemon juice, and salt. Bring to a boil over high heat and place the artichokes in the pot right side up. Add the olive oil, if desired, to give a little extra taste. When the water returns to a rolling boil, cook, uncovered, for 25 to 35 minutes, or until the artichokes are tender when pierced with a skewer or fork and a leaf comes away easily from the base of the artichoke. Spoon the mayonnaise into a small dish and mix it with the lime juice, basil, and more salt, if needed, and pepper.

Lobster Tails

MG TIP: Buy your lobster the same day you plan to eat it, and don't refreeze it.

1/4 cup (1/2 stick) butter

3 teaspoons chili powder

1 lemon or 2 teaspoons lemon juice

2 thawed lobster tails, shells on

MG TIP: If you're pregnant, talk to your doctor about eating or preparing raw seafood.

Preheat the oven to 400°F. In a small bowl, mix the butter, chili powder, and lemon juice and microwave for 2 minutes on medium-high so that the butter is completely melted. With a sharp, heavy knife, split each lobster tail down the middle, leaving a clean cut but keeping the shell on. Place the lobster tails in a baking dish and generously baste with the chili-butter sauce. (If you don't have a basting brush, a spoon also works.) Bake the lobster tails for approximately 20 minutes, or until they're cooked through.

Chocolate-Dipped Strawberries

2 cups water
6 ounces bittersweet chocolate, chopped
3 tablespoons heavy cream
2 tablespoons butter
1 teaspoon vanilla extract
10 large strawberries with long stems

MG TIP: For added wow, you can roll your strawberries in chopped-up Oreos, nuts, or coconut 5 seconds after you've dipped.

Cover a cookie sheet with wax paper and set it aside. Pour the water into a medium saucepan. Find another heatproof bowl that can sit on top of the saucepan without touching the water (this is a makeshift double boiler). Add the chocolate to the bowl and turn the heat to medium-low. *Do not let the water touch the chocolate, or it will "seize" and be ruined.* When the chocolate is melted, add the heavy cream, butter, and vanilla extract, and whisk. When the mixture is smooth and the butter is melted, hold each strawberry by the stem and dip it into the mixture, twirling it carefully when you're done to shake off the excess. Set the strawberries on the wax paper–covered cookie sheet and refrigerate for at least 30 minutes to set.

Faking It

Okay, now that I've given you some great menus to work with, let's get real: Sometimes disaster strikes and you accidentally torch your main course. Or your cat leaps on the counter and turns your pasta into pet chow. Meanwhile, your guests are coming in less than two hours. My solution? *Cheat.* Here's how:

- To serve (4 to 6), buy a fully cooked rotisserie chicken from your local gourmet food shop or grocer. Once your guests arrive, pop it into a preheated oven at 250°F for 10 to 15 minutes. Slip in a few sprigs of rosemary, sprinkle fresh parsley on the top, and garnish with halved lemons.

- Pick up fresh, pregrilled fish or seafood from your grocer—whether it's swordfish, shrimp, or salmon. Drizzle with olive oil and heat under your broiler for 2 minutes, or until warm. Garnish with fresh herbs and lemon slices.

MG TIP: Ruin a cake? Make cake in a jar by using mason jars or mugs. Put scoops of cake and frosting in individual cups and it will look deliberate.

MG TIP: Here's some advice on how to frost your cupcakes like a pro from Candace Nelson, founder of Sprinkles and host of *Cupcake Wars:* "Always make sure your cupcakes have fully cooled before attempting to frost them. So many times on *Cupcake Wars* contestants short on time would frost warm cupcakes. By the time the plate arrived to the judges' table, it was a melted mess! I prefer to use an offset spatula rather than a piping bag to frost my cupcakes. The spatula gives me control of the frosting and allows me to cover the top and sides of the cupcake. I believe that the frosting-to-cake ratio should be equal in every bite you take! When using an offset spatula, twist the cupcake without gripping too hard and smooth the frosting around the top of the cupcake until you create an elegant swirl."

- Who says you have to cook your own veggies? Go to your local grocery store's deli counter and see what vegetables they've prepared for that day—such as steamed asparagus, grilled zucchini and peppers, or marinated artichokes—and give them a quick reheat before guests arrive.

- Chinese takeout *can* look chic. Just take everything out of the containers and transfer onto clean-lined, rectangular plates. When the food is paired with fabulous vino and a dessert like chocolate-dipped fortune cookies or green tea ice cream, guests will forget they're eating takeout.

- Instead of making your own dessert, buy one from your local bakery. Serve it on a platter with some fresh berries, and no one will know the difference (as long as you don't choose the most ornate cake in the case).

- Mashed potatoes go fabulously with steak and salmon, but who wants to be churning spuds all afternoon when you could be getting a pedicure instead? Buy takeout mashed (KFC has the best ones, but the grocery store—deli variety isn't half bad) and add one special ingredient, such as wasabi, horseradish, pesto, or Cheddar cheese. Reheat and garnish with chives.

- When in doubt, garnish. Use deep pink and red rose petals, herbs, crab apples, figs, apricots, parsley, arugula, baby cherry tomatoes, gourmet olives, or drizzles of olive oil and cracked pepper around your entrées . . . it will give everything a more "homemade" touch.

The Drinks

Modern Girls like to have fun, especially when they go from shake-shake-shaking their bodies to music to shake-shake-shaking drinks for their guests. And while elegance and epicurean feasts are important, a party can live or die by the cocktails served.

How to Stock a Bar

Before you can start mixing up your cocktails, you've got to have the proper supplies. Of course, it's always easier to offer one specialty cocktail (like a mojito or a cosmopolitan) and then serve beer and wine. If you want to do a full-blown bar with variety, here's a starter kit for creating your own liquor lair:

The Hard Stuff

Vodka (splurge on a pricier one so you don't get a hangover) and store in the freezer. That way it's ready to go—and chances are you have more room next to the ice cream than you do in your pantry, thanks to your newly stocked cupboard, per the list at the beginning of the chapter.

Gin (ditto above on the pricey part)

Rum (dark rums are sweeter but light rums are more commonly found)

Tequila (these days your guests may be looking for *añejo*)

Whiskey (see pages 272–75 to pick the perfect scotch)

Other Basics

Imported beer

Wine

Angostura bitters

Triple sec

Amaretto or Bailey's Irish Cream

Vermouth

Mixers

Tonic water

Club soda

Ginger ale (you can get by with just tonic, but it's nice to have around for future tummy aches)

Grenadine

MG TIP: Serve your expensive booze first . . . Bring out the cheap stuff as the evening goes on, since people will probably be too drunk to notice.

MG TIP: Don't have time to make the trip to the liquor store? Have it come to you with the help of alcohol delivery apps Saucey and Drizly. Delivery usually takes under an hour and prices aren't more than at your local bodega.

Garnishes

Lemons
Limes
Oranges
Olives
Cocktail onions

MG TIP: The distinction between a good and a great martini is the "chill" factor. *Great* martinis are chilled and not watery. That's why many prefer shaken to stirred, since stirring leaves more time for the ice to melt and won't get your drink optimally cold.

How to Make a Martini Bond Would Kill For

There's something sexy about a woman who can make a great martini. It says "old school," "elegant," and "party girl" all in one potent little glass. But with the advent of watermelontinis, passionfruittinis, and chocolate chiptinis, true Modern Girls know that a classic is best. She needs no fancy ingredients to prove her mettle.

For such a simple drink, though, martinis certainly require quite a production. The best advice is to invest upfront. Get a decent shaker and strainer. Buy a large bottle of vermouth (trust me, you'll never see the bottom of it), keep the pantry stocked with jumbo pitted green olives, and stick at least one bottle of vodka in the freezer. As for fancy vodkas versus cheap ones? There are myriad different expert opinions, but the fact is that premium vodkas just might be worth the money. Finer, more expensive vodkas are produced in smaller batches, distilled several times, and then filtered, a process that leaves them purer and, consequently, better. They make for smoother mixers and are even delicious straight up. The unique purification process of premium vodkas usually leaves them with fewer congeners (natural by-products created during the alcohol fermentation process), which may mean a kinder, less punishing hangover (if there is such a thing).

But any Modern Girl will tell you that somehow, hangovers from snazzy labeled bottles just feel better than those from torrid cheap ones.*

---

*I will refer purely to vodka martinis after having had such a dreadful experience after a night of gin martinis that I feel I can't ethically pass on the recipe.

The Perfect Vodka Martini

2 ounces vodka (a little less than a quarter of a cup)
A dash of vermouth
Olives (or cocktail onions)

Before you plan on drinking, rinse your martini glass. If you don't have a martini glass, the best substitute is a wide-mouthed glass. Shake off the excess water and stick it into the freezer. If time is pressing, fill it with cracked ice and water and let it sit a few minutes.

Take four or five large ice cubes and crack them into somewhat smaller pieces. Put each cube in the palm of your hand, grab a tablespoon, think of an ex, and give a good whack. Don't use crushed ice, as it will melt too fast. Place the ice in a martini shaker and add the vodka and vermouth. Shake sharply for 10 seconds (no cheating). Strain into a frosted glass (or at least a clean one) and garnish with an olive (or onion). Repeat as desired.

When You're Caught Unprepared

Now, I sometimes feel the mood isn't right for a shaker . . . or I can't find it. In this case:

Fill a mixing glass with ice cubes and water. Stir the ice alone in the glass until the glass is chilled. Tip out the water, and top again with ice. Add the vermouth and continue to stir. Add the vodka. Stir thoroughly but try not to chip the ice, as this will dilute the vodka. Strain into a frosted glass and garnish.

When Your Drinker Wants It Dry

Hopefully it's that he likes his beverage dry, not that he himself is dry. When it comes to martinis, "dry" is about the amount of vermouth. The less vermouth, the drier the drink (basically, he's asking for straight vodka). Should your companion ask for "extra-extra-dry," consider adding no vermouth to his drink but simply dabbing a touch on your body. That way, he can decide for himself how dry he's willing to go.

The Negroni

Since not everyone goes Bond bonkers for martinis, it's good to know another chic cocktail to whip up for your guests. The Negroni is an oldie but a goodie, and it welcomes inventive interpretations.

MG TIP: One ounce = 3/4 shot, or 2 tablespoons

2 ounces gin

2 ounces Campari

2 ounces sweet (red) vermouth

Orange zest for garnish

Combine all ingredients except orange zest in an old-fashioned glass filled with ice; stir gently for 10 seconds and garnish with orange zest. More formal types may serve it in a chilled martini glass. For something a little different, top it off with soda water or champagne, or opt for a flavored gin.

Moscow Mule

Conceived in the forties as a way to introduce Americans to vodka, the Moscow Mule is so easy to make you can continue whipping them up after you've thrown a few back. Plus, you'll earn points among your hipster friends for serving this trendy comeback cocktail.

MG TIP: For added complexity, substitute rum or gin for vodka.

Half a lime

2 ounces vodka

4 to 6 ounces ginger beer

Squeeze lime juice into a collins glass or copper mug and drop in the lime. Add 2 or 3 ice cubes, then add vodka and fill with cold ginger beer. Serve with a stirring rod.

Wine

Sangria: A Sweet, Refreshing Tipple

Sometimes gin and martinis are too stiff to serve—and don't quite go with your meal. This brings me to sangria, a refreshing mix of wine, brandy, and fresh fruits, served over ice. It instantly makes a party feel festive, especially in the summertime—and because it's on the sweet side, you can get away with not serving a dessert if you prefer. It's a red-wine punch, although it can also be made with white wine (known as *sangria blanco*).

Super-Fruity Sangria

1 bottle red wine (I like Rioja or Shiraz best)

2 cups orange juice

2 cups ginger ale

1/4 cup brandy

1/2 cup Triple Sec

1 thinly sliced orange (keep a few pieces for garnish)

1 thinly sliced Granny Smith apple

1 thinly sliced lime

Other fruits, if you so desire

Combine ingredients in a pitcher and keep in the fridge overnight. Before your sangria shindig, add ice cubes to the pitcher, pour into glasses, and garnish with an orange slice.

Buying Wine

Is it true that cheap women drink cheap wine? Certainly not. But there are some facts that might help you feel more confident next time you buy and serve wine. While a $100 bottle probably isn't ten times as good as a $10 one, a $20 bottle may be ten times better than a $5. So your best bet is to stick within $17 to $25 if you can afford to. Here are a few tips from *Wine Spectator* to follow when looking for wine:

* Don't be a wine snob. Trust what you like and don't get caught up in high prices or critic's awards.

MG TIP: Consider downloading one of the great new wine apps to store favorite bottles, compare prices, and find other suggestions. Vivino and Delectable are two of my favorites.

• When you've found a wine you like, buy it by the case. Some retailers give you a 10 percent discount, or one bottle free.

• Having said that, shop around for different styles. As Mikey would tell you, "Try it, you might like it." There are many new types of wines, and you may find one that better suits you.

• Shop for values. You can get great prices on very good wines. Find a shop you like, build a relationship with the owner or sales clerk, and ask them to alert you to new specials.

• Like you, wine should never get old. Unless you're buying super-expensive bottles, most should be consumed within ten years.

What Wine to Serve?

MG TIP: If a guest brings you a bottle of wine as a gift, don't feel compelled to open and serve it. The guest should understand that you have probably selected the best wines for your meal, and the gift is more of a thank-you. If you think your guest is expecting it to be opened but you don't want to serve it with the meal, serve it for cocktails.

Modern Girls know that when it comes to matching food and wine, you should forget about "The Rules." After all, you'll drink most of the wine before and after dinner, so just find a wine that you like and would drink by itself.

According to *Wine Spectator*, the old rule about white wine with fish and red wine with meat is a bit outdated. It used to be that all white wines were light and fruity and red wines were heavy and weighty; but that doesn't hold as true today. It is true that hearty food usually needs a full wine because robust food will make a lighter wine taste dull. With lighter food, a light wine fits better, but you can also use light food to bring out the fuller flavor of a heavier wine.

Storing

MG TIP: When entertaining at home, it's up to you whether you want formally to "taste" the wine. Unless you are having a tasting, it isn't mandatory or even necessary. But when experimenting with a new bottle that you are unfamiliar with, you may want to taste or ask one of your guests to taste it for you.

Unlike me, wine hates heat. Keep bottles out of direct sunlight (total darkness is best) and store them on their sides. If you don't have wine cases or racks, store them as low to the ground as possible in a cool, dry space that doesn't get much light. A low cabinet you don't open often is ideal.

Anything over 70° F will affect a wine, resulting in flatter flavors and aromas. In addition, rapid temperature fluctuations (and I don't mean between you and your date) may cause pressure changes within a bottle, moving the cork upward and allowing air in the bottle. This can lead to oxidation, which produces a brownish color and makes it taste icky (that's a technical term).

Serving

For most of the wines I serve, a plastic cup wouldn't change the way it tastes. But occasionally even I splurge on (or receive) a fine bottle. In this case, the glass matters. The size and shape of the bowl of the glass will affect intensity and complexity of the bouquet. The rim matters because it determines where the wine lands on your tongue, affecting the taste.

The stem of the glass should be long enough so that your hand doesn't touch the bowl. Not only will you get unsightly fingerprints on it, but you might warm the wine when you shouldn't. The stem should be almost as long as the bowl is tall. As for the bowl, the clearer the glass is, the richer the wine's color will appear.

Unless you're looking to get yourself and your date really drunk, fill a wineglass no more than half full. This leaves enough space to release the aromas.

Many glasses are too small; few are too large. A good red wineglass will have a capacity of at least twelve ounces (that's a full soda can). Generally, glasses for red wines are wider than those for white. Champagne flutes should hold six and a half ounces or more (smaller than your red wineglass) but should be filled two-thirds of the way up to the top. They have smaller openings to conserve the bubbles. Because port and sherry are stronger wines, they are usually served in smaller glasses. Brandy snifters have little to no stem, because your hand should cradle the glass to heat the brandy slightly.

Hangover Help

What about that wicked hangover headache the next day?

While many of us believe a hangover is nature's way of paying us back for a good time, in truth, a hangover is caused by a combination of dehydration, a depletion of vitamins (A, B, and C), and the toxic by-product of alcohol metabolism (acetaldehyde).

While hangovers are hard to escape entirely, some drinks give you worse hangovers than others. The ethyl alcohol (ethanol) gets you drunk, but how brutal the hangover will be can depend on the impurities or congeners (amyl alcohol, butyl alcohol, methyl alcohol, propyl alcohol, and isopropyl alcohol—they even sound hostile).

Due to their filtering processes, clear liquors such as vodka and gin are generally lower in congeners than whiskey, rum, and bourbon. Freshness also matters. Liquor that has been around a while (particularly an open bottle of wine) will have produced more hangover-causing acetaldehyde.

To keep you from praying to the porcelain gods the next morning, follow these tips:

How to Prevent a Hangover

- Have a preparty meal. Before you imbibe, load up on a low-sodium combo of complex carbs, protein, and fat, which will be digested slowly. Try a whole-grain pita stuffed with grilled chicken, veggies, and cheese.

- Take a Berocca vitamin supplement before you start drinking (consult your doctor first). You can purchase a bottle of Beroccas at the pharmacy. This gives you additional vitamin B, which can help you better combat a hangover.

- Skip carbonated alcoholic beverages. The alcohol in beer, champagne, and wine coolers is absorbed faster than in noncarbonated drinks.

- Alternate fruit juice or water with your drinks.

- Beware of sugary libations. The sweet flavor masks the alcohol, which can make you consume more booze than you think.

- Drink lots of water before bed to help prevent dehydration.

Hot Hangover Remedies

While I can't promise a full-blown recovery, consider serving this hangover-crushing New Orleans secret as a nightcap at your next party. Your guests will thank you in the morning.

- Mix a drop each of lemon juice, heavy cream, and powdered sugar with equal parts orange flower water (which you can buy at pretty much any upscale food store), egg whites, gin, and soda.

- Should you not have the forethought (or the damn flower water), try to stock up on the energy powder available at most health food stores. It's typically used to ward off a cold, but can work wonders on the "too-much-partying" flu.

Setting the Mood

Now that you've mastered your menu—or at least how to fake it—it's time to pay a little attention to the table. I've found that if my guests walk into a nicely set room, it puts them in a good mood and makes them feel pampered—before they've even had a bite.

Table-Setting Savvy

When you're throwing a dinner party, think of your table as the gift-wrapping and your food as the gift. You want to give your guests a knockout visual presentation so they get excited about tucking into the delicious spread you've prepared. But all you really need to pull off the effect is a runner for a semiformal dinner (you and your guests are wearing jeans and cute tops) or a fabric tablecloth for a formal one (everyone's asked to wear cocktail attire).

If you don't have a runner (which is basically just a long strip of fabric laid down the center of your table), a quick makeshift idea is to use a long scarf. I've even used a black brocade scarf of my grandmother's before. Another option is to run a row of fabric place mats down your table. With your flowers and olive oils and other small dishes on top of them, no one will notice they're not all one piece.

For a formal table, splurge on a tablecloth. White is always a safe bet because it won't clash with your plates or food. But don't worry about getting the finest quality. What's more important is that it's ironed and crisp-looking. If you'd sooner have your teeth drilled than iron, send out your napkins and tablecloth to be pressed.

A truly formal setting implies having all of your cutlery, dishes, and glassware already on the table at the beginning of the meal. What I like about this—whether I'm actually serving a formal meal or not—is that not only does it pass the Miss Manners test, but as the hostess you don't find yourself scrambling for more glasses during the meal.

Traditionally, cutlery is laid smallest to largest, working toward the plate. Forks go to the left of the plate, spoons and knives to the right. The exceptions are the dessert fork and spoon, which go above the plate, spoon on top. There is great debate among my friends as to whether you should put out a full set of cutlery even if you don't need it (i.e., a salad fork if there is no salad). My feeling is, put out whatever you think a guest might use (who knows, she *might* want to cut her rigatoni with a knife). But skip anything that will lead a guest to think a course is coming that isn't. (I once left a dinner party extremely hungry, thinking, given the plethora of forks, that the entrée was the appetizer.)

Place the water goblet right above the tip of the knife, and set the wineglasses slightly in front. For more formal parties, preset for as many different types of wines or champagne as you plan to serve.

I prefer to set the napkin in the center of the plate, with a nice napkin ring. Many people like to place the napkin *in* the water goblet, but after breaking a friend's Tiffany crystal stemware trying to remove it, I now try to spare guests of mine—and my fine crystal—the same fate.

After you remove your napkin from the ring, place the napkin on your lap and the ring to the left of your plate. After you have finished your meal and get up to leave the table, you can place the napkin to the left of your plate, or once your plate has been removed, you can place it where your plate had been, but not back in the napkin ring. However, it's proper etiquette to leave your napkin on your lap until you get up from the table . . . even if you're finished eating. If every-

MG TIP: Forget which side to put the bread plate and which side to put your drinking glasses? Make an "okay" sign with both hands—you'll see that your left hand makes a "b" for bread, and your right hand makes a "d" for drink. Easy!

MG TIP: Remember that all food and drinks should be served on each diner's *right* (that's why the glasses are all on the right), and cleared from each diner's *left*.

one stays at the table and chats after the meal, it is considered rude to have your dirty napkin in sight.

Don't have napkin rings on hand? Here's how to fold a napkin like a pro:

Fold the napkin into a triangle. Fold in the two bottom corners one quarter of the way. Fold both of the corners over one another so they meet in the middle. Fold the top point down and flip the napkin over, and you have a chic envelope shape. You can leave it as is, or insert your silverware, a pretty flower, or chopsticks if you're serving an Asian menu.

The Centerpieces

Part of entertaining is just making things look pretty—you, your pad, your food. It's not about spending tons of money; it's about showing guests that you made an extra effort to have things feel a bit more festive for them. While everyone knows that flowers can make a room, unless you're sent a magnificent bouquet, do not feel obliged to take out a second mortgage to make your living room look like the botanical gardens. In fact, when it comes to arranging flowers, here's the best advice I've been given: Don't. When possible, avoid arrangements. Truth is, it's hard to make cheap flowers look expensive and remarkably easy to make even expensive ones look cheap.

Instead, consider alternative arrangements that make guests think you're far too creative to resort to flowers or have held so *many* dinner parties already that you've run through the entire botanical repertoire. Another bonus to these alternative arrangements is that they are all fairly low to the table, making it easy to talk over them.

Snazzy Alternatives to Flowers

* *Fruit:* Bowls or vases filled with one variety of whole fruit (Granny Smith apples, lemons, and limes are my favorites) are as colorful as most flowers but last longer . . . and certainly come in handy

should your bar run short. I've even seen a row of pineapples lend a fun tropical touch!

* *Cacti and Succulents:* Not only are these beautiful plants afford-able and easy to maintain, they make for a diverse and interesting table setting when you mix and match different kinds.

* *Shells:* You don't have to live by the beach to use shells at your next dinner party. Most local craft stores sell them by the bag, and they look extra cute when turned into a DIY candle.

* *Candy:* Nothing is as tempting as a vase or bowl filled with multi-colored jellybeans, childhood favorites, or sweets in bright wrappers. The added bonus is that after dessert, you'll have little to clean up.

One of my favorite party decoration ideas comes from Joy Cho, the master of Pinterest and the blog *Oh Joy!*, who says, "The dollar store is filled with things you can use to decorate for a party that look chic when clustered together. For example, buy a few bags of balloons in a mix of colors, blow them up in different sizes (they don't all have to be totally full of air), and tie the ends to a string so that you have a long chain of balloons in different colors and sizes. Then string them over a doorway for an instant 'pop' of cheer."

The Real Deal

Okay, sure, they're cute ideas, but sometimes you're just going to want to use flowers. After one party when my candy centerpiece was half empty before my guests arrived, I figured I might need to switch strategies. So when arranging flowers, here are a few things to remember:

* Invest in a nice short vase. Sure, it's easy to pull out the big, tall one your ex sent you stuffed with long-stemmed roses when he wanted to convince you to take him back, but as with him, it's not the size that matters. Keep it low. While tall arrangements are eye catching, they can ruin dinner conversation. Flowers need to be low enough to allow guests to see one another.

- In general, flowers should be one and a half times as tall as the vase they are in.

- Go for a single bloom. One of my favorites is to put three or four low square vases on the table with one blossomed rose in each. It makes a dramatic statement, but requires little work and even less skill.

- One color is easier to make look good than many. Try to pick three similarly hued flowers for an arrangement.

- One of the easiest arrangements is a "hedged" or vase-top arrangement—in which the flowers are bunched together right at the top of the vase. Get a bunch of one type of blossom and cut the stems down so that the bud is just resting on the vase. Repeat with the remaining flowers until the vase is full. You may cringe at cutting long stems off flowers like roses and calla lilies, but it will look elegant and doesn't really require arranging. Showcase the blooms in a short, squat vase. Big blossoms (like hydrangeas) can be done in a more statuesque vase if you prefer.

- Use that green Styrofoam to arrange your flowers. It keeps flowers in the place you want them and if the best florists use it, why shouldn't you? But the trick is to make sure the foam isn't visible. Use in an opaque vase, or if that's not available, try to get a big banana or palm leaf (florists have them) to wrap around the inside of the vase. Or cut lemon, lime, or orange slices and place on the inside of the vase for cover.

- Similarly, use bubble wrap or newspaper to fill in areas of an opaque vase and make a few flowers seem like more.

- To get grime out of vases: Pour in ice and rock salt (or table salt if rock salt isn't available), then rinse. It leaves the vases shiny. Alternatively, soak the vase in water and Clorox for thirty minutes.

- Just like stylists don't get plunging necklines to stay in place through magic, florists use floral wire to make flowers stay where they want them. This is a great tool when making your arrangement.

MG TIP: Arranging flowers is much easier without water. Get all your flowers positioned, and then add the H_2O. It's more likely that the buds will stay in place.

MG TIP: Ever wonder what to do with cloning vases? If you're like me, there are two things you have more of than you could ever need: wire hangers and cheap glass vases from flowers sent to you by adoring fans (read: your parents). While I have yet to figure out what to do with the hangers, here's an idea for the vases. Go to a thrift store or fabric store and buy different attractive fabrics (heavier cottons and silks are the best). Get a glue gun (or a tube of superglue if glue guns make you feel too crafty), place a small amount of glue on each corner of the fabric, and wrap the vases in the fabric. Depending upon the shape of the vase, you may need to precut the fabric, but chances are you can just wrap up the vase in it. Then give the new, more original vases to friends, or use one of them as your centerpiece and send a lucky "winner" home with the whole thing (put a gold star under a plate).

Picking and Maintaining Flowers

- *Don't cut with scissors. Get a real pair of garden cutting shears.* I used to use kitchen scissors all the time. Who owns flower cutters anyway, and a cut is a cut, right? Wrong. Scissors crush the stem and prevent the flowers from getting water. Invest in garden shears and use them only to cut flower stems, or they will get dull.

- *Bacteria are what kill flowers fastest. Put a few drops of Clorox in the water to keep blooms fresher longer.* (I know, you really should change the water every other day, but I'm lucky if I take a shower that often.)

- *If it's an extra-special bouquet, use bottled water.* Or if you're cheap like me, at least use water from a Brita-style purifier. This cuts down on the bacteria.

- *Tips for particular flowers:*

  - *Roses:* When choosing roses, squeeze them. If the petals feel tightly bunched, chances are the flowers will bloom. If they are loose, it's safe to guess they'll droop before dessert. Also, look to see whether the tiny leaves surrounding the bud are pointing up. As in many other situations, pointing up is a good thing.

  - *Tulips:* To keep the stems from bending, roll them in wet newspaper, and then submerge them in cold water up to the head. When you are ready to display them, switch to a vase with cold water and ditch the newspaper.

  - *Irises and daisies:* Treat with three drops of peppermint oil in a quart of water. (You can buy peppermint oil at most natural food stores.)

  - *Lilacs:* Scrape the bark off the bottom of the branch, smash the end with a hammer, fray it, and soak in cold water with the powder packet you get at the florist's.

  - *Lilies:* Add ¼ cup vinegar per two quarts of water.

The Modern Girl's Flower Kit

Garden cutting shears
Green Styrofoam
White vinegar
Bleach
Water jug
Peppermint oil (if you're a big iris and daisy fan)
Bubble wrap
Flower food (stock up on the packets you get from your florist)

Lighting

Just as important as your centerpiece is the kind of lighting you use at your party. Your food (and your guests) will look twice as attractive if you take a few steps to ensure sexy mood lighting. So turn off those bright, wrinkle/zit/cellulite-emphasizing halogen lamps and replace your regular 60-watt bulbs with soft, 40-watt amber bulbs (or, better yet, install a few dimmer lights [see page 179]). Everyone looks just a little tanner and healthier under that gold light. Put votives everywhere you can—bookshelves, windowsills, coffee tables, lining a staircase, on the floor of your entryway, in the bathroom—these little light sources dance off skin and make everything look more inviting. Another small touch that adds a magical feel is using white twinkle-lights—wrap them around a staircase or line them inside a window or around a mirror.

Maximizing Party Space

Don't *not* throw a party just because your place is a little cramped. To accommodate as many people as possible when they're mingling before dinner, push your couch all the way against the wall and bring in chairs from other rooms to cluster in various areas. That way, everyone won't be crowded around your coffee table. Clear any

MG TIP: A great way to get tapers to burn longer is to pop them in the freezer for a few hours before your party. Right before guests arrive, take them out, place them in their holders, and light them. You'll get twice the burn time out of them. Always trim all candle wicks to one-quarter inch.

MG TIP: Tired of your cylindrical candles looking like lopsided mushrooms after the first few uses? Burn them for no less than three hours the first time you light them. This creates an even ring on the top.

MG TIP: We all know not to cry over spilled milk, but what about spilled candle wax? No sweat. For hard surfaces, let the wax cool and harden, then scrape it off with a credit card. For difficult-to-reach spaces such as moldings and creases in tables, use a hair dryer to melt the wax and wipe clean. For rugs, heat up an iron and place a brown paper bag over the wax spot. Run the iron over the bag. The paper will absorb the wax. Be sure not to use a hair dryer or iron on anything flammable.

MG TIP: Don't have a dining table, or your kitchen table seats only two? No problem—either buy a cheap card table and put a pretty tablecloth over it or make your coffee table your dining surface and have guests lounge around it on large, cushy pillows. Wrap couch pillows in saris and scarves for an exotic look.

furniture that may be blocking a window—guests (especially smokers) crave that space. Set up hors d'oeuvres and drinks at both ends of the room so there will be traffic back and forth and people won't just huddle in one corner.

Music

Like lighting, music can either make your party sexier . . . or seriously put a cramp in it. The first thing to consider is pacing: The faster the music, the faster people will drink (I've learned this the hard way as a hostess). So start out the night with your slowest grooves because this is when your guests will be drinking cocktails on empty stomachs. When you sit down, build to something a little more upbeat, but make sure the beats don't go faster than a normal heart rate. Otherwise, people will subconsciously eat faster to keep up with the pace of the music—not what you're going for! You can finish off the evening with something a little more fun and wild because this is when people are loosened up. Another tip: If you're not into playing deejay, choose a soundtrack without lyrics. No one will know if that album has been playing four times in a row.

MG TIP: To avoid the déjà vu effect with a repetitive soundscape, overprogram your playlist. If you anticipate your dinner party will be three hours, plan for five hours of music.

Next, consider the vibe of your menu, decorations, and guests. If creating a playlist is adding too much to your plate, there are plenty of sites that have already done the work for you. I am a big fan of Songza, which allows you to select a list based on mood, genre, or decade, but the Indie Rock channel on iTunes Radio is another safe bet. On Spotify, you can even stalk your audiophile friends and borrow their expertly curated playlists for your next party.

The Guests

MG TIP: Don't invite more than twelve people to a dinner party. It is intended to be an intimate affair, not a fraternity function.

What's the point of great food, music, flowers, and booze if the right people won't appreciate it? When you're putting your party crew together, there are a number of moving parts to consider:

Who to Invite

Mix It Up
It's better to bring a few fresh faces into the mix than to solely invite couples or friends who've known each other forever. So don't be afraid to diversify—whether it's by age, profession, or simply people who don't know each other. The best, wildest dinner party I ever went to had both an eighteen-year-old and a sixty-year-old at the table. Who knew?

Don't Designate an Oddball
If you invite a bunch of couples and one single person, he or she may feel out of place.

Keep an Even Male-Female Ratio
Why? It will help keep the conversation balanced and looks more even.

Get a Support Team
If this will be one of your first dinner parties, make sure to have one or two close friends on hand who won't be critiquing whether or not your risotto is al dente—and will be there for moral support (and cleanup duty).

How to Invite Them

Knowing your numbers is crucial for a dinner party, and sending out formal invitations is the best way to get your guests to respond. Since most people only check their mail when anticipating a new shoe delivery, I usually go the digital route for invites. Paperless Post has great designs for every occasion, so try to pick one reflecting the theme of the party—bright and colorful for an outside barbecue or a hand-drawn wine logo for a rustic Italian dinner in autumn. I prefer sending out invites two or three weeks in advance and asking guests to RSVP no later than a week before the party. That crucial window allows you to invite some backup friends should others drop out.

MG TIP: When you are about to rudely bail on a dinner at the last minute by text, remember how much preparation you put into your own dinners. And think twice. But since others may not be as courteous as you hopefully will be, you may want to keep an eye on your phone just to make sure there are no last-minute cancellations.

Making a Smart Seating Chart

A swank dinner party isn't just about presentation; it's about positioning your guests at the table for maximum mingling (and minimal blowups). Here are some points to keep in mind:

Make Pro Place Cards

They can be as simple as heavy-stock paper stuck in a wine cork, or guests' names written on pieces of fruit in a silver pen. For a fun touch, take a Polaroid of each guest during the cocktail hour and slip it onto their place setting. A friend of mine does this at all her dinner parties, and it's always a good icebreaker. It adds a seasonal decoration to the table and lets everyone know where they belong.

Seat Everyone Male-Female-Male-Female

It keeps a better convo flow. Otherwise, you could wind up with four women at one end of the table and four men at the other (which means giggly gossip at one end and nervous grunting at the other).

MG TIP: Make the menu fun by presenting it in an unexpected way. One of my favorites is printing it on a paper bag, which you can then fill with appetizers or snacks. Just remember to lightly tape the top of the bag before running it through your printer to avoid any jams! You can carefully cut it open once it's out.

But Don't Go Noah's Ark

If you seat couples next to each other, all they'll do is talk among themselves. Instead, seat them just across from each other at a rectangular table, or a few seats away from each other at a round table. That way when they do talk to each other, they'll include the others between them.

Know Your Place

As the hostess, you should sit at the end of the table that's closest to the kitchen so you can get up easily. Your boyfriend or husband should sit at the other end of the table. This also makes your guests feel more comfortable. I have friends who always insist on placing guests at the head of their table. While they're trying to informalize the situation, they end up making two guests feel like they have to lead the evening, which usually flops.

Keep Strong (and Muted) Personalities in Mind

You're looking for balance here. While it's probably not smart to put Rowdy Randy smack next to Shy Sheila (she'll probably get a panic attack), you also shouldn't put all the most outspoken personalities at one end of the table. Why? By the time the main course is served, they'll be having a great time while the rest of the guests simply stare and watch the show. Seat an interesting "wild card" personality diagonally from an outspoken political type. That way, if they get into a debate, other people will automatically be invited into their space—and diffuse the squawking.

What Happens When Guests Aren't Clicking?

It sounds basic, but tell them something they have in common—even if it's just by a thread. After all, you're the one responsible for bringing these two together, so you should know something about them that you can toss out to get them gabbing. Dig. Do whatever you have to do. If you've done all you can and you see people just aren't talking to each other, squeeze in between them and start a little small talk.

Topics to Avoid

These days, it's almost impossible not to talk about politics or world issues, but be sensitive to who's at your table. If you've got a brazen left-winger babe chewing out your man's Republican college buddy, it's your job to steer everything back into neutral territory . . . and don't get involved yourself. Other topics that can sting: child-rearing, abortion, religion, layoffs, the prices of people's homes, and, depending on who's at your table . . . plastic surgery.

Happy Endings

How to Make a Decent Cup of Coffee

Nothing can ruin a good meal like a bad cup of coffee. I've gotten a few looks that suggest "Clearly she couldn't have cooked such an elaborate dinner if she can't make a good cup of joe." (Tablespoon, teaspoon, sometimes a girl gets confused.)

If the secret to a good martini is about being cold, the secret to a good cup of coffee is about being hot. The hotter the water, the more flavor it will extract from the coffee grounds. Many say that's why you should invest in a great maker (experts suggest the Cuisinart DCC-1200 Brew Central).

Now, I hate coffee grinders and can't see the merit in freezing beans. It just seems so *elaborate*. But the truth is that if you buy pre-ground coffee, know that it will be stale. Typically, whole beans stay fresh about two weeks after roasting. Keep a can of coffee in your pantry for emergencies, but do your best to stock up on beans every two weeks or so. Keep the beans in an airtight container. Store in the freezer over the long term (over a month) and in the fridge in the short term (two weeks or less). Invest in a decent grinder, but you can get away with a relatively inexpensive one. Don't grind it too fine. That will make the coffee bitter.

There is some debate over paper versus metal filters. The metal ones are reusable and you'll never run out. Paper filters will absorb some of the oils from the coffee and make it taste less rich. However, these oils may also raise levels of LDL cholesterol. Go for the paper and if guests dare complain, tell them you're just looking out for their health.

Start with cold water (preferably filtered). Measure two level tablespoons of ground coffee per six (not eight) ounces of water. Ideally you should use a coffee scoop, but you may want to measure it against a tablespoon to see how accurate your scoop will be in a pinch.

Rather than leaving the unused coffee on the warmer, pour it into an insulated carafe. The longer it sits on the warmer, the worse it will taste, because the coffee is actually cooking for a second time (the first being when it was brewed), which technically "burns" the coffee. So don't get ahead of yourself and turn on the coffee when you start the appetizer. Guests would rather wait a few extra minutes for a fresher cup.

Don't clean your coffeemaker with dish soap. It's really hard to get that last bit of detergent out. Instead, use a nonabrasive scrubber and about a teaspoon of baking soda and rinse thoroughly.

How to Gracefully Boot Guests Who Have Stayed Too Long

Getting guests to leave is a tricky business. I suggest making a series of subtle hints that the party is winding down. I've found saying, "I've loved having everybody and can't wait to do it again soon," works wonders. Especially if you open a coat closet or start collecting glasses. My godmother simply says, "Time for everyone to go now," and shoos us out. The thing is, it's direct, it doesn't play favorites, and chances are everyone is wondering when the right time to exit will be. If your guests are that desperate to stay together they can head to a local hangout or someone else's house. Best to kick 'em out on a high note before you resent that they ever came.

MG TIP: Never do the dishes during the party (it's a total downer).

The Cleanup

Now that you've successfully thrown your dinner party and the guests are no doubt talking up your entertaining skills on their way home, it's time for the dreaded cleanup. And when it comes to loading a dishwasher, Modern Girls know that it's all about *heat*. The water temperature in the dishwasher should be at least 120 degrees. The problem is—beyond the fact that few Modern Girls actually *know* how hot their dishwasher gets—that it's the hot water that first preconditions the dishes for the wash cycle. So to be sure, run the hot water in your sink before starting a dishwashing cycle as this will flush out the cold water in the lines.

You shouldn't have to wash the dishes, but at least scrape them, and a rinse is never a bad idea either. Any surfaces that are not exposed won't get clean, so don't pack them too tightly or have plates touching or spoons, well, spooning. Items should face down. Cups, bowls, or containers that face up will simply fill with water. Wineglasses must be anchored to something (many appliances have racks preset for them). Otherwise they will be bandied about by the water and break. And be careful. While many glasses and china patterns can go in the dishwasher, if instructions say wash by hand, do it. Otherwise you're likely to ruin them.

There is great debate over silverware in the dishwasher. To get it cleanest, you should load it handle down, allowing the utensil part to get the most cleaning. However, if you have small children, consider their safety, give an extra rinse, and load them handle up. Every toddler I know has reached into the seeming treasure chest of glistening items. You don't want your child grabbing the blade. (And frankly, I've never figured out how to unload without getting my hands on the perfectly cleaned cutlery anyway.)

For extra credit, give each silverware item its own compartment (forks together, spoons together). This will save you time in the inevitably badly timed unload phase. Don't overload the dishwasher. If there is no room for the grub to get out, it will settle where you are least likely to notice it (until your mother in-law stops by and picks a bit of crusted macaroni from your serving bowl).

Typically you don't have to fill both cups with soap, unless you're morally opposed to scraping and rinsing. But do make sure the one you fill is latched. If your glasses are spotty, try JET-DRY rinse conditioner. Otherwise, buy one of those plastic white baskets your mother had that allows you to put in spot reducing tablets. Attach it to the lower rack. It works.

Sleep Tight

Chances are it's around midnight now. And you, darling, have done a fabulous job of cooking, greeting, wine pouring, awkward-silence saving, wax removing, dessert dishing, cleaning, and being an all-around dining diplomat. So go to sleep. As in, put your head on your pillow, shut your eyes, and don't stay up all night wondering whether people had a good time or not. They did. Whatever little appetizer you forgot to serve or playlist you overplayed, no one noticed. And the best part is, you've always got another shot to make it better next time.

CHAPTER 3

Mod-Girl Etiquette—Because Good Girls Do (Mind Their Manners)

Etiquette has no doubt changed a bit since Emily Post first made us sit up straight and take notice. After all, we live in an age in which saying "Shut up!" means "You're kidding!" and where people send e-mails for everything from a thank-you to a wedding invitation. And while some of these new rituals make life a little simpler, some are simply rude (Hint: The wedding invite is *not* a good idea). The problem lies in distinguishing which is right and which is wrong. This chapter will help you make sense out of these old-school-meets-technology-age rituals. If you get confused, just err on the formal side because a Modern Girl should never forget her manners. Like champagne and a little black dress, they never go out of style.

Online Etiquette

When I reread this book in its original form with some girls (far younger than me) in my office, they just about busted their well-toned guts at the section on writing love letters. The idea that one would put one's feelings on paper, put that in the mailbox, and trust the postal service to carry it to one's beloved was beyond farcical to them. In the age of hookups, you might go through three or four relationships in the time it takes the missive to get there. And even if you *were* still together, your paramour might consider getting a restraining order when anything more than planning a get-together hours in advance is considered today's sign of ultimate romance. So how, then, does one navigate the online mores in a world where everything from breaking up to becoming a breakout star can happen before you download the hottest new app? Here's the Modern Girl's cheat sheet:

Breaking Up by Text

Just because your relationship started with a text booty call doesn't mean it should end the same way. The text breakup is the true coward's way out for many reasons. For one, you can't control the situation. You have no idea where, when, or how the recipient will get your poisonous pop-up. Will he or she be at work, driving (be honest, we all check), or with a group of buds who will rib him or her mercilessly? Whatever response you get, you will have no way of knowing whether it is true, false, or anything in between, because no matter how clever the use of emoticons, an emoticon is a representation of a facial expression. It is *not* a facial expression. So you won't really *know* if he or she is "totally fine with it," hurt, sad, or overjoyed. Breaking up is not easy, but you *owe* it to your soon-to-be-ex, and to yourself to give each other the respect you deserve and have a real live conversation, not one taken over by cute characters. Russell Brand broke up with Katy Perry by text. Need I say more???

Now, there are a few exceptional cases in which I do think it is okay to break up by text. That's when:

- They're abusive. In that case, don't go near them. They're lucky you're texting them.

- They're avoiding you. Not that they didn't text you right back in three seconds, but they're not returning your calls and clearly don't want to hear from you. Fine, dude. Be that way.

- They were cheating on you. Bastard. I still prefer a good old face-to-face, but if you prefer to dump them by text, that's your prerogative.

- They're a serious liar. Similar to the cheater, but say they're married or a criminal or something big. You don't have to see them if you don't want to.

- It's super early in the relationship . . . like you've been on one date and having a sit-down would be . . . well . . . sort of awkward.

Calling in Sick by Text

Here's the thing . . . it's in the title . . . Most employees and employers are not on a texting basis. So if you want to use text as an added backup, by all means do so. But it should be your secondary, not primary, line of communication. In fact, you may be required to call or e-mail your head of HR to let him know you are out. Plus if your boss doesn't check her phone often while at work, you'll be doubly in the doghouse as she waits, annoyed, for your never-happening arrival.

Resigning by Text

Sure, it *happens*; in fact, there's even an app called Quit Your Job that helps you come up with ways to say it by text and then look for new jobs. But personally, I wouldn't really recommend it. After all, it's quite possible your new employer or a future employer will call your previous one for a reference. They're probably not going to *text* them. So don't let this be the way your employer remembers you. Do it the right way. Write a letter, then sit down with your boss. No matter how much you hate her.

Cell Phone Etiquette for the Modern Girl

We all think that it's just one call, just one text, or just going to be "one sec." But the truth is, whenever you take your attention away from the person you're with to take a call, send a text, or check your phone, you're telling the person you're with that he or she is less important than whatever is on the phone (which, by the way, might be a picture on Instagram). So while you might know much of this, here are a few tips to keep in mind:

- Just because you can't sleep doesn't mean everyone is awake. And not everyone remembers to silence his or her phone. So if you send a text message at 2 A.M., you may be waking someone out of a techless dream.

- Don't believe the hype. I appreciate that you want me to have good luck and that you're worried something bad will happen if I don't send this text to ten other people, but come on! We all have too much to do to be spamming each other with these messages, right? Unless you're sending me something so funny I might spit out my drink, don't send it.

- Sarcasm isn't funny. And I'm not being sarcastic. It's just too hard to read emotion. No matter what emoticons you use. Avoid the drama. Lose the sarcasm.

- Even though you're not leaving a message, it doesn't mean they can't see you called. In fact, the phone will start counting for you. Either call once and leave a message (though no one seems to actually check messages anymore), or text. Repeatedly calling will just make you annoying.

- Don't make waitstaff or sales staff wait. It's rude. Take the phone away from your ear, be considerate, and let the people who are trying to do their jobs do their jobs. If you don't, and they overcharge you, you deserve it.

- Stop YELLING. Turns out the average person talks three times as loud when they are on a cell phone. So take it down a notch and speak at a normal volume. The people around you—and on the other line—will appreciate it!

- Kp it rl. In other words, don't do what I just did. Unless you know absolutely positively that your recipient knows your shorthand, don't use it. My mother-in-law wrote to my children that their great-uncle was very ill and signed it "LOL," and they couldn't understand why she was "laughing out loud." I had to explain that she thought it meant "lots of love." Oops.

- Don't bring your phone into the bathroom. Even if the fact that one in five people has dropped his or her cell phone in the toilet doesn't deter you (which it probably should), remember that you never know who is in a public restroom and will hear what you're talking about.

- Guess who's not coming to dinner. Don't put your cell phone on the table at dinner. I don't care if your friend is in labor or you're waiting for your boss to text. Simply putting it on the table invites everyone in your contacts to dinner, and did you mean to have that many people at your meal? If you have urgent business, simply apologize at an appropriate moment and check, then put it back away.

- Sorry, Grandma, that was meant for Greg, my boyfriend. When sending a photo, e-mail, or text, imagine that the worst possible person could receive it and see it (e.g., the person it's about, your grandmother, your partner). If you're okay with that, go ahead and send. If not, rethink.

- And finally, please, please—and I know you know this—don't drive and do anything. Don't text, don't read a text. Don't check your likes or like or chat or anything. Just wait. Until we have self-driving cars, just let the phone be.

Thank-You Notes

With the convenience of e-mail and text, who has the time (or hell, even the interest) to pen a handwritten thank-you note when you can just type, hit Send, and not even bother with a stamp?

Easy answer: *You* do . . . sometimes. A handwritten thank-you is classy and sincere, and says, "I'm making the effort to acknowledge the effort you made on my behalf." Plus, it practically guarantees you'll continue to get the kinds of fabulous gifts/dinner party invites/job leads you were thanking the person for in the first place. For a quick "thanks" e-mail is fine, but it should not be your go-to.

If part of the reason you're afraid of writing a thank-you note is that your literary style is more George W. Bush than John F. Kennedy, then read on for tips on how to craft a few all-important notes.

Writing Perfect Thank-You Notes

To your mother-in-law (even when she's sent you the most hideous gift ever):

Dear Mrs. Buckingham,

Thank you so much for the lovely set of cat figurines and bumblebee napkins. They add a whimsical touch to our dining room, and the hint of yellow really cheers things up.

It was so nice catching up with you over dinner as well. I love hearing all of your decorating stories . . . they have given Marcus and me some inspiration to finally renovate the guest room! I look forward to our next visit.

Love,
Jane

Hot Tips:

- If in doubt, address your mother-in-law by her married name.
- Do praise specifics about the gift, even if it's gathering dust in your closet.
- Do say you look forward to seeing her, even if you don't.
- If she's spent time with you, do try to mention at least one enjoyable conversation you had together—even if you didn't find it especially enjoyable.
- Don't insult her son, even as a joke.
- Send the letter no later than three days after receiving your gift.

To a couple you've stayed with for the weekend:

Dear Angie,

What a fabulous weekend Marcus and I spent at your beautiful home in Santa Barbara. Please extend our thanks to Brad as well for your hospitality (and those incredible scones). We haven't felt so relaxed and pampered since our honeymoon!

When Brad finishes shooting and you are back from your latest UNICEF trip, we'd love to have you to our country home, or, if your schedule is crazed, at least let us take you to dinner.

Again, thank you for a truly lovely weekend—you are incredible hosts.

Fondly,
Jane and Marcus

Hot Tips:

- Address the note to both of them or just the wife. If you do the latter, mention her hubby somewhere in the letter.
- Use the word *home* instead of *house*.
- If you got into a tiff while you were there, don't rehash it.
- If you don't want to reciprocate the houseguest invitation, at least acknowledge how you'll return the favor.
- Send this letter no later than two days after your stay.

To a prospective employer:

Dear Ms. Head Honcho:

Thank you for taking the time to meet with me today. I enjoyed speaking with you about the senior management opening at Company X (and the benefits of St. Lucia over the BVIs . . . how could I have been so wrong all these years?!).

Our conversation reinforced how much Company X prides itself on excellence and demands the best of its employees. I feel that with my skills in Y and Z, we would make a perfect fit.

I look forward to speaking with you soon. If there are any additional references or information I can provide you with, I would be happy to do so.

Sincerely,
Jane Buckingham

Hot Tips:

- Send an e-mail thank-you *and* a physical one as well. Type up your letter and send it out the day of your interview. The e-mail should go out the day after your interview.
- Use a colon following the greeting, not a comma.
- Add a dash of humor that refers back to your conversation—but skip clichés.
- Restate key points from the interview.
- Don't put anything in writing that you couldn't say in person.
- Stick to "sincerely"or "best regards"—anything else sounds like a kiss-up.

Who Else to Send Thank-You Notes To

There is no hard-and-fast rule about who gets and who doesn't get a thank-you note. Suffice it to say that if anyone goes out of his or her way for you—it could even be as small as a friend lending you her chandelier earrings for a date—jot it down and send it in the mail. No one has ever been upset by getting a kind piece of mail.

Do You Give a Thank-You Note for a Nice Thank-You Gift?

The best response for a nice thank-you gift is a phone call or an e-mail. Let the sender know that you received the gift and are touched by the gesture. Tell the person once again that it was more than your pleasure to do whatever it was that he or she is thanking you for. If you are really intent on writing a note, then by all means do so, but it *definitely* isn't necessary.

When Is It Okay to Send an E-mail Note to Thank Someone?

The answer is, almost never. Most etiquette experts agree that it is inappropriate to thank someone via e-mail, whether it's for an engagement gift or a weekend stay at someone's home. The only exception seems to be e-mailing a thank-you note for a job interview, or for very small presents given in a business situation, but even then a proper, handwritten thank-you note is preferable. You don't want to wonder whether you didn't get the job because of an etiquette faux pas.

How to Give a Good Gift

Now what happens when you're on the other side of the gift-exchange fence and need to choose the perfect present for someone? Whether you're giving a gift certificate or a store-bought item, the secret to good gift-giving is giving something you know the recipient would like, not something you want for yourself or something you think they desperately need. Don't give your best friend Pilates classes. You may think it's trendy, but she'll just read it as, "Oh. She thinks I'm getting fat." Steal a few of my surefire ideas below, and the guesswork will be over forever.

Perfect Gifts

For the Friend Who Has Everything

Since she doesn't need yet another knickknack on the shelf, consider these options:

- Give a must-consume-now gift. Think a dozen cupcakes in her favorite flavors; my go-to is always Sprinkles cupcakes. There's something spontaneous and festive about a gift that's asking to be enjoyed within the next twenty-four hours.

- If you're not a DIY maven, don't stress about creating the perfect scrapbook. Instead, order a professional photo book online (www.apple.com/mac/print-products) for a friend that centers on loved ones or an important time in his or her life. Add a personal touch with a handwritten note in the front.

- A beautiful basket of artisanal treats is sure to please your foodiest friend. Start with a bottle of nice wine and pair with a box of nutty crackers, marcona almonds, sea-salt caramels, or an exotic-sounding chocolate bar. Consider opting for a rustic crate and some kraft crinkle paper for an updated feeling.

- Order an item such as a pochette or a tote (like the fashionable ones from Clare V.) and personalize it by adding a monogram. Or buy a book by an author you know a friend loves and inscribe it with a note. You also can order custom-made stationery with a friend's name on it from various websites—I love www.sugarpaper.com, www.alisonspaperie.com, and www.pspaper.com. Their stuff is adorable and looks homemade.

Great Guy Gifts—At All Stages of the Relationship

Gifts for guys are often trickier than those for girls, especially at the beginning of the relationship, because they may signify more than you want them to. Going overboard is a cardinal sin, and when you've been together longer, it doesn't necessarily get easier. How do you balance out a nice piece of jewelry a few years into the relationship? And what if you spend way more than he does, making his cute picture of the two of you in a frame he made himself seem dopey? Here is a good rule of thumb on how soon to give, and how much you should.

Good Options at One to Three Months

I remember giving a boyfriend an ID bracelet with his name inscribed on one side and "I love you" on the other side. Great gift, except that I was eighteen years old, we'd been dating just three months, and it cost $100. He dumped me a week later for a girl named Amanda. Did the gift scare him away? Maybe. Did I feel like an idiot? Definitely. The worst part was that he gave me back the bracelet. What was I supposed to do with a bracelet that read, "Kyle, I love you"? Wait until I met another Kyle? From this I learned two things:

- Don't engrave or monogram any gift for a guy you've been dating less than a year. Simple as that.

- Don't spend more than $100 on a present for a guy you've been dating for three months or less.

Maybe I'm paranoid because of Kyle, but I've learned that in the beginning stage, any gift can be construed as loaded. Even a Valentine's card can be misconstrued (How do you sign it . . . Love?). Your best bet is to give him something disposable that he can't ponder the meaning of back at home. The perfect option is to take him out to dinner at a hip, midpriced restaurant.

Best Buys at Three to Six Months

The secret here is to get him something that is thoughtful, but doesn't have "you" written all over it. Otherwise, he may think you're trying to push the relationship along too fast. Try:

MG TIP: Do *not* buy him any clothes at this point. He might read it as too "mothering."

- A book on a topic you know interests him

- A new set of chips for his poker night

- Pilsner glasses for a beer drinker

- A fashionable shave kit subscription (www.harrys.com)

- A streaming music service subscription so he can jam out sans commercials

Significant Gifts for Six Months to One Year

He's probably taken you away for a weekend trip at this point and perhaps introduced you to his family at a holiday gathering. So go a little more personal:

MG TIP: Steer clear of "makeover" gifts, such as an electric shaver (i.e., you don't like his "facial hair"), a gym membership, or a body-waxing gift certificate.

- A photograph of the two of you in a great, masculine frame

- A cashmere sweater or scarf

- A nice bottle of something he really enjoys, like scotch, or a bottle of the expensive wine the two of you shared on an early date

- Tickets to a sporting event or a concert you both want to see (but keep in mind, this is his gift, not your chance to check out Taylor Swift.)

- A high-quality leather wallet

- His favorite player's jersey

What Works at One to Two Years

You're a solid couple, no question. So this gift should celebrate the two of you, without getting too-too serious.

- A wine-tasting or mixology course

- A ski or beach weekend away, your treat

- Golf or dancing lessons for the two of you. (But don't torture the poor guy if he has two left feet. This is his gift, remember.)

- A couple's massage

- High-thread-count sheets (300+) . . . for the two of you to enjoy

MG TIP: Do not buy him a pet. I know he said he likes chocolate labs, but the only chocolate you should be getting him at this point is truffles.

What Works at Two to Four Years

If you're not engaged already, people are probably bugging you with that annoying question. So you want to give him something that says "permanence" without being stifling. You also know what he could use by now, so don't be afraid to go practical:

- Monogrammed cuff links

- A watch

- A carry-all or briefcase (Coach makes a great, affordable line)

- Electronics: That new Bluetooth speaker he's had his eye on, the gaming console he drools over, or, if he's super particular and you're a bit too intimidated, a cute IOU for the stereo or TV of his choice. Keep in mind, electronics are to men what jewelry is to women.

Five Years and Up

Get him something that shows you still value the individualistic side of him, before he met you, possibly married you, and forgot what it means to spend a Sunday without hitting Bed Bath & Beyond.

- A fabulous grill and all the accessories (a man and his meat have a very sacred bond)

- Tickets for a fly-fishing weekend away with his buddies

- A paid-for tee time at his favorite golf course

- Skydiving/race-car driving/sailing lessons

Gift Wrapping 101

No matter what gift you give—whether it's for your guy, your best friend, or your boss—presentation is everything. Okay, your guy probably won't know the difference, but at least *you* know it looks good. It's easy to make an original, inexpensive gift wrap with a few shortcuts:

The Brown-Paper Package

Wrap Step 1
Use brown paper from an office supply store as your base (for a guy's present, even grocery-bag brown paper can look chic if you fold it sharply on the creases). Measure your box on the paper, then place it top side up, making sure to fold the ends of the paper in at least a half inch to hide rough edges. Use double-sided tape for a clean, flawless look.

Wrap Step 2

MG TIP: Looking to save on wrapping paper? Look no farther than your neighbor's recycling bin. Last week's newspaper serves as great wrapping paper in a pinch.

Don't have ribbon? No problem. Just take a ball of cotton string or twine and wrap it around the box three times to create a cool pattern. Then find an ornament to slip under the twine. Clip a leaf or fresh flower from your garden, or attach a fun trinket that corresponds to the gift (for example, a cute olive fork if you're giving a friend a martini set).

The Gift Basket

Have a pretty basket you never really use? It makes the perfect gift vessel for bath, kitchen, and gourmet items (regifted utensils especially . . . since you likely won't have the original box).

Wrap Step 1
Fill your basket with gift items and sit it on a large square of clear or colored cellophane (three times the size of the basket's base). You can pick up cellophane at most party or gift stores.

Wrap Step 2

Pull the cellophane straight up over the edges of the basket, then give it a twist to the left and secure with a rubber band. Tie a ribbon around the cellophane, then clip the rubber band off. Trim the edges of the cellophane if necessary.

The Wax-Paper Present

I know—the only time you'd think to use wax paper is when you're baking. But the milky feeling of the paper gives your gift a sophisticated, Zen-like vibe.

Wrap Step 1

Simply wrap your box with wax paper, being careful to make sharp creases and fold under any zigzag edges. And avoid boxes that have writing on them. But don't be afraid to use a colorful or black box—it looks great peeking through the wax paper.

Wrap Step 2

To dress it up, add a strip of decorative gift paper. This technique is called "the cummerbund." (It's a great way to use any beautiful bits of paper you've saved from past gifts.) Just make sure you fold the edges of the cummerbund under to achieve smooth edges. For an extra kick, tie a skinny ribbon through the top of the cummerbund, and top with a fresh-picked flower.

Should You Ever Give a Gift Certificate?

MG TIP: *Always* include a 15 percent tip with "spa-type" gift certificates. There's nothing tackier than making your giftee chip in a tip for his or her own present.

Giving gift certificates and gift cards has become not only acceptable but downright preferable for many people. The key today is making sure it comes from a store the person really likes or is for something he or she will use and doesn't have hidden restrictions. An in-law who just had a baby may love a gift certificate to her favorite restaurant once her pickles-and-fried-chicken cravings are over. Your friend who's been stressed out but never indulges herself? A pedicure or a massage certificate may be more welcome than a purse she doesn't like (but feels compelled to wear in front of you). And sometimes, when it comes to electronics and your guy, you can do more harm than good by doing it by yourself. Most guys won't scoff at an Amazon gift certificate.

The Rules of Regifting

Regifting (aka giving a present you've received to someone else) is slightly risky, but a Modern Girl can pull it off if she does it right. After all, why should you be expected to keep a closet full of great presents that don't work for you . . . but might for someone else?

Regift Rule 1

Never regift a present you've already used . . . even once. Sure, she may never know you dipped into the fancy jar of honey bubble bath just one itty-bitty time, but it's just beyond tacky.

MG TIP: If you happen to be a lucky girl who attends many events where swank goodie bags are handed out, set aside the nice candles and bottles of lotions you receive. Wrap them up immediately in pretty paper or tissue so they are always ready for service at a moment's notice as excellent and unique hostess gifts. But just remember, don't bring them to someone who may have attended the same event.

Regift Rule 2

Inspect before you wrap. Look for things like fingerprints on a bottle of wine, old "sell by" dates on food, missing warranty cards from appliances or electronics, or notes to *you* from the original giver.

Regift Rule 3

Rewrap the present in a plain white box with tissue paper or a decorative gift bag. If your regift contains a few separate items, opt for a cellophane-wrapped basket, tied with colorful ribbon.

Regift Rule 4

Do *not* go back to the store you know it's from and try to get a bag. Should your giftee go to return it, she'll be in for a big surprise when she finds out that the product hasn't been around for the past two years.

Regift Rule 5

Keep a list of who's given you what. Wedding presents can make great regifts . . . as long as you don't give that bread maker back to Pam and Steve, who gave it to you in the first place. Also avoid regifting items to anyone who is close friends or family with the person you received it from. This can easily backfire.

Regift Rule 6

If someone asks you where you got the gift, you can either fib and say you bought it in this little ol' store in _____(fill in a state that's far away from you), or you can fess up and hope she won't delete you from her contacts.

MG TIP: Never regift a totally tacky item. After all, you wouldn't want the recipient to think that you have terrible taste and actually bought that dog-shaped cookie jar, or worse, that you think the recipient is as hideous as the gift you've given them.

The Tao of Tipping

Another important gift you need to give people on a regular basis are tips. Yeah, yeah, you already paid 150 big ones for a cut and color job. So why oh why should you have to shell out more cash on top of that? Because it's the right thing to do. And also because a lot of times, these people make a low base wage because they *count* on being tipped. Here's how to shell it out the right way:

Tipping at the Hair Salon:

Your hair washer/blow-dryer: $5.00
Your stylist or colorist: 20 percent of the bill
Your manicurist or pedicurist: 15 percent of the bill

MG TIP: Never tip the owner of the salon.

Tipping at Restaurants

15 to 20 percent of the bill. If you've had expensive wine, you can keep it at 15 percent. If the service is terrible, I recommend leaving 10 percent, but mention the bad service to the manager on the way out. That way you don't look like a cheapskate, and the waiter's poor performance won't go unnoticed.

Tipping at Bars:

15 to 20 percent of the bar bill (but never less than a dollar)

Valet Parker:

$2.00

The Coat-Check Person:

$1.00 or $2.00

The Ladies' Room Attendant:

$1.00 or $2.00 if she did something great like find you the last tampon in her secret stash drawer or helped you get a cosmo stain out of your dress

Your Doorman:

$25 to $150 at Christmastime, depending on how long you've lived in the building and how close you are

A Doorman at a Hotel Who Gets You a Cab:

$1.00 or $2.00

Your Cleaning Lady or Nanny:

One week's salary if she's been working for you a year or less; after that, two weeks' pay or more is appropriate at Christmas

Your Mailman:

MG TIP: If you're picking up food or having it delivered it's best to still tip 5 to 10 percent of the bill.

You actually should not tip a federal employee, as it's not allowed. A small gift is acceptable.

Your Paper Boy:

If you're lucky enough to have ever seen him, $10

Hotel Bellman:

$1.00 per bag, but never less than $5.00 if they've come all the way up to your room, shown you around, and told you where things are.

Hotel Maid:

$2.00 per night stayed

Airport Skycap:

$1.00 per bag ($2.00 for your entire boot collection), but chances are, if you're using a skycap, you have several bags, so you should usually give $5.00 or more, depending on the load

Cabbie:

Tip around 15 percent, then round up to the nearest dollar.

MG TIP: *Tipping* originated as a British word meaning "to ensure promptness."

Party Etiquette

Sometimes the best gift you can give to someone is being a fabulous guest at their parties. And believe it or not, your fabulousness starts with what you put on before the party even starts. For most shindigs, all you need to do is don something sexy that you feel comfortable in. But when there's a dress code specified on the invitation, ignoring it is an insult to your host . . . and will make you feel awkward when you're there. Here's how to decode the most common dress-code lingo:

When Your Invite Says "White Tie"

Girl, all I can say is I'm jealous: You're either headed to the White House for dinner or going to one hell of a wedding.

You wear: A full-length dress—steer clear of lightweight floral prints and opt for richer fabrics in jewel tones, neutrals, or black (avoid anything too risqué; this is not the time to show how great your cleavage is). Pair it with elegant jewelry (think diamonds and pearls, not turquoise and coral, however stylish), plus long gloves (which you take off when you eat).

Your guy wears: Black tux pants, black dress shoes, a stiff wing-collar shirt (a store employee can point out the difference), studs, cuff links, white waistcoat (aka vest), white tie, and black tailcoat.

When Your Invite Says "Formal" or "Black Tie"

Most evening weddings and galas require formal dress. Technically, "black tie" is not worn before 6 P.M. Of course if your host didn't get that memo and calls a wedding "black tie" at 4 P.M., by all means comply.

You wear: Conservative etiquette dictates a floor-length dress, but a fancy knee-length dress or dressy tuxedo pants and a fancy silk blouse can pass. If you're wearing pants, pair them with skinny stilettos, not chunky heels.

Your guy wears: A tuxedo with a white dress shirt (i.e., pointy collar with no buttons underneath it), a cummerbund or waistcoat, studs, cuff links, a black bow tie, or, for a more contemporary look, a dressy silk necktie in black, silver, or white. Hint: Steer clear of colored cummerbunds and matching bow ties. They were "amusing" at frat formals in college; now they're just tacky.

When Your Invite Says "Black Tie Optional"

You wear: The same as if it was black tie, above.

Your guy wears: A tux or a dark suit, white dress shirt, and dressy tie. It's always better to be overdressed than underdressed, so if he owns a tux, he should play it safe and wear it.

When Your Invite Says "Semiformal"

You wear: A little black cocktail dress or a slinky sheath, with fun jewelry, strappy shoes, a great handbag, and a wrap if it's chilly out.

Your guy wears: A dark suit, white dress shirt, and tie. Remember, dark shoes and socks go with dark suits and light shoes and socks go with light suits.

When Your Invite Says "Cocktail Attire"

You wear: A short, elegant dress, plus nice accessories (see semiformal, above).

Your guy wears: A dark suit, white dress shirt, and tie, or a navy blue blazer with a fancy white dress shirt, tie, and dress pants or khakis.

A Note on Dressing

The "why rent when you can buy" theory does not always apply to clothing. I admit I was somewhat skeptical when Rent the Runway came into being, but take a lesson from Cinderella and send that ball gown back! Here's the thing: When it comes to special events, you want a showstopper, right? Something so fabulous and gorgeous that people will say *wow* and remember it. But the catch is that then you won't want to wear it again! So, instead of laying out the cash to own it, rent it! I have to say I've now done this for three black-tie events and I've never gotten more compliments. I'm more likely to wear gowns I wouldn't buy (when you buy you are more practical), I am more likely to get something perfect for that occasion (the place, weather, theme), and because Rent the Runway lets you get two sizes, no matter how my skinny jeans are fitting at the moment, I can get a dress that looks perfect. I know I'm sounding like a commercial and if there are other sites, by all means use them. Just saying, this one, and this whole idea, works for me.

Two tips:

- Rent in advance. My only issue has been when the dress I wanted was not available in my size when I wanted it.

- Don't be embarrassed! If anyone asked where I got the dress, I told them. I felt super savvy and they felt not so super having laid out a lot of cash for a dress they might wear only once!

How to Be the Best-Ever Party Guest

Want to get invited back again and again? Besides wearing the right attire, being effortlessly fascinating, and complimenting the hostess on her pad, follow these tips:

Party Pointer 1

If you are going to someone's home, always bring a gift, such as a bottle of vino. Champagne is festive and always makes a good impression (just stick to the $25+ range or everyone will be reaching for Advil).

Party Pointer 2

If you want to bring someone with you to the soiree, yet your invitation didn't specify a "plus 1," call the host and ask if it's okay ahead of time. If it's a dinner party, do not ask to bring anyone but your significant other—the host has already worked out her head count and seating chart.

Party Pointer 3

If you're a smoker, ask the host's permission before lighting up a cigarette, even if you see others smoking.

Party Pointer 4

Once you enter someone's home, turn your cell phone on silent (or better yet, leave it in the car). If you absolutely have to have it on because you're expecting an important call, duck into a hallway or patio to use it. Chances are, if you're taking calls at the table during an intimate dinner party, your host will think you're uninterested in her event or you have other plans for later in the evening and may skip out.

Party Pointer 5

Try not to be the first or the last guest to leave. Few hosts appreciate guests who arrive early, but never show up more than fifteen minutes late for a dinner party or thirty minutes late for a cocktail party. Heed your host's signals for when it's time to leave. If she starts yawning, doesn't begin new conversations, or starts to do the dishes, chances are she's ready to see the back of you.

Party Pointer 6

Give your host a follow-up thank-you call or e-mail the next day.

Mingling No-No's

Don't Text and Talk

While texting and driving is deadly, doing it at a party is socially lethal. It not only makes you unapproachable but makes you look like you just don't want to be there. Even though we have all felt socially awkward and used texting as a crutch, resist the urge and put your cell phone away.

Don't Be a Walking Résumé

After being introduced to someone, don't make your second question, "So, what do you do?" Asking this off the bat makes people feel judged, and both of you will feel awkward if his answer is, "I'm unemployed, actually."

Resist the Urge to Window-Shop

Sure, it's tempting to ask that random girl by the sangria station where she bought her fabulous top and how much it was, but this is a no-no. Simply compliment the item and say you haven't seen anything like it anywhere—it's a more gracious way to encourage her to fess up.

Do Not Velcro Thyself to Thy Date

There's nothing more nauseating at a party than the Glued-Together Couple. They laugh on cue, they drink in simultaneous sips, and worst of all, they create disgusting PDA moments. I know he's hot. I know *you* know he's hot. Don't share the love in public.

Don't Have a Wandering Eye

No, this doesn't mean don't scope out other men when you're standing with your honey—I assume you already know this no-no. What I do mean is don't be the person in the room always looking for the next better person in the room to talk to while you're still in conversation with someone else. We all know the type, and it's no fun when it happens to you, so don't do it to others.

How to Work the Room as a Host (When All You're Really Thinking About Is What Time You Need to Take Out the Chicken)

The trickiest part of hosting a party, believe it or not, is having a good time yourself. Oftentimes you get so tied up in what you're doing to pull off the party that you forget to actually *attend* the party. Here are a few tips on how to be a perfect hostess:

Plan Ahead

Sure it's fun to wow your friends with tricky recipes that will make them think you're the next Julia Child, but they didn't come over to sit alone in the living room. Plan menus that just involve taking something out at the last minute, or moving into the kitchen fifteen minutes before dinner to put on finishing touches. And allow a bit of a cocktail hour before the meal so that when your guests arrive, you have time to mingle before you step into the kitchen.

Work the Room Like a Bride

Make a concerted effort to spend a few minutes with each guest. Your friends will understand you're in "host mode" and won't mind if you duck out of conversations to check on something in the kitchen, as long as they've had their face time.

Recruit Help

Not only will this make your life easier in the kitchen, but sometimes it's a great way to catch up with a friend who needs a little bit more attention. Simply say, "Heather, could you be a doll and help me with the salad—and we can catch up at the same time. I want to hear all about your blind date last week."

How Not to Forget a Name . . .

I could give you a lot of tricks to remembering names; but the truth is, most of us don't remember people's names because we never actually *hear* the name to begin with. We're too busy assessing the person or thinking of something else. ("He's cute—do I look okay?"

"She came with *him*?" or "Oooh, that waiter has mini-quesadillas!") But Modern Girls pay attention. They listen when someone is introduced to them, and if they do doze off, then they simply, *immediately*, say, "I'm so sorry, what was your name again?" and smile.

Now if you *are* paying attention, there are two tricks that remain pretty tried and true:

- Repeat the name immediately. Nothing forces you to pay attention like having to use it. So say, "Nice to meet you, Joe." Do it again before you leave the person's company: "Nice talking to you, Joe, I'm going to grab a quesadilla!"

- Associate the name with a celebrity. If the person's name is Heather, think Locklear. Sounds weird, but it may help you remember.

. . . And What to Do When You *Do* Forget a Name

- Greet them with, "Hey, hon" or "Hey, handsome" when you see them, and then when your good friend Mark is mingling in your vicinity, use him as a prop. Look at what's-her-name and say, "Have you met my friend Mark yet?" He'll extend his hand and say hi, and your mystery person will in turn offer up her name.

- If you don't have someone to use as a prop, simply re-ask it. I know, that seems mortifying (especially after you've practically told them your entire sexual history), but come up with some excuse. You've had a long day, you've had too much wine, or the understandable "I'm just terrible with names." In doing so, also restate your name, lest they think you are so far above your station that names don't matter to you but do to them. ("Gosh, I am so terrible with names, please tell me your name again—I'm Jane.") Keep in mind, the only thing worse than apologizing is being caught faking an introduction by slurring over their name. And everyone knows when you're looking at a name tag— so if you do peek, do so long before you will be making an introduction.

What to Do When You're Stuck with a Snooze of a Guest (Yawn)

Keep Your Composure

It's tough, but listen, smile, and give your companion the courtesy of thinking you are enjoying his or her company. Do not keep glancing over the person's shoulder hoping for someone better. If there actually *is* someone better, you'll have time to find them. Even if someone is rude or pushy, try to remain nice and excuse yourself after five minutes.

Remember the Selfish Social Secret

People *loooove* talking about themselves. If you meet a guy who likes sports, try to take an interest in it and ask how a particular game is played. If you meet a girl who is into travel, ask where she's been or is planning to go. Taking the conversation from small talk to specifics will at least be more intersting in those few minutes before you manage to slip away.

Make an Escape Plan

If you're going to bolt from an obnoxious guy, don't leave him hanging with no one to talk to. Consider introducing him to someone you know and saying, "Margaret, you must talk to Dylan, he has the funniest stories." Or suggest that you both head to freshen a drink or check out the appetizers. That's being inclusive, but also gives the other person a gracious out to go about his own business. If you simply must get away, the bathroom is one place you know they can't follow.

What to Do When You're Surrounded by Mensa Scholars and You Thought Mensa Was the New Manolo . . .

Should your fellow guests seem supremely intellectual and demand the same of you, don't take the bait. Just because Rhodes Scholar Rhonda is annoyed that you look cuter in your dress than she ever could doesn't mean she can make you look stupid. If you don't have a position on politics, the economy, or the newest art house film, simply say, "I can't say I know a great deal about the subject, but I'd love to hear more of your thoughts." It's (relatively) honest and it allows the other person to keep talking.

In the future, if you feel your IQ supply is tapped dry, before you go out, quickly scan the headlines at www.wsj.com or www.nytimes.com, then actually read one or two articles that interest you. This way you'll be packed with current topics and have some insight into an issue or two.

How to Sound Smart at an Art Gallery Opening or Benefit

Cocktail parties seem like a cinch when you compare them to off-site soirees, such as art openings. Not only do you have to look good, you actually have to know what you're talking about. And while no one expects you to know the date of every painting in Monet's haystack series or that one of Edward Hopper's paintings inspired a movie set (it's the house on the hill in *Psycho*, by the way), flexing your knowledge of old-school masters and funky modern styles alike shows your host and your company that you can swing it at the most sophisticated events. If you're invited for a museum date and don't want to sound clueless, here are the Cliff Notes:

Impressionism
This nineteenth-century technique spearheaded by Monet, Renoir, and Degas (water lilies/people in hats at picnics/anorexic ballerinas) uses broad strokes of color that give a natural "impression" of the light, tone, and color of a scene, rather than trying to look true-to-life perfect.

Pointillism
This technique, made famous by Seurat, uses pinpoints of color to represent shapes. Consider it a more anal form of Impressionism. And remember the rhyme: Seurat the Dot.

Cubism

See a painting that reminds you of your high school trig class, with lots of sharp angles, fragmented objects, and people's bodies in funky geometric shapes and proportions? Spaniard Pablo Picasso became the Cubist king for his work *Les Demoiselles d'Avignon* in 1907. Impress your date by telling him that Picasso's works have been auctioned off more times than any other artist's, totaling $1.23 billion in sales.

Surrealism

Think: Art on an acid trip (weird staircases, melting clocks, floating flowers in a desert). Dali, the mack-daddy of surrealist artists, was known to paint what he saw in his own dreams.

Bauhaus (Bau-house)

Just using this word ups your cool factor. Bauhaus describes the 1920s industrial-chic German school of art that influences everything from hotel lobbies to IKEA furniture today. Their question was, "Why should art be limited to flat canvases—why can't art be found in functional objects?" You can see Bauhaus style in sleek steel coffee tables, funky plastic chairs, and geometric light fixtures.

MG TIP: There's no "correct" distance from which to view art, but stay a minimum of five to ten feet away. Should you want to take a closer look at details, view them from a diagonal angle—otherwise, you're blocking everyone else's view. But never get so close that you could sneeze on the installation. Squint your eyes a little, throw your hand on your hip, and slowly sip from your Chardonnay glass to signal deep thinking.

What to Say If You Can't Seem to Remember the Styles

If you're still confused, here are a few pointers on phrases that will wow 'em.

If you're looking at a modern piece of art that has . . .

Cartoons

Say, "Mmm, that's very Lichtenstein" (*"Lick-ten-stein"*). Roy Lichtenstein was one of the major players in the pop art movement, alongside Warhol. He's best known for doing giant comic-strip depictions of men and women.

Wacky Objects or Pieces of Furniture

Utter, "How derivative of Duchamp" *("Du-shaamp")*. Duchamp is famous for displaying a urinal as art, and painting a mustache on the Mona Lisa. You'll really blow 'em away if you throw in: "That's very Dada." Duchamp has been called the daddy of Dadaism, an antitraditional art movement that labeled random objects as "art" with a wink-wink sense of humor.

One or Two Solid Colors

Say, "How Rothko." His minimalist paintings have been said to look like "television sets for Zen Buddhists."

Splatter Paint

"I appreciate its Pollock-esque vibe." Jackson Pollock was one of the most famous American painters in the 1930s. Extra snob points if you comfortably use the term "Ab-Ex" (not to be confused with AmEx). It's short for Abstract Expressionism, and is used to describe art like Pollock's and Rothko's, which finds meaning via forms and colors, rather than subject matter.

Movie Credits

There have been several movies made about great painters. While they tend to be hit or miss critically, they at least give you some insight into the time period and the artists' inspirations. You can watch them to brush up on the artists and their time period. Try:

- *Basquiat* (1996): Tells the story of the meteoric rise of New York City graffiti street artist Jean-Michel Basquiat in the early eighties. Extra bonus: It goes into great detail about Andy Warhol, who discovered Basquiat, and was written and directed by Julian Schnabel, a painter and sculptor known for his "broken plate" paintings. Broken plate paintings are (true to their name) paintings on a series of ceramic fragments, which give a feeling of texture and disjointedness.

MG TIP: Try to be open-minded when you're viewing art, but it's okay not to like everything you see. Should someone ask your opinion, don't lie and say it's wonderful if you don't think it is. Just find an interesting detail to point out, even if it's a critique. Still, refrain from saying "They call *that* art?" At a benefit, gallery, or museum show, you never know who's listening.

- *Surviving Picasso* (1996): It's the story of the painter circa 1943 and the various romantic affairs he had over the years, as told through the eyes of one of his lovers, Françoise Gilot. Think of it as a movie about torrid affairs with an art history lesson thrown in.

- *Pollock* (2000): Ed Harris stars as the American painter, with Marcia Gay Harden playing his wife and fellow artist, Lee Krasner. Gives an interesting look into his tortured world from the late 1940s until his death in 1956.

- *Frida* (2002): Salma Hayek stars as the Mexican painter Frida Kahlo. It not only goes into depth about her lifelong pursuit of art before and after a tragic accident, but it also gives a good picture of her famous lover, painter Diego Rivera.

- *Factory Girl* (2006): Sienna Miller stars as a young party girl turned model whose close relationship with Andy Warhol (played by Guy Pearce) takes her on a wild ride through the art scene of New York City in the 1960s.

Opera 101: How to Sound Smarter at the Opera

Another equally daunting social venture is the opera. Sure, if you're Julia Roberts in *Pretty Woman*, all you need to make a fabulous impression at the opera is a horsey laugh and a gorgeous red dress. But for the rest of us, a little background information will make the night flow more smoothly.

Who Are the Major Composers?

Mozart (1756–91): This Austrian bigwig is arguably the most versatile composer. His most famous works are *Don Giovanni*, *The Marriage of Figaro*, and *The Magic Flute*.

Verdi (1813–1901): Consider this Italian stud the BMOC: Big Man on the Opera Circuit. He's famous for *Aida*, *Otello*, *Rigoletto*, *Macbeth*, and *La Traviata*.

Wagner ("Vog-ner") (1813–83): Talk about serious! This German composer is famous for complicated operas such as *Tristan und Isolde, Die Walküre*, and *Parsifal*. I don't recommend a Wagner opera as your first.

Puccini (1858–1924): His finest operas, *La Bohème, Tosca,* and *Madame Butterfly*, are strongly emotional and romantic. (The hit Broadway play *Rent* is based on *La Bohème*.)

What Are the Styles of Opera?

Operas are either comic (*opera buffa*) or serious (*opera seria*). How do you tell which is which? Trust your senses; a *buffa* will have lighter banter and less sweeping arias than a *seria* will.

What Are the Parts of an Opera?

The Aria: Long, uninterrupted solo vocals that sound like songs ("*Mio Bambino Caro* . . .")

The Recitative: Dialogue that sounds like two Italians rapping back and forth. But don't think you're in for a short night; full-length operas can be three acts or more and are usually four to five hours long.

What Do I Wear to the Opera?

Back before World War I, the opera was the most formal event around. Women wore floor-length dresses and men wore white tie. Now the rules are more relaxed, but you should still wear a cocktail dress and your date should don a jacket and tie. If you're going to opening night or a benefit, break out the black-tie garb.

When Do I Clap?

Applaud when the conductor takes the podium and whenever the curtain comes down. It's also routine for there to be applause at the end of a famous aria. But wait to stand up and applaud during the final curtain call. The people seated behind you won't be able to see the stage as the performers take their bows. If a standing ovation does happen, go ahead and stand.

What Do I Do at Intermission?

If your date bought the tickets, buy him a drink. You can also switch to better seats in your section if no one claims them. Just be sure to ask the usher first.

How the Heck Do I Keep from Falling Asleep?

Even the most polished Modern Girl can be overcome by the Opera Snooze around the third act. Have a coffee before the performance, keep Altoids and chocolate-covered espresso beans in your purse, and skip the bubbly at intermission. Also, sit up straight so you'll be less likely to slouch into a nodding-off position. If all else fails, tell your date that you were so engrossed, you just had to shut your eyes and throw back your head to truly savor the experience. Just watch out for drool spots on your dress.

"Wediquette"

Okay, now that you're keyed up on how to gracefully handle everything from cocktail parties to art exhibits to arias, I'm going to discuss the most important social function of all: a wedding. Look at it as a super-size soiree that requires you to follow a set of decorum rules. And trust me; I know how confusing it can all be. Between the gifts, the engagement parties, the showers, and the ceremony, you may be a bit frazzled as to what is expected of you. Whether you've been to one wedding or twenty, here are answers to etiquette issues that often crop up.

So, Can I Wear White to a Wedding or What?

Nope, not even ivory. The worst wedding faux pas besides making out with the groom is outshining the bride. I don't care if she's the most laid-back woman in the universe and it's a scorching 110°F at the air-conditionless ceremony. Pick a flirty pastel color or print instead. The reason not to wear ivory? Unless you're fond of snotty glares from the mother of the bride, best to stay away from *her* color.

Agh! What's the Difference Between a Wedding Reply Card and an RSVP?

Wait, you may say to yourself: Is there even a difference? Yup. Most wedding invites have a reply card that will be three and a half by five inches and will look something like this:

> *The favor of a reply is requested:*
> *Mrs. Jane Buckingham*
> *Will——X——attend*
> Check or "X" it if you can come.
> Write in "not" if you cannot.

Some invitations will ask you to RSVP on an enclosed blank card. The most old-school, proper way to reply, however, is to write it on your personal stationery to the sender of the invitation (i.e., the parents of the bride). If you ever receive an invitation with no reply card, this is why. Take it as your cue.

Formal Acceptance Is:
Jane and Marcus Buckingham accept with pleasure the kind invitation of (name of the parents of the bride—see the top of the invite for this).

Formal Decline Is:
Jane and Marcus Buckingham regret that we are unable to accept the invitation of (name of the parents of the bride).

Can I Add My Guy's Name to the Reply Card?

No! This is considered bad taste. If it says your name and "guest" on the invite, he will be included. The only time you may want to ask the bride if you can bring him along is if you haven't spoken to her in ages and she doesn't know you now have a fiancé or husband. But don't be offended if she refuses to include him; brides typically have to limit their guest lists because of cost and space concerns.

How Long Do I Have to Respond?

Respond immediately, especially if you are unable to attend. That way the bride can give an accurate head count to the caterer.

Belle of the Ball?

If you are just so popular that you are invited to more weddings than your budget allows, you may have to make some tough choices, particularly if a wedding requires you to travel. If you choose not to attend, respond quickly with a sincere note and send a gift, but do remember that if you don't show up to theirs, they are quite likely not to show up to yours.

Can I Go Off the Registry?

You're not limited to the registry, but it is a smart option, especially for the shower and wedding. Look at it this way: This is the bride and groom's one chance to get that blender, set of knives, and vacuum cleaner that are too unsexy to buy each other as birthday gifts. Since the invitation shouldn't specify where they are registered, ask someone else involved with the wedding, such as their parents, siblings, or a member of the bridal party. You can typically locate registries through www.theknot.com. Also, don't be surprised if it's not a blender they're asking for, but instead a honeymoon. Honeymoon crowdfunding sites often allow you to earmark your gift for a certain use, like a couple's massage or a nice dinner out, making the gifting experience a little more personal.

MG TIP: If you're invited to two or three showers for the same bride-to-be, bring a bona-fide gift to the first gathering and a smaller token for those thereafter, such as a framed photo or anything homemade.

MG TIP: If the bride or groom is a close friend, send a separate wedding card in the mail in addition to the free gift card that comes with your online registry purchase.

Help! I Have to Give a Shower Gift, an Engagement Gift, Another Shower Gift . . . Gift, Gift, Gift!

First, breathe. Second, think of a wedding as a three-act play: the Engagement, the Shower, and the Ceremony. Keep your piggy bank intact by deciding on the total amount you want to spend on everything, and divide that number by three—although you may choose to weigh it more toward the actual wedding gift.

Act I: The Engagement Party

These gifts are geared toward the bride and don't have to be practical. Go with something feminine, like a silver clock, a pretty champagne bucket, great stationery, or a silver heart-shaped case. Just be careful about monogramming items, unless you know whether she intends to take his last name. Or stay on the safe side by choosing the first letter of her first name. In fact, Emily Post actually says that only immediate family and the closest of friends need to give engagement gifts, especially if there is no party.

Act II: The Shower

By the time the shower rolls around, the bride and groom will have registered. The shower will likely have a theme, which will help narrow your choices. If the theme is a "kitchen shower," buy their requested coffeemaker, and give it a cute twist by adding a variety of exotic coffees. Bring the gift to the shower instead of having it sent to the bride.

Act III: The Ceremony

This should be the nicest, most practical gift, so choose it from the registry and have it shipped to the address specified. Don't show up with a gift in hand. The last thing a bride and groom need to worry about is how to schlep all that loot home. If you've stayed well under your budget for the first two gifts, this is where your surplus should go.

What's the Lag Time I Have for Sending a Gift?

Everyone says you have a year to send it, but this really isn't true. It should always arrive before the wedding. Don't let more than a month go by between receiving your invitation and sending the gift. Put an alarm in your calendar to remind yourself. Here's another reason not to wait until the last minute: All that will be left are plastic spoons and $350 bedspreads.

Do I Need to Send a Gift If I'm Not Attending the Wedding?

Yes. There's no excuse for not sending a gift.

Can I Give Cash?

Cha-ching! You can send it as a check, gift certificate, U.S. government bond, or stock certificate, but don't send cash through the mail. Unlike regular gifts, you can present your envelope to the couple at their reception, made out to both the bride and the groom. If you're sending them a check before the wedding, make it out to either the bride or the groom (depending on whom you know better).

How to Host a Bridal Shower Without Having a Panic Attack . . . or Going into Debt

A bridal shower is rarely given by the bride's mother, sister, or grandmother because it's considered bad taste (i.e., a family ploy for more presents). Either the maid of honor or another close friend typically throws it.

If you're the lucky one and are freaking out because the closest you've come to throwing a shower is getting into a shampoo-induced tangle with your plastic curtain, remember this: You have help, and showers are meant to be casual and fun, not wedding-photo perfect. Here are the steps to help you pull it off:

MG TIP: Looking for a shower in a box? P.S. XO will send you all the decorations, crafts, and supplies you need to throw a perfect shower at a reasonable price.

Shower Step 1: Powwow with the Bride

Some showers are planned as surprise parties, but who wants to deal with that much stress? It's much smarter to talk to the bride about the guest list, the location, and get hints about shower themes she'd love.

Shower Step 2: Get Your Backup Singers Ready

No one expects you to single-handedly orchestrate the shower. You have her mom, the groom's mom, and her bridal party to help, so delegate away. Can't cook but want the shower to be a chic country brunch? E-mail your arsenal of women asking who makes good scones and who knows where to pick up fresh peach juice for Bellinis. Keep everyone in the loop about their duties via e-mail. Create a file on your computer that says "Shower Details" so everything is organized.

Shower Step 3: Pick a Theme

Most showers have a theme, which can dictate the type of presents people give. Chances are, the bride will say, "Oh, anything is fine!" when you mention theme ideas. So think about what kinds of things she loves (whether it's Mexican food, massages, or *The Great Gatsby*) and base it on that. Here are some trendy ideas:

A Spa Shower

What could be better than a day of pampering and pedicures? Call up local spas in your area to find out what their "off-peak" hours are (Sunday morning might be cheaper than Saturday afternoon, for example) and if they can give a group rate. A less expensive option is to throw a spa shower at home. Hire a massage therapist and a manicurist-pedicurist to treat your guests (skip the facialist, as many women don't want to be seen sans makeup). Serve maki sushi, fruit salads, mimosas, and lemon cake. Many hostesses give guests a token of appreciation as they enter or leave the party. Cute spa options are terry slippers, a set of nail polishes, body lotions, or soaps.

Tea Party Shower

Is your friend a classy girl who would fit in among the likes of Lady Mary and the Earl of Grantham? If so, give the shower a tea party theme. Avoid alienating the common folk by mixing the old world with the new, juxtaposing mismatched flea-market china against a modern bold floral tablecloth. Set the party in the midafternoon and serve a tower of treats, including scones, tea sandwiches, and cakes. While you should of course have tea, consider offering adult cocktails as well, like a grown-up limeade or summer punch. Leave your guests walking away with their own miniature tea sets, ready to try the Downton tradition on their own time.

A Scavenger-Hunt Shower

Is the bride a true adventurer? Are her friends and family the kinds of casual chicks who'd pass up tea and crumpets for a good challenge? Make up a list of riddles for guests to figure out, such as "Where did Karen and Bryan go on their first date?" and "What is their favorite thing to do together?" Split your party into two groups, pass out two digital cameras, and have them take photos of themselves at those various locations. When you all meet up later in the day over lunch, give the winning team their prize. Collect the cameras and compile all the photos that were taken for a scrapbook for the bride.

A "Jack and Jill" Shower

Coed showers are becoming incredibly popular. Including the groom and his groomsmen can lend a more fun, less prissy vibe to the party (and gives all the single bridesmaids a primo chance to flirt). Think of your total crew: Are they casual, sporty types, or foodie sophisticates? If they're the former, go with a barbecue. If they're the latter, try a wine-tasting party, where guests are instructed to bring different types of vino. Do a blind tasting where guy-girl teams compete to guess varietals and vintages. The winning team gets to take home a bottle of their favorite Cab or Merlot.

Shower Step 4: Plan Your Party Date

Most showers take place between a month and two weeks before the wedding. Travel details can figure in too. If you and most of the guests are on the East Coast and she now lives out West, talk to her mom about when she'll be back East for a final dress fitting or to get her marriage license. That way she won't have to buy yet another plane ticket.

Shower Step 5: Devise Your Guest List

Invitees should include the maid of honor (who may be you), the bridesmaids, the mothers and sisters of the bride and groom, and close friends and relatives who are invited to the wedding. Don't invite men unless it's a coed shower. Also, avoid inviting too many out-of-town guests unless they fall into the categories above. Doing so starts to look like you're just digging for gifts for the bride.

Shower Step 6: Write Up Your Invites

To be on the safe side, send out your invites a month before the shower date. More and more people are sending Web invitations, as it is a great way to track the responses and get the word out. Paperless Post and Evite do great ones. If you prefer printed ones, I love Tiny Prints.com, which does adorable wedding shower invitations, baby shower invitations, and thank-you notes. Here's an easy way to word it:

You Are Invited to Attend a Bridal Shower

With a "Kitchen" Theme* [or whatever the theme may be]

In Honor of [bride's name]

on [date] at [time]

at [address]

Kindly RSVP to Jane Buckingham by [date, spelled out]

[your phone number and e-mail]

*The bride's colors are sage and cream.

Shower Step 7: Chip in with the Other Bridesmaids for a Grande Gift

Pooling your assets guarantees she'll get one of the major items from her registry. If you plan to purchase the gift in person from a department or specialty store, agree on a price point and ask the girls to chip

MG TIP: These days more and more people are sending e-mail invitations. While many people will always prefer the more traditional route, it is a great way to save costs and sometimes gets better responses.

MG TIP: Whatever you do, don't list her registry information on the card.

MG TIP: It's customary for the bride to be "fashionably late" to her shower, so ask guests to come half an hour before she arrives. That way, all her presents will be out on a display table when she walks in.

MG TIP: To make the party more fun, plan to give the bride a gag gift along with your regular gift. The best moment I ever had at an otherwise "proper" bridal shower came when the groom's sisters presented the bride-to-be with a set of white cotton bikini underwear with hilarious junior high photos of the groom silk-screened on them. The bride promised to wear them on her wedding night. We all hoped she didn't.

in their share in advance. That way, you won't have to chase everyone down after the fact.

Shower Step 8: Appoint a Gift Recorder and a Bouquet Maker

As the bride unwraps her gifts, she'll need someone to write down who gave her what (so that she doesn't go blank at thank-you-note time). Then, designate another relatively artistic friend to collect all of the ribbons and make a "rehearsal bouquet" by stapling them to a paper plate. If you're the maid of honor, save it and bring it to the rehearsal, where the bride will carry it down the aisle.

How to Give a Great Wedding Toast Without Getting Booed Back into Your Seat

MG TIP: If you are asked to give a toast but are public-speaking phobic, jot down your speech on three-by-five note cards, practice in front of a friend, and bring the cards to the wedding in your purse. Make sure to write your words in pen, because most receptions have low lighting, and you won't be able to read pencil. And try to look up after every other sentence and not hide your face in the cards.

Now that you've shone as the host of the shower, it's on to the main event. While most of the time it's the best man who gives a speech, it's becoming more common these days for the maid of honor or sister of the bride to give a toast as well. At formal lunch or dinner receptions, speeches are given after the dessert has been served. If you're called on to give a speech, you'll be told long before the reception date. Otherwise, save your words, however clever and touching, for the bride and groom's ears only.

Sure, it's cute in movies when the speech giver clinks his or her glass to get people's attention, but not only is it considered in bad taste, you might land the bride's parents with a hefty broken-glass caterer's bill. Take the microphone if there is one, and pause for a moment. Someone will likely say, "Toast!" or people will start saying, "Shhhh . . ." Introduce yourself, say how you know the bride or groom, and tell three great things about her (or him), backed up with funny stories. It's best if you can incorporate both the bride and the groom, but if you don't know the groom very well, focus on your relationship with the bride. Don't tell inside jokes, don't mention ex-boyfriends, don't discuss politics, don't insult the bride even in a joking way, don't mention anything that has to do with the sexual exploits of the couple, and for the love of brevity, don't yammer on longer than one or two minutes. Let everyone know when it's time to toast by saying, "Let's raise our glasses to . . ."

When Can You Leave the Wedding?

I don't blame you for wondering. Your feet are hurting in those 3½-inch skinny heels, you're bloated from the buffet, and the only good-looking, unmarried groomsman is gay. It's acceptable to depart any time after the cutting of the cake. (Oh, and kiss your no-carb diet good-bye for the night—it's considered bad luck if you don't at least have a taste of the wedding cake.) Before slipping out, make sure to find a member of the bride's immediate family and thank him or her. If you can't find a host to personally thank, pop a short thank-you note in the mail. This is one place where I wouldn't recommend an e-mail, as the last thing a bride or parent of the bride wants to deal with the next morning is a bunch of e-mails.

CHAPTER 4

Home Chic Home

Every Modern Girl deserves to live in the most stylish digs possible. Maybe you dream of living in a loft with thirty-foot-high ceilings, a wall of double-height windows overlooking the city, and a room full of ridiculously mod furniture. Coming home from work every day would be pure bliss as you listen to jazz, relax on your terrace, and sip cocktails with all your sophisticated, equally domestically superior friends. Or perhaps you see yourself in a charming country abode with vanilla-scented candles and freshly cut flowers, mountain views, and a classic furniture collection so luxe, *Elle Decor* editors from far and wide would be scrambling to photograph you, your dog, and your perfect guy whipping up breakfast in your professional chef's kitchen . . .

Whoa, reality check! Much as we'd all love to own sprawling, Pinterest-worthy pads, very few of us actually live in that fantasy world. Take my first apartment, for example: It couldn't have been more than four hundred square feet total, even though it technically had three rooms. My bedroom was an embarrassing little square that just squeezed in my bed (literally—it was so tight I could only exit from one side). My bathtub was so pint-size that I had to keep my knees bent at a ninety-degree angle to lean back in it. And my faux "kitchen" consisted of a mini-fridge and an electric stove in one corner of the wall, while the only window in the living room faced a dark airshaft. After giving my brother a tour of the apartment (which took all of ten seconds), he asked where the rest of it was. Not funny.

Since homestead-hopping was not an option, I went on a guerrilla mission to make my cramped space more livable. Determined to transform my bedroom from claustrophobic to calm, and to punch up my living room from dorm dump to cocktail party-ready status, I started reading catalogs and design books, scouring antique shops, and experimenting with different furniture and color combos. Shockingly, my shack took a stylish turn. And I've carried those tricks I employed in that Mini-Me first apartment on to bigger and better living spaces.

Painting: The Easiest—and Cheapest— Way to Transform Your Pad

Think about how you feel right after you've put on makeup in the morning. Your face looks brighter, fresher, and more alive, doesn't it? Well, slicking a spanking-new coat of paint on your walls has the same effect. Color adds a wham-bam kick to an otherwise boring abode and serves to separate rooms—giving the illusion of a larger living space. For example, if your kitchen and living room happen to all be in the same open space, opting for two colors to distinguish between the rooms makes it instantly appear to be two rooms. And the best part about painting is that it's inexpensive, relatively easy to do, and will set the tone for decorating the rest of your home. But before you bust out the overalls and paintbrushes, you need to decide on the type, finish, and colors that work best for you.

Picking the Right Type of Paint

Navigating your way through a paint store can be a dizzying whirl, but not when you know exactly what you're looking for. First, you'll notice two popular kinds of paint: latex-based and oil-based.

MG TIP: If you are re-painting white walls with white (common when redoing ceilings), then CIL's Magic White is your savior. The new line contains special additives that make the paint go on pink, allowing you to see where you have added a fresh coat. When you are all done, grab a beer and watch it magically turn to the fresh white you wanted.

MG TIP: The people over at Dutch Boy are making big advancements in the world of paint storage and I could not be happier. Their new one-liter and 3.7-liter plastic square containers are equipped with twist-off lids, side handles, and easy-pour spouts, making those rusted, circular cans an artifact from the past that won't be missed.

MG TIP: You'll also see a type of finish called gloss, which is one step shinier than semi-gloss. Use it only on door and window trim and moldings—its shininess will illuminate imperfections on your wall.

Latex-based paint is easier to work with because it's water-based. If you accidentally dribble it across your floor (or wipe it across your forehead, as I have), it quickly comes off with soap and water.

Oil-based paint, on the other hand, requires turpentine in order to be removed. The appeal of oil paint is that it's almost totally stain-proof once it's on your walls, though, and lasts longer than latex. If you opt for oil, be sure to use heavy gloves to protect your hands and to cover your entire floor with a thick drop cloth before painting, so you don't accidentally do any Jackson Pollock splatter painting around your feet. Also, as geeky as it sounds, you may want to wear a paper mask (available at any hardware store) to prevent yourself from inhaling toxic turpentine fumes (you'll need those precious brain cells for arranging your furniture later). And if you're pregnant, check with your doctor before working with oil paint or turpentine.

Finish is the texture your paint will have on the wall. The most popular finishes are flat and semi-gloss.

Flat paint has a smooth, matte finish, and won't reflect light, so it's a good choice for your bedroom or another large, soothing space, like your living room. But keep in mind that it's tough to remove stains from flat paint—rubbing the wall with cleanser or just water often leaves a dark mark.

Semi-gloss gives a subtle sheen to your walls by reflecting light. It's great for kitchens and bathrooms; should you accidentally kick the wall with your shoe or a chair, or splatter spaghetti sauce or makeup on it, you can easily wipe it clean with a rag and a little cleanser.

Choosing Colors

Now that you've decided on your paint type and finish, it's time for the fun part: picking your palette. Do you go with funky tangerine or cool celery? Deep crimson or peach blush? It's easy to get seduced by the Crayola array of colors out there, but before putting those cans in your shopping cart, do the following:

Decide Your Vibe

It's important to figure out what mood you want to create with paint so that your walls aren't fighting your furniture—or your mental state! Do you want your pad to be a cool, minimalist den of Zen? Stick to cool neutrals like light gray, light charcoal, muted gray blue, pale celadon green, amaretto, and taupe. These colors promote relaxation and team well with sleek chrome and rectangular, espresso-stained furniture. However, if you dream of your place as an upbeat entertaining pad that instantly makes you feel energized, consider creamy yellows, rich oranges, sexy reds, or eye-popping greens to contrast with your white walls and give a boost to plain old wood furniture.

Confused about what your color vibe is? Start ripping out pages of catalogs and magazines with rooms you like. Think about hotels you've loved staying in, or TV characters' pads you've adored, whether it's Olivia Pope's crisp, demure Washington, D.C., apartment on *Scandal* or Hannah Horvath's eclectic boho digs on *Girls*. Last, look at your closet—besides black and white, what colors do you feel happiest wearing? That color cue could tip you off to a shade you'd love to see on your walls.

Beware of Color Clashing

Even though you may fantasize about painting your bedroom violet and your living room red, consider what that visual combo would be when you're standing in one room and looking at another. If you plan to paint all of your rooms, your safest bet is to go with neutral tones that will flow from one room to the next. If you do go with brights, choose colors that complement each other, and think about leaving a room in between two bright rooms white. The white will act as a visual "break" between the two vibrant tones.

Consider Painting Just One Wall

A great alternative to color-drenching the entire room (especially if you're a little spooked about adding so much new hue or afraid of color commitment) is simply adding color to one wall, often called an

MG TIP: Consider attending a "faux finish" class at Home Depot. "Sponging" your walls can add an easy, interesting texture.

MG TIP: Primary colors are red, yellow, and blue. Secondary colors are orange, green, and violet.

MG TIP: The one-painted-wall effect works best with cool, subtle shades. Do it with one shocking wall of red, for example, and it may look like you got lazy after painting wall number one and just called it a day.

accent wall. It creates a little drama and depth without overpowering the room. The best wall to paint is the longest one with the least going on. So if you have a couch, end tables, and a chair against one wall, and just a TV and framed photographs on the opposite wall, paint the latter for balance. If you paint the wall loaded with furniture, the rest of the room will look stark and unfinished. You'll probably want to repaint the other walls in your old color as well, so the old walls don't look dirty and faded next to your fab new colorful wall.

Buy a Few Small Cans of Paint and Test Your Colors First

MG TIP: Keep in mind that under the bright (often fluorescent) lights of a paint store, the sample card is going to appear much lighter than it will at home on your walls. So buy your test colors a few shades lighter than you think you'll need.

It may seem like a huge pain, an extra expense, and well, just a boring way to spend a few hours, but trust me, testing a shade before you commit goes a *long* way. I once bought several gallons of what I thought was the perfect shade of latte. After getting all the paint home and smearing just one brush stroke on the wall, it was clear that unless my latte had been blended with Welch's Grape Juice, this was not the color I was looking for. The worst part was that since the color was custom mixed, I was out $200 for the four gallons of paint. The lesson I learned is that $15 or $20 on a small can is a lot less to lose if the color's wrong than $200.

Another reason you'll want to test-drive your paint is to make sure it looks great under all types of light. For example, a cool celadon could look gorgeous at night with your dimmed lamps and candles glowing, but once the natural light of the next morning streams in, it could look closer to split pea soup. I suggest buying a quart each of the two shades that look closest to what you want. Then apply both colors in a patch about the size of a laptop to several places in the room. (Try one spot by the window where the most light hits it, one spot in the corner that is the darkest, and one spot by your couch that is a nice mixture of the light.) Let the paint dry, and then check out the colors in both daylight and nighttime. Like 'em both? Go ahead and paint those walls, baby.

The Best Colors for Each Room in Your Crib

Now that you have a few tricks and tips up your sleeve, it's time to do some picking. Some hues are perfect for morning lattes and cappuccinos and others for kicking back on the couch. And some shades just make you wanna go *zzz*. This palette primer will get you started:

Reds and Oranges

Rich brick reds, crimsons, and burgundies go well in entryways, powder rooms, kitchens, and dining rooms (and no wonder . . . studies say that the color red increases appetite). Warm oranges follow the same rules as reds do, but look better in living rooms than kitchens. Don't paint your bedroom red or orange if you want to get any sleep, as it might not only stimulate you, but cause 2 A.M. munchies.

Yellow

Energizing and soothing at the same time, yellow works well just about anywhere and has a magical brightening effect in dark apartments. Go for a pale creamy yellow instead of a bright canary yellow. The more muted the shade, the more design options you'll have.

Green

Calming a color as it is, green can be tricky. Celadon or pale green with slight gray undertones looks cool and refreshing in the living room and bedroom, but lime green should be reserved for smaller spaces. Moss green can just look murky if it's not done perfectly. Keep your furnishings full of creams and cognac browns if you plan on painting a room moss.

Blues and Purples

In their most concentrated forms, these colors can easily overpower. So skip the royal blues and violets—the subtler the shade, the better. Reserve soft blues, pale plums, and muted lavenders for your bedroom to induce sleep.

MG TIP: You can try a light blue ceiling in a white or cream room to add some color, but be careful not to go too dark. This will make the ceiling seem lower and the room smaller.

MG TIP: If you're lucky enough to have a room with crown moldings, (or at least trim around your doors) play them up. Snow-white moldings add crispness to a room painted in a vibrant color like rich red, navy, or brown, and soothe more subtle walls like pale yellow. If you find white boring and are feeling daring, paint your moldings a few shades darker than your walls within the same color family. So if your room is light gray, go for charcoal trim. If your walls are latte, try espresso trim. Just avoid contrasting "opposite" hues on the wheel, like green walls and red trim, or yellow walls and purple trim. Though these colors are considered complementary, having the combo on your wall can feel suffocating. Better to introduce them in smaller splashes via a pillow, piece of artwork, or rug.

Gray

If you want to instantly add mood to your room but don't consider yourself a "color person," gray's the way to go, whether it's in your living room, foyer, or bedroom. But make sure to get it *at least* three shades lighter than what your eye tells you. With low lighting, it can easily look black. Eek.

Cream

A painting staple, cream looks great everywhere, especially lighter hues like linen and ivory. Creams are great if you'd rather use fabrics and pillows to add color to your room.

Amaretto

This shade is neutral, but nutty and rich at the same time. A pale latte color can look equally great in a modern living room with white sofas and a traditional one with rich browns and reds. A deeper shade of amaretto in the bathroom can also make a white sink and bathtub look even brighter by contrast.

Colors to Skip

Black

Great to wear on your bod, a nightmare to have on your walls. It's dark. It shows flaws. And, for the most part, it's just plain creepy. If you're craving a sleek, dark color, consider charcoal and offset it with clean white moldings.

Mustard

Keep it on your burger. About 5 percent of people on earth can pull this color off in a room—and they're often high-concept designers. Save yourself the style headache.

Kelly Green

Can we say St. Patrick's Day?

Pink

It worked for Reese Witherspoon in *Legally Blonde*, but that alone should tell you something. Random fact: Maximum security prisons reportedly painted their cell walls pink because the color supposedly had a calming effect on the prisoners. Over time it had the opposite effect and actually drove them mad!

Let's Get This Painting Party Rollin'

Now that you've picked the perfect colors for your place, it's time to get them up on the wall. Don't be daunted—with a helper or two you'll be done before the day is out . . . and will be saving yourselves upward of a hundred bucks. (Hey, if the clueless couples on *Trading Spaces* can do it, you certainly can.)

Supplies You'll Need

- *Paint:* Measure your walls first; one gallon covers about four hundred square feet.
- *Paintbrushes:*
    - *Small brushes:* One half to one and a half inches is ideal for trim work, corners, and touch-ups.
    - *Medium brushes:* Two inches is great for baseboards and cupboards.
    - *Large brushes:* Three- and four-inch brushes are ideal for flat areas such as walls, ceilings, floors, and doors.
- *Edger:* Allows you to "edge" near ceilings, corners, baseboards, and trim.
- *Paint roller:* Size, thickness, and texture depend on the paint you're using and the texture of your walls; ask the paint store pros.
- *Disposable paint roller inserts and a metal tray:* This makes cleanup easy. Don't try to skimp and get the flimsy plastic insert alone. It's likely to buckle and spill paint all over your floor.

- *Masking tape:* Two inches wide (or wider).

- *Drop cloths:* Old sheets, tarps, or anything else thick that can cover the floor.

- *Ladder:* Whatever you do, wear shoes when you climb one, and it's better not to climb when you're the only person at home—have someone spot you. More than 350,000 people fall off ladders every year. Another option is a paint roller extender that may offer less control but more reach.

- *Old sunglasses or ski goggles* to cover your eyes.

- *Shower cap/bandana* to protect your hair.

- *Rubber kitchen gloves* so that you don't need a new manicure.

11 Goofproof Steps to Perfectly Painting Your Room

Step 1: Clear Your Work Space
Move all the furniture out of the room, or at least to the center of the room. Roll up the carpets and take down art. Put your sheets or tarps over the furniture and the floor. If you run out of sheets, just tape a few layers of newspaper to the floor.

Step 2: Open the Windows and Doors
Don't be stupid like I was and forget to open your windows and doors before painting. If you're painting window trim, the wet paint can seal windows so tightly you'll have trouble opening them again. Also, keeping doors open will air out the room.

Step 3: Wash Your Wall
If you're painting over a greasy surface (such as your kitchen walls) or painting over the previous tenant's hideous old paint job, clean it with a sponge and gentle household cleanser. The new paint will stick better to clean surfaces.

Step 4: Tape, Tape, Tape

Line your masking tape around all doors, windows, trim, and the edge where the wall meets the ceiling to create straight lines and to separate moldings.

Step 5: Get Primed

Primer is the first coat used to seal the wall. It works kind of like a base coat of nail polish—it creates a smooth surface for your topcoat to stick to. Ask the paint store pros to tint your primer so it's closer to the color of your paint. You'll save yourself from having to paint additional coats of your color.

Step 6: Dip It

Fill up your paint tray with one to two inches of paint and dip your roller into it. Roll it back and forth on the ridged part of the tray. This squeezes out the excess paint and evenly spreads the paint all the way around the roller. If the roller drips when you lift it, there's still too much paint on it.

Step 7: Hit the Ceiling

Paint the upper corners of the room first, and with your roller lightly dipped in paint (but not dripping), move across the ceiling in long, rolling strokes. Cover small spaces until you're finished.

Step 8: Coat Your Walls

When painting your walls, move your roller in broad up-and-down strokes, then go over it side-to-side so the lines won't look streaky. Keep tackling small spaces until you've covered the entire wall. Let the paint on your walls completely dry for at least a day before moving on to moldings.

Step 9: Trim It Up

Now it's time to pull the tape off your moldings so they can be painted. Remove the tape slowly so that you don't rip a layer of paint off your wall. Also, watch out for wet paint on the tape. Paint the doors and window moldings—and remember that you're using semi-gloss here.

MG TIP: If you have "popcorn ceiling," (that bumpy, nubby plaster finish frequently sprayed over a concrete ceiling to hide its imperfections), be sure not to roll back over your paint while it's wet. It will remove the paint you just put on and make some of the debris fall.

MG TIP: Whatever you do, don't decide to take a painting hiatus when you reach the middle of the wall. It will be hard to make the lines match hours later, after the first half has dried.

MG TIP: If you'd rather dispose of your leftover paint, keep in mind that paint is actually considered chemical waste, so you can't just toss it in the garbage with your Sunday paper and Chinese takeout. Most towns have monthly toxic-waste drop-off drives (gee, wonder if they take toxic ex-boyfriends, too?), so store your paint until then. In cities where there aren't drop-offs, you may have the option of pouring the paint in a nonrecyclable container, putting the container in the trash, and the empty paint can in a recycling bin. For more detailed info, call your local solid-waste office or hazardous-waste collection site.

Step 10: Hands Off!

Resist the urge to feel the wall to see if it's done—this isn't baking! Simply wait four hours for the first coat to dry before applying a second coat (if you forgot to have your primer tinted). If it's a rainy or humid day, allow for another few hours, because the moisture in the air will make the paint take longer to dry. Now pat yourself on the back. You've set the stage for a fabulous new room.

Step 11: Store Smart

When you're all done painting and getting ready to dispose of your paint, make sure to save a little bit for touch-ups in small Tupperware containers, empty plastic ketchup bottles, or small jelly jars. Then, label the containers (living room paint, living room trim, and so on). This way, you'll have easy access to the color should you nick a wall, and you don't have to store a bunch of half-full paint cans. If you want to be *super*organized, type out a list of colors you've used and keep it somewhere safe.

Hot Hints for Furniture Hunting

So now you've got a splashy set of walls just waiting to be showcased by some swell new furniture. But before you go put thousands of dollars of goods in your online shopping cart, remember that the biggest decorating mistake you can make is not taking your time. In a mad rush to furnish every square inch of your pad, you can easily wind up settling on pieces you're only half-jazzed about. You wouldn't make a rash decision to move in with a guy or accept a job offer across the country, so why rush into buying permanent pieces you have to live with every day? Instead, let your style slowly take shape by scanning Pinterest, home décor blogs (Apartment Therapy and Design*Sponge never disappoint), online furniture sites (I like West Elm, Urban Home, and even IKEA), and lots of design mags and only *window-shopping* in a variety of furniture showrooms—that way you'll be confident about every single purchase you make.

Once you develop your taste and style, stick to it. The second biggest decorating mistake people make is chucking their own style instincts and getting swayed by the fad of the moment. Although that popular pin might look hip and cool at the time, you might have a panic attack once that orange eight-person sofa and polka-dot rug are in *your* space.

When to Splurge, When to Skimp

Now that you've honed your style, it's going to take a little willpower not to blow a wad on everything from lamps to leather benches. The key is knowing what items you can get away with going low-budget on, and what items will give the most style wattage to your digs.

Splurge On: Your Couch

Think of your sofa as the crown jewel of your living room. It's one of the first things people will see when they walk into your home, and like shoes, it can either make or break the look you're trying to achieve. For example, a luxe sofa can draw your eye away from a plain coffee table and add depth and texture to a room that's otherwise sparsely decorated. But if you have a cheap, futon-looking couch, even the most expensive TV set, sound system, chairs, and rugs won't make up for it.

Order your couch before any other item in your pad. It will set the tone for the rest of your furniture, and takes the longest (generally six to eight weeks) to arrive. When choosing styles, go with a fabric that is durable and doesn't show dirt. Leather is classic and will last you a lifetime if you care for it properly. Or consider getting a slipcovered sofa in a durable fabric. Not only can slipcovers be easily washed, you can change the entire look of your place should you get tired of your choice. If you want a more modern look, nothing beats an L-shaped sofa. Look for one in Supersuede or Ultrasuede—it looks and feels like the real thing, but its nonporous surface is highly stain-resistant.

MG TIP: If you're looking for help but don't want to lay out the cash for a decorator, go online. There are countless free interior decorating sites and blogs to help you get inspired and get decorating. And of course, we can't forget about virtually everything on Pinterest.

MG TIP: Be sure to measure your doors and the building's elevator before purchasing furniture to make sure you can get it in. You don't want to get yourself into a situation where you have to grease the couch (or your movers!).

MG TIP: When you order your couch, you'll have the option of signing up for a "stain protection plan." Shell out the extra bucks to get it. Should you spill something that absolutely won't come out, the manufacturer will send people out to fix it.

MG TIP: Ever wondered how to feng shui your bedroom? Position your bed so that you have a clear view of anyone entering your room. The foot of the bed should *not* face the door. Also, don't place a mirror opposite your bed. It might work in porno movies, but in feng shui it just fouls up your *chi*.

When choosing a couch for your living room, remember that scale is very important. Be sure to measure your available space before purchasing your dream sofa. Cut out sections from a newspaper and arrange them on the floor to mark your traffic patterns, making sure you will have enough room for a walkway; then measure the remaining space for your sofa.

Splurge On: Your Bed Linens

Just as your couch is the main eye-catcher in your living room, your bed is the focal point of your bedroom. But it's really the color and style of your pillows, duvet, and bed skirt that can change the vibe of your room . . . not the bed itself.

To get started, think about the color that you've painted your wall. A good rule of thumb is if the wall is wild, the bed should be mild, and vice versa. So if you were daring and painted the walls lilac, you could buy all your linens in cool charcoal, and offset it with a pair of deeper lilac-colored shams. If you're working with simple cream walls, consider a duvet with a crisp striped pattern or print. Love the all-white look? Invest in a high-quality duvet cover plus shams and bed skirts in fabrics that add depth and texture, such as matelassé.

Another way to make a quietly bold statement is to go monochromatic. If your walls are pale green, go with a pale green comforter in a slightly lighter shade, freshened up with cream sheets. At the very least, buy quality "show pieces" (pillows and throws that simply look good). Whether they're sequined, striped, polka-dotted or monogrammed, that little burst of color will add visual punch. (For tips on buying a quality mattress and sheets, see pages 51–52.)

Skimp On: Your Coffee Table

Some stores, like Jennifer Convertibles, will often throw in (or seriously slash) the price of a coffee table with your couch purchase. If you can't find a deal like this, consider using a flat-topped trunk, a set of wine barrels, two skinny benches covered with an exotic sari, antique drums you find at a flea market, or go to a garden store for a large stone pot, then top it off with a thick, unbreakable piece of glass from a local hardware store. When guests come over, fill the pot with water and float rose petals on the top. They'll get a pretty surprise when they look through the glass.

When it comes to choosing between a glass or wood coffee table, I tend to go for wood. Glass, because of its transparency, will give the illusion of more space, but it's much colder. Glass is also harder to keep clean and quickly looks untidy—not cozy—if magazines and books are left on it. Solid wood surfaces, on the other hand, look rustic and stylish with the odd vase, candle, or stack of books . . . and the big plus is that they give a feeling of solidity to a room.

When choosing a wood coffee table, make sure it suits the size of your room, couch, and rug. If your room can handle the chunky look, a coffee table with storage space underneath is the perfect option. Baskets for magazines, books, and floor pillows can also look great under a coffee table and will make the space more homey and inviting. Leather, square bench-style coffee tables can double as cocktail-party seating.

If wood isn't your bag and you're feeling creative, consider another option: a mosaic coffee table. I saw a very pretty coffee table once that had been made out of heavy slate tile in different muted tones. It will instantly give your pad an exotic, Mediterranean vibe—perfect for serving sangria and some of the tapas-style appetizers you mastered in chapter 2. It's very pretty and fairly easy to do.

To make your own tiled coffee table, you'll need:

- About ten to twelve slate or faux marble tiles, eight by eight or twelve by twelve (the larger the tiles, the less work you'll need to do)

- One three-quarter-inch-thick piece of exterior plywood (cut to size to accommodate the tiles)

- Border wood strips with ends cut at an angle to meet up with partner strips (to cover the plywood on the edges of table not covered by tiles)

- Mastic (to match the color of your grout)

- Notch trowel

- Grout (I recommend a dark gray grout. It will show fewer imperfections than a lighter one.)

- Float (grouting spreader)

- Large sponge

- Plastic floor covering or an old sheet

- Bucket

- Wood sealer

- Wood stain (optional)

- Wood glue

- Finish nails (small, short nails with a barely perceptible head)

- Antique/thrift store "table" stand. (If the support is wide and solid enough you may only need to center your tabletop, not cement it. Ask your salesperson for advice.)

Directions

Arrange your tiles on the floor as a mock-up of the size and shape you want for your table. Measure it and then head to Home Depot. Pick out a three-quarter-inch-thick piece of exterior plywood and have a helpful member of their staff cut it to the dimensions of your mock-up. Next, get four strips of wood for the border of the table and have your helper cut each strip to the size of your four table edges (there should be plenty of choices from molded strips with a curve to straight and narrow pine strips). Purchase a bag of grout, a grout float (an inexpensive one will work just as well as an expensive one for this project), and a grouting sponge (but any large natural sponge will work). Purchase a container of mastic (the tacky stuff that helps tiles adhere to a surface) and a notched trowel suited to the particular size of your tiles. Be sure to take in a sample tile to show the Home Depot staff so they can help you match it with the right trowel.

Once you're home, lay out a large piece of plastic or an old sheet to protect your work area and place your wood piece in the center of the sheet or plastic. Follow the directions on the mastic container, spreading the mastic with a trowel. Pace yourself! Apply mastic and arrange tiles a section at a time. (Do not apply mastic to the entire surface all at once. You don't want your mastic to dry before you place your tiles.) Let it dry overnight.

After you've let the mastic and tiles dry for a twenty-four-hour period, mix your grout with water according to the directions on the container, then apply the grout to the tile with your float, spreading it over the entire surface, and filling in all the gaps among the tiles. Don't freak if it looks super messy; just keep spreading. If there are any gaps remaining between the tiles, pack the grout in with your sponge. Wet your sponge and wipe it over the tiles several times until they are completely smooth and grout-free.

While the grout is drying, lay out your wood strips and spray with a wood sealer. If you want them to be a different color, you can also stain at this time. Let the strips dry for about two hours, or until they're no longer tacky to the touch. Apply the wood strips to the table edges with the wood glue and reinforce them with the finish nails (three to four per side spaced evenly).

Center your new tiled tabletop onto your antique stand and voilà—you have your own beautiful, homemade "mosaic" coffee table.

Skimp On: Your Bed Frame

There's no point in dropping tons of dough on a bed that comes with a headboard and footboard built into a wooden, leather, or iron base when you can buy a freestanding, detachable headboard. The headboards look clean-lined yet plush, and will save you hundreds of dollars. Stores such as Pottery Barn sell headboards with slipcovers so you can change the look of your bed whenever you please . . . a chic and cheap alternative.

More Cash-Saving Tips

Another way to keep your piggy bank plump is to consider alternative furniture styles, creative venues, and wise buying tips. Making smart choices can save you hundreds—even thousands—of dollars.

MG TIP: To give an antique wood table an instant makeover, tile the top of it following the same steps. It's easy and you won't have to bother with buying and cutting wood and finding a table base. You can use tiles (you may need to have a couple of them cut to fit the table-top) or broken plates and china in a variety of colors for a more festive look.

MG TIP: You can make your own headboard at practically no cost with items such as standing screens, bookcases, tapestries, and draped fabric. Multiple shams and pillows will also give height in the absence of a headboard.

MG TIP: Consider a cute area rug as a headboard (hang on the wall behind your bed). I got a great one at Target.

WHAT TO DO BEFORE FURNITURE SHOPPING

You need a whole lot more than just your credit card if you want to make a smart buy. Luckily, everything you need fits in your laptop or cell phone.

Let Your Fingers Do the Walking

If you are like me and get tired before you make it through the sofa section of the local furniture store, consider going online for your shopping needs. Great sites like One Kings Lane and 1stdibs curate a wide variety of products, from high-end furniture to kitchen needs. Though you are not always getting a bargain-basement price, you get carefully selected products, fabulous customer service, and the chance to shop at two in the morning. Plus I have never purchased something from One Kings Lane that has disappointed me, and the one time something arrived broken, OKL took it back in a heartbeat.

Pinterest

Be sure you have this loaded on your phone's Internet browser before you go in case you have bad cell reception in store. You'll be reminded of exactly what you need to pull off that look you've always wanted for your room. Plus, a picture is truly worth a thousand words in this case, and it will be way more helpful for your salesperson or shopping buddy to see the look you're ultimately going for rather than listening to you describe it.

Camera

You've done your homework online, and you've saved your room measurements in your notes. Now that you're taking the time to actually visit a store, make sure you take enough pictures! We tend to overestimate how much space we have, and looking back at your pics when you're actually in the store will clue you in to how much room you really have.

continued

The Right Apps

Your living room inspiration board is filled with beautiful pins, but sometimes it's still difficult to imagine what pieces will look like once you actually put them in your space. You can use an app called SnapShop to visualize any piece of furniture in your house. Hold up your phone, drag and drop furniture from the app's catalog so it looks like it's in your room, then take a photo. You can save the arrangement and even e-mail it to friends for feedback.

Buy in Bulk

Think of it as an all-you-can-eat buffet, but with furniture. Get three or more major pieces of furniture from the same place and they'll often give you a markdown on the bottom-line price. Stores may also waive the delivery fee altogether if you butter them up enough.

Go DIY

My dresser, nightstand, TV console, kitchen table, and wine rack are all manually assembled by *moi* . . . and no one would ever guess. With all the money I saved (more than $2,000) I was able to splurge on more items I wouldn't have otherwise been able to. Crate & Barrel has a particularly good line of DIY furniture at a fraction of the cost of their preassembled items.

Get Items That Do Double Duty

The more functional an item, the more you save. Two leather cubes can work as both a coffee table and extra seating. An L-shaped couch will hug your coffee table on two angles so that you won't need to buy an armchair to fill the space.

MG TIP: Flea market and antique finds are great in wood and metal, but often fabric items can be dusty and moldy and wreak havoc on allergy sufferers. I'll never forget crashing on a girlfriend's couch and waking up in the middle of the night with my throat closed up. It turns out her couch was bought from a cat-infested antique store. Make sure your item is in great condition or can be reupholstered before committing to a used couch.

MG TIP: Don't go to a flea market hungry; MGs need to be in tip-top bargaining shape! Bring an energy bar to combat any midmorning cravings.

MG TIP: Bedbugs give me nightmares, and there is *no* guarantee that used furniture is safe. But one thing you can do is try to check for them. Bedbugs deposit small black spots after feeding. You can sometimes see groups of pinpoint spots on hard and soft surfaces, and fabrics may also show reddish streaks or smears. But honestly, I'd stick with small items that are safer.

MG TIP: Looking for luxe vintage? Check out 1stdibs and One Kings Lane for statement pieces that will pull a room together.

Tips for Scoring at the Flea Market

With a little luck and a lot of strategy a Modern Girl can outfit an entire apartment with just one trip to the flea market. But buyer beware: There are a number of day-ruiner rookie mistakes that could leave you headed home empty-handed. Stick to these tips I've picked up over the years for a day of treasure hunting that ends with you taking home the loot.

Leave your Louis at home: If you want to have a shot at bargaining, leave behind flashy accessories or else vendors will suspect you have more cash in that purse than you're letting on.

Layer up! If you're a serious flea market shopper, you may be scouting from dawn to dusk, which means you'll need to bundle up in the morning, then strip down to face the midday heat.

Time it right: If you want to snag the best stuff, go early. Some even recommend arriving thirty minutes before the gates open. If brunch or the snooze button has gotten the best of your morning, do not fret! The end of the day is a great time to get deals on merchandise that sellers don't want to cart home.

Bring a friend: A trip to the flea market is no solo mission for the Modern Girl. Bring a friend who can help you divide and conquer the seemingly hundreds of booths. Bonus if they have a truck and big muscles!

Bring cash: It's easier to budget and bargain with cash in hand at the flea market. While some bigger-ticket vendors will accept credit, sometimes you can snag a steal if you offer cash instead.

Do a loop: You've finally arrived at the market and you're excited to dive into every booth. Stop! Before you do, take a quick lap around the perimeter to develop a plan of attack.

Talk to the vendors: The easiest way to land a great piece (and get a great deal on it) is to cozy up to the sellers. If you a seller one you like, ask her if she has a showroom with additional product, because often they do, and that's where you'll find the hidden gems.

Bargain like a pro: Yes, we all want to get the best deal (mostly for the bragging rights), but it's important to be respectful of the seller when you're haggling for a piece. Consider starting at two-thirds to three-quarters the initial price and go from there. If you buy in bulk from one vendor, you're even more likely to score a sweet deal.

Be willing to walk away: Whether your bargaining skills are a little rusty or the piece isn't the perfect one you were looking for, there are many instances in which the right thing to do is to walk away. Don't worry, there's always next weekend.

Speaking of Which . . . Check eBay

You know it's the one-stop shop for bargain shoppers—just make sure you read the fine print before you bid on an item, however. Many sellers don't pay for shipping costs, and sending large pieces state-to-state can quickly add up.

Get Inspired

Although it's a lot easier to just browse through online sites like Pinterest and Houzz, think about getting offline for a little inspiration. Go to top-rate home design stores, such as ABC Carpet & Home, and just wander around. When you see something you like, think about how you might create that item yourself. For example, a $600 exotic silk pillow you find online can be duped by cleverly tying a few thrift-store-bought silk scarves around a standard square pillow. Also, if you know a great upholsterer, you can find a cheaper fabric and have them make a knock-off for you.

Small Touches That Make a Big Impact

Whether you want to add some major pizzazz or just make a few tweaks to your place, it's all in the details. Here are items that will instantly liven up your space:

MG TIP: According to Dr. Alan Hirsch of the Smell and Taste Treatment and Research Foundation, the combined scent of pumpkin pie and lavender stimulates the male libido—so go for candles in these flavors. For women, a combination of cucumber and Good & Plenty is the top aroma. You might not be able to find this exact combo, but Tocca makes a fabulous cucumber and fig candle that comes mighty close.

Scarves, Pillows, and Candles

Want to give your room a minor face-lift? Purchase pretty throw pillows, blankets, and afghans. They're a great way to add texture and color and are sometimes all you need to jazz up a tired sofa or chair before your room is ready for a full makeover. Lamps are another easy way to alter the feel of a particular space. You can often find beautiful ones at thrift stores relatively cheap; slap on a new shade and you'll give your antique lamp (and your space) a whole new vibe.

And while some might say that candles are the Modern Girl's equivalent of cats—too many say "crazy lady"—they're probably the easiest and most effective way to touch up a tired room. A friend of mine turned her first New York apartment (from shabby to chic) by placing large candles in her nonworking fireplace. The effect was beautiful; suddenly her bare-bones railroad apartment was lovely and cozy.

Eliminating Clutter

Giving your space a quick pickup is often as simple as picking up; nothing brings down the mood of a room more than clutter. Find storage spaces for excess knickknacks, papers, CDs, and other odds and ends. If you're short on storage space, antique/thrift stores are usually overflowing with cheap (but adorable) bookshelves, chests, and all kinds of vintage-looking containers.

Uplighting

Want to add a little drama to your room at a minuscule cost? Take a cue from trendy restaurants and hotels and try uplighting—a sophisticated way of illuminating space. All you need is a canister-sized light holder (around $10) fitted with a floodlight-style halogen light bulb (around $14). Simply set it on the floor behind an end table in the corner of your living room. Put a tall vase of flowers on top of the table and flip the light switch. Light will flood from the floor to the ceiling, casting a warm glow on the wall and illuminating your greenery.Choose an amber bulb instead of a soft white one for added warmth.

Dimmers

Nothing sets a mood like a dimmer. It won't change the size of your place, but it puts the mood in "mood lighting." They're super easy to install. Please keep in mind that the following is meant to be a general guide for installing a dimmer; installation may vary a bit depending on the brand and model of your dimmer switch. So be sure to read and follow the instructions, diagrams, and safety precautions that come with your particular switch.

Tools and Materials You'll Need

- Flat-head screwdriver
- Circuit tester
- Wire cutter/stripper
- Dimmer switch
- Needle-nose pliers
- Wire nuts (plastic twist-on wire connectors/caps)
- Dimmer switch plate

Directions

Turn off the circuit you will be working on in the breaker box. Be sure to double-check it by trying to turn the light on; if it remains off, you're good to go. Remove the old switch plate with a screwdriver. Although you've turned the switch off at the breaker box, as an extra precaution use a circuit tester to make sure that the switch is not receiving power before beginning work on the wiring.

Disconnect the wires that are connected to the light switch. There should be three wires in all: a black wire, a white wire, and a ground wire, which is usually red. If the exposed wire ends look worn, strip the wires using wire cutters. First cut off all the bare wire to just below the plastic insulation on all three wires. Then use your wire cutter to strip off three-eighths inch of the insulation. This will give you clean pieces of wire for the new connection.

Connect the black wire from the workbox on the wall to one from the dimmer switch by placing the bare wire ends next to each other. Then twist them together in a clockwise direction with the pliers, and twist on a wire nut (a plastic twist-on wire connector). Do the same for the white set of wires as well as the ground wires.

Bend all the wires into a zigzag pattern to fit them easily into the workbox. With all three wires connected, you're ready to install the new switch in the wall box. Just make sure the switch is oriented so that up is on and down is off (believe me, I've made this mistake before). Push the switch into place; tighten with the workbox screws to hold it in position, and screw on the switch plate. Turn on the breaker and let there be light!

LIGHTBULB AND LAMP BASICS

Choose the Right Wattage
Find the right wattage bulb for your lamp. Burning a 100-watt bulb in a lamp designed for 60 watts is a fire hazard. Most lamps have wattage instructions written along the socket, so be sure to read them. Use three-way bulbs only for lamps with three-way switches, as there is also a potential fire hazard when using a regular bulb with a three-way switch.

Save Money with Halogen Bulbs
Instead of a traditional incandescent bulb, consider buying a halogen bulb, which will provide more light and will last longer. Halogen lights are more expensive, but they can save money over time. Just be cautious and keep halogen bulbs away from flammable objects like curtains; they heat up to a higher temperature, making them more of a fire hazard.

continued

How to Remove a Broken Light Bulb

If you're ever removing a light bulb and the glass breaks off the base, don't worry—it's easy to remove. First turn off the power to the light at the breaker panel, then firmly jam the most narrow end of a potato into the socket, and twist out the broken base. Be sure to wear gloves and safety glasses to protect eyes and hands from the glass.

Create a Softer Light

The inside of a soft white bulb is coated so that the light is less focused. This type of bulb omits just as much light as a regular bulb with the same wattage, but will give a softer feel and will add warmth to a space.

Choose the Right Lampshade

Lampshades can change the look of an entire room. For example, a linen shade provides general diffusion for good ambient light. Opaque shades are best for lighting an isolated area. When choosing a table lamp, be sure to pay attention to the light output in terms of lamp size, bulb wattage, and shade type. Lamps that use 150-watt, three-way bulbs will provide more light and versatility. Lamps that use lower-wattage bulbs (60 watts or below) will give off a lovely ambient light.

Plants

Nothing gives a room instant freshness like a plant—whether it's a housewarming gift or one you brought home from the nursery. But then again, nothing says "I'm a sloth" like a pot of sun-scorched, crumpled brown leaves you forgot to water (or droopy ones you practically drowned).

MG TIP: If you go on a lot of business trips and simply can't deal with a high-maintenance plant, buy a succulent. They require only moderate watering and TLC. Skip delicate ferns or ficus plants; they demand mucho attention.

To Keep Plants Looking Vibrant

- Keep them in a naturally well-lit area, but out of direct sunlight. (Flowering plants require more light than your big, leafy green variety.)

- Steer clear of drafty areas, open windows, and heating vents.

- Always water your plants in the early morning. Water doesn't evaporate as readily then as it does in the heat of the afternoon. Check with your florist or look up your houseplant directions to see how often.

- Overwatering is the most common way to kill plants. The soil gets soggy and prevents oxygen from going to the roots. To check if a plant needs water, stick your finger in the soil about an inch. If it's moist, don't water.

- Make sure your pot has drainage holes so that water doesn't collect in the bottom, which can lead to root rot and kill the plant.

- Mist your plants with a water-filled spray bottle to ward off insects.

MG TIP: Hang your mirror so that it reflects something interesting: a beautiful hanging light fixture, a painting, or a window (which will increase the room's natural light).

MG TIP: If you want to reflect most of your room (creating the maximum feeling of space), buy a large rectangular mirror and hang it two or three feet above eye level (depending on the ceiling height) and give a few inches of slack to the hanging cord, allowing the mirror to tip forward slightly from the top.

Mirrors

The best thing about mirrors is their magical way of making a room look bigger. Place one over your couch and anchor the look with a pair of modern-looking sconces. You'll score double spatial points if you can catch your windows in the reflection. Or triple the ante by placing one mirror in a hallway and another one inside a room, so when you look into one, it bounces off the other, instantly multiplying depth. Position a freestanding one in the corner of your bedroom—much chicer than sticking one of those flimsy ones to your closet door. Or mount two or three small mirrors—go with sleek silver or funky gold ones—in succession along the wall in your foyer to expand its dimensions. To give a more artsy feel to your space, find an old window with several panes at an antique store or salvage yard and have mirrors cut at a glass shop to fit inside the panes. Your homemade "antique" mirror will add charm and warmth to a stark wall and will look terrific resting on a fireplace mantel.

Art

The biggest misconception about having art in your home is that for something to look substantial, it has to cost a lot of dough. Granted, a framed poster of Monet's *Water Lilies* isn't going to come off as unique, but whatever moves you deserves precious wall space. Frame four similar-looking images—even pieces of fabric. Have them framed with wide matting around them for a clean, polished look that will make the images pop. Or consider black-and-white prints a photographer friend has taken. Group them on the wall and call it your "installation" (hey, you might even make money on your investment if he or she becomes famous one day). Once you have your masterpiece ready, here's how to hang it:

Find the Perfect Spot

Because your pictures will be the focal point of your room, they will work better within a large expanse of wall space. Allow five to ten inches from the top of a sofa or other furniture. Otherwise, hang them about five or so feet from the floor, typically at eye level. You could also try propping your art against a mantel, chest, or—if it's big enough—an empty corner of a room with a few clustered votives to illuminate it from the floor.

Make a Paper Mock-up

You can master mistake-free art placement by marking the wall first with paper. It's a bit time consuming, but it saves newly painted walls. Get butcher paper or wrapping paper and trace and cut the outline of your piece to be hung out of the paper. Mount the paper to the wall with masking tape to figure out the spacing. Nail directly through the paper, rip the paper away, and boom—you have perfect placement.

Use Special Picture-Hanging Hooks

Choose an appropriate hook such as a two-piece nail and hook. Heavier art should be hung with a hollow-wall anchor, which will protect your walls and bear the weight of the picture. You can usually find inexpensive special picture hanging hooks at your local drugstore, but if not, your local hardware store is sure to have a picture-hanging kit that will contain everything you'll need.

MG TIP: The thicker the glass, the more accurate the mirror. But if accuracy isn't necessarily what you're after (and hey, before a hot bedroom session or after a long dinner party it often isn't!), tilting a mirror out a bit from the bottom a few inches should give a thinning effect.

MG TIP: Hang pictures on two hooks instead of one. Your art or mirrors are more likely to remain level.

MG TIP: Help prevent the plaster or drywall from cracking by placing a piece of Scotch tape on the wall where you insert the nail.

Make Sure Your Picture Is Level

Once you've hung your work of art, take a few steps back and eye it to make sure it's level. For a more accurate read, use a carpenter's level.

Rugs

While area rugs can make the biggest difference to the feel of a room or space, the prospect of rug *shopping* can make a girl break out in hives. Because there are so many different kinds of styles of rugs at almost every price point, I find it extremely helpful to first establish a budget and target price before shopping. Once you've picked your price point, the following rug basics should make your shopping experience a little less confusing and a lot more successful.

Handmade Rugs: Hot Investments

While handmade rugs are almost always preferable, they can be extremely expensive. They are made with natural fibers like wool or silk and can take up to nine months or longer to make. So if you are wondering why a particular rug costs $8,000 or more, it's likely because of the slow, intricate weaving process. Just remember that this type of rug is a real investment and will most likely grow in value; many antique silk and wool rugs go for hundreds of thousands of dollars today. If you want an heirloom-quality rug, stick to handmade.

Machine-Made Rugs: More Affordable Threads

If budget is an issue (and heck, when isn't it?), you should consider a machine-made rug. These types of rugs can be made in several styles and sizes quickly and easily, and are, as a result, much less expensive than handmade rugs. Higher-end machine-made rugs are often quite durable and can be very beautiful. Look for one made with natural fibers; wool and silk rugs are typically more expensive, but are durable, naturally flame-resistant, and deter bacterial growth. Wool even purifies indoor air by locking contaminants deep in the fiber. If wool and silk are too pricey for your budget, look for rugs made with less expensive natural fibers such as cotton, flax, and linen. Don't pass up a synthetic rug that you love, but do avoid

MG TIP: The density of your carpet has a lot to do with how long it will last. A good rule of thumb is that if you can see the backing through the fibers, the carpet won't last as long.

MG TIP: One way to tell that your rug is handmade is to check the nap or pile. Pile or nap is what the strands of material that stand above the base of the rug are called. Spread the pile apart and look down. If you see knots at the bottom of the pile, the rug was most likely made by hand. A handmade rug's pile is fixed on the base thread with a knot, while a machine-made carpet's pile is either glued on or simply stuck between the base and the wefts. Also check the fringe. On a machine-made rug, the fringe will be sewn onto either end. This is a clue that it was applied after the rug was completed. A handmade rug's fringe is woven in and naturally sticks out at the end.

extremely low-priced rugs made with acrylic that are likely to pill and fall apart by the time you get them to your car. Look for nylons and double-ply, higher-quality olefins (otherwise known as polypropylenes) that are often more durable than acrylics. But avoid single-ply olefins, which are just about as cheap as you can get.

Rug Placement and Size

Rugs are like bras—sometimes you want 'em to give you more coverage, sometimes you want 'em skimpy so you can showcase certain assets. If you have beautiful hardwood floors, for example, you aren't going to want a full-floor rug to cover them up. But if you're going for warmth, the larger the rug, the cozier your room will feel. There is no hard-and-fast rule, but do keep these things in mind:

- Know your boundaries. When using one large rug in a living or family room, make sure that there is an even amount of flooring around all four sides once it's placed, or so at least the opposite sides of flooring space are even. Don't get a rug so large that it touches or rides up the wall or baseboard of a room.

- Double up. If you want to define two different areas within one room, try using two coordinating (but not matching) rugs.

- Back off. As a general rule, put the front legs of furniture pieces (like a buffet or a side table) on the rug and the back legs off. However, as long as the rug is placed in a balanced way in the room, the furniture can fall either on or off of it.

Super-Simple MG Decorating Tips

Fake it in the bedroom: If you want an inexpensive headboard, just paint one on the wall! A simple rectangular shape in a fun color adds pop and flair to your bedroom.

Get framed: Buy inexpensive poster-size frames and beautiful wrapping paper in single sheets. Buy several different ones that look artistic. Frame the paper and voilà! Instant art.

MG TIP: To prevent your rug or carpet from wearing out, just vacuum weekly. It will add years to its life.

MG TIP: Eighty-five percent of dirt that comes into your home comes from shoe soles. If you don't want to subject your guests to ped-nakedness, at least have a mat outside your door so your home—and rugs—stay clean.

MG TIP: A dining room rug should be four to five feet larger than the width of the table so that it is large enough to accommodate moving the chairs away from the table without them falling off the edge. Surrounding dining room furniture, such as a buffet or china cabinet, should be off the rug and on the floor.

Go au naturel: No, don't walk around naked (although that would take the attention away from your lack of furniture!) . . . Instead, purchase inexpensive shells of all types. They make great décor that brings the outdoors in.

Commitment-phobe: Temporary wallpaper is a great way to spice up your walls at a lower cost and without making your landlord see red.

Plate spinning: Well, actually more like plate hanging. Hit the flea markets, buy some inexpensive vintage plates, and hang them in a collage on your wall. It's a colorful way to add art and a story.

Window-shopping: Get a stained-glass effect by placing colored-glass jars and vases on windowsills.

The Trickiest Piece to Fit into Your Home:
Your Man

Even more daunting than choosing a rug, hanging a picture, or painting every wall in your place is dealing with the guy who *shares* that living space with you—even part time. Whether he's your boyfriend, fiancé, or husband, three things are constant: He will create chaos; he will try to get you to love his (often) awful taste; he will have odd and seemingly backward housekeeping habits that will drive you abso-freakin'-nuts. When my husband and I first moved into an apartment (we were engaged but not married), I thought I might have to call off the wedding because he (gasp) folded his towels in half, not thirds. Now one might think having a handsome, kind, employed, loving man would be enough, but no. . . . I fold my towels in three so that you can't see the seam. I begged, I pleaded, I threatened. Nothing I did could make him change his ways. So what happened? We got married, and I refolded his towels for about a month. Then he started doing it too. And I imagine we moved on to argue about something else. Here's how to deal with his other testosterone habits that affect your chic home:

MG TIP: The bad towel-folding husband from above has a great tip. If you always characterize someone by what they don't do, you'll forever be frustrated. Instead, try to think about the things they *do* do. When I realized how often *he* changed the light bulbs and *he* emptied the garbage, it made me feel less resentful about the things he *didn't* do around the house.

Consolidate Electronics

Does he really need *five* remote controls for his TV? Try programming them into one handy universal remote that can sit, undetected, on your coffee table. If not, this is a great excuse to find a cool decorative box for your table that can hide the ugly remotes.

Make Clothes Dumping Easy

Get two hampers: One for dry-cleaning items and one for laundry. This way, he'll be less likely to put his work clothes on the bed, on the couch, on the . . .

Play Hardball with Furniture

If he just happens to be a metrosexual stud who knows as much about home design as home runs, you're in luck. But for the greater male population, futons, gold entertainment consoles, and easy chairs are considered quality items. You must intervene. But let him hold on to the one thing that bugs you the least, whether it's a leather chair or his six-speaker sound system (which is probably better quality than yours). As for warming him up to buying new items, give him the option of shopping *all day long* with you so it's a joint effort, or to kick back at home watching football and simply trust your opinion. Either way, it's a win-win situation for you.

Buy Dark Towels and Dark Bath Mats

Don't ask. Just do it.

Try One-Stop Stocking

It's no mystery that men love making piles—piles of clothes, piles of books, piles of nickels. What's with the love of clutter? If you clearly set up spaces for him (a change cup inside his nightstand, a magazine filer next to the couch) he'll be more likely to clean up and compartmentalize.

Make It Man-Friendly

Stubborn and style-challenged as your man may be, you still want him around, don't you? Keep him sated with a big TV and Netflix

MG TIP: Men, biologically speaking, aren't as prone to pick up on dust or crumbs lying around. Supposedly, the rods in their eyes aren't as long as ours so they don't notice details. *Hmm.*

account (it's that simple). When it comes to food, remember to pick up regular Coke, ice cream, and regular salad dressing . . . not just the low-cal versions for you.

Keep an Open Mind

Shocker, I know, but sometimes your guy may have a brilliant decorating idea of his own that you could benefit from putting into action. So before you shoot him down ("What? You want to put the couch *there*?"), slowly visualize what he's suggesting. Who knows? Maybe he's been secretly watching *HGTV* and could teach you a thing or two.

Moving Like a Pro

Of course no matter how attached you become to your abode, there may be a time when you need a change of temple. And when you do, try to remain calm. While the whole process of schlepping your items from point A to point B is stressful, knowing how to pack your stuff properly will save you time and headaches:

Stock up

Buy duct tape, heavy-duty scissors, a set of colored markers, small, medium, and large boxes, Styrofoam "popcorn," and tissue paper, and save old newspapers.

Sort

Pack heavy items like books in small boxes and light, bulky items like pillows in the largest boxes.

Stack

If you have a big mixing bowl, wrap it up and stow another smaller item inside it.

Wrap

Don't be afraid to wrap up your best plates in several sheets of newspaper—it's more durable than tissue and can withstand jostling just as well as foam popcorn can. If you're shipping it, you must pack it well. Although you can go a little lighter if it's being moved by a truck, you never know when a clumsy mover may drop a box, so it's better to be safe than sorry.

Pad

Use as many fillers as you can in fragile-item boxes. A pillow, robe, or bath towel can do double duty as a shock absorber and buffer between breakables.

Roll

For minimum wrinkling and maximum space-saving, roll your clothes instead of folding them. For coats, dresses, and suits, ask your movers ahead of time for boxes with metal rods across the top. (You can often get these at a discount if you pick them up yourself from a local storage facility.)

Cover

Drape old sheets over anything suede, silk, or light-colored. Oils from the movers' hands can leave permanent marks on the fabric.

Label

Mark the top and sides of each box—for when they're stacked and you want to see what's there—with the room you want it to go to in the new place and a number. Take an additional step and color-code your boxes with a distinguishing dot of marker. Everything marked RED is kitchen, BLUE is bedroom, and so on. That way you can quickly tell the movers which room to put each box in so *you* don't have to later.

MG TIP: Don't label what is in the boxes; it's an invitation for theft: A box marked SILVER is too easy to be true.

List

Type a corresponding list for your labels: One column gives the box's contents (let's say "Glassware, Kitchen") and the other column gives its number (let's say #14). This way, you'll be able to check off each box as it arrives in your new home and quickly know if a box is missing.

MG TIP: Fill your regular suitcase with the items you know you'll need for the next three days (toiletries, toilet paper, clothing, nightclothes, shoes, underwear, alarm clock). Otherwise, you'll be digging into ten boxes at once trying to find things.

MG TIP: Pack a set of sheets, pillows, a blanket, and towels in a carry-on and bring it with you. Knowing you can sleep and shower comfortably no matter what state of disarray the rest of the place is in is a godsend.

MG TIP: Having your goods unpacked signals a solid transition into your new pad, but don't forget the other details—like making sure you're getting your mail. Six to eight weeks before your move, fill out change-of-address forms (you can get them at the post office) so your work payments, regular mail, credit card statements, insurance and tax forms, and magazine subscriptions get to the right place, on time. Call the new utility company, phone company, electric company, etc.

How to Unpack

- Unpack the bedroom items first—you know you'll need them for the first night you move in.

- Don't unpack delicate boxes while standing up, and always open an item over the box it came in. Why? Because it's too easy to unroll your packing paper only to have your champagne flute or glass vase slip out the opposite end and hit the floor. Check off your typed list of the boxes as you plow through each box.

- Tackle the boxes for one room at a time.

- Don't get tempted and open more than a few boxes at a time. You'll wind up overwhelmed.

- Save some of your boxes—you can use them to store Christmas decorations and other seasonal items.

- As soon as you unpack your kitchen utensils, dishes, and glassware, put them straight into the dishwasher. Give all other kitchen items a once-over with antibacterial spray.

Hiring a Mover

The first time I hired movers (to move from the Mini-Me apartment I told you about to a Slightly Larger Mini-Me apartment), I must have made every mistake in the book. Desperate because I had to be out of my apartment within the week and had just broken up with my six-foot-three boyfriend a few days earlier (trust me, I was kicking myself for not keeping him around just to be my personal pack mule), I jumped at the first movers I found. They were posted on a flyer in a health-food store in my neighborhood, and I figured I'd be able to save at least a few hundred bucks by giving them a call. I never met them in person or got to see their website (they claimed it was "under construction")—but agreed to it anyway . . . even their provision that I needed to pay a quarter of the fee up front to hold the space.

Well, the Saturday when they rang my doorbell, I got a *small* surprise: The "moving company" was comprised of one tiny van and two wimpy guys, obviously college kids who were trying to make money on the side. But it was too late to ditch them; I had to move and had already given up some of my dough. After watching them spend an hour and a half trying to break down my bed and wiggle my mattress through the front door, I got so frustrated I pitched in just to make the slugs move faster. As we lugged and banged everything up four flights of stairs to my new place (the turning point that made me go for an elevator building for my third apartment), one of them cracked my gold mirror. "Oops, uh, sorry," he muttered, and knocked a hundred and fifty bucks off his fee. But at that point, I was so pissed off I actually wanted to put *him* through the mirror. Oh, and the money I saved by hiring the guys dirt cheap? I wound up blowing it on a two-hour deep-tissue massage to put my neck back in place. So please, for the love of duty-free lifting, follow these tips:

Do Your Research
Start looking for movers at least 2 months before your move. The more time you give yourself to do your research, the more likely you are to find good movers.

Size It Up
Estimate the size, distance, and timing of your move. How much stuff do you have? How far are you moving? How much do you plan to do yourself? How much do you ideally want to spend? Being armed with these facts will make it easier to get a cost estimate and will help you to choose the company that's best for you.

Gossip
Ask your friends for recommendations. You can also double-check with local consumer protection groups on the performance history of the movers you're considering.

Check Up
Avoid companies that aren't licensed. Double-check by going on safersys.org to make sure who's legit. Many of the best moving companies are also members of local or national moving trade associations. Ask the mover if the company is a member of any

MG TIP: Call the FMCSA's Safety Violation and Consumer Complaints hotline at 888-368-7238 and inquire about the complaint history of your moving company. At the very least, check Yelp!

associations and contact the association for further information so you can check into their business practices. Or do a little sleuthing on the Federal Motor Carrier Safety Administration's (FMCSA) website to get crucial info on your movers (www.fmcsa.dot.gov/factsfigs/moving.htm). Make sure your movers have enough insurance—the minimum is $750,000.

Shop Around

Check out several companies and request a free home visit for an accurate estimate.

Get It in Writing

Insist on a written contract and be sure that you understand it fully. Read between the lines, watching out for any hidden costs.

Cover Your Ass(ets)

Get insurance to cover any loss or damage during the move (damn that gold mirror!). While it might add to the total cost, it will be well worth the extra peace of mind. With every other facet of her fabulous life to juggle, a Modern Girl can't afford *not* to make life a little easier on herself.

CHAPTER 5

Looking and Feeling Fabulous

There are days I think I'm fabulous. Days I think I have great hair and a killer bod. Days when I think I have it all together. Did I say days? I meant day. Did I say day? I meant hours. Maybe minutes. You know, I don't know why I even said that. My hair sucks, I could lose ten pounds, and . . .

Well, you get my point. The second we start feeling great about ourselves, this thing called Me So Flawed syndrome kicks in and makes us zero in on all the freckly, flabby, or fashion-challenged problems we're convinced we have. Sometimes all it takes to trigger the syndrome is a photo of Gisele shaking her skinny bon-bon in a magazine spread (someone get that girl a cheeseburger), or just comparing ourselves to friends and coworkers who have thicker hair, clearer skin, bouncier boobs, and swankier wardrobes. Don't we have better things to obsess about, like George Clooney or world peace? Of course. But that still doesn't make it any easier.

As a generation we've been told to be the best we can be and that we can do anything we want to. But despite all that bolstering and incentive it's easy to feel like you're not projecting the kind of image that will take you to the top. And the truth is, no one's putting more pressure on us to look great than us. But a Modern Girl doesn't stress about what Mother Nature stiffed her on in the looks department—she takes action. From cleverly upgrading your wardrobe to getting the most bang out of your makeup buck to Pilates for Pasta Addicts, I'm going to share a few shortcuts that will help you cheat your way to being a chic, toned, traffic-stopping version of you.

Building a Modern Girl Wardrobe

Let's face it. Most of us open our closets and see three groups: clothes we don't wear (80 percent), the six pieces we do wear (15 percent), and the two "skinny outfits" we'll only fit into if we have our jaws wired shut and go on liquid diets (5 percent). Doesn't leave much room for looking fabulous, does it? The trick to cultivating a great clothes collection isn't having a gazillion new items, but having key classic pieces that mix and match well together, giving the illusion that you have a fatter, richer wardrobe than you really do. Here's what you need to get started:

The Basics

It's hard to imagine that when I first wrote this book, Spanx was just a young company, and today we don their wares (almost) as regularly as we brush our teeth. Body-shaping garments can do everything from slim a booty to trim a muffin top, tighten your tummy to tone your thighs. I have so many Spanx you'd think there were three of me. But not all shapewear is the same:

- The higher the nylon content, the more a garment will alter your shape. If it's lightweight and thin it will smooth you out but not really hold you in. If it's heavier, it will suck and tuck you into shape.

- Bodysuits are great because they will give you a head-to-toe streamlined shape, plus they can minimize a larger chest.

- Be careful—shapewear can make you feel hot, not just look hot. It's usually made of nylon and spandex, synthetic fabrics that don't breathe. So if you're wearing it in the warmer months, look for a brand that includes cotton for moisture absorption and breathability, and microfiber for odor control, like Wacoal.

Dark Denim Jeans That Make Your Butt Look Amazing

Semidressy, slim-fit jeans are an MG must for their sheer versatility. Great booty-slimming brands are J Brand, Frame, Rag & Bone, Citizens of Humanity, Hudson, and Paige.

High-Quality T-shirts and Camisoles

They go under everything from blazers to sweaters and are inexpensive enough to buy in bulk. Try a few daring color choices to make a neutral wardrobe pop.

Crisp White Button-Down

Simple and clean-lined, these shirts are a layering must.

Fitted Blazer

Whether cotton, wool, tweed, or velvet, a fitted blazer adds sharpness to any outfit—and has an instant slimming effect. Opt for styles that cinch in at the waist and have well-defined lapels, rather than boxy numbers that chop your torso in half.

Thin V-Neck, Scoop-Neck, Turtleneck, or Cardigan Cashmere Sweaters

Get these in multiple colors. Cashmere sweaters are one of the best investments an MG can make. They cost a pretty penny but will hold their shape, not pill, and last for years. You can often find price slashes on cashmere at beginning-of-summer sales, when stores are trying to unload their winter and spring merchandise. But beware: Not all cashmere is the same. The best cashmere comes from the throat and belly of the animal, where the fiber is longer and denser to keep the animal's vital organs warm. Cheaper cashmere manufacturers use the short fibers from the back and legs, where it is coarser, but which also costs less to buy and produce.

MG TIP: If white is more your thing, stock up by buying two or three of your favorites—that way, you won't be in a fashion dilemma should you spill, which you will. Don't be afraid to spend a little more on T-shirts, as the investment ones (like Petit Bateau) will last much longer than cheaper ones that might lose their shape.

MG TIP: In cashmere, softness does not equal quality. The inferior short fibers may make the sweater "fluffier" but will also make it more likely to pill and wear out faster.

MG TIP: With cashmere, go for as many "plys" as you can afford: two- or three-ply cashmere is sturdier than single-ply.

MG TIP: Don't dry-clean cashmere; the chemicals can ruin it. Hand-wash it in cold water with a mild soap or baby shampoo. After rinsing, lay your item on a dry towel and roll, pressing excess water out. Shape it on a second towel and let it air-dry. Do *not* hang it up to dry.

One Fabulous Suit

Even if your job doesn't require you to suit up, every MG should own a lightweight wool gabardine suit in black or gray. Even better, for optimum versatility, get a suit jacket that goes with both a pencil skirt and a pair of slim pants.

Black, Lightweight Wool Trousers with Give

What I mean by "give" is that if your weight goes up by five pounds, these pants will be able to camouflage it. The primo pair of pants shouldn't cling to the bottom of your tush; they should be snug and smooth at the top and slightly fall away midway down your buns.

Chinos or Cargo Pants

Pay attention to fit first when opting for more casual styles like chinos or cargo pants, or else you run the risk of looking more schlub than chic. Look for styles that sit comfortably on your hips, as opposed to ones that hit you mid-tummy. High-waisted chinos make your butt region look bigger. If you like a slightly more fitted look, skip the 100 percent cotton khakis and go for ones that are 97 percent cotton and 3 percent spandex. As far as cargoes go, the more slim-fitting (with flat, form-fitting pockets) the better. Sure, Jennifer Aniston and Gwen Stefani can get away with wearing army gear, but the rest of us just look schlumpy.

Sexy Sweats

Skip the hot pink styles and go for black, navy, or gray . . . you'll be able to get away with wearing it more often. Also, avoid velour. Although it too has had moments of hipness, it's heavy, fast to get "uncool," and most likely to look like the track suit your grandma wears religiously. Instead, look for more modern details like a contrasting drawstring and a slim cut with gathered hems.

MG TIP: If your dress takes a sexy "V" dive and doesn't allow you to wear a bra, make like a celeb and use a self-adhesive bra. There are a number of versatile styles out there to hide under any plunge, so drop the tape and invest in a good one!

Little Black Dress

This elegant classic will take you from cocktails to first dates to holiday parties. For optimum versatility, choose one that skims your knees in an A-line cut. If you're tall and slim, go for a sheath.

Jeans Genius

Given that jeans have crossed over from a weekend staple to a day, nighttime, and date-night must, here are a few tips to make sure this fashion perennial lasts as long as you need it to:

- Jeans that are mostly cotton are less likely to stretch and sag than those that have 20 to 30 percent Lycra.

- To keep your jeans from stretching and fading, wash them inside out and don't put them in the dryer. If you're like me, though, and don't like that crunchy air-dried texture, throw them in the dryer on the air-dry setting (which has no heat) for ten minutes, which will soften them up.

- If your jeans shrink from the dryer, spritz them with water all over, then put them on to stretch them out.

Five Easy Pieces That Make You Look Richer Than You Are

Okay, if you can't drop a fortune on cultivating absolutely all the brand-spanking-new items listed above, at least stock up on these sophisticated staples. Not only will they give more mileage to what's already in your closet, you'll look so glam, people will assume you've entered a new tax bracket.

A Classic Trenchcoat

Nothing elevates your look like a traditional trench. This iconic staple has graced glamazons like Brigitte Bardot, Audrey Hepburn, Gwyneth Paltrow, and Princess Kate. No need to shell out for a movie-star-budget Burberry trench—stores like the Gap and Target make more affordable versions. For the most classic look, skip trendy pinks and flashy fabrics and opt for a traditional tan cotton style that hits just below your knee. You can throw it over everything from dresses to jeans—and the best part is, trenches can often double as raincoats.

MG TIP: Beware! Avoid a double-breasted jacket. While it may be a classic that's back in style every ten years, you'll have nine years in between where you'll look like you missed the fashion memo.

Crisp Button-Front Dress Shirt

Classic, chic, polished, and wearable anywhere, a crisp white button-front dress shirt is something you may not have thought of, but it can go from the boardroom to the summer soiree. You'll know it's better quality if it's 100 percent cotton with a single seam down each side and under each arm rather than double stitching. And go for the standard pointed collar, which is a design that never goes out of style.

Faux Diamond Studs

MG TIP: Buy the latest faux diamonds, called "Moissanite," which cost one-tenth of what real rocks do and look real.

They shimmer, glimmer, and go with absolutely everything (even your birthday suit). Clearly diamonds are a glam girl's best friend . . . especially when you can fool everyone into thinking you've dropped a fortune on them. The trick is not to get your ice too big. Each stud should be no bigger than a pencil eraser, the equivalent of "two carats," or it will be a giveaway that your bling-bling is bogus.

Stylish Daytime Bag

A great tote is an easy way to pull an entire outfit together. The perfect bag will be roomy enough to fit your life, but structured so you don't look schlumpy. Camel, brown, and black are safe colors because they're neutrals, but don't be afraid to go for an eye-popping color like red if your wardrobe is filled with whites, grays, and blacks.

MG TIP: Always have these things in your purse in addition to your wallet: baby wipes (they clean anything), mini–sewing kit, pain reliever, cell phone, pen, gum or mints, pocket mirror, shades, lip balm or gloss, and a condom . . . just in case. Fill a small cosmetic bag with them so that they're easy to transfer from one bag to another. A shortcut: Pick up a Pinch Provisions kit (www.pinchprovisions .com), which has all of the emergency essentials.

A Chic Clutch

Whether it's beaded, sequined, or just simple satin, a tiny handbag is a going-out essential. Black is a great investment because it will match virtually any outfit and work for any event. If you'd rather go for a metallic or bold color, make sure you opt for a simple style like an envelope, which will easily pair with your existing wardrobe.

Investment-Worthy Essentials

Since I wanted to make sure my style savvy was on track, I checked with the ladies who are the go-to experts on the Internet for all things fashion, Hillary Kerr and Katherine Power, the cofounders of WhoWhatWear. I have yet to see these girls *not* look put together. Not once. Ever. If I didn't like them so much it would be irritating. Here's what they had to say:

WHAT TO WEAR FROM THE GIRLS AT WHOWHATWEAR

When it comes to shopping, there's one strategy we swear by: always invest in versatile, understated, timeless pieces that will serve as the foundation of your wardrobe. These items should be elevated basics that you can wear for a wide range of occasions, and they should work with your lifestyle and personal style.

There's no hard-and-fast rule about which essentials you should own—a stay-at-home mom's must-haves will be very different from those of someone who works in a law firm, for example—but whatever you buy must fit you perfectly. (A good tailor is worth every penny.)

Our three investment-worthy essentials include:

Pointy-Toe Pumps
Whether you go for classic black, leg-elongating nude, or a bright pop of color, this shoe style is always flattering and adds polish to any look. Plus, you can style them with everything from slouchy jeans on the weekend to a tailored dress for work.

Leather Moto Jacket
Whether it's adding a touch of edge to an otherwise feminine frock or styled with a striped T-shirt and cigarette jeans, an un-fussy leather motorcycle jacket is a must-have. Basic black is always a good choice; just be sure to stay away from too much trendy hardware, as this can date your investment piece.

Clean, Dark Skinny Jeans
A pair of simple skinny jeans in a dark wash—no rips, distressing, or embellishments, please—can solve any number of outfit conundrums. They go from the office to off-duty drinks with ease and are ideal for everything from a concert to a plane trip. Just make sure they're hemmed correctly (we like them to hit just above the ankle bone, so they can work with heels, boots, and flats alike) for maximum wear.

How to Shop Like a Stylista Online

Online Shopping

I love shopping online. Sometimes I can just shop, fill up my cart, feel like I've somehow refreshed my wardrobe, and not even have to purchase anything to feel satisfied. It's weird, I know. Other times (usually at work or two in the morning) I find nothing more satisfying than getting a great deal on a pair of shoes I've been coveting for months or a handbag I didn't know I needed to have. But then there's nothing I like less than realizing the great deal I thought I got was actually just a retailer offloading merchandise they didn't want, something I would never have gone near in the store, or something I could have found at a deeper discount in person. So how can you tell the real savings from the ruse?

Sample Sale Sites

If you love clothes you are likely to already love online sample sales. But let's not confuse these with true sample sales. A sample sale used to be when designers had to sell the clothes they used on fit models or in showings. This is not what modern sample sales are selling. Typically, a designer today is unloading merchandise that they can't sell. That doesn't mean it isn't great. They may have produced too much or gotten returns in late—whatever. But make sure you are getting a real deal by checking the sale price against a Web discounter, like www.bluefly.com, or the designer's own website.

Personal Shopper Sites

I think I would like these sites more if I were a little more discriminating. The way these sites work is that you tell them your size and the brands you like and how often you want them to deliver to your inbox, and then they will scour the Web for sales based on everything you've told them. My problem is I like a *lot* of brands, and even though I'm a size 8, I'm pretty confident I can squeeze into a 6 if the price is right.

But lots of people find great success without all the scouring, on sites like Shop It to Me and MyPerfectSale. Plus I do love that they hit all the big department stores, which means that I don't have to.

Her Closet Is Better Than Mine

I guess the real name for this category is Gently Used, but somehow sites these days have made gently used feel far more personal and somehow less—how can I say this delicately?—gross. The RealReal describes itself as "a luxury resale store. Offering authenticated, pre-owned, designer fashion including Chanel, Hermès, Manolo Blahnik and Cartier—all at up to 90 percent off retail prices." While I never really loved the thrill of the hunt in a vintage store, I can browse for hours on the RealReal or Shop Hers. Plus all the merchandise is authenticated. Perhaps we've become a disposable society where no one expects to hang on to an item for more than a year or two, or we all get tired of everything far before its expiration date. Whatever the case, I'll buy just about anything from these sites, and I get some pretty good deals too.

MG TIP: If you plan on visiting these sites regularly, I would recommend joining their "first look" program, which typically runs about $5.00 a month and gives you "pre" access to merchandise—usually twenty-four hours before non-first-look members. Otherwise some of your favorite items may be gone.

Group Shopping

In some ways, group shopping maximizes what the Internet does best: It harnesses the power of the group. After all, if only one person wants to go to a Pilates class, they pay full price. But if you bring fifty friends with you it stands to reason that you should get a discount. That's the premise behind sites like Groupon, Tippr, and LivingSocial. Typically the deal only goes into effect if a certain number of people purchase it, and it's often limited to your particular city. Like flash sales, though, the deals typically last only one to three days, so you have to be careful not to be too impulsive and not to miss out. It has yet to be seen whether the business model for these sites really works. So hopefully this won't be one section I'll be removing in my next update!

Bigger Is Better

Looking for a cute pair of undies? Chances are you might hit Amazon first—*and* find what you're looking for at the right price. And I sort of keep thinking that Zappos is going to show up at my door soon telling me I need to stop ordering from them as I have exceeded their limit. Sorry, but the free shipping and free returns just make it a little too easy to buy something on a whim. In two sizes. Just be careful not to fall into the "I meant to return it but then I forgot" trap. I once realized my car's trunk was a veritable returns junkyard full of items I should have returned but hadn't. By the time I got to it, some were past the return date and some were so beat-up from, well, my driving that I was too embarrassed to send them back.

Online Coupons

Repeat after me: "Do not make a purchase online without searching for a coupon code." Got it? Say it again. All you have to do is search for the store name and "coupon code" and voilà, lots of coupon codes will show up. Sometimes they'll work, sometimes they won't. I've saved a *lot* of money on everything from clothes to photos to vitamins (no judgment, please) by simply searching for coupon codes and finding a special promo I didn't even know existed. RetailMeNot is one of the best; Coupon Cabin is another. Now again, repeat after me . . .

Tweet Deals

Though I sometimes get tired of the endless chatter on Twitter, I never get tired of the deals I can find. Though the best ones can change, here are some of my favorites:

@AmazonDeals

I'm a pretty big Amazon fan. Now, that doesn't mean I don't frequent mom-and-pop shops. I do. But when I remember at 3 A.M. that my daughter needs a daisy headpiece made within forty-eight hours, Amazon is usually where I go first. And AmazonDeals tweets Lightning Deals, which are pretty sweet prices that typically last about an hour.

@DealsPlus

This is a coupon and deals aggregator that searches the Web for discounts and tweets them to its followers. I've seen deals for Nikon, Prada, Xbox, Starbucks, Apple, and even a doughnut maker (yum).

@AppleDiscounts_

Though it's *not* authorized by Apple (it's a third-party aggregator), this Twitter account scours the Web for all coupon codes related to Apple products.

@JetBlueCheeps

If you're a last-minute traveler this is a great one for you. JetBlue tweet great deals on last-minute flights each Tuesday.

@AmericanExpress

What's great about this is, unlike most companies, who discount only their own products, AmEx can discount any merchant's product. Basically you need to: Visit sync.americanexpress.com/twitter to sync your AmEx account with your Twitter account. Then when AmEx announces a "special offer" hashtag (which they do several times a day), if you retweet that hashtag, you'll get a discount at that merchant. You can also make it more personalized by signing up for the "Deal Stream," where you check off the categories (fashion, tech, entertainment, food) you're interested in, but beware, you will get a *lot* of deals . . .

UNLEASH YOUR VINTAGE VAMP

While vintage can mean awesome retro cuts and hard-to-come-by craftsmanship, vintage gone bad can leave you looking like a grandma reliving her glory days (not pretty). If you're just dipping your toe in the vintage world for the first time, consider sticking to more recent decades (with the eighties being an exception) and opting for pieces that will easily integrate into your existing wardrobe. After a few shopping trips, you'll be a vintage vamp ready to take bigger wardrobe risks.

Spot It!
Do a thorough scan for spots and stains before investing in a piece. While a suede cape would seem like an obvious yes, a few stains will most likely mean it's going straight from your closet to Goodwill faster than you can say Shout!

Fabric Check
Seventies garb may catch your eye with bold prints and bright colors, but step away from the polyester! Stick to breathable fabrics like cotton that won't leave you sweaty (and smelly). Also, be sure to feel the fabric to make sure it's in good condition; it's not uncommon for old fabrics to easily tear.

Don't Halt for Hardware
If the item you're buying is missing a button or two, think of it as an opportunity to give a piece a modern update with a full new set! As a general rule, making small changes to a vintage piece can make it fit more seamlessly into your current wardrobe.

continued

Get Fitted

If you're diving into the world of vintage, it's best to have your tailor on speed dial. When you find a piece that is just perfect, but not a perfect fit, you'll want to bring it in immediately or risk its disappearing to the depths of your closet. Always remember, it's easier to take it in than let it out.

Buy these vintage . . .

- Denim jackets

- Handbags

- Coats

- Jewelry

- Sunglasses

- Leather boots (unless, like me, this totally grosses you out)

And steer clear of . . .

- Shoes (not boots)

- Basics

- Silk blouses

- Suits

- Cashmere

- Leather jackets

Style Tips for Tricky Situations

Having a closet full of chic basics will make dressing easier, but sometimes you find yourself in circumstances that require a little more fashion forethought. Whether you're about to walk into a high-stress meet-his-parents moment, find yourself bloated to the size of a beach ball, or know you'll be caught on camera, here's how to cope:

Looks That Ace a Job Interview

The trick is to look stylish and confident without being distracting. To get the best sense of your prospective company's dress code, do your research. Do you know anyone else at the company who could give you the style scoop? If not, check on glassdoor.com for the insider skinny or stroll through the building's lobby a few days beforehand to get the lowdown on what people are wearing.

If none of those options prove fruitful, consider the industry of the company at which you're interviewing and dress from there.

Corporate/Finance
Put down the statement necklace and step away from the lipstick! As much as I'd like to say you can show your personal style in a business-formal environment, it's best to play it safe when interviewing in more traditional industries. I recommend wearing a suit—either a slim pant or a pencil skirt will do—and opting for neutral colors that won't attract attention. Closed-toed shoes are your best bet, and be sure that the heels are less than three inches and the shoes are scuff-free to keep it extra professional.

Marketing/PR Agency
Marketing, advertising and PR can be a fashionable place, but that doesn't mean you should be dressed for the runway at your first interview. Consider wearing something professional but chic: a conservative dress paired with a blazer or a pair of trousers with a tucked-in blouse. Top off your look with one trendy accessory—note, *one*

accessory—that will add a punch of personality to your look and let them know that you know what's up.

Start-up

If you're interviewing at a start-up you should get a little more relaxed with your outfit, but beware of going too casual. It's still important to look put together and polished. Consider a pair of dark denim jeans or printed skinnies and pair with a tucked-in blouse and sleek belt. For shoes, still steer clear of sky-high heels and platforms and instead slip on a polished pair of flats or sandals with a shorter heel. As for accessories, feel free to show your personal style, but again avoid anything too distracting as you'll be there to highlight your strengths, not your style.

MG TIP: No matter the office environment, avoid bright makeup, heavy eyeliner, red talons, chunky jewelry, etc. Basically, if you would wear it out at night, don't wear it to an interview.

The Perfect Garb for Meeting His Parents

A cashmere sweater and skirt or pants are just conservative enough to let them know you won't kidnap their son and flee to a sleazy Vegas wedding chapel. Just make sure you wear a camisole underneath the sweater. There's nothing worse than sweating buckets and having no cotton material to soak it up underneath, or having your headlights pop on in front of his dad. Trust me.

Slimming Styles for Bloated Days

You've already heard that wearing all black works wonders when you're packing extra pounds—and it's true. But you can also get away with wearing a splash of color under a slimming piece, such as a baby pink tank underneath a fitted tan cotton blazer. Another trick is going monochromatic—wearing a charcoal sweater and charcoal pants, for example—which has an elongating effect.

A V-neck top will slim you down on top and draw attention away from big hips, as will an A-line skirt. Fuller pant legs can camouflage a big booty or ample thighs, but make sure they don't have pleats or a button fly—they instantly add bulk to your middle. Flats will make you

MG TIP: Many women make the mistake of going for the cheapest, most disposable maternity clothing out there. But why would you go for shoddily made duds when you feel your most unflattering and you're putting the most stress on your seams? Drop a little extra dough and get a few well-made basics like jeans and black pants and a great white shirt. You won't regret it, and you can always pass them on to your sister or good friend later. Check out the Liz Lange line at Target . . . stylish and affordable.

MG TIP: Most women seem to try to stave off wearing maternity clothes as long as possible, some-how seeing it a failure to have put on weight. Forget it! Don't bother with your favorite designer in bigger sizes. You're pregnant and your body is changing in different places. Bigger sizes will usually just make it look like you've gained weight, not another human! Instead, go for maternity clothes that will fit in the right places. And start wearing them early! You have a pretty short window to wear these clothes, so the sooner you start, the lower cost per wear.

look squattier, so throw on a sexy pair of heels to visually shave off a few pounds.

Dressing Sexy When You're Preggers

Gone are the days where pregnancy meant you'd be a walking fashion crisis for nine months. Everyone from Reese Witherspoon to Kate Hudson has broken all the rules and made belly bumps beyond chic. So instead of going with sacky items that hide your body (which, by the way, will only make you look bigger), learn how to play up the geometry of your curvy new shape. If you go for a tight top that draws attention to your chest and tummy, opt for a pair of looser-fitting cargoes on the bottom. If you wear a more boho, blousy top, go for a skinny pair of black pants or a skirt that shows off your legs. When you wear an evening dress, choose a V-neck or empire waist. Your décolleté will be highlighted and your tummy minimized. No need to convert to flats, but kitten heels or low wedges will be sexy yet comfortable when your legs and back are absolutely not in the mood to teeter on four-inch stilettos.

Looking Hot in Front of the Camera

When you know you'll be photographed at a party or wedding, it's good to know what styles work and what doesn't so you don't wind up cringing when you see the developed prints. For starters, skip super-sheer fabrics in light colors. They might look good at the event but under the bright lens, they will draw attention to any lump, bump, bra strap, wiggle, or jiggle you have. Tans, creams, whites, and patterns tend to have a widening effect if they aren't paired with slimmer pants or skirts in dark solids.

Body language can go a long way in slimming you down, too. Rule number one is not to put your hands on your hips; they'll draw attention to them rather than hiding them. Instead, keep your arms loose and try to angle yourself to the camera just a little by easing one shoulder toward the photographer and bring your chin around that shoulder. Also keep one leg a little in front of the other to elongate your bod, and bring your hip around the point with that same favored toe (practice your poses in front of a mirror to see yourself). If you have a bit of a belly, casually hold your purse or shawl in front of you to camouflage it. Tuck in your butt, throw your shoulders back, and smile.

How to Take a Great Instagram Photo

Let's start by saying not every meal you order or person you meet needs to be captured on Instagram. And don't think that every great photo was taken on the first shot! Some of the Instagrammers with the biggest followings will tell you (if they are telling the truth, anyway) that for every post it took at least ten tries.

MG TIP: Holding your head down makes your eyes look bigger (and your jaw line smaller) and your eyebrows darker, but your nose will look bigger. Keeping your head up makes your eyes look smaller, but can have a slimming effect on your nose. Pick your poison.

- Take pictures with your camera app. Not only will you be able to save the original photo, but you can use the HDR function for shots of still objects, of landscapes outdoors, in super-sunny conditions, or in high-contrast lighting situations.
- If you don't want to have to crop your photo, set your camera to "square," otherwise it won't have the aspect ratio used by Instagram.
- Try to use your grids (um, if you even knew you had them) to take straight shots. But if you don't, use the straightening tool. I'll be honest: I didn't even know this was there for a while, but once I found it I didn't know how I lived without it. It's great if you have a horizon line, beach, or sunset. Trust me, your photos will look a lot better once you've used it.
- Go natural! With your lighting, that is. When you can, try to avoid the flash. If what you are trying to capture looks dark, try tapping on the darkest area of the photo and you'll see it gets more light.
    - If you do need light and just don't have enough, see if you can borrow your friends' phones. Have them turn on their flashlights, and voilà, you'll have plenty of wattage.

- Consider an editing app. Some of my favorites are:
  - Snapseed
  - VSCO Cam
  - Camera+
  - Diptic

How to Take a Great Selfie

According to www.izzigadgets.com, over one million selfies are taken a day just among eighteen-to-twenty-four-year-olds. So if we're going to be adding to that number, we better make sure the ones we post are some good ones.

- First, look for a neutral background. Anything too chaotic behind you will just detract from you!
- You might be surprised to learn that for the best-quality photo, you shouldn't hit the flip-around button. You should turn the whole phone around and aim the main camera lens at yourself. That lens has better resolution and takes better pictures. And you can look at them *after* you take them . . .
- If you must do the whole camera flip-around thing, tap your finger on your face (on the phone, silly) or wherever you want the camera to focus. That will better balance the light around you.
- For lighting, try to use a friend's phone's flashlight feature and shine it up toward your chin. That's how they do it in modeling studios (okay, not exactly), because it casts a better shadow on your face. Tilt your face up at the ceiling for a second or two *right* before your shot. Experts say it stretches the muscles under the chin and sucks in that wiggly skin. If you look over your shoulder, that will stretch it nice and taut too.
- To help your arms look toned, put your hands on your hips. If you cross them, it will make your muscles look bigger.
- Don't expect to get it right the first time! Take a bunch! Work the camera like a supermodel with different expressions and poses . . . no one needs to see the rejects but you!

- When in doubt, try a filter, a blur, or a glow. Some of the best photos use editing devices like Snapseed, Lo-Mob, Photo fx, or Afterlight.

What to Pack for a Weekend Getaway

Even more stress-inducing than dressing for the camera or strategically picking out "fat blaster clothes" is bringing myself to pack for a vacation—even if it's just for three days! I always cram in too much, and then lament the fact that there's no room to put in any items I've shopped for while I was there. The trick, I've learned, is to spread out everything I want to bring on the bed, and only put in items that I can wear at least twice (either because they're practical or won't wrinkle or stain easily). Also pick a color "theme" and build around that—matching jewelry, makeup, and shoes accordingly.

Weekend by the Sea

- Trench
- Striped nautical T-shirt (long-sleeved and fitted)
- 2 T-shirts: 1 white, 1 black
- Bootylicious jeans
- Denim shorts or skirt
- Chinos or cargos
- Workout gear
- Flirty cocktail dress
- Thin cashmere sweater
- Windbreaker
- Bikini, sarong
- Bras, undies
- Medium-size tote
- Strappy sandals, thongs, sneakers

MG TIP: I sleep in the buff . . . if that's not you, go for some sexy pj's with a cami you can also wear by day.

MG TIP: Roll your clothes in your suitcase instead of folding them. On your bed, lay out a stack of tops (one above the other, lying flat), with the least delicate one on the bottom and the most delicate ones in the middle. Roll the shirts in one fat roll from neck to base, rolling the arms inward as you go. Do the same stack-and-roll with pants (jeans on the bottom, khakis and dress pants in the middle, sweatpants on top). The loose rolling action keeps your clothes from getting creased and wrinkled— which easily happens with folding. You'll also save space in your suitcase, which will come in handy for vacation purchases.

MG TIP: Wrap your shoes in clear shower caps to protect your clothes.

MG TIP: Make sure to keep all your prescription meds in your carry-on or purse, in case your luggage gets lost. And *don't* transfer medication to another container; medicines are more susceptible to heat and sunlight, and in an emergency, others will need to know what you're taking.

MG TIP: Now that airport security is tighter, be sure to pack valuables such as jewelry in your carry-on or purse and protect things in your bag that you don't want touched by placing them in clear plastic Ziploc bags. This works great for undies, toothbrushes, and even sex toys. (For more air travel tips, see pages 405–7)

MG TIP: If you have a high status on one airline but find yourself suddenly flying another—due to a new route or location—you can often call the new airline and ask them to match the status given to you by the other airline!

Weekend in the Snow

- Long wool coat
- Faux fur vest
- 2 superwarm sweaters in cream and black
- Sexy deep V-neck cashmere sweater
- Wool pants
- Bootylicious jeans
- Bikini (hot tub at the lodge, anyone?)
- Bras, undies
- Scarf, hat, gloves
- Medium-size leather tote
- Tall leather boots (snowproof)
- Après-snow slippers
- Oh, and should you be going skiing, go for fabulous black ski pants and jacket and pick two brightly colored turtlenecks to make them feel different.

If you travel frequently, consider getting global entry at www.cbp.gov/global-entry/how-to-apply For $100, preapproved, low-risk travelers get expedited clearance upon arrival in the United States. It also gets you higher TSA clearance on *all* airlines, not just ones you fly frequently, which means you will be whisked through security lines much more quickly. It will require you to fill out a lot of forms and give an interview, but trust me, it's worth it!

Shoes: A Modern Girl's Best Friend

Unlike selecting clothes, looking fabulous in shoes is a no-brainer. Besides polishing your outfit, a great pair of heels or boots will make your legs look longer and stronger, lift your butt a little higher, and help you walk with a sexier strut. (What I love most is that my shoes still love me when I've gained ten pounds.) But it's easy to get suckered into buying shoes that don't fit correctly—and subsequently get banished to the back of your closet. Here's how to make smart purchases you'll wear and wear and wear:

Buy Your Shoes in the Late Afternoon

Your feet will have swollen a touch from walking around all day, which gives you a more accurate sense of the kind of fit you'll need.

Go Snug

Shoes often stretch, so it's better to buy the eight and a half that's a little snug than the loose nine. I like to break them in by wearing a pair of thin socks with them around the house. If this still doesn't make them stretch, take them to a shoe repair store and they can do the job for just a few bucks.

Buy Quality

One pricey pair you love wins over two so-so pairs—otherwise you'll always be lamenting not getting "the ultimate pair" . . . and wind up splurging on them a month later anyway.

Choose Leather Over Suede

I know, the soft stuff looks luxe and conforms to your feet, but suede can be surprisingly high maintenance. No matter what your salesperson promises, suede does not look good after it's seen the rain. It also draws in stains; black suede begins to look grayish over time, lighter colors like tan and pale pink show dirt.

Don't Pressure Yourself

When you're walking around the store, note how much pressure you feel on ball of your foot. The more weight that's jammed to the front of your shoe, the more uncomfortable a pair of heels is going to be. Most of us aren't blessed with high arches, but a shoe that fits your foot will closely align with your arch—meaning there isn't space between the bottom of your foot and the shoe itself. The more alignment in your arch area, the less weight you'll feel pushed to the front of your foot . . . and the easier it will be to dance in them all night (or heck, at least walk three blocks).

Wait Twenty-four Hours

Not sure you can justify the purchase? Put them on hold for a day before you plunk down your plastic. During that downtime, go into your

MG TIP: Find a hard floor. Ever wonder why so many shoe departments are carpeted? Because it makes walking in heels more comfortable. Find a patch of hard wood or marble and take a stroll before buying. You need to make sure you can work all surfaces.

closet and think about all the outfits these shoes will realistically go with. If the number's higher than five, splurge.

Give the Boots and Stilettos You Already Own an Inexpensive Shoe Lift

Hey, sometimes a good shoe splurge just isn't in the cards. But that doesn't mean you can't revive the shoes you already have (instead of wanting to replace them the second they get a little shabby). With these easy SOS tips, your current kicks will carry you from season to season.

Find a Sole Mate
Have thin rubber soles put on the bottoms of your shoes. Not only will they add to the lifetime of your heels, they will make them easier to walk in over slick floors and in bad weather.

Heel!
Have the little black plastic covering of your heel replaced when you see it's gone down a few millimeters. Don't wait until you see a metal rod poking through the heel because you've worn them so much. It costs only a few bucks and will stretch out the lifetime of your shoe.

Shine On
Have your shoe repairman shine them up on a regular basis. Vaseline on a soft cloth will work in a pinch too.

Be Supportive
Put shoe pads inside the soles at the balls of your stilettos and boots. They'll cushion your feet and absorb shocks. They'll also keep the insides of your shoes clean and help maintain their original shape. I like Foot Petals (available at www.footpetals.com).

MG TIP: When I've just bought a pair of shoes I truly love, I add soles and heels *before* I've even worn them. It's an added expense after a pricey purchase, but it really keeps them in shape. As hey say, prevention is the best medicine.

Pretty Up Your Ankles

If the ankle strap on your stiletto is broken or frayed, replace it with a pretty satin ribbon in the same hue as your shoe. If they're pumps, wrap the ribbons under the dips just before the heels and crisscross them up your ankles. Tie in bows at the back of your ankles.

Makeup Tricks for Busy Chicks

Fact: No matter how killer my shoes, slimming the outfit, and chic the purse, some days my face looks blemished, blotchy, or just plain blah and I just don't feel like I look good. Thank God we girls have makeup on our side to quickly give us a little gloss and glow. The trick is knowing what products to splurge on and how to correctly apply them so you make your skin look fresher, your eyes brighter, and your lips plumper—basically a cleaner, prettier version of your natural self.

Makeup and the Internet

I'm pretty sure that when Al Gore "invented" the Internet he had no idea that one of the best outcomes would be the explosion of makeup tutorials. That's right, among us Modern Girls, Michelle Phan is considered sort of a superhero. Without her, we would still be botching our cat eyes and couldn't go bronze or look like a beach beauty. But here's the thing about Internet beauty tutorials: You need one that really shows you step-by-step how to do what you are looking to do. Not one that just *tells* you or shows you the before and after. Plus look for one that points out mistakes to avoid and one without an assistant—unless you plan on having an assistant. There are some amazing ones out there; some of my faves are:

Bethany Mota
Bunny Meyer
Ingrid Nilsen
Kandee Johnson
Wayne Goss

5 BEAUTY GAME CHANGERS TO HELP KEEP YOU FROM EVER LOOKING TIRED, ACCORDING TO BEAUTY EXPERT YING CHU, EXECUTIVE BEAUTY DIRECTOR AT GLAMOUR MAGAZINE

Eyebrow shaping: Your brows truly do frame your face—and if they are the right shape, they can help create the look of high cheekbones and well-rested eyes. The best way to get there is to seek the help of a pro. After a session or two, you can maintain the shape yourself.

An eyelash curler: Splurge on a sturdy metal one (I like the classic Shu Uemura curler) that fits the shape of your eye and practice using it. For women with short or droopy lashes (most Asian women), this means you will never suffer from raccoon eyes again.

A perfect blush: If you wear one makeup item on the weekends, make it this. It beats even concealer and foundation at making you look healthy, alive, and glowy. I'm all for testing dozens to find the most flattering shade for your skin tone. A pretty universally flattering one I swear by is Nars Blush in Orgasm.

A caffeine-laced eye cream: Store it in the fridge and when you put it on in the morning, massage it in by tapping the pads of your fingers around your eyes (like you're typing on a keyboard). This will help get the blood flowing and take down the puffiness.

A sunscreen you actually love and will put on your face every single day: Wearing it will drastically improve the way you age—preventing spots, lines, enlarged pores, you name it. It's proven by science and endorsed by beauty editors everywhere.

MG TIP: Though I'm a fan of most loyalty programs, I'm a superfan of Sephora's. Their point system lets you quickly rack up the ability to "buy" trial-size samples of products you genuinely want. I *highly* recommend joining.

Your Skin

If you have a small makeup budget, leave room to splurge on a good tinted moisturizer, BB cream, or foundation and concealer. Higher priced brands have a higher level of pigment and less filler. That means truer color and even fewer breakouts, because more pigment keeps your skin looking (and staying) clear.

For the most even coverage, moisturize beforehand and apply the foundation in small *downward* strokes with a makeup sponge, blending carefully just below your jawline. For a dewy, less made-up look, opt for the tinted moisturizer. I stick to the easiest application method possible, dotting some of Jouer's tinted moisturizer on the back of my hand and applying it with Hourglass's No. 7 finishing brush, which you just rub in circles on your face until it is flawless. Dot concealer over pimples and other problem spots with a tapping motion (rubbing it in will only smudge it off), and finish with a light dusting of translucent powder to set.

MG TIP: When choosing the right color of tinted moisturizer, and powder, test it on the inside of your wrist—it will give the closest match to your face. Testing it over the makeup you already have on your face won't give you a true picture.

MG TIP: You can prolong the life of your foundation by applying it with a fresh makeup sponge instead of your fingers (which have bacteria on them). Wash sponges weekly and discard them monthly.

Your Eyes

I'll admit it: For a number of years I did that little cat's eye eyeliner upturn at the corner of my eyes, thinking it made them look bigger. *Oops.* Once I had a professional show me the way, I learned that using the thinnest amount of eyeliner only along your upper lashline actually makes your eyes look bigger and far more natural.

I also learned these tricks from my cosmetics guru friends:

MG TIP: Before sharpening your eyeliner, place it in the freezer for ten minutes. It'll harden a bit and not break when you sharpen it.

- Light-colored eye shadow in the inside corners of your eyes can make close-set eyes look farther apart.

- Lining the insides of your lower lids with a white liner blends into the whites of your eyes, making your irises look brighter and your eyes larger.

- The more light your lids reflect, the more wide-eyed you'll appear. Blend a pearly or bronze shadow across your lid, and blend a slightly darker shadow in just the outside corners of your eyes for

MG TIP: Try putting Vaseline on your eyelashes before going to bed. When you wake up your eyelashes will be silky soft and ready for mascara.

MG TIP: On a lazy Saturday, swing by your favorite department store makeup counter for a free makeover. You don't have to buy everything suggested. You might just walk away with an eye pencil, but you'll have learned invaluable application tips that you can replicate with cheaper brands.

MG TIP: If you do choose to use a brow pencil, it's best to go two shades lighter than your brow color. Then, apply the pencil working against the natural growth of your hair (from the outside of your eye to the inside of your eye). This puts the color underneath your brow, which makes it less Tammy Faye and keeps it in place longer.

definition. I love Make Up For Ever's eye shadow because it sticks to my lids, seemingly, forever!

- Highlight your brow bones with a pearly or champagne powder—it will give your eye area the illusion of having more height.

- Wiggle your mascara wand at the base of your lashes, then extend the wand to the tips. The extra color the wiggling deposits will make your lashes look darker and thicker. For a special occasion, placing a few individual faux eyelashes on the middle-to-outside stretch of your eye gives va-va-voom volume.

Your Brows

Gone are skinny matchstick brows—full arches are back (think: Cara Delevingne, Amanda Peet, Salma Hayek . . . but not when she starred in *Frida*!). To keep yours from looking like an overgrown thicket, invest in an angle-tipped pair of tweezers. Each brow should begin above the inner corner of your eye, so tweeze any hairs that fall into unibrow territory.

Next, locate your natural arch (the highest point of your brow) by holding a pencil vertically in front of the outer edge of your pupil. Then pluck underneath that arch to create an upside-down V shape, which will define your brows. Next, hold the pencil diagonally against the outer corner of your eye, pointing up to the brow bone. Your brow should extend slightly beyond the eye and taper slightly down—pluck anything past that. To finish, fill in any sparse patches with a light brown powder—pencil can look too harsh—and finish with a brow-grooming gel to hold in place. (In a pinch, you can use a bit of hairspray on a new toothbrush.)

Your Cheeks

Blush can be tricky. If you don't have Sarah Jessica Parker's cheekbones, it's difficult to know exactly where to apply it. For starters, sweep the blush just *below* your cheekbones, not on top of them. Otherwise, you're just depositing color, not highlighting the contours of your face. A great brand to try: Nars Blush in Orgasm. And it's not just because I like the name.

Another popular choice is cream or gel blush. You have more control because you rub it into your cheeks with your hands—and it's much more convenient to apply on the go. Just squeeze a dot of it into your hands and blend into the apples of your cheeks (when you smile, it's the highest, fleshiest part) for a dewy, fresh-faced look.

MG TIP: Blush doesn't go on as evenly with a dirty brush—and can even contribute to breakouts. Wash your makeup brushes once a month with special brush cleaner or baby shampoo.

Your Lips

I am blessed with many things, but gorgeous, supple lips is not one of them. When I nibble on the corner of my lips I don't look all sexy and pouty; I wind up with chapped, flaky, irritated lips that look like I just fought a round with braces and lost. I pretty much said hallelujah when I found Sara Happ's lip scrub and somehow got the kind of lips I'd only dreamed about. Sarah created a multimillion dollar cosmetic company—beginning in her kitchen—and makes the best products around. So now that lips are back to being a major trend, I sought her advice on all things lips. Here's what she had to say:

Get your lip products to wear the way they should
There's no way around it. You must prep. This means exfoliation to remove dead skin. (And we're not just talking visible flakes . . . You know how sometimes your lips look a little gray? That's skin that needs to be swept away.) Massage a gentle, sugar-based lip scrub onto lips and watch their natural color come to life, because a) that old skin is gone, and b) you've stimulated blood flow (blood is after all what gives lips their color). All things lip will adhere to baby-smooth skin in a more even, long-lasting way.

Achieve the perfect pout
It's three simple steps, and don't let anyone tell you otherwise. Once you've prepped your lips by exfoliating, dab the tiniest amount of highlighter (shimmery nude eye shadow works like a charm) onto

your cupid's bow and directly beneath, at the center of your bottom lip. Go just beyond your true lip line to create that lit-from-within, angelic glow. Then slather on a rich, emollient gloss. It'll appear effortless yet totally flawless. Every time.

Pick the perfect shade

Every girl needs two lip colors (not the twelve that may be floating around your handbag right now, though I completely understand the obsession): A perfect pink and a perfect nude will work in every situation, from beach day to black tie. A subtle, blue-based pink makes teeth appear whiter and looks understated yet polished. For nudes, sheer is the rule, or you risk looking like a corpse. Go for something that's slightly darker than the shade of concealer you'd buy for your specific skin tone. Then enjoy the freedom of being that girl with just a couple of wands in her clutch.

Make your lips legendary

Alcohol is the lip industry's dirty little secret. You apply your gloss, balm, or lipstick, and three minutes later, you want and need to reapply. Truth be told, most lip products are created to dry your lips out, so you need more. So you buy more. Ouch, right? Rise above that trick and seek out products loaded with essential oils (sweet almond, jojoba, and grape seed are my favorites) along with beeswax. These truly hydrate and protect your pout, which is what that delicate skin deserves.

Put on lip balm before you apply your lipstick (I love Hourglass No. 28 Lip Treatment Oil), and use a little pressed powder just before you apply your liner and lipstick to set the color. If you prefer a lighter, less lipsticky look (find it on everyone from Lauren Conrad to Jennifer Aniston), opt for a long-wearing gloss like Chanel's. I like Dior's Diorific Long-Wearing True Color Lipstick as well. Sephora also has a great lipstick sealant that keeps it on for ages.

MG TIP: Ever wonder what to do with extra lip balm you've put on with your fingers? Rub it into your cuticles for a little extra moisture.

WHEN GOOD MAKEUP GOES BAD . . .

Unlike food, cosmetics aren't required by law to have expiration dates. From the moment you open it, bacteria will start to grow and its effectiveness will decrease.

• Concealer should be replaced every six to eight months, foundation every three to six months. Powders can last a year. Wide-mouthed bottles expose it to more air, and should be trashed even sooner.

• Toss your mascara after just two to three months. By then your tube is teeming with bacteria, thanks to the pumping action of the brush (can anyone say eye infection?). Throw out powder eye shadows every nine to eighteen months, and cream eye shadows every six to twelve months. Dip your eye pencils in alcohol every week to kill germs.

• Lip gloss and lipsticks can last a year (but frankly I've either used it all or tired of it by then).

MG TIP: Keep makeup in a dry, cool area, and remember: Any cosmetic that changes texture or smell should be discarded immediately.

Your Nails

Just like with blowouts, these days you can get a decent manicure at a reasonable price. But just because a manicure is cheap doesn't mean it's good. If you're lucky, you've got a fabulous salon like Olive and June, the hottest nail salon in L.A., where they keep your shape, color, and any experience preferences on file, and though you feel like you're at a spa you're paying reasonable prices. Since gels are all the rage, I asked the owner and founder, Sarah Gibson Tuttle, for the honest truth on getting gelled. According to Sarah you need to remember that gels are basically plastic on your nails, so if you are a gal

MG TIP: If you're headed to a sketchy salon, bring your own polish. Some salons will add acetone to theirs to make the supply last longer.

MG TIP: Looking for fewer chemicals in your polish? Go for five-free polishes, which don't include dibutyl phthalate (DBP), toluene, formaldehyde, formaldehyde resin, or camphor. All pretty yucky. Some of the big brands that are five-free include Givenchy, Dior, Chanel, Deborah Lippmann, and Jin Soon. But note that some feel that these polishes chip faster.

MG TIP: Never apply nail polish in the sun. It turns into a goopy mess that takes forever to dry. Also, try storing your nail polish in the fridge to make it last longer.

MG TIP: Dip your nails in a bowl of cold water and ice cubes after you finish them. It will harden your nails and keep the polish from chipping.

who's into organic polish, five-free polish, or anything natural, these are not for you. According to Sarah:

- If you have a choice of UV vs. LED light, LED is definitely better, but the gel that cures with UV solely (CND Shellac) typically lasts the longest on the greatest number of women. If LED light scares you as well, Sarah recommends sunscreen before you start or just avoiding gel manicures altogether.
- The biggest problem is often not the gels themselves but the removal; most salons want to rush through this, so they are tearing up nails. At Olive and June they allow the acetone to soak in longer so the gel lifts easily from the nail bed. So you *must* go someplace where they remove the gels properly!
- The biggest no-no when you have gels is to try to peel your own gels off, which is very bad for your nail bed.

If you don't want to spend money on manicures and aren't blessed with a hand model's naturally strong, healthy talons, take the no-fuss approach. File them into a clean, squared-off shape; give them a coat of clear polish with a strengthener ingredient; and put two coats of a super-pale pink over the top. The hint of color will make even the shortest, most brittle nails look clean and pretty, and is subtle enough that if you paint outside the lines or get a few air bubbles, no one will notice.

Taking Your Look from Day to Night

When you have tons of time to carefully apply your makeup in your own bathroom, it becomes second nature, almost a ritual. But in an MG's go-go-go lifestyle, heading back home to prep for a big night out is often impossible. Jetting to a swank holiday party or hot date after work requires the ability to transform your look right in the office or car. Here are a few fast moves that instantly update your look from afternoon to evening:

Day-to-Night Tip 1: Get High-Drama Eyes

Add intensity to your orbs with a smoky shadow at the outer corners of your eyes, or a charcoal pencil along your upper and lower lash lines.

MG TIP: Rub a little petroleum jelly on the tip of your charcoal eye pencil to make it glide on with more shimmer.

Day-to-Night Tip 2: Amp Up Your Lips

If you're playing up your eyes with charcoal, slick on a nude gloss. If you'd rather play up your lips than your eyes, line your lips in a berry tone, slick on your lipstick, and then dab a little gloss in the center of your lower lip. Delicious.

MG TIP: If you're playing up your eyes, downplay your lips and vice versa. You don't need your face competing with itself for the spotlight.

Day-to-Night Tip 3: Sexify Your Skin

Keep sample sizes of stronger, more sophisticated perfumes in your desk drawer or makeup pouch to dab on your wrists and behind your ears. If your top permits, create a little hint of cleavage by dusting bronzing powder between your breasts.

Day-to-Night Tip 4: Heat Up Your Hair

Put a little hand lotion (about the size of a dime) in your palms and run it on the ends of your locks to get rid of frizzies (it works!). Then decide: Are you going to go for wild or slicked back? If you're going wild, throw your head over and brush it backward to create volume at the roots. If you choose slicked back, put a little more hand lotion on your strands, part your hair just a little off center and pull back into a low chignon or sleek ponytail with a rubber band.

Day-to-Night Tip 5: Accessorize

Always have a statement necklace, a cuff, or a pair of fancier earrings stashed in your office or glove compartment. They instantly kick up even the most casual work duds.

Solving Mini–Beauty Disasters

Sometimes, despite much preparty beautification and primo product usage, the Beauty Gods throw you a big, ugly curveball. Here's how to undo the damage:

MG TIP: If your pimple is large, red, and feels like a rock when you touch it, don't squeeze—it won't work and prodding it will do mucho damage. See a dermatologist who can inject the bump with cortisone, which will make it dramatically shrink over the next two days.

Big, God-Awful Zits

You've heard it everywhere: Don't pick your face! And whoever told you that is right, by the way. But when you've got a mammoth white-head on your chin that looks like it's about to pop any second (and subsequently scare your guy, your coworkers, and small children on the street), a little intervention is necessary.

Soak the area with a warm washcloth for five to ten minutes. Then, with a tissue wrapped around each of your index fingers, gently press down on the area around the pimple. (Don't squeeze the pimple itself, or you'll only push the bacteria down deeper and cause scarring.) If nothing happens, soak the pimple again, then push down around the area again to coax out the offending pus (now Windex the mirror, please).

Once you're a triumphant pop princess, you may find that your bump bleeds a bit. Wrap a few ice cubes in a washcloth and hold it on the area for five minutes. The coldness will shrink the bump and help the blood coagulate. Wait a few more minutes, and then apply a benzoyl peroxide zit cream, and later, your concealer. Finally, take a Tylenol, which has an anti-inflammation agent that will help the zit shrink further.

Under-Eye Bags and Dark Circles

Whether you went wild at a party or just woke up on the Dark Side, you can combat puffy eyes by holding the back of a cold spoon to each lid for a minute, or by slipping on a refrigerator-chilled gel eye mask (just six bucks at Origins). Reduce dark circles by using an eye cream with retinol or vitamin C—it will stimulate collagen production to thicken the skin. To camouflage dark rings, use a yellow-based concealer (to counteract the blue). Dot your concealer on—don't rub—with your ring finger.

A Hideously Botched Self-Tanner Job

Looking like you went to St. Tropez: good. Looking like you're auditioning for the tiger cage at the Bronx Zoo: bad. To tone down unsightly orange streaks, rub a Stridex face wipe over the area. If you're looking for a natural solution, a mix of lemon juice and baking soda also works wonders. Then hop in the shower with a loofah to buff off the remaining color. If it's still obvious, blend a little liquid bronzer into the lighter areas around the streak so the contrast isn't as evident. To prevent future orange freak-outs, make sure to exfoliate before applying self-tanner, use it sparingly around your hands, elbows, knees, and ankles, and wash your hands immediately in warm soapy water (or use gloves to apply). Also choose a brand like Ban de Soleil Streakguarde that darkens instantly, so you can fix your mistakes on the spot.

Hairs Sprouting in All the Wrong Places

I know. All it takes are a few wayward spikes to make you feel like an extra from *Planet of the Apes*. But the good news is, nobody else ever needs to know about your extra fur:

- *Nipple hair:* Run, don't walk, into the bathroom and pluck away. Same goes for moles with hairs poking out (don't worry; it doesn't cause cancer).

- *Dark, furry arms:* Three words: Jolen Cream Bleach. It's less painful and less expensive than waxing or lasers. Also, arms with no hair can look a bit odd.

- *Mustache maladies:* Whatever you do, don't shave! Here are your options:
    - *Waxing:* rips the hair out of its root, but wait for the spikes to grow out before you wax again.
    - *Bleaching:* will lighten the hair, but won't remove it. This can work well in combination with waxing.
    - *Depilatories:* such as Nair for Face or SurgiCream dissolve the hair just below the surface.
    - *Electrolysis:* kills the hair with an electric pulse. It is effective, but can be painful, pricey, and leave tiny scars.
    - *Lasers:* paralyze the hair at the root using a handheld machine that glides over your skin. Laser treatments are pricey (anywhere from $75 to $250 per session for an average of four to eight sessions), but they're the best permanent hair removal option around.

MG TIP: Ever wonder why the stubble from a razor seems so much sharper than any other? Because you are cutting in the middle of the hair, which is thicker than the end, at a blunt angle (as opposed to waxing, where the hair that reappears is the tapered end), so it feels sharper and may actually look thicker!

MG TIP: Try using hair conditioner instead of shaving cream to shave your legs! It will soften the hair and may give you a closer shave.

MG TIP: Don't clench or hold your breath as your waxer is ripping the cloth strip off. This only makes the hairs hang on more, causing more pain. Relax and gently exhale as she's pulling and it will hurt a ton less.

- *Bikini line bushiness:* The smartest treatment for your bikini area is waxing or lasers. Lasers can be expensive and tend not to work on dark skin or pale hair, because lasers target the melanin in the hair, so the laser needs to be able to lock on to the dark pigment and needs to differentiate the dark hair from the skin.

Dermatologists recommend leaving waxing up to the pros, especially if you want a Brazilian (a skinny landing strip with everything else cleaned out). The week before your waxing appointment, gently exfoliate the area to slough off dead skin. (See chapter 8 for more Brazilian tips.)

Hot Hair Hints

MG TIP: Shampoo shouldn't actually get into a big bubbly lather. In fact, you'll find the cheaper the shampoo, the more it lathers. All you need is slight foaming action. Massage your head in tiny circles for optimum cleansing.

MG TIP: Sometimes you need an expert to craft the perfect coif, and for those occasions I always turn to the pros at the local blow-dry bar (my favorite right now is Drybar).

Now that you have a game plan to get your less-than-desirable hairs zapped, plucked, waxed, and out of the way, let's talk tresses. We all know the meaning of a good hair day and a bad hair day—and how much it can affect our moods. In fact, according to a recent study by the Dove Self-Esteem Fund, two-thirds of women reported withdrawing from activities when they were feeling bad about their appearance (hair included). Here's how to make sure that happens as seldom as possible:

Washing It

- Shampoo your hair every other day, and if you can get away with it, every third day. Too much washing will strip your hair of its natural oils and make it dry and dull.

- To get rid of styling-product buildup and shampoo residue, try washing your hair once a week with a cup of apple cider vinegar.

- If your hair is greasy but you don't have time to hop in the shower (that damn alarm clock), sprinkle baby powder or Bumble and Bumble hair powder on your roots. It will absorb the oils in your hair in a pinch, and give it a softer, thicker texture. Powder also works if you're blonde and want to brighten up your roots in between highlight appointments.

Blow-Drying It

After shampooing and conditioning, wrap a towel around your head to absorb excess water, then squeeze, don't twist. Spritz a protein spray that has heat-protecting elements onto your hair and run through it with a boar-bristle brush or wide-tooth comb. Now separate it into sections (clip one at the crown, two on the sides, and two in the back, upper and lower). Start at the front of your head with a large round brush (doing this section first, when you're still paying attention, guarantees you'll do a good job). As you're gliding through a section of hair, follow it with the nozzle of the dryer, holding it horizontal to your brush as you move from the roots to the ends—this will keep your strands as sleek as possible. Then dry the sides, and finally, the back. When you're finished, apply a dab of styling cream and run it over your hair for maximum shine. Give your hair a final shot of cool air to minimize flyaways and frizzies.

Healthy Hair Tips

- Try to keep your hair in a rubber band as little as possible—it makes hair more brittle. The only thing that doesn't damage it is a fabric scrunchie, but those are so eighties. Better to twist and hold it loosely in a small tortoise plastic clip with teeth.

- Don't follow the hundred-strokes-a-day rule. You'll overstimulate the oil glands in your scalp. All you need are twenty strokes a day.

- Use a deep conditioner once a week that contains proteins and moisturizers to soften and strengthen your strands—especially if you're a highlighting junkie.

- Try to get your hair trimmed every six to eight weeks—even just a quarter inch and even if you're growing your hair out. The more often you trim it, the more polished you'll look and the less likely you'll be stuck with straggly split ends that can break your hair up the shaft.

- If you're raring to try a new look, bring a ripped-out magazine photo of your desired hairstyle to the salon. Even though you may not wind up looking exactly like the picture, your stylist will get an idea of the vibe you're looking for—which equals tress success.

Advice from the Blow-Dry Demigoddess

Now, if you're anything like me, even with these tips, endless YouTube tutorials and a third arm, you *still* would rather get your hair blown out for you. Luckily, Alli Webb went ahead and did the best thing ever and created Drybar. Call it the women's clubhouse—where we can get an inexpensive, fabulous blowout in thirty minutes, watch a chick flick, have a glass of bubbly, read a magazine, or chat with girl-friends. It is, simply, heaven. With over forty locations in nine states, I hope you're lucky enough to have one close to you. So I asked Alli for her best tips on keeping a great blowout once you get it. Here's what she had to say:

Some Things Can Last
One thing that drives me absolutely crazy is getting a blowout that doesn't last. Staying power is one of the things we constantly work on and train our stylists to achieve. Fortunately, there are some techniques and tricks to maximize how long your blowout lasts.

Keep It Clean, Ladies
While it's not something that quickly comes to mind, starting your blowout with super clean hair is the key to a great, long-lasting blowout. If there is any oil, dirt, or product residue left in your hair, your blowout will come out flat and lifeless no matter how good your technique or products are. Always start clean!

One Product Does Not Fit All
It's also essential that you use products best for your hair type. If you have frizzy, curly hair (like me!) you need a good smoothing/hydrating cream (I'll admit I'm partial to ours, the Cream Soda Smoothing Cream, which will help you get through your hair with ease and save you some serious time!). If you're going for volume and

curl, be sure to use a great mousse. And always use a good heat protectant. These products really do make a difference!

Size Does Matter

And the brushes you use make a big difference, too! For more curl and volume, use a smaller barrel brush. Less curl, straight and smooth styles, use a big barrel brush.

Patience Is a Virtue

Take your time and work in small, manageable sections (about two to three inches) and use professional quality clips to hold the rest of your hair out of the way! Perfecting each and every section will help ensure a long-lasting blowout (rushing through your sections or using too large of sections will leave you with an unfinished look that will not last).

Tricks of the Trade

- Be sure to use professional tools starting with a blow-dryer with nano-ionic technology—it makes all the difference and will leave your hair shiny and bouncy (a cold shot after your blowout is complete will really help lock in style and shine, too).

- I also love using a curling iron as finisher in case my blowout is a little frizzy and needs a touch-up. A good iron will do the trick!

- Finish your blowout with a smoothing oil or shine cream on the mid-shaft to ends (never on the roots) and a spritz of a humidity-blocking hair spray. Voilà, beautiful hair for days!

As a Drybar devotee, I can tell you that I swear by Alli's methods and products—check 'em out in a store or at Drybar.com.

Finding a Fabulous Hairstylist and Colorist

Whether you're scouting for your first bona-fide stylist and colorist, or you're breaking up with your old ones (and honey, it really does feel like a breakup), here are a few strategies to help you on your search:

Ask Around

This seems so simple, but we don't do it nearly enough. When you see someone on the street or in your office with a hair shade or texture similar to yours, whose cut or highlights you love, ask her where she gets her hair done, and—most important—which stylist she goes to. She may feel a little protective at first, but say you'll go to the stylist saying she recommended him or her. She'll get the ego boost and you'll get the crucial number.

Screen the Salon

Start online with review websites like Yelp and StyleSeat. These will help you narrow the field before doing the in-depth research. Do they have an internship or apprentice program for training their new stylists? What kind of degrees and certificates do the stylists hold? Are they required to go to salon training programs or an advanced academy? All these questions can be answered over the phone if you ask to speak with the assistant manager.

Get a Consultation

Top-notch salons won't skip over the consultation process—this is where you sit down with your stylist and really get a sense of whether you click or not. Tell him or her what you're looking for, and ask tons of questions to get insight into the person's background, training, and general personality. Beware of extremes: If the stylist or colorist refuses to give you a certain cut or color, or goes with your request without discussing the details, you might wind up with a cut and color you're not happy with. If at any time you are made to feel uncomfortable, simply say you have to go to the ladies room, ask to speak to the manager, and explain that this isn't a good fit for you. Remember, you're the customer.

Start Subtle

When trying a new hairstylist, don't request a Miley Cyrus chop or a baby-blonde dye job. Test them out with a trim or a blow-dry and take it from there. Don't book an appointment just before a wedding, holiday party, or when you're seriously wigged out from work. That's more pressure than an MG needs.

Getting the Most for Your Money

So now that you've found your salon, how can you stretch your dollar as far as it'll go? Try these tips:

Milk the "New Customer" Discount

When you go in, ask if you can get a discount for being a new customer with a particular stylist or colorist. When I switched colorists, I was given a 25 percent discount for my first two visits—but I never would've gotten it had I not asked.

Check the Pecking Order

Many salons allow their star stylists to charge upward of $50 or more per haircut than their colleagues. The way you often can tell is that they're wearing street clothes, as opposed to any sort of a uniform. If you know you're in a top-notch salon, chances are that all the stylists are competent. Go for a mid-tier stylist and save your money.

Go for a Half-Head of Highlights

I learned this lesson very quickly—if you can get away with it, have your colorist only do a half-head. What it means is they'll lighten the top of your hair and leave the underneath darker (which only shows if you're wearing a ponytail). I'll get a half-head during the fall and winter, and a full head during the spring and summer, and save between $400 and $500 per year.

Don't Buy Hair Products In-House

I know, it's tempting. After you've had your fabulous cut, color, and blowout, your stylist will often lead you to a wall full of products, boasting that you can replicate the same silky effects you have now by buying a mousse, spray-gel protein spritz, grooming mist, yada yada. Note the products he or she mentions, then go online and see if you can find them at a cheaper price. Often, stylists have told me that the most important thing to buy post-color is a deep conditioner specialized for your hair type. So if you're picking up one product only, go for that.

MG TIP: If you're going for the beachy look, ask your colorist for balayage: a French hair-coloring technique in which the highlights are applied by hand rather than with foil. An added benefit of balayage: You can wait longer between visits to the colorist because there's no demarcation line.

MG TIP: Don't judge a stylist by his or her haircut. Yes, the stylist should be well groomed and work at a neat, well-maintained station, but some of the best cut-and-color jobs I've had were from people with far "wackier" hair than mine.

Ask for a Free "Treatment"

When I get an expensive color job, I'll often ask if they can throw a quick protective treatment on my hair after the color is rinsed out. (This is normally a $30 value.) At the very least, many salons have coupon booklets where you can redeem a free "treatment" with your next cut or color.

Waive the Blow-Dry

Some salons give you a free blow-dry with your cut and color, but other upscale salons actually require you to pay a stylist for a blowout for $30 to $40, plus tip.

More on Hair Color

My whole life I've wanted to be a blonde. And some of my life I've been one. And some of my life I've been a pretty bad one (No, not what you're thinking!). Just not a good *shade* of one. I've been brassy, I've been green, I've been Barbie blonde, I've been just plain old bottle blonde, so when I met Mèche Salon's Kari Hill, who makes pretty much every A-list celebrity the perfect shade of blonde (or brown, or red), I couldn't help asking her for some tips. Here were her words of wisdom:

Long-Lasting Hair Color

There are many tips out there offering help to keep and maintain long-lasting hair color. The way to keep it simple is to know less is more. For example, deep conditioning or at-home masks sound good but can fade a rich brown or vibrant red. The conditioner/mask is designed to get deep in the hair follicle to moisturize; however, when the conditioner/mask is rinsed out, it takes the color molecule with it, resulting in the color fading. To avoid this, a good daily conditioner not left on an excessive amount of time is perfect. One analogy for protecting hair color is to compare it to preserving a beautiful fabric. You wouldn't wash it with harsh detergents or leave it in the sun unprotected and expect it not to fade. Consequently, a fantastic way to think about taking care of your hair color, whether it be high-lights, lowlights, reds, or browns, is to treat and protect it like you would your skin: Invest in a cleanser specific to your hair type; use a moisturizer that isn't too light or too heavy; and, most of all, protect it from the sun with hats, scarves, and SPF sprays or creams.

Communication

It is important to have great communication with your colorist. When I'm consulting with a new client, I of course like to ask what they like or want. Surprisingly, clients are usually not so sure what they want and are generally vague or unclear with their answer. A more precise and revealing question to ask is "Can you tell me what you don't like?" The client usually responds with revealing and definitive boundaries that the hair colorist can use to guide and achieve the desired result. For example, the client might dislike reds or brassy tones or, vice versa, ashy or gray tones. Also, when clients know what they *don't* like, their feedback is often very specific and emphatic concerning how fine, subtle, bold, or natural they want their highlights.

My top advice for clients going to a new colorist or making a significant change with their current colorist is to bring in pictures (eg, what is ashy or brassy to you may be completely opposite to someone else). Agreeing with the semantics of the tones encourages communication and avoids undesired results. Also, the technique and desired application of highlights can be different from what the client is anticipating and what the hair colorist is strategizing.

A common language clarified through pictures speaks volumes and allows a photo to communicate what the client is attempting. Taking a little time to either tear a picture out from a magazine or research on Pinterest before your appointment is truly worth it.

A very important and surprisingly common form of miscommunication with your colorist comes from a reluctance to tell the truth. Always be candid with your colorist about what products you're using, what chemical treatments you've done (straightening), and if you've colored your hair yourself at home. The previous procedures or chemicals on your hair may impact the outcome and/or health of your hair—just be honest!

A common misconception that needs clarification is that color takes better on dirty hair. No, it doesn't! The only time in which an oily scalp may be desired is when you're very sensitive to color applied directly on the scalp. In this case, don't wash your hair (it agitates the scalp) or exercise (sweating; opens pores) the day of your color service. Color also takes more evenly from root to end if it doesn't have obstacles such as grease/oil or product buildup to break through.

Last, but very important, don't wear your highest-end clothes, shoes, or handbag to get your hair colored. It's always good to let your stylist/colorist see your personal style, but be aware that color or water from shampoo bowls can splash and possibly ruin your high-end purchases.

Hard Water Is Hard on Your Hair

Beware of hard water! Just because you have a fancy filter doesn't mean you won't have hard water. And hard water can turn beautiful blonde hair a dirty, dingy green! Even in just one washing with hard water. Luckily your colorist can do a simple (inexpensive) process that can take the green out. So if you're feeling dingy a few weeks after getting your color done, go see your stylist. Your color might not be bad, your water might be!

Treating Your Body Right

Gorgeous hair? Check. Man-melting makeup? Check. Stylin' wardrobe? Triple check. But your beautification process doesn't stop there. Look at your body like a luxury car—all the cosmetic things you do to shine up the outside certainly make a difference, but the inside has to run well for peak performance. Here's how to transform the inside of your body so you look like a lean, mean, sexy machine.

The MG's Pocket Guide to Not Stuffing Thy Face

To look good, you need to eat lots of macaroni and cheese, potato skins, and french fries (just checking to see if you're still reading). Okay, the truth is, if you want to have glowing skin and look fabulous in those new cigarette pants of yours, eating the right foods—at the right times, and in the right quantities—is a must. Don't worry . . . you'll still have room to splurge on chocolate.

Get the Right Ratio

At each meal, envision your plate being divided into three parts—one half of your plate with vegetables, one quarter of your plate with protein, and the other quarter with complex carbs (brown rice or sweet potatoes).

Use the Rule of Thumb

Portion control is the secret to surviving at parties and dinners out—and all you need is your hand. The palm of your hand is a reasonable size for protein like chicken, fish, or steak. This means the thickness of your hand too. If it's a two-inch-thick steak, cut down the size of your portion considerably. Cup your hand, and that's equivalent to a cup of pretzels or chips. Your thumb would be about an ounce of cheese. The tip of your thumb would be about a tablespoon (very helpful when you think about dips). The tip of your finger would be about a teaspoon.

Play the Twenty-Minute Game

It takes twenty minutes to fully digest your meal, so even though you think you're hungry, buy yourself time before wanting to have seconds. Call a friend—or if you're at a restaurant, excuse yourself to freshen up in the bathroom. Have a decaf coffee or drink herbal tea . . . by the time you finish, your craving should pass.

Chug Water

Drink eight glasses of water—eight to ten ounces each—per day. Not only will it improve your skin and help move toxins out of your body, downing a glass of water after a meal will help keep you fuller so you don't ask for seconds.

Eat Fiber

Forget geriatric prune diets. Noshing on high-fiber fruits, whole grains, and bran cereal for breakfast will fill you up faster—and keep you full longer—than a starchy, sit-in-your-stomach bagel can.

Pig Out on Protein, Not Sugar

When you chow down on sweets, your blood sugar takes a hike and then drops a few hours later, which makes you cranky, tired, and craving more-more-more licorice whips. Better to have a slice of turkey or some low-fat cheese.

Be Party Smart

Half the time at parties, you don't even notice what you're eating—you just have the urge to pop something in your mouth to quell nervous energy. Do it by chomping on a crudité and lean protein instead of egg rolls and dumplings. Another trick: Fill up a plate instead of standing by the buffet picking at things. If you're picking, you won't realize how much you're consuming.

Steer Clear of Faux Health Foods

Shopping at a health food store doesn't guarantee waistline-whittling eating. For example, a single serving of dried fruit can have up to sixteen grams of fat—and banana chips, fried in coconut oil, can pack in as much fat as a big old burger.

Try Not to Eat After 8 P.M.

When you load up your body with tons of grub after dark, and then fall into bed, you can't burn the calories off easily—so they sit with you all night. Ugh. Even if you have a few hunger pangs, tell yourself you'll load up on a big breakfast in the morning. People who make breakfast a key meal of their day wind up eating less overall.

Kiss the Bread Basket Buh-Bye

I know it's hard, but if you want to slim down quickly, stop reaching for the doughy white dinner rolls. They have little nutritional value and make you retain water. And instead of sating your appetite,

MG TIP: Have a healthy snack *before* you go to a soiree so you're not prone to party pig-outs.

MG TIP: At a party, carry a clutch and get a glass of water (or wine). With both hands filled, you'll *really* have to want the food to do the necessary acrobatics to grab it.

chowing on bread can actually stimulate you to eat more during your meal. Conspiracy!

Color Code

Weight-loss plans suggest putting food on a blue plate or placing a blue light in your fridge. That's because there aren't many blue foods in nature; therefore our appetites aren't triggered by the color.

Give in to Mini-Cravings

If you are dying for a fro-yo with toppings at 2 P.M. and deprive yourself all day, chances are you'll be diving into a pint of Ben & Jerry's come midnight. Also remember that when you're craving a giant piece of chocolate cake, all your body may truly want is a small piece of chocolate. So savor it. Love it. Chocolate even contains serotonin, which boosts your mood.

Sugar, Gluten, and Other Foods You've Been Wondering About

Sugar

I still love you, Sugar . . . but we may have to see less of each other for a while.

I tried. I really tried to find someone who would tell me that sugar wasn't that bad for you. After all, I *love* sugar. I mean, I grew up on a bowl of Froot Loops at breakfast, some Hostess cupcakes at lunch, and some M&M's at dinner. Sugar has never failed me. And now everyone wants to gang up on it? Well, I'm no fair-weather friend . . . And turns out it's in my DNA. Researchers have found two sweet-receptor genes that can predict a preference for sweets. So here's the deal . . . The bad news: The American Heart Association links added sugar to obesity, type II diabetes, and cardiovascular disease. The good news? Um, not as much as I had hoped. But like most things, in moderation, sugar is okay.

The American Heart Association recommends most women get no more than twenty-four grams of added sugar per day. That's about six teaspoons (hello, that's me before breakfast), or one hundred

MG TIP: Remember the "Rule of Two" when dining out: Pick your entrée and sides, then pair with two other things to eat or drink. This could mean two glasses of wine but skipping the bread basket, or opting for an appetizer and dessert and skipping everything else. Trust me, it's worth it. People following the Rule of Two end up eating 25 percent less on average.

calories. But the average American woman gets about eighteen teaspoons daily.

So what's so bad?

- Not only can sugar increase your overall risk for heart disease, but a 2013 study in the *Journal of the American Heart Association* gave evidence that sugar can hurt the pumping mechanism of your heart and increase your risk for heart failure.

- If the liver is full of glycogen, eating a lot of fructose overloads the liver, forcing it to turn the fructose into fat.

- Though I don't want to just blame sugar, people who drink sugar-sweetened beverages have up to an 83 percent higher risk of type II diabetes.

- There is some evidence that sugar, due to its harmful effects on metabolism, can contribute to cancer.

- The fact that sugar releases dopamine in the brain means it can cause addiction in a lot of people. In fact, I think I can honestly say I'm an addict.

- A 2009 study found a positive relationship between glucose consumption and cell aging. WHAAAT?? Seriously, sugar? Now you're giving me wrinkles? That's not cool. There's also evidence that sugar may affect the aging of your brain. A 2012 study showed excess sugar consumption was linked to deficiencies in memory. I think. I can't remember.

Some good news? Well, naturally occurring sugar—in fruit, some veggies, and milk—is healthy. *Yay!* It's sweeteners put in during processing that aren't so much. And it is almost impossible to get too much fructose by eating fruit.

Agave

Before you look for more "natural" solutions, beware . . . just because something looks and sounds like it belongs in Whole Foods doesn't mean it's necessarily the answer to your sweet prayers. Or as Cara Natterson, MD, pediatrician and bestselling author of numerous books, likes to say, "Just because it's natural doesn't mean it's good for you." Most agave is made from the blue agave plant, the same succulent used for making tequila. The good news is it is typically "natural," meaning that while some odors and flavors are removed, no colors or artificial flavorings are added. Agave syrup is about 25 percent sweeter than typical sweeteners, like honey and refined sugar, so you'll need less in your coffee. But with sixty calories per tablespoon, it has about 25 percent *more* calories than mainstream sweeteners (forty-five calories). So to get the same sweetness, you wind up with the same number of calories.

And while people say it's more healthful, about 70 to 85 percent of the sugar in agave syrup is fructose versus about 50 percent in refined sugar and high-fructose corn syrup. While fructose may have a low glycemic index, it still encourages weight gain and irregular blood sugar. Fructose *also* increases your "I'm hungry" hormone (ghrelin) and interferes with your body's ability to absorb blood sugar.

Stevia

So stevia is the darling of the sweetener market for the moment. Stevia has no calories, and it is two hundred times sweeter than sugar in the same concentration. Stevia is derived from a plant that grows in Paraguay and Brazil. There, people have used leaves from the stevia bush to sweeten food for hundreds of years. They've also used the stevia leaves in traditional medicine for burns, colic, and stomach problems, and even as a contraceptive. Though I wouldn't recommend using your stevia sweetener packets for any of these purposes, it's part of why there is a lot of buzz around the potential health benefits of stevia.

Aspartame

I have a lot of aspartame panic. I really do. In addition to my love of sugar, I also love diet soda. What is aspartame? Well, aspartame is one of the most common artificial sweeteners. It is sold under the brand Equal. Aspartame is made by joining together the amino acids aspartic acid and phenylalanine. I have tried to either ignore or find evidence against many of the articles about the dangers of aspartame that people have sent me. Here's the deal. If you go to the American Cancer Society website they say aspartame is safe and there are no links to cancer or health issues. But . . . an awful lot of companies seem to be getting out of the aspartame business. So you may just want to ask yourself if you might want to as well.

There are a zillion sites and people who will tell you that aspartame is evil and they had headaches, nausea, temporary blindness, or any number of issues from ingesting it. So here's my thought. If it freaks you out, there are enough other sweeteners that you don't have to have it. Right? So the choice at this point is really up to you.

High-Fructose Corn Syrup

In the great sweetener debate, high-fructose corn syrup is the Chris Brown of sweeteners: Nobody seems to have anything nice to say about it.

The biggest controversy is about how your body handles HFCS. And there is much controversy over that. Some studies show that with HFCS you can't satisfy your hunger (whereas with regular sugar you will), hence it contributes to your eating more. Other studies have shown that it contributes to obesity in rats far more than regular sugar. Whatever the case, it tends to be found in highly processed foods, and you might want to stay away from those either way.

Gluten

Nothing seems to make you look more in shape than spending the day running around in athletic wear (even if you're not exercising). And nothing makes you sound like you're eating healthy more than saying you're gluten-free. So why are we all giving up gluten, and should we be?

Fact is, experts estimate only about 1 percent of Americans have actual celiac disease, which is caused by an abnormal immune response to gluten and can damage the lining of the small intestine, which can prevent important nutrients from being absorbed. But if you don't have celiac disease, should you give up your gluten? Be careful, because a gluten-free diet can lack vitamins, minerals, and fiber (including B vitamins, calcium, iron, zinc, and magnesium). Though gluten itself doesn't offer that many special nutritional benefits, many of the whole grains that contain gluten do. And just because it's gluten-free doesn't mean it's healthy. Some gluten-free foods are high in saturated fat, calories, or cholesterol.

Five Foods That Might Be Secretly Making You Fat

Low-Fat Yogurt

The low-fat yogurt you pick up at the supermarket is typically highly processed and has artificial sweetener, high-fructose corn syrup, and sugar—ingredients that make you gain weight rather than lose it. Plus, it's not fat that makes you fat; it's sugar.

Whole Wheat Bread

Sure, it sounds healthy, but according to the watchdog group the Center for Science in the Public Interest, the label is just a marketing ploy. Half of the products marketed as whole wheat bread have enriched flour as their second ingredient. And as we MGs know, enriched flour contains no nutritional value and lots of sugar!

Diet Sodas

This just bummed me out. But diet soft drinks contain aspartame, and according to a journal published by the U.S. National Library of Medicine at the National Institutes of Health, aspartame boosts your appetite. Sigh. Well, back to water.

Dried Fruit

As someone who can eat an entire bag of dried mangoes in one sitting, I was not so happy to learn that even though dried fruits are good for you, you may be consuming far more than you thought, as they are more concentrated in calories and carbohydrates. Plus, according to the Mayo Clinic, the 250 calories you get from eating them on a daily basis can result in a two-pound weight gain in two months. It's not that dried fruit is worse than other foods (it may be better, yay!) it's just that, like any food, you need to be careful about portion control.

Turkey

I love me some turkey, but while it's a good source of protein, the packaged turkey slices sold in grocery stores often have a ton of sodium! In some brands, a mere two-ounce serving can have around two-thirds of your recommended daily dose of sodium.

Vitamins That Keep You Gorgeous

They say the best way to get your vitamins is through the nutrients in your food, but let's face it: Some days subsist of pizza and Starbucks. That's why a multivitamin has you covered. When choosing, look for one that provides 100 percent of the Recommended Daily Allowance (RDA) of these vitamins and minerals:*

- Vitamin A
- Vitamin B
- Vitamin B_2
- Niacin (Vitamin B_3)
- Vitamin B_{12}
- Vitamin C
- Vitamin D
- Vitamin E
- Copper
- Chromium
- Iron
- Selenium
- Zinc

---

*Please note: I'm a Modern Girl, not a doctor; and it's always best to check with a professional before starting any supplements.

But even with a multivitamin, you still may have deficiencies that need to be addressed. You should talk to your doctor about taking a supplement if . . .

You Bruise Often

If you're prone to bruising, with your doctor's okay, take the mineral zinc (in tablet form), which is vital to wound healing and immune system function. Also rub in a dollop of cream fortified with vitamin C or vitamin K.

You Want Better Skin

Take vitamin A, or include more of these skin-boosting foods in your diet: carrots, citrus fruits, sweet potatoes, winter squash, broccoli, spinach, and kale. Also, the omega-3 fatty acids in fish such as salmon and mackerel add luster to your skin. Hazelnuts and almonds will improve your skin as well—they're packed with vitamin E.

MG TIP: Though chocolate and potato chips actually don't worsen your skin, shellfish such as shrimp might. Their high iodine content can contribute to breakouts in some people.

Your Nails Peel and Split and Your Hair Is Brittle

Talk to your dermatologist about taking the B vitamin biotin. The most concentrated food sources of biotin include liver, egg yolk, soy flour, cereals, and yeast. Salmon and leafy greens are also a good source of B vitamins.

You're Anemic or Energy-Depleted

Iron keeps red blood cells healthy, but since women lose about 15 to 20 milligrams of iron each month during their period, their levels can dip, which can lead to fatigue, lethargy, and other more serious problems. Your doctor may prescribe an iron supplement to take regularly to combat anemia—but don't diagnose yourself and just start popping iron pills because you're feeling tired and bleed heavily during your period.

Why? Because too much iron can keep your body from absorbing calcium and zinc, and possibly lead to other problems, so speak to your health care professional if you're thinking about taking an iron supplement for the long term.

According to the Harvard Medical Institute, food is the best way to boost your iron intake because it's easier for the body to absorb iron from food than from pills. Meat and fish are good sources of iron, as are leafy green vegetables, beans, dried fruits, prune juice, nuts, and whole grains. Iron is absorbed better with vitamin C, so try to eat them at the same time. For example, eat orange segments in your spinach salad, or tomatoes with red meat. Steer clear of tea and coffee; they limit the absorption of iron.

You Frequently Get Colds

Consider taking 100 to 500 milligrams extra of vitamin C. Some multivitamins contain extra C, but if yours doesn't, you may need a separate supplement. Check with your doctor.

MG TIP: If you don't get enough vitamin D, the calcium you're taking doesn't get absorbed in your body. We get vitamin D naturally from spending time in the sunlight, but that often isn't enough, especially during winter. Compensate with a supplement.

You Get Mega-PMS

It's not all in your head—those crazy mood swings are caused by interaction between your brain's neurotransmitters and sex hormones. Besides making sure that you meet your requirements for vitamins E, B_6, zinc, and magnesium, load up on calcium. Doctors say that 1,000 milligrams of calcium a day (equivalent to four glasses of milk) can help alleviate mood swings, tension headaches, and cramping. Low-fat dairy foods, salmon, tofu, broccoli, peas, and beans are good sources of calcium.

You Like to Drink Red Wine

Take folate. Though moderate amounts of red vino prove beneficial, just one drink a day can reduce the amount of folate in your body. Too-low folate levels have been associated with breast and colon cancer.

You're Pregnant

Again, folate's your supplement *du jour*. If you think you might become pregnant at any point in your life, you need folate (400 milligrams daily; 600 during pregnancy). It can vastly reduce your risk of giving birth to a child with certain spinal and neurological defects. You'll also find folate in many fortified cereals, citrus fruits, liver, collard greens, dried beans, and peas.

You're on the Pill

If you take birth control pills, you could be deficient in vitamins B_6, C, folic acid, and calcium. Luckily, a multivitamin will usually make up for the pill's interference.

You're a Vegan

If you're a strict vegan, you risk having deficiencies in calcium, iron, zinc, vitamin D, and the B vitamins, especially B_{12}. B vitamins help to convert carbohydrates into usable energy.

You Frequently Get UTIs

If you're prone to urinary tract infections, drink plenty of water and take vitamin C and cranberry-concentrate pills. A common dose is between one and six 300- to 400-milligram capsules twice daily by mouth taken with water one hour before or two hours after meals. They are more effective than cranberry juice, which contains a lot of sugar—an ingredient that might inhibit the effectiveness of curing UTI symptoms. Also, the single easiest way to avoid a UTI is always to urinate immediately after sex.

You Get Constipated

With high-protein diets all the rage, sometimes it is a little hard to be regular no matter how many salads you're eating. Try taking two 1,000-milligram capsules of omega 3 (sometimes referred to as fish oil or salmon oil) before you go to bed and you should be moving just fine in the morning.

You Love Sushi or Foods with Tons of Salt

I adore sushi, but I hate that bloated feeling I get the next morning thanks to all the soy sauce I dipped my spicy tuna rolls in. To avoid the bloat, I pop two B_6 tablets before I go to bed. I may get up one extra time in the night to pee, but I feel much better in the A.M., since B_6 helps stop the retention of water.

MG TIP: Beware of too much vitamin A intake when you're pregnant. Getting enough vitamin A (5,000 IU) early in pregnancy is critical for a baby's development. But more than 10,000 IU can be harmful.

MG TIP: If vitamins make you nauseous, taking them before bed can help out.

Vitamin-Taking Tips

- In general, the best time to take vitamins is in the morning, with food and plenty of water. When your digestion is most active, there is the opportunity for maximum absorption, and there is less chance they will hurt your tummy. But check the back of the bottle to make sure the effectiveness won't be diminished by certain foods or supplements.

- Don't buy vitamins in bulk—they will expire and lose all effectiveness by the time you use them all.

- Your vitamin should disintegrate quickly and completely dissolve. "Time release" vitamins, though they sound good, can actually inhibit the absorption of folate, so skip 'em.

- Don't overdose on vitamins; more isn't necessarily better. Excess vitamin C will simply pass through your system, but other vitamins taken in high doses can be toxic.

- Don't store vitamins in the fridge—they can lose their effectiveness. Keep them in a cool, dark space in your cupboard or pantry.

Home Remedies That Really Work

Some feel-good ingredients don't have to come from the drugstore. In fact, they can all be found in your fridge or pantry right this second. Sure, you probably rolled your eyes when you mom told you to eat chicken soup when you were sick, but the truth is, these concoctions really have positive effects:

Yogurt

Eating yogurt with active cultures of L. acidophilus can help prevent yeast infections. Make sure, however, that the yogurt has active cultures and is not pasteurized. You can find this yogurt in health food stores and large grocery stores.

Aspirin

You know it works for headaches, but it also softens calluses on your feet. Crush five or six pills and mix in a bowl with a half teaspoon water and a half teaspoon lemon juice. Coat your calluses with the mixture and cover with a warm cloth for ten minutes. The solution will soften the callus and make it easier to remove with a pumice stone.

Garlic

Garlic can kill the viruses and bacteria responsible for colds and flu. Chop it up and put it in stir-fries and pasta.

Hot Sauce

Feel a cold coming on? Spicy sauce and hot mustard act like expectorants. Eating spicy foods regularly helps thin out secretions of colds and allergies. It also can boost your metabolism.

Milk and Honey

Pour a mixture of a half-cup liquid honey and three cups powdered milk in a bath for a soothing soak.

Oatmeal

Mix up a half packet (or one-half cup) instant oatmeal with hot water, let it cool slightly, and spread over your face. It will act as both a skin soother and a mild exfoliant. Leave on for ten minutes and rinse with cool water.

Eggs

Whip up one egg white and spread it over your face for a firming mask that combats oily skin (add a few drops of lemon juice to beat blackheads). If you have dry skin, use an egg yolk instead, and add a teaspoon of honey. Let it sit for ten minutes and rinse with cool water.

Mayonnaise

I never eat it, but it's a fabulous deep-conditioning treatment for your hair. Coat your strands with it, cover your hair with a plastic shower cap, and let it sit for 15 minutes. Rinse with warm water.

Exercise Tips . . . When All You Want to Do Is Channel Surf

Looking good and feeling fantastic can't come from food and vitamins alone. (Damn.) But if you look at exercise as a drag, consider this: Scientists (and Elle Woods) believe that the endorphin rush you get from exercise hikes up your mood. Running and aerobic exercise can help combat everything from PMS, stress, and depression to morning sickness during pregnancy. Here are some sneaky strategies to actually get you excited about working out:

Mix Up Your Menu

Let's be honest here: Half the reason we don't like to exercise is that it gets boring. This is why you shouldn't expect yourself to go on the same run or do the same elliptical workout every single day. Plus, studies show that mixing things up actually tones your body better than working the same muscles in the same way every day. Thankfully we live in an era where new exercises are abundant! Try hot yoga one day and do a YouTube-led ten-minute abs video the next. Throw in a spin or barre class here and there. Increasingly you'll find more local run clubs and boot camps. Consider checking one out—you'll not only get a workout, you might meet some new friends. The more diversity you give yourself, the more likely you'll see exercise as a fun release, not a chore

Tone Up in Front of the TV

Sometimes you just can't get to the gym to pump iron. But you can still do some fast exercises at home while you're watching *Scandal* or *Game of Thrones* (c'mon, is it that much worse than parking your butt on the sofa?). Throw down a towel, and do these three calorie-torching workouts three times a week. Don't get fancy, don't expect daily vigilance, just do them when you're watching a ridiculously thin actress pretend to eat and you'll find there's nothing more motivating than noticing little definition marks forming in your arms, and dropping a little junk in your trunk.

WHICH WORKOUT WORKS?

Here's some advice on finding a fitness regime that works for you from Amanda Freeman, exercise guru, CEO and founder of SLT, one of the hottest fitness trends on the East Coast: "I recommend trying out a few workouts, classes, or pieces of equipment that have some appeal to you. Once you find one or two you like, put them in frequent rotation (say two or three times a week). But also make time to try other things that might help to keep it fresh and confuse your muscles. I also recommend making workout plans with friends. You'll be much less likely to flake on a workout if it also means bailing on a friend . . . or client. You should also make realistic goals for yourself and stick with them or penalize yourself when you slack. Maybe every time you skip a workout, you have to donate twenty-five dollars to charity."

And as for picking cardio vs. toning, seems that's the Sophie's choice of exercise. According to Amanda, "Both are important! It's ideal to incorporate a mix of the two workout types into your regimen. That can be done within a single workout or you can alternate days (cardio on Monday, toning on Tuesday, etc.). While cardio burns more calories per minute, toning (or strength training) workouts increase your metabolic rate for hours after your workout, leading to continued calorie burn throughout the day."

And of course, one other tip is that just looking good might help you to, well, keep looking good. Gabby Etrog Cohen, the VP of PR and marketing for my other go-to exercise of choice, SoulCycle, says, "Frankly, for me it is more about how you feel. If you feel good in your exercise clothes, then you actually want to exercise! I invest in my workout gear because if I feel great, I am even more excited (and incentivized) to exercise."

• **Butt Boosters:** Get on all fours and extend one leg back. Keep it straight out behind you. Lift just a little higher and a little lower than your butt. It's the mini-motions that will help melt the fat. Switch legs and repeat. Try to set your own pace, working up to four sets of twenty reps on each side. Next, bring your knee down and do thrusts into the air, with your toe pointed. Don't bring your knee all the way down to the floor; just pull it down a few inches and then thrust it higher. Switch legs and repeat. When you feel your lower cheeks burning, you know you've done enough.

• **Ab Strengthener:** This Pilates-based move called the Roll Back* will give you an all-over tummy-smoothing effect. Sit in an upright position with your knees bent and your feet together, so your legs create an upside-down "V" with the floor. For support, grip the backs of your legs where your thigh meets your knee with your hands. Lengthen your back as much as possible, and "scoop" your abs in by squeezing your butt muscles inward and upward. Now inhale slowly and begin rolling back so your back makes a forty-five-degree angle with the floor. Hold the position for a few seconds as you slowly exhale. Now inhale and begin rolling up to the upright position. Start with ten roll backs, and work up to two reps of ten.

• **Tricep Toner:** If, like me, you're worried about having a little jiggle underneath your upper arms, this move will turn them from cottage cheese to solid marble. Move your coffee table out of the way, face away from the sofa, and position the palms of your hands at the edge of the sofa. With your butt at a forty-five-degree angle off the floor, your knees bent, and your feet out in front of you, slowly lower yourself toward the floor. Go down almost until your butt touches, and then bring yourself up again, using only your arms to support your body weight. Start out doing two reps of twenty, and work your way up to three reps of ten.

---

*Move courtesy of Brooke Siler, author of *The Pilates Body*.

The MG's Definitive Workout Guide

Frequent exercise keeps Modern Girls physically and mentally fit, but I'm the first one to admit that you can only force yourself on the treadmill so many times. These days, I prefer to take a variety of different workout classes so I can mix things up and make sure my muscles are always challenged. The best part is that many classes are offered at independent studios, meaning you won't need to spend big bucks on a monthly gym membership to feel the burn.

Barre

While this is a ballet-based workout, you don't have to be a prima ballerina (or even *that* coordinated) to get benefits from a barre class. Typically lasting about an hour, the classes are a mishmash of workouts that will leave your arms, core, butt, back, and legs (are there any other body parts?) burning. As far as results go, expect a longer, leaner figure, as the high-repetition, low-weight exercises will build strength and skip the bulk. There are a few basic moves you need to know, so be sure to hit up a beginner's class before joining the big leagues.

    Good for: Building a long and lean bod

    Average calorie burn: 400–500 calories per hour

Spin Class

Get ready to leave it all on the bike when you enter a spin class. These high-intensity workouts will leave you with a red face, sweaty bod, and huge sense of accomplishment. Typically lasting forty-five minutes to an hour, a spin class will guide you through a number of intervals on a spin bike set to heart-pumping Top 40 jams. Right now I'm addicted to SoulCycle, where they add in a quick weight session on the bike, which not only tones your arms but also gives you a moment to catch your breath mid-workout.

    Good for: A heavy sweat

    Average calorie burn: 500–750 calories for a 45-minute class

Yoga

There are a number of different options when it comes to yoga and each will offer its own set of benefits. If you're looking to chill out, opt

MG TIP: Lululemon offers great yoga, spinning, and fitness classes for free throughout each month. Check them out as a way to experiment with your workout.

for yin or hatha yoga, which focus on breathing through long poses. On the other hand, vinyasa flow and power yoga will keep you moving through a series of poses, thus amping up the energy. If you're willing to brave the heat (105 degrees and up), Bikram yoga will push you to your limits and leave you super sweaty.

Good for: Balancing both mind and body

Average calorie burn: 175–630 calories per hour

Zumba

Known for its "fitness party" vibe, Zumba is a high-energy dance class that dishes a full-body workout with no fancy footwork required. Typically dances are set to Latin beats, so be prepared to move those hips while blasting away calories. The Zumba brand offers a number of different classes, from Zumba Toning to Aqua Zumba, meaning no matter your mood there's a Zumba for you!

Good for: People looking for a nonworkout workout

Average calorie burn: 350–650 calories per hour

CrossFit

If you like to max out and are looking to build muscle, CrossFit may be for you. This fitness phenomenon has gained steam in recent years thanks to its nontraditional exercises and tight-knit community. In place of treadmills and weight machines, at a CrossFit gym you'll find five-hundred-pound boxes, plyo boxes, and dumbbells that enable the functional fitness workouts at the core of CrossFit. There are some risks associated with CrossFit, as people in the midst of the "go hard" mentality can push it too far, leading to injury and sometimes rhabdomyolysis (a terrifying syndrome where your muscle cells explode!).

Good for: Building muscle and making friends

Average calorie burn: Varies depending on workouts

Power Pilates/SLT

To call this Pilates would be a misnomer, but it is based on the premise of strengthening the core of your body through Pilates principles. This fast-paced workout functions off of a "mega machine" that allows you to work and strengthen, lengthen, and tone (SLT—get it?)

your entire body. It's one of the best workouts I've found for men and women who are looking to get lean but build strength without having to bother with dance moves.

Good for: Strengthening, lengthening, and toning

Average calorie burn: Varies depending on workouts

Modern Girls Should Exercise Their Brains Too

To say meditation is a trend is a little bit demeaning. After all, whole continents of people have been practicing meditation for thousands of years. But while I used to believe that exercising would calm my mind far more than meditating, I've come to realize that the two pursuits really aren't equal. So I talked to Suze Yalof Schwartz, the founder of Unplug Meditation, an innovative and rapidly growing center for drop-in guided meditation in L.A. helping to spread the meditation word one person at a time.

According to Suze, the three reasons people say they are hesitant to meditate are:

1. They are afraid they won't be able to stop thinking.

2. They don't have time.

3. They can't sit still.

But I'll add a fourth. I'm achievement oriented. And to me, well, meditating just seemed like . . . um . . . okay . . . I'll say it . . . a waste of time. I know. I'm a terrible person.

Well . . . according to Suze:

1. **You _don't_ have to stop thinking.** Hmmm . . . Of course you are going to be thinking . . . it's all about not judging your thoughts and then bringing them back to your focus point.

2. **You can meditate in ten minutes or even one minute; just connecting with your breath is meditation.** Fine, I will sacrifice one checking of Instagram.

3. **You don't have to sit entirely still.** Really? Okay. I'm in . . . sort of . . .

4. **You actually achieve something!** Suze explained that meditating is actually partly about exercising your brain. You are training your prefrontal cortex—which helps you to be more logical and less emotional. So when you meditate you are not just being all spiritual and mindful, you are getting better at *thinking*! As Suze put it, meditating teaches you how to deal with your thoughts and access your inner pause button. So before you send an angry e-mail or lash out at a boyfriend, your ability to calm your brain may come in handy. Call me crazy, but suddenly meditating makes sense. And I should try to get *good* at it.

Plus there are all kinds of benefits, such as:
    Reduced blood pressure
    Reduced overeating
    Reduced sensitivity to pain
    Lowered risk of heart attack and stroke
    Decreased stress and anxiety
    Decreased loneliness in older adults
    Increased awareness
    Better sleep
    Improved grades
    Improved memory
    Improved productivity
    Increased brain growth
    Improved mood

I'm sold. So then the question is, how do you do it? So here I turned to my brother, who, rather handily, has been a practicing Buddhist his whole life and has written two bestsellers on the subject. But while he's my little brother and I can't really take him seriously, that doesn't mean you shouldn't, so here's meditation according to Lodro Rinzler, Shambhala Buddhist teacher and author of the bestselling book *The Buddha Walks into a Bar*:

The Four Steps to Meditation

1. *Take a dignified but relaxed posture.* When you sit down to meditate, you want to feel balanced and grounded. Before you sit on your cushion or chair, take a few deep breaths or take a moment to stretch your body, so you are relaxed as you enter the practice. If you're on a pillow or cushion, sit in the center with your legs loosely crossed. If you're on a chair, place your feet firmly on the ground, hips-width apart. From that strong base, stretch your body upward. If it's helpful, imagine a string at the top of your head pulling you straight up, elongating the spine. You don't need to tighten the muscles in your back or shoulders; just relax with your natural skeletal curvature.

Your head sits at the top of your spine, with your chin slightly tucked in. Relax the muscles in your face. Your jaw can hang open, with your tongue against the roof of your mouth. You can close your eyes if you like but I recommend you let your gaze rest in a loose and unfocused manner about four feet ahead of you on the ground. You want to simultaneously feel uplifted but grounded when you sit down to meditate.

2. *Connect with the breath.* Having made a connection with your body, turn your full attention to the act of breathing. You don't need to alter your breath at all; just allow it to flow as it normally does. The only difference between now and the rest of your day is that you are tuning in to this natural act. The breath is always fresh, it's always what's going on right now, so it's an excellent anchor to the present moment. The more you can be present with something as simple as the breath, the more you can be present with all of the pleasurable and painful aspects of the rest of your life.

3. *Stay in the present.* Everyone has trouble just staying present with the breath. When you get lost in thought, either reliving something from the past or planning for the future, you can gently and silently say, "Thinking," to yourself. Use that word to propel yourself back to the present moment and the breath. Thoughts are not good or bad here, but the goal is to come back to the present moment.

4. *Repeat.* Meditation is hard! If it was easy everyone would do it. The good news is that it does have a major payoff in terms of allowing you to be more in the moment and live a kinder and more compassionate existence. It's said that any new habit gets easier to follow if you do it for eleven days in a row, so I recommend you try meditation for ten minutes a day for that long and see if it works for you.

MG TIP: After you've washed your workout clothes and they're almost dry, soak them in one part vinegar, four parts water for twenty minutes to kill the last of the bacteria. This will eliminate the sweaty smell and make them last longer.

Getting the Right Gear

With the rise in fashionable fitness apparel, one of the best parts of working out today is shopping for the gear. That said, it's easy to drop a pretty penny, so follow these guidelines to make sure you're getting the right gear:

- Skip the baggy shorts and promo T-shirts. Not only will they slow you down (aerodynamics, anyone?), they will also make it harder for your instructor to spot essential alignment adjustments. Instead opt for stretchy, moisture-wicking, and breathable fabrics that will keep you cool and dry during sweaty situations.

- Whenever possible, try on workout clothing in the store, for a couple of reasons: First, sizing varies drastically from brand to brand, meaning you might be a small at Gap and an 8 at Lululemon. Second, the staff at the store can typically direct you to the most popular and flattering pieces that will be best for your body.

- If the staff isn't particularly helpful that day, pay attention to the seams: Look for seaming in pants and shorts that wraps around the sides of your booty, and look for tops with seams that curve inward.

- As with any outfit, black will be the most flattering, but if you're against the ninja look, opt for a piece with a pop of color or a patch of print.

GET THE RIGHT ATHLETIC SHOES

Sometimes all you need to kick-start an exercise regime is great gear. If you're working out frequently, top-of-the-line sneakers are a smart investment. Old, worn-out trainers can lead to blisters, muscle strain, sprains, and micro-tears in your foot tissue—so it's key to buy often and buy right.

• *Measure your feet.* It's very common for women to have one foot a half-size bigger than the other. When you buy shoes, judge the fit by your "big" foot. You want room in the toe with athletic shoes, enough to fit your thumb. As you move around from side to side, you'll need that extra bit of space. Also, keep in mind that your feet swell when you work out, so always err on the larger side.

• *Invest in running shoes* if you run more than two miles at a time. Replace them every four hundred miles, or after six to nine months.

• *Go for a cross-trainer* if you like to mix up your workouts between the treadmill and weight lifting.

• *If you're a tennis player*, you need more lateral stability than you do if you're just running. Be sure to buy shoes that are heavier and more rigid. All tennis shoes have light-colored, non-marking soles to keep the court scuff-free.

• *Get ankle support.* If you have weak ankles, a midheight shoe will give them more support, which means less chance of twisting them.

• *Buy two pairs of the same shoes* and rotate them every few workouts—it sounds like a splurge but will actually save you money overall. And don't forget sports socks for cushioning and support.

MG TIP: Think getting the perfect sneaks isn't worth it? Well, every step you take puts three times your body weight on each foot.

Prepare Yourself for Quality ZZZ's

Looking great starts and ends with good sleep. And after a long hard workout (or heck, just a day running around like a crazy woman at the office), an MG deserves to unwind. But I'm often so frazzled at the end of the day that I can't shut my mind off come 10 P.M.—whereas annoyingly, my husband seems to nod off anywhere, from airplanes to shopping malls. Though I know I'll never be as snoozable as he is, I've used these tricks, and they work:

- Start dimming the lights a few hours before bedtime. Putting yourself in a darker atmosphere will help increase your natural melatonin levels, preparing you for sleep.

- Put down the phone, stow the laptop, and stop checking e-mails. At first you'll have a little separation anxiety, but trust me, it will be worth it!

- Don't watch Fallon, hoping he'll put you to sleep. You might think that dozing off to TV is the answer, but putting on soft music before bed will give you a more restful snooze.

- Light some candles and take a soothing bath with a few drops of lavender essential oil. Lavender is scientifically proven to help induce sleep and relaxation. If you love bubbles, try Origin's Float Away Sleep-Inspiring Milk Bath. Soak for ten to fifteen minutes.

- After your bath, slather on some self Sanctuary Body Butter by Mark, then drink a cup of chamomile tea or warm milk with honey. If you're still a little wired, have a couple of crackers. The carbs in them will boost your serotonin level and stimulate sleep.

- Once you're in bed, don't let your mind drift to the laundry list of things you didn't accomplish today, or tasks you need to get done tomorrow. An MG's precious brain and body need to mellow the hell out. Instead, slowly pay attention to your breath, in and out, feeling yourself sinking deeper and deeper into your bed like it's one giant marshmallow. If that doesn't work, start dreaming about the next pair of Louboutins you're dying to buy. One Louboutin went over the moon, two Louboutins, three . . . zzzzz.

HAVING TROUBLE SLEEPING?   zzz....

Caffeine may be part of the problem. Absorption of caffeine is rapid. About fifteen minutes after you take your first few sips, your heart rate increases by at least 10 percent and it takes thirty minutes for you to feel its full effects. And it will be another three hours before you're back to square one. Although everyone has a different reaction, 200 milligrams is a strong stimulant for most people. While you know if you need to stay away from coffee (the average cup has 135 milligrams of caffeine), be aware of other places caffeine may be lurking in your diet:

- Tea has almost half the caffeine in coffee.

- Soda can have up to 55 milligrams.

- Coffee-flavored yogurt and ice cream can have caffeine (35 to 75 milligrams).

- Chocolate: Milk chocolate has 3 to 10 milligrams of caffeine per 1.4-ounce serving; dark chocolate has 28 milligrams.

- Nutritional drinks like Boost (5 milligrams) and Ensure (10 milligrams) have smaller but relevant amounts of caffeine.

- Medications such as Excedrin (130 milligrams), and Dristan (30 milligrams) might not only make you feel better, but might also keep you awake.

Feeling Fabulous for the Long Haul

Some would say that your twenties are your throwaway years before settling down and getting serious about your career. And while I understand how that's certainly the case for some, I found them to be a time of truly getting to know myself and what I wanted for my life. It's inevitable that we will make mistakes and sometimes have regrets as we grow, so I created a list of the things I wish I had known during my twenties in hopes that these won't make it onto your list.

Twenty Regrets from My Twenties

20. Sporting a muffin top and a bare midriff
19. Skimping on sunscreen
18. Using the excuse "It feels better without a condom"
17. Not starting to invest, even a little bit
16. Forgetting to pay the bills (hello, bad credit!)
15. Spending too much time looking at screens
14. Flaking on friends at the last minute for no reason
13. Being too scared to move to a new place
12. Forgetting to be grateful
11. Trying to be everyone's best friend
10. Not taking care of my body . . .
9. But worrying about my weight
8. Being afraid to say no
7. Staying in the wrong relationship
6. Not reaching out to friends in need
5. Holding grudges
4. Not traveling when I had the chance
3. Spending too much time worrying about the future instead of sitting down and setting goals
2. Giving up too quickly
1. Worrying too much about what other people thought

CHAPTER 6

Bond, Jane Bond

I'll admit it, I like having the door held open for me by a man as much as the next girl (although somehow it irks me when my man holds the door *for* the next girl). But the real reason I feel comfortable playing the doted-on female is because I like that little bit of dying chivalry, not because I depend on it or need it in any way. In a pinch, I could do just about anything that a man can do—from using a power drill to changing a tire to drafting a fantasy football team.

Truth be told, my quest to acquire those skills normally reserved for the testosterone set started (dare I admit it?) because I wanted to impress a man. He was a scotch drinker, and I figured one of the best ways to cover up my girlie-girl nature was to show him I could be the cool girlfriend and hang out like a guy friend. I downed two scotches (simply nodding at the first one the bartender suggested), puffed twice on a cigar (and, mind you, I won't even smoke cigarettes), and quietly excused myself to go to the bathroom, where I promptly threw up the dinner I had insisted we split the bill for. Lying (alone) in bed that night I vowed, like Scarlett O'Hara, not only never to go hungry again, but never to pretend to be like a man. Instead, I'd learn the things men know to make me a better woman.

Sports Basics for Bombshells

Every MG should have a little knowledge of the rough-and-tumble sports in her repertoire. It's not just knowing how to talk the talk when your man's friends are coming over for Super Bowl Sunday. More and more, corporate events (that you're running, of course, CEO diva that you may be) are centered around sports. And at the very least, Leo DiCaprio might invite you to a Lakers game. Here's a mini-view of several major professional sports, including a history of the game, the basic rules, the players you should know, and a little trivia that will wow even a cynical "Oh, chicks don't know football from fencing!" sports fanatic at your next corporate event or party.

Basketball

Basketball season is October through June (when the NBA Championship is played, it's referred to as the postseason). The games are fast-paced, with a set time limit, and the rules of basketball are a cinch to understand. Games average two and a half hours in length.

MG TIP: The Boston Celtics have won the most NBA championships (sixteen), including eight straight, from 1959 through 1966.

Teams

There are currently thirty NBA teams, split into two leagues, the Eastern Conference and the Western Conference, each with two divisions. If you know geography at all, you should be able to guess what conference your team is in. These leagues vie each year to win the championship.

Basics of the Game

Professional basketball is played on a ninety-four-foot-long court with a ten-foot-high basket ("hoop") at either end. Two teams play a total of four 12-minute quarters. The object of the game is simply to have more points than the other team when the time is up.

The team with possession of the ball (offense) attempts to advance the ball near the defending team's hoop and score points by shooting the ball in that hoop. Players move the ball by passing and dribbling but may not run with it (called traveling).

Meanwhile, the team without possession of the ball (defense) is attempting to prevent the offense from scoring in their hoop. Each field goal, or basket, scores two points, or three points if shot from beyond a specified distance (slightly longer than twenty feet from the hoop—there's a big horseshoelike ring on the court that marks the three-point line).

Players

Each team has a full roster of twelve players with five on the court at any given time. Most NBA teams use the following positions in their lineup:

- *The center:* He's usually the tallest player on the court (think the seven-foot-tall Shaquille O'Neal). The center generally stays close to the hoop for rebounding, blocking, or altering shots, and easy dunks.

- *The power forward:* He's usually tall (six foot eight inches or so) and is used for rebounding and shooting close to the hoop (think LeBron James).

- *The small forward:* He does a little bit of everything—he passes, he dribbles, and he shoots (think Larry Bird).

- *The shooting guard:* He's the best shooter on the team (think Dwyane Wade)—he's the one who goes for the long-range three-pointers.

- *The point guard:* He's seen as the team leader (think Chris Paul); he dribbles and passes the ball more than any other player. The point guard tries to set up his teammates for close-range baskets.

Basketball Terms Every MG Should Know

- *Air ball:* A shot that completely misses the rim and the backboard.

- *Assist:* A pass to a teammate who then scores a field goal.

- *Brick:* An unsuccessful and ugly shot—as in, "Man, Shaq's laying bricks up there."

- *Dunk:* To throw the ball down into the basket with the hand above the level of the rim.

- *Hook shot:* A one-handed shot where the player arcs the ball over the head of the opponents.

- *Lay-up:* A shot made by driving as close to the basket as possible, then bouncing the ball off the backboard into the hoop.

- *Nothing but net:* A shot that goes into the basket touching neither the rim nor the backboard (aka "swish").

- *Rebound:* When a shot is made toward the basket that doesn't go in, and members of both teams scramble to get it.

- *Turnover:* Any loss of the ball without a shot being taken.

Major League Baseball

MLB is played from early April until October (when the World Series takes place). Unlike basketball, there is no time limit in baseball. If they're tied after nine innings, the teams will just keep on playing extra innings until one team wins. So theoretically, a game could last forever (yeah yeah, I know, ugh. But just think: You have *that* much more time to ogle Matt Kemp in his tight white pants).

On average, however, games are completed in just two and a half hours, so if you go to a 7:05 P.M. game, you'll get out just in time to make your 10 P.M. reservation at the trendy new restaurant in town—if you have room after all those peanuts and beer. At the end of the nine innings, the team with the most runs wins. The home team always bats last (called "last licks").

Teams

There are currently thirty Major League Baseball teams split into two leagues, the American and the National, that vie each year to win their league's pennant and eventually the World Series. The only difference is that the American League has a designated hitter who bats for the pitcher.

MG TIP: The New York Yankees have won the most World Series championships of any baseball team in history, with twenty-seven to date.

Basics of the Game

A baseball game is divided into nine periods of play, called innings. Innings are divided into two halves, referred to as the "top" and "bottom" of the inning. During the top of an inning, the visiting team is at bat while the home team is in the field. After the first team at bat has three outs, the two teams switch roles, and the bottom of an inning begins. If the game is tied after nine innings, the teams continue to play until one has scored more runs at the end of an extra inning.

Players

A baseball team fields nine players but can have as many as sixteen more guys waiting on the bench in the dugout, making it a grand total of twenty-five guys.

- *Batter:* The batter tries to hit the ball as far as possible, to get a run. After he hits the ball, he tries to get to first (single), second (double), or third base (triple), before the opposing team gets the ball back to where he is. If he makes his way around all of the bases, he has hit a home run.

- *Pitcher:* The pitcher throws the ball for the batter to hit. Top pitchers like strike-out machine Clayton Kershaw or Cliff Lee can throw the ball as fast as 100 mph, and are attempting to prevent the opposing team from getting any hits or scoring any runs.

- *Catcher:* The catcher (think Buster Posey or Yadier Molina) works directly with the pitcher in an attempt to strike out the batter.

The catcher makes a lot of the decisions about what kind of ball the pitcher will throw—a fast ball, a curve ball, a slider, and so on.

- *Infielder:* Includes the first, second, and third basemen, and the shortstop, who plays between second and third base.

- *Outfielder:* There are three outfielders: left field, right field, and center field. Yasiel Puig and Mike Trout are famous outfielders.

- *Umpire:* He crouches or stands behind the catcher and calls balls and strikes on the pitcher. He works for neither team.

Baseball Terms Every MG Should Know

- *Bases drunk:* Bases are loaded (i.e., when there is a player on first, second, and third base, with a hitter at bat).

- *Base hit:* When the batter hits the ball and reaches first base safely.

- *Bunt:* When a batter hits a baby hit on purpose by turning the bat sideways and grabbing both ends with his hands.

- *Double:* When the batter makes it safely to second base, usually by making a strong hit to the outfield.

- *Triple:* When the batter makes it all the way to third base.

- *Home run:* When the batter hits the ball (usually over the fence) and gets to home plate. This scores one run if there are no other teammates on base. If there is one runner on base, it scores two runs, and so on.

- *Grand slam:* When a hitter hits a home run with the bases loaded. His team gets four runs.

- *Walk:* When a pitcher throws four balls to the batter that are deemed out of the strike zone (i.e., unhittable) by the umpire and the batter gets a free pass to walk to first base.

Football

Ah yes, good old pigskin (and grunting and butt-slapping). Football is played September through January, and culminates in the Super Bowl, played in late January or early February. Like basketball, there is a time limit in football. The game spans four 15-minute quarters. At the end of the four quarters, the team with the most points wins. Don't get too excited, though; it doesn't mean the game lasts an hour. There are tons of time-outs, and the average football game lasts three hours. If the two teams are tied at the end of the fourth quarter, there will be one "sudden death" fifteen-minute overtime. Sudden death means the first team to score wins. If no team scores, it's a tie (unless it's the playoffs, in which case they keep playing until a team scores).

Teams

There are currently thirty-two National Football League (NFL) teams split into two leagues (the American Football Conference and the National Football Conference—the NFC is older, but there is little difference between the two) that vie each year to win the coveted opportunity to play in the Super Bowl championship game.

MG TIP: The Pittsburgh Steelers have won the most Super Bowl championships, with six to date.

Basics of the Game

Offense
The basic offensive object of the game is to either carry or pass the football across your opponent's goal line (aka the end zone). A touchdown earns six points, plus an extra point by doing a short-range kick through the goalposts, or an extra two points if the offense passes or runs the ball back over the end zone from two yards. A team has to advance at least ten yards in four plays, called downs (first down, second down, and so on). If it doesn't, it must punt (i.e., kick) the ball to the other team. If it looks like the team isn't going to make the correct yardage by the fourth down, but they're within kicking range of the opponent's goalposts, the team will try to kick the football through

the opponent's goalpost to score a field goal through the posts, which counts for three points.

Defense

The basic defensive object of the game is to prevent your opponent from advancing up the field by defending your goal line and goalpost. You do this by tackling the ball-carrying opponent. The only way for the defense to score is by tackling a ball-carrying opponent in the offensive team's end zone (called a "safety"). The other way you can get points on defense is via a turnover (due to a fumble or an interception) and a run with the ball into the opponent's end zone for a touchdown.

Players

There can be up to sixty-five players on the team, but there are only eleven on the field at a time. Half the team plays offense, half the team plays defense. Typically, offensive players are the quick, fast guys, while the defensive players are the big, blocking-type guys. The following three positions are the key offensive roles. (Don't stress over learning who the other guys are.)

* *Quarterback:* He is the team leader for the offense. He decides what the strategy will be: whether to hand the ball to the running back, to throw the ball down to the wide receiver, or to run with the ball himself. Top NFL quarterbacks are Tom Brady, Peyton Manning, and Cam Newton.

* *Running back:* Running backs are seen as the workhorses of the team, and there are always two on the field. The running back is expected to carry the ball many times in a game and as such the position is one of the most injury-prone. Great running backs include the Seattle Seahawks' Marshawn Lynch and the Minnesota Vikings' Adrian Peterson.

* *Wide receiver:* There are two wide receivers on the field, and they hold slightly more finesse than the straight-ahead, bruising

running backs. Wide receivers attempt to elude the defense by cleverly sprinting away in order to get open for a toss from the quarterback. Top wide receivers like Michael Crabtree have trained with ballet companies in the off season to help strengthen their jumping and spinning abilities. (Geez—and I can barely get my butt to yoga.)

Football Terms Every MG Should Know

- *Down:* A play that starts when the ball is put into play and ends when the ball is ruled dead. A team has four downs to make ten yards.

- *First down:* The first chance out of four that a team on offense has to advance ten yards down the field; as soon as it gains those yards, it earns a new first down.

- *Field goal:* If you are unsuccessful at getting a touchdown, your team may attempt to kick a field goal (worth three points).

- *Fumble:* When a ball carrier loses possession by dropping the ball or having it knocked away before a play ends; the first player to get possession of the loose ball is said to make the recovery, and his team becomes the offense.

- *Interception:* A pass caught (stolen, kind of) in the air by a defender whose team immediately gains possession of the ball and becomes the offense.

- *Punt:* When the offense has been unsuccessful at advancing the ball down the field after four downs, they're forced to punt (i.e., drop-kick) the ball straight to the other team. This happens when the offense isn't close enough to try for a field goal.

- *Tackling:* Contact with a ball carrier that causes him to touch the ground with any part of his body except his hands, thereby ending the play. In other words, it's wrestling an opponent to the ground.

- *Touchdown (TD):* When a team crosses the opponent's goal line with the ball, catches a pass in the opponent's end zone, or recovers a loose ball in the opponent's end zone; it earns a team six points.

Golf

What MG in her right mind would pass up the chance to spend a sun-drenched spring Saturday afternoon playing a round of eighteen among meticulously manicured greens at Carmel's Pebble Beach? Uh, me. A few years ago, I was so intimidated by all things golf—from basic rules of the game to proper driving technique, club selection, and even etiquette—that I turned down a primo invite from a few colleagues of mine. Instead, I wandered through stores in Carmel all day, feeling useless (I guess shopping really isn't a sport). Frustrated, I resolved to learn the basics over the next year so that I too could enjoy and participate in a sport that's increasingly important in the professional world—as well as a cool family sport. (And hello—how cute are those preppy-chic golf outfits?) So read on. I promise, once you're out there on that crystal-blue-sky afternoon, driving two hundred yards off the tee straight up the fairway on that final par five of the day, you'll feel as fabulous as Tiger Woods (okay, maybe not that fabulous, but you get my point).

Basics of the Game

As you probably already know, the objective of golf is to get the golf ball in the hole in the fewest number of shots from the tee. Most rounds of golf are for eighteen holes and last anywhere from three to four hours. If you don't want to make the full-time commitment, most courses allow you to play just nine holes.

Shots are referred to as "strokes." The fewer strokes it takes a player to get the ball in the hole, the lower the golf score. (Unlike every other sport we've discussed, the lower the score in golf the better.)

The golf course is split into eighteen holes, with three main sections on each hole. The first section is the called the "tee box," a defined area where you hit your first shot of the hole. This is where you "tee off," and here you're usually going for distance and accuracy. The goal of the tee-off is to hit the ball cleanly onto the second area of the hole, known as the "fairway." This is an area of medium-height grass (think Ryan Seacrest's hair) that provides a smooth surface to make your approach shots onto the final main section, known as the "green." The green is the area of short-cropped grass (think Brad Pitt's buzz cut) that surrounds the flag marking the cup (hole).

Sprinkled around the course, you'll find various other sections of tall grass (the rough), trees, and large pools of water or sand (hazards). Avoid these areas! They will cost you strokes to get out of them. It is extremely difficult to hit a ball out of the rough or a deep sand trap, and you will incur a penalty if you hit the ball into a water hazard, which will increase your score.

In Da Club

A golf club has three components—the head, the shaft, and the grip. (Oh, get your mind out of the gutter!) A standard set of golf clubs consists of three woods (the driver, three, and five), seven irons (three, four, five, six, seven, eight, nine), a pitching wedge, and a putter—twelve clubs in all. The rules of golf allow you to carry fourteen clubs in your bag, so many golfers add another iron or a specialty wood.

Wood: For Your First Shots

A wood is a hollow-bodied, large-headed golf club. Woods are used to hit the long shots. If a golf hole is 175 to 450 yards from tee to green, most golfers use a wood to hit off the tee. The driver (also called the one wood) is typically used for your longest tee shots. Most golfers also carry three and five woods in their bag. The higher the number you see on the golf club, the higher the loft or arc on the shot (how high it will go). As you get closer to the hole, the higher-numbered woods will give you more arc to get over hazards (like sand traps or water traps) but you won't hit the ball as far—which is good, because as you near the hole it's all about precision, not power.

MG TIP: Since the 1980s, woods have actually been made of metal.

Irons: Getting Closer

Irons are generally used when you are less than 200 yards away from the green (the short grass you putt on). The closer you are to the green, the higher the number iron you will use.

Wedges: Getting You onto the Green

Wedges are really just specialty irons, and they're extremely useful to your game. Because of the angle of the club head, the ball goes very high, but not very far. The wedge is used for those special times when you're too far away from the green to putt but too close to the green to use one of your regular irons, which will have too much power for the shorter distance.

Putters: When You're Right Next to the Hole

A putter is a golf club with a special purpose: getting the ball into the hole. The putter is used on the green and there are many styles of putters: short, belly, long, bent, heel-toe, mallet, and so on.

Scoring in Golf: Getting on Par

Each of the eighteen holes on a golf course is a par three, par four, or par five. The par number refers to how many strokes it should take a very good golfer to get the ball in the hole, based on the distance and the difficulty of the specific hole.

Par

If you hit the ball into the hole on the third stroke of a par three, the fourth stroke of a par four, or the fifth stroke of a par five, then you've "shot par" for the hole.

Birdie

If you shoot the ball into the hole with one less stroke than par—i.e., on the second stroke of a par three, the third stroke of a par four, or the fourth stroke of a par five—then you've made what's referred to as a "birdie" for the hole. (Try to do this every time, and call yourself Tiger or Annika.)

Eagle

If you've shot two below par, you've made an "eagle." This is a pretty darn good thing.

Hole in One

This is just what it sounds like. Many say it comes from massive talent; I'd say it's more like luck. If you get one, quit the game and consider yourself a winner.

Bogey

If you shoot the ball into the hole with one stroke more than par—i.e., on the fourth stroke of a par three, the fifth stroke of a par four, or the sixth stroke of a par five—then you've made a "bogey." As you take additional shots, you can refer to it as a double bogey, triple bogey, and so on . . . but you may want to stop keeping track at that point.

Tallying Your Score

At the end of the eighteen holes of golf, you add up all your pars, bogeys, and birdies and get a final score. On most courses, if you shoot a par on every hole, your score will be a seventy-two. This is considered extremely good, and if you do it regularly you're known as a "scratch golfer." If you shot more bogeys than birdies in your round of eighteen, then your score will be some number "over par."

Your Handicap

After playing golf for some time (several rounds), you'll begin to develop an average score over par. Take your average score and subtract seventy-two (par) from it and you get an approximation for your handicap. For example, if my average score is ninety-two, then I have a twenty handicap. The handicap is a useful way to measure yourself against other golfers and allows players of varying skill levels to compete against one another. For example, if I'm a twenty handicap golfer and I'm playing with my friend who's a more experienced and skillful ten handicap golfer, then she must beat me by ten strokes to win in some types of friendly play.

Key Rules to Remember

Fourteen-Club Limit

The USGA (United States Golf Association) allows a maximum of fourteen clubs to be carried in a bag. Less than fourteen is okay (and lighter).

Tee Markers

When teeing off on a hole, the ball must be behind the tee markers, which are usually represented by colorful enlarged balls or wooden posts. Usually the women's are a bit farther in than the men's, so the women don't have to hit as far.

As It Lies

Playing the ball as it lies means you may not improve the way the ball sits at rest (damn!). If you are on the green, you may mark the space with a tee and pick up your ball to clean it, but while on the fairway, you must play the ball as it lies.

Shot Order at the Next Tee

The person with the lowest score for the hole has "the honors," and plays first on the next hole.

Shot Order on the Green

The ball farthest from the hole is played first.

Sand Traps

Since this is a hazard, you may not clear a pathway in the sand with your club prior to taking your shot.

Out of Bounds

If you hit your ball into a water hazard, you may play it (though it may be messy), or take a one-stroke penalty to your score and play another ball from the same spot you swung at for your first ball. Option three is to drop another ball where the original ball entered the hazard, incur a one-stroke penalty, and play on.

Golf Etiquette

Experienced golfers take the sport *very seriously*. Anyone who is willing to spend four hours hitting a little white ball must love the game, so rules are important. Trust me, I pretty much blew it with a potential mother-in-law when I bungled a few of the below:

- Don't swing your club until you know that others in your group are a safe distance away from you.

- Don't hit the ball until you are certain that the group ahead of you is out of range.

- If your ball appears headed toward another player or another group, give them a warning by yelling, "Fore!" (Not "Omigod, watch out!")

- Keep your cart off the grass as much as possible.

- Do not spend too much time looking for a lost ball, particularly if there is a group behind you ready to play. If you insist on taking the full five minutes allotted to look for lost balls, golf etiquette says you should allow the group behind to go ahead and "play through."

- Always try to keep pace with the group ahead of you. If space opens in front of you, allow a faster group to play through.

- Repair all divots (the kicked-up soil and grass).

- Always rake sand traps after hitting to erase your footprints.

- Never talk during another player's swing.

- Be aware of your shadow on the putting green. Don't stand in a place that causes your shadow to be cast across another player or that player's putting line.

- Never walk through a playing partner's putting line. Your footprints might alter the path of a partner's putt.

Scotch Secrets Every Modern Girl Must Know

I learned the hard way that single-malt, straight-up scotch doesn't jibe well with my body . . . *burp*. But that doesn't mean that the rich, amber-colored spirit is banned from my cocktail cabinet. It's a sophisticated occasional aperitif or after-dinner drink that goes well with cold nights (and hot dates). My secret weapon for staying just this side of *el baño* is drinking on a full stomach and buying a scotch *blend*. And if you still can't stomach the idea, read on, because scotch makes a great gift for a guy. Here's the difference between single malts and blends:

MG TIP: Scotch whisky must be distilled in Scotland in order to be called scotch, although it can be bottled elsewhere. If it isn't, you'll notice that *whisky* is spelled *whiskey.*

MG TIP: If you are looking to cut down on carbs, scotch is a good choice. It has the lowest sugar content of all liquors.

Single-Malt Scotch vs. Scotch Blends

Single malts come from one distillery (hence the "single"). They are distilled from 100 percent malted barley, which gives them the purest flavor, according to connoisseurs. But they are incredibly strong and tough to stomach. Scotch blends are much lighter and female-friendly. They're comprised of grain whisky and anywhere from fifteen to fifty single-malt blends (which make them more mildly flavored).

How to Order Scotch Blends at a Bar

Just like testing out fragrances, the best way to discover your favorite blend is by sampling a variety yourself. A good rule of thumb is to aim for the middle ground pricewise. Don't buy a $4 scotch, but you needn't go for the $25-a-glass Johnnie Walker Blue either. Stay in the $10 to $12 range. You'll get a quality drink, but it won't break your bank. Here are some "starter scotches" you'll find at most bars and lounges:

Light Blends
Cutty Sark
Dewars Twelve-Year-Old Special Reserve
Famous Grouse

Heavier-Bodied Blends
Ballantine
Chivas Regal Twelve-Year-Old
Johnnie Walker Gold Label Eighteen-Year-Old

Easy Tasting Tips

Once you're holding your drink in your hand, it's key to sip it correctly so that you can get the maximum flavor benefits.

Be Nosy
Take a whiff of the aroma, but keep your nose a bit off the glass (you don't want to burn out your nostril hairs).

Sip, Don't Chug It
Let it coat your tongue and feel it roll down the back of your throat. Think about how smooth or pungent it tastes. This is called getting a "mouth-feel."

Detect the "Flavor Notes"
You might taste and smell hints of dark chocolate, citrus, smoky peat, honey, or even green grass. It's not that different from wine tasting in that you'll see some are full-bodied, some are light, some are sweet, and some are more bitter.

Buying Scotch for Your Home

If you find that you like scotch blends a lot more than you thought you would, consider keeping a bottle on hand at home for cocktail parties or after-dinner drinks on chilly fall nights. A few guidelines:

Sample, Sample, Sample
If you don't know your Cutty Sark from Royal Salut, some specialty liquor stores hold "scotch tastings" that allow you to try a variety of brands and hone your sniffing skills. Bring along a notepad so

MG TIP: Test your charm by asking the bartender to give you a taste of a few different brands before you commit to a full glass.

MG TIP: Order your scotch on the rocks, with water, or with soda. Sure, scotch snobs may balk that you're watering down the flavor, but the truth is, adding a little extra liquid will make it easier for your mouth and stomach to handle. Ask to have your glass filled with equal parts scotch and water if you're a nervous first-time tippler.

MG TIP: Ordering your scotch "neat" means you don't want any water, ice, or beverages added. I don't recommend becoming a "neat" freak until you've gotten more used to scotch's strong bite.

you can remember what you liked (and what smelled like Vicks Formula 44).

Buy Quality

I'd shell out for a $60 bottle over a $20 bottle. Look at scotch as a year-plus investment—you're not going to plow through it like a bottle of wine.

Understand Aging

Don't buy a young scotch and figure you'll store it away for a few years so it will age. Unlike red wine, scotch stops aging once it's been bottled. The age depends only on how long it's been aged in barrels.

Know Your Numbers

The youngest a scotch can be by law is three years, and any good scotch will be aged for a minimum of ten years (choose a twelve-year if you can). By the way, the age marked on the bottle of blended scotch is the age of the youngest scotch in the blend, not the average age of the scotches.

Store It in a Dark, Cool Place

If you don't have a bar, keep it in the bottom kitchen cabinet close to the floor, where it's cooler.

MG TIP: Single-malt scotches require a specific type of glass with a flared lip and a wide, tulip-shaped bowl, but blended scotch can be served in a standard eight-ounce or nine-ounce tumbler. A chic and cheap option: double old-fashioned tumblers from Crate & Barrel ($6.95 a glass).

Sweeter Ways to Serve Scotch

I'm all for giving my scotch a girly-girl kick when I'm not in the mood for the stiff stuff. Here are two classic-yet-simple drink recipes your guests will appreciate. (You'll be surprised; men may gravitate toward the sugary drinks more than the women do.) I like to use Dewar's scotch in these two recipes.

Mod Girl Whisky Sour

2 ounces Dewar's scotch
1 ounce sour mix
1 maraschino cherry
1 orange slice

Combine the Dewar's and sour mix in a shaker filled with crushed ice. Shake, shake, shake, and pour into a highball glass. Add the cherry and orange slice (plus an extra cherry and a wink if he's lucky).

Funky Old-Fashioned

1 1/2 ounces Dewar's scotch
Splash of spring water
Splash of sugar or "simple" syrup (at select grocery stores or make your own
    by boiling 2 parts water to 1 part sugar—should be gooey but not as thick
    as honey)
Bigger splash of Angostura bitters
1 maraschino cherry

Combine the Dewar's, water, sugar syrup, and bitters in a tumbler half-filled with ice. Mash the cherry into the bottom of a glass and pour the drink over the cherry.

Walk Like a Man, Talk Like a Man

I don't really want to walk like a man; given a choice I'd rather walk like a supermodel. But I do find that while men are seemingly totally at ease mixing a drink and working a room, we gals might be totally at ease among ourselves, but once you throw some guys into the mix we can clam up. So how can we work a room like they do and feel comfortable? Well, as I mentioned in chapter 2, everybody likes to talk about themselves, but that doesn't mean you shouldn't have an

MG TIP: Mixing scotch drinks will be easier if you invest in a jigger: It's a metal cup that measures one and a half ounces. That way you won't over-pour and wind up with guests doing the backstroke on your floor (or worse, your dear friend Anna in bed with your greasy neighbor Dan the next morning).

interesting story or two about yourself to toss in. In general, it's better not to start with questions about work, politics, or relationships; instead go for more interesting questions. Here are a few to consider:

- What would you do if you only had twenty-four hours left to live?
- Do you believe in luck?
- What is your favorite movie of all time?
- What is the worst movie you've ever seen?
- What is your favorite meal of the day?
- What is the craziest food you've ever eaten?
- Where do you plan on going for your next vacation?
- If you could live anywhere in the world, where would it be?
- Where did you grow up?
- What would be your last meal?
- If you could have any superpower, what would it be?
- Do you believe in miracles?

And if all else fails, here are five jokes to have up your sleeve for emergencies:

What washes up on tiny beaches? Microwaves.

What do you call fish with no eyes? Fsh.

What did Jay Z call his girlfriend before they got married? Feyoncé.

I renamed my iPhone the Titanic, so when I plug it in, it says, "The Titanic is syncing."

Q: Why does a chicken coop have two doors?
A: If it had four, it would be a chicken sedan.

Why can't you take a Pokémon to the bathroom? He may Pikachu.

What did the fisherman say to the magician? Pick a cod. Any cod.

How to Play Poker with the Boys

What other men's-club pastime pairs well with sipping scotch? Poker, of course. And there's nothing more impressive than beating a guy at his own game. While men seem to think they're the only ones who hold the key to the casino, the MG can hold her own at the card table too . . . once she knows the basics.

How the Game Works

The most basic version of poker is called Five-Card Draw. Each player puts an "ante" (a token bet) into the middle of the table before the cards are dealt. Then the dealer deals out five cards to each person and puts the rest of the stack in the middle of the table. (The dealer always deals herself last.)

Here's the juicy part: betting. Everyone looks at his or her cards, and the person to the left of the dealer places a bet. Let's say the bet is $5.00. You can "call" the bet, meaning add $5.00 to the pile so you can stay in the game. Or, if you have a particularly good hand, you can "call" the bet and "raise" it by putting in more money (let's say $2.00). Now everyone at the table has to throw in $7.00 to stay in the game. If you have a really lousy hand and you think it's best to get out, you "fold."

Your aim is to get the hand with the highest value. Depending on how good a hand you're originally dealt, you may want to get rid of up to three cards you don't want and take up to three new ones from the deck. After every player gets a chance to get new cards, the betting starts again. Here is the breakdown of winning hands, from lowest to highest value:

- *High card:* If none of the players has a good hand, the player holding the highest-value card wins (two is the lowest; aces are always the highest).

HOTSHOT TERMS THAT MAKE YOU LOOK LIKE A POKER PRO

- *Bet* means to begin the betting process.

- *Call* means to match your opponent's bet.

- *Checks* are poker chips.

- *Fold* means putting your cards face down on the table because you have a bad hand or the betting pool is getting too high and you want out of the game.

- *The muck* is the discard pile in the middle of the table, where everyone throws their castoffs. When you fold your hand, you can say you *muck* your cards.

- *The nuts* is the highest possible hand; as in, "Nobody can beat me, I've got the nuts."

- *Raise* means to add more money to the pot.

- *One pair:* Two cards of the same numerical value.

- *Two pair:* Two sets of pairs, plus a random card.

- *Three of a kind:* Three cards of the same numerical value.

- *Straight:* Five cards in a row not of the same suit (clubs, hearts, spades, or diamonds).

- *Flush:* Five cards of the same suit.

- *Full house:* Three of one kind (number, that is), plus a pair.

- *Four of a kind:* Four cards of the same numerical rank, plus a random card.

- *Straight flush:* Five cards in a row of the same suit.

- *Royal flush:* Ace, king, queen, jack, and ten, all of the same suit. This is the mack-daddy of all poker hands.

Bluffing

Bluffing is a tricky (but often highly successful) strategy in poker. Basically, you're giving the impression that you have a better hand than you do (you can do this by "raising," as discussed above). The point is to freak out everyone else at the table into thinking their hand is worse than yours . . . and to subsequently "fold."

"Tell" Signs

"Tell" signs are those facial indicators that hint to everyone what your hand really is—your aim is not to let any "tell" signs slip out! For example, your eyebrow might raise if you see you have a royal flush in the making; or you may bite your lip if you realize your hand sucks. But keep your poker face on—be as neutral as possible no matter how crushed or elated you feel. Kinda like how you'd act if you bumped into your ex and wanted to seem perfectly indifferent to the fact that he'd gotten engaged to a twenty-two-year-old actress/model with legs like Heidi Klum's.

MG TIP: Before you play for cold, hard cash, hone your skills by hosting a girls' poker night at your place. Play for each other's cast-off designer bags, random makeup, and bad birthday gifts. (Just make sure none of them came from the girls at the table.) Or, the winner with the most chips (or Oreos, if you don't want to spring for a poker set) gets treated to brunch.

How to "Man" a Barbecue

I'm not sure how barbecuing became such an extreme sport for the male population. Chalk it up to caveman psychology—the sweaty pleasure of grilling a large carcass (okay, maybe just a few burger patties) that he caught out in the wild (or more likely bought at the local grocery store) is his showy way of providing for his brood. His way of being manly. *Whatever.*

I say it's high time MGs left the heart-shaped pancake recipes to the guys and took hold of the grill once in a while. *Grrrr.* Not because we all want our bras to reek of hickory sauce, our hair to get singed, and our pores to get clogged with charcoal, but because the grill is not something to be feared but feted—if you learn how to handle the beast. And the only tools you need are tongs, a spatula, and a sharp knife. But beware, the guys may put up a fight over this one, so tread with caution.

Go Gas over Charcoal

A gas grill uses propane or natural gas, so you don't have to worry about buying coals, or lighter fluid, or dumping the ashes when you're done. (Modern Girls like that!) And the risk of scorching your skin and hair is lower, because you use a dial to control the heat and flame level. Just make sure the propane tank in your barbecue is full. Most modern grills have gauges on them to indicate when you need to refill the propane; hardware stores carry the gauges too.

Marinate Like a Madwoman

For tougher cuts of meat, a marinade (a combo of liquids and herbs) will help tenderize the meat. Steaks and chicken are best if marinated overnight in plastic Ziploc bags in your fridge.

Simple Marinade for Chicken and Beef

1/2 **cup cooking oil (canola is most healthy)**
1/3 **cup soy sauce**
1/4 **cup lemon juice**
2 **tablespoons mustard**
2 **tablespoons Worcestershire sauce**
1 **clove minced garlic**
1 **teaspoon freshly ground pepper**

Whisk the ingredients and pour them into a large Ziploc bag. Add about 2 pounds of meat and marinate overnight before baking or grilling.

Simple Lemon Soy Marinade for Fish

1/4 **cup freshly squeezed lemon juice**
2 **tablespoons soy sauce**
1/4 **teaspoon garlic powder**
1/4 **teaspoon hot sauce**
3 **twists cracked black pepper**
1/4 **cup olive oil**

Blend the first five ingredients in a blender, and then slowly add the olive oil with the motor still running. Pour into a shallow dish and marinate 1 to 1½ pounds fish steaks or fillets for half an hour before grilling, roasting, or baking. Don't marinate longer than a half an hour before or the fish will get mushy.

Preheat

If you don't preheat so the grill gets to a hot enough temperature, the meat will stick to the grill. To avoid stickiness, rub the racks with a paper towel and some vegetable oil or spray with nonstick cooking spray (but don't use spray if you're using charcoal) before you heat the grill. Then preheat it to close to 400°F. If you don't have a temperature gauge on your grill, preheat it for fifteen to twenty minutes.

MG TIP: For dry rubs, coat the food with olive oil and pat on the rub (dried rosemary, thyme, crushed red pepper, fennel seeds, dill, and cracked peppercorns are good places to start).

Don't Think "Fat-Free"

Having the right balance of fat, acid, and salt is key. So you'll want to grill your chicken with the skin on even if you want to eat skinless chicken to cut calories. Place the meat skin side down to get the skin crispy, add richness and flavor to the meat inside, and keep it moist. You can peel the skin off *after* you grill.

MG TIP: If you're pinched for time, marinate at room temperature, as the flavors will soak in better. But for anything over an hour, definitely fridge it or the food could go bad.

Be Patient

You may get the urge to flip your salmon steak or your chicken over and over because it makes you feel like Bobby Flay. But frequent flipping lowers the temperature of the food and prevents a proper sear. Turn your meat with tongs once, halfway through cooking (don't use a fork—it will pierce the meat and let the natural juices escape). The average chicken breast takes six to eight minutes per side. Salmon takes five minutes per side, steak six to eight minutes on each side, veggies fifteen minutes, and bread three to five minutes (try to put it on a higher grill rack out of direct heat). Also, resist the urge to push the meat down into the grill with a spatula to hear that great sizzle sound. You're only pushing all of the juices out of the meat.

Lay Off the Heat When Necessary

I know I said that to avoid stickiness, heat the grill as high as possible. But when you're cooking a thick piece of chicken, you don't want to scorch it too much in the beginning or it will be charred and leathery on the outside before it's even cooked through on the inside. So start it on high heat to sear it, and then turn the gas down a bit or move your food aside until the coals cool down a little. Also, you don't want to have a hellishly hot grill when cooking delicate foods like shrimp, vegetables, or breads.

The Diva's Guide to Using a Power Drill

MG TIP: Find out what material your wall is made of first. If it echoes when you knock, it's probably Sheetrock. If not, it could be made of cement or brick, and you'll need a more heavy-duty drill, plus larger drill bits.

Besides grilling, another Tarzan activity I learned to master is *drilling*. Albeit absentmindedly. You see, when I wanted to make the transition from post-college IKEA slob to urban sophisticate, I decided I would start with a set of very modern, very hotel-style sconces. And all I needed to mount them was my trusty hammer and nails from college!

What an idiot I was. As soon as I opened the (nonrefundable) lights, I read the fine print: *must assemble with power drill*. Ugh! I let the box of sconces sit in my closet for two months, until my friend saw them and said, "You know, Jane, it's really not that hard. I'll bring mine over and we'll do it together." My friend had her own drill? Was it pink with rhinestones? Did they make Prada drills? I was shocked.

But what I learned is that operating one isn't hard. It's actually pretty damn fun. In fact, I got so drill-addicted, I asked my then-boyfriend, now-husband, to buy me one for Christmas.

The Best Power Drills

DeWalt DCD710S2

This one is bit on the pricey side at $150, but it is easy to handle and lightweight, making it ideal for the power drill novice. It is also equipped with an LED light for visibility in dark places, and the hot bumblebee-yellow color makes it easy to spot in your crowded closet.

Ryobi Twelve-Volt Cordless Drill/Driver Kit

It's a drill and so much more: It is equipped with a built-in level and the handle has a small magnetic tray to store extra screws (so you no longer have to hold them between your teeth). It will cost you around $81, but when you think of the extra perks it is totally worth it.

Pink Power PP182 Eighteen-Volt Cordless Drill Kit

If you are worried your man might try to take your tools for his own, keep him at bay with this pink power drill. But don't be deceived by the girly color; it's got some serious power and is the cheapest of the group at about $55.

Tool Terms You've Gotta Know

Torque

You may hear the word *torque*, which is the measure of a drill's twisting power. Most drills let you adjust the torque with something called a "clutch." Check your manual for details on your specific model.

Bits

You use drill bits for drilling holes and screw bits for pushing through screws. Most drills come with a small assortment. Ask your salesperson what the most popular sizes are. Also keep in mind that you need different drill bits depending on what you're drilling into: wood, dry wall, masonry, and so on.

MG TIP: Go for a cordless if you don't mind paying a little more and recharging batteries. It's great if you want to tackle projects outside (since there may be no outlets). But corded ones can give you more power (and can even be lighter, since the cordless kind also hold a battery terminal).

MG TIP: Twelve-volt drills (with at least four amps) are the best to buy because they aren't too powerful, but not wimpy either. They can do small jobs (like drilling pretty knobs onto your shabby chic dresser), but they're powerful enough to assemble furniture.

MG TIP: Keep your receipt! Unlike buying pricey, heel-pinching shoes that wind up sitting in your closet because you can't return 'em, you can often return drills for up to thirty days, no questions asked. Also, find out what the warranty is. Many drill manufacturers will replace any damaged parts in the first year.

MG TIP: More and more home superstores are offering DIY classes that teach you how to handle power tools. Devote a Saturday (did you need to go to brunch and shop anyway?) to learning the basics.

Chuck

Once you meet Chuck, you'll be impressed with all the variety he'll give you. A chuck is what holds the different bits on your drill and expands or contracts to fit them. Go for a three-eighths size; that's all you'll need. Some drills have keyless chucks, which means you don't need to use a chuck key to open it every time you want to use a different-size bit.

8 Simple Drilling Do's

1. *Read your manual. Really.* Yeah, yeah, I know it's boring, but you don't want to use the wrong size bits for the wrong jobs. Or put a hole in your thigh. I recommend reading the manual while your nails and toes are drying or while you're waiting for your bath to fill; it won't feel like such a time-suck.

2. *Get familiar with switching speeds.* When you pull the trigger of the drill, you'll feel a surge of power, and it's good to be able to distinguish power levels fast. High settings are for drilling holes into hard wood and cement, and low settings are better for drilling in screws.

3. *Set the "clutch" correctly.* The clutch is the big dial on your drill that gives it the right tension (so the bits don't move around and strip surfaces). See your manual for details.

4. *Practice on a piece of wood* before you make your first hole. You might be a shy drill-handler, or shock yourself and be a *Texas Chainsaw* madwoman. (Not that I know anything about that.)

5. *Get handy.* Before you pull the trigger, make sure your hands are in the most comfortable spots. With a corded drill, put your dominant hand on the handle and the other on top of the drill to steady it. With a cordless, put your other hand on the battery base for support.

6. *Let the drill do the work for you.* My mom always told me not to "push too hard" with guys, and the same applies for drills. Apply enough pressure so that you can feel the drill making progress. Don't try to muscle it through; you may break the bit or burn out the motor.

7. *Anchors away!* You can't just drill a hole in the wall, insert your screw, and expect whatever you're hanging—a mirror or a painting or a sconce—to stay in place. You need to put an anchor in the wall so the screw stays in tight. An anchor is a plastic yellow shell that looks like a screw that's been hollowed out on the inside (they're super cheap at the hardware store). It has the same effect as a plaster cast on a broken leg—it holds everything together so there's no jostling around. That means your screw won't slip within the hole and let fall to the floor whatever you're hanging on the wall.

8. *Drill a smaller hole* than you think you'll need. Let's say you're drilling a hole in the wall. Once you put in your plastic anchors (which hold the screws in place), they'll expand the hole and fit snugly as they must.

Drillin' SOS

- *Watch out!* If the drill gets too hot, it could be burning out. Take it back to Home Depot (or wherever you purchased it) and they'll help you better assess the problem.

- *You knotty girl.* When you're drilling into wood, you may hit a "knot." You'll know if the drill suddenly feels like it's not moving, and you feel a ton of resistance. Shift to a lower speed so that it doesn't make your hand shake out of control (and scare everyone around you). You may have to drill another hole nearby instead.

- *Messed up?* Buy spackle (aka hole-filling goop) the same day that you buy your drill. If you accidentally drill holes in the wrong spots (like I did), it could wind up looking like the Terminator just paid you a visit.

How to Drive Stick Shift

Fact: The biggest gadget a guy has isn't his Plasma TV screen—it's his car. Second fact: Many men—my stubborn husband included—wouldn't dream of driving an automatic (too wussy). But for many women who were told in high school driver's ed that we didn't need to bother learning stick (also called "standard" or "manual" transmission), automatic seemed like the only choice.

But here's the thing: Driving stick gives you power and options. Once you learn, you'll be prepared to drive in *any* car in *any* emergency situation, have better traction going up hills and around curves, save thousands of dollars (standard transmissions guzzle less gas and cost less to buy), and develop fabulously toned calf muscles.

Stick Shift 101: Getting Started

Congratulations for being badass enough to join (or at least read about) the world of Manual Transition Mamas. But before you ride your wheels off into the sunset, know the following lingo:

The Fab Five Gears

In an automatic car, when you go into "D" (aka Drive) the gears shift automatically. But with a manual transmission, you have to shift the gears yourself. You'll find them labeled 1 through 5 on the gearbox of your car, located between the driver's and the passenger's seats. Each gear has a different function:

First Gear (up to 15 mph)
This gear gets the car moving, but when you want to go faster, you have to shift to second . . . otherwise the engine will screech.

Second Gear (15 mph to 30 mph)

This gear helps you round sharp curves and climb hills with rough terrain, but if you want to go more than 30 mph, shift to third.

Third Gear (30 mph to 45 mph)

You can travel at a good pace with this gear and still stay in control when you round curves and go up gradual hills.

Fourth gear (45 mph to 60 mph)

You don't take a big curve in fourth, and you wouldn't go full speed in it either. You use it for quick transitions. Sometimes you won't even use fourth at all. Say you're going fast in fifth gear and see a sharp curve. You'll instantly slow down and drop into third to take the curve with more control.

Fifth Gear (60 mph and above)

Perfect for going straight ahead on the highway. Downshift to third gear before taking turns.

The Clutch (wait, isn't it just a trendy purse?)

The clutch is located to the left of your brake. Remember "CBA": Clutch, Brake, Accelerator. Think of it as your key to switching gears. You can't switch gears unless your left foot is down on the clutch (if you try, you'll hear an awful noise). Note: The clutch and gas work oppositely from each other. When your left foot is completely down on the clutch, your right foot is completely off the accelerator.

Neutral: Your Best Friend at Stoplights and in Traffic

Neutral is not a gear; it's actually the absence of a gear. It's what you use when you don't want the car to move, but you still want to keep the engine running. Ever notice how people wiggle the shifter back and forth when they're waiting for a light to change? It's to make sure they're in neutral, because you can't jiggle it when you're in gear.

MG TIP: You want to ease your foot off the clutch, not lift it abruptly. This will cause the car to lurch and stall. Majorly uncool.

Va-Va-Vroom! Getting Behind the Wheel

Now that you know vital stick-shift vocab, it's time to put it to use. Find a laid-back instructor because there's nothing worse than learning stick from someone with a stick up their butt. Boyfriends and husbands can be good teachers as long as they aren't ridiculously overprotective of their wheels, or expect you to go from novice to NASCAR overnight.

When it's time for your lesson, wear comfortable shoes. Heels, flip-flops, and sandals will make it hard for your left foot to easily and firmly push down on the clutch. Learn to shift the gears without the car running, practicing pushing the clutch in each time. Then, from the passenger seat, try it with someone else driving the car and using the clutch. Once you're comfortable, it's time to go.

Step 1

Put your right foot on the brake, put your left foot all the way down on the clutch, turn the key in the ignition, and shift into neutral to let the car warm up.

Step 2

Shift into first gear to start going forward, or reverse if you need to back out of a parking spot. Quickly move your right foot off the brake and onto the accelerator while slowly lifting your left foot off the clutch at the same time. Picture your legs as a seesaw; when one goes down on the gas, the other comes up off the clutch. You'll feel the car begin to move forward.

Step 3

MG TIP: Many cars have a light pop up on the dash, telling you when to shift. Or glance at the tachometer (a dial on the far left of your dashboard). It shows your RPMs (revolutions per minute) on a scale of 1 to 9. Aim for 3 (3,000 RPMs) and don't exceed 5.

When you want to go beyond 15 mph, shift into second by putting down the clutch and *then* shifting the gear. You'll feel the stick click into a groove. As you continue driving, you'll frequently need to switch gears depending on your speed. If you hear the engine straining and making a high-revving sound, shift up—you're in too low of a gear. If it's making a cough-cough sound, you're in too high a gear, so downshift. After you've driven a few times, you'll naturally know when to shift.

Step 4

Learn to slow down smoothly. When you're coming to a complete stop (such as when you're pulling into a parking spot), apply pressure to the clutch while you brake and shift into neutral. If you don't press down on the clutch when you're stopping, your car will stall and give you and your passengers a jolt (not fun if they're applying mascara or sipping lattes).

Step 5

Use the emergency brake when parking. Manual transmissions don't have "P," or "Park," so unless you pull up the emergency brake and keep your car in gear, you may find your cute little auto isn't where you parked it earlier that morning.

Troubleshooting for Icky Moments

Just as important as knowing how to make your car go is mastering minor disasters:

When You Stall the Car

When you lift up too fast on the clutch before giving the car any gas (commonly called "popping the clutch"), the auto will just stop. Solution: Put your right foot on the brake and your left foot all the way down on the clutch and start the car again.

When You're Rolling Backward Down a Hill

A mortifying thing that can happen to a Modern Girl is driving déjà vu (aka realizing that your car is rolling backward). It often happens when you lift your right foot off the brake and let too much time lapse before you switch to the gas pedal while simultaneously lifting your left foot off the clutch. Your secret weapon: the emergency brake. To go, shift into first, accelerate slowly as you release the clutch pedal, then release the emergency brake as you feel the car move forward. This way you are using the brake to keep you from rolling back. (This is a great tip if you live anywhere hilly, like San Francisco.)

MG TIP: If you stall in bumper-to-bumper traffic, don't hyperventilate. Yes, you'll probably have rude people honking at you, but I've found the best thing to do is wave to them, then tune 'em out as you get down to business and restart your car.

How to Change a Tire in Stilettos

In addition to holding a high-powered job and raising a family, I'd love to say I'm a natural automotive dynamo. But the truth is, I managed to learn how to drive and maintain my car by doing the absolute minimum . . . and stayed that way until one summer day a few years ago.

My friend Sharon and I were cruising through the countryside in her red Volvo, on our way to our friend's bridal shower, when we felt the right side of the car go *ba-ba-bum*. She'd gotten a flat tire. (Ugh! Weren't Volvos the kinds of cars that never had problems?!) So there we were, stranded in the countryside, Sharon in a chiffon top and skirt, and me in a Cynthia Rowley cream dress with three-inch strappy stilettos. Talk about the true meaning of fashion *emergency*. We had three options:

1. Ask the cows for help.

2. Call AAA.

3. Change the tire ourselves.

Truth be told, I was pushing for option 2. After all, I was wearing a dress designed for mingling, not grease-monkeying—and what are my yearly AAA dues for anyway? But Sharon decided that we could do it on our own. We'd be power chicks on the open road! We'd change the tire in a half hour instead of waiting in Nowheresville for a tow truck and arriving three hours late to the shower! And we had all the tools in the back of the car! I asked her if she'd done this whole tire-changing thing before, and she said yes, *of course*.

I didn't find out until we'd safely made it to the shower that Sharon had lied. She'd only seen her uncle change a tire once before. But she winged it so well, and gave me such good instructions, that the mechanic at the gas station we drove to on our spare tire was flabbergasted. "What? You ladies did this? Nooo." Oh yeah, buddy, we did. And the best part: We only got a single grease stain each on our outfits. But they were battle wounds, baby.

Tools You Need to Change a Tire

The Doughnut
It ain't a Krispy Kreme, but the sweet news is, it'll get you home. This is the mini-tire (aka the "spare"), found under the rug in the trunk of most compact to midsize cars. Some people keep a regular tire in their trunk, if it fits. If you have neither, buy one at your local Michelin, Goodyear, or Goodrich distributor.

The Jack
This tool opens like an accordion to prop (or "jack") up your car so you can take off your busted wheel and put the spare on. Most modern cars come equipped with jacks and lug wrenches (see below), but if yours didn't, buy them from your local automotive supplier.

The Lug Wrench
This cross-shaped tool is used to loosen the lug nuts holding your tire in place. (You'll see between four and six lug nuts per tire.) You also use it to remove your car's hubcaps.

What to Do the Moment You Get a Flat

Flash 'Em!
Pull over to the right side of the road and put your hazard lights on (even in broad daylight) so that other cars can easily maneuver around you as you're working. Also make sure your car is in Park or in "gear" if you drive a stick shift.

Give It a Squeeze
Pop the trunk and check the pressure of your spare tire. Is it as firm as Pamela Anderson's implants, or saggier than Ozzy Osbourne's face? If your spare is too flat, you won't be able to use it and will need to call AAA (if you're a member) or a tow truck. (In the future, check your spare tire pressure every time you have your other tires checked by a service guy at the gas station. Experts say once a month.) If it's firm (meaning you can't squeeze it no matter how hard you try), take it out and set it to the side.

MG TIP: Look into buying a good emergency roadside kit, available at any automotive repair store. Keep it in your trunk at all times.

MG TIP: Pull your hair back and make a deal with yourself that you won't touch your face or clothes. Keep baby wipes and paper towels in your car to save you from getting grease on your outfits. Roll up your sleeves and sarong-knot long skirts (or use the change of clothes in your kit, if you have one), and keep your shoes on . . . you'll need 'em later.

Tool Out

Look under the rug in your trunk for the jack and the lug wrench . . . they're often underneath your spare tire. And whip out your manual (which is in your glove compartment, right?). It'll give you specifics about your car, like if you have "wheel locks" and show you the right tool in your kit to unlock them.

MG TIP: Don't get conned. When Sharon and I drove to the gas station on her spare, they recommended buying a new tire (which cost triple what they do elsewhere). But instead of blindly agreeing, we asked questions and learned that it would be perfectly safe to drive on the patched wheel. Your best bet: If the hole is small, ask if they can patch the tire so that you don't have to spring for a new one that minute. Then, the next morning, take your car to an auto body shop you trust. They can give you a better selection of new tires to choose from.

Eight Steps to Being a Tire-Changing Goddess

1. *Pry off the flat tire's hubcap* using the flat end of the lug wrench. Or, if you have a flat screwdriver in your car (bonus points for you), it can make the job much easier.

2. *Loosen those lug nuts.* To loosen the nuts, turn the lug wrench counterclockwise about one turn. Don't take the nuts off completely. If you don't have enough muscle power with your hands alone, put your stilettos to use: Step on top of the wrench (use the ball of your foot), and push all of your body weight into it as you turn.

3. *Place the jack in front of the wheel* if you have a rear flat tire or behind the wheel if you have a front flat tire. Your manual should point to the exact spot (called the "lifting point") where you should place the jack.

4. *Jack up the car.* Wait, isn't it impossible for little you to lift up that huge car? Nope—the beauty of the jack is leverage. All you have to do is pump. Stick your lug wrench into a groove on the jack (it's pretty obvious where it is) and pump up the car until it's about three inches off the ground.

5. *Remove the loosened lug nuts and pull off the wheel.* Now this is the part where you could go from a cream dress to a chocolate dress, as I almost did. The secret is grabbing the wheel at the sides (it's a heavy sucker) and squatting, using your upper thighs to support yourself, not your back. That means sticking your butt out J.Lo style (c'mon, it's fun). Roll the tire off to the side. Don't drop it, or dirt and mud may ricochet onto your outfit.

6. *Lift the spare tire* (it's gonna seem a lot lighter than the old wheel) and slide it onto the axle hub of the car (there's only one way it can fit, so this is really easy). Screw the lug nuts back on tightly.

7. *Lower the jack* (use your feet again for leverage if you have to). Slip the wrench out of the jack and use it to tighten the lug nuts (remember, "right equals tight"). Pick up your flat tire and stow it in the trunk, along with your tools. Now pat yourself on the back. Somebody's getting a spa treatment tomorrow!

8. *Drive* to the nearest auto body shop or gas station. They will check out the spare tire and look at your flat one. If they can't easily find the hole in your tire, they'll immerse it in water and look for where the bubbles are coming from (that's where the hole is).

MG TIP: Sure, you *could* do it, but don't try to change a tire at night, especially if you're alone. Being outside your car makes you a potential target for attackers. Lock your doors and call a tow truck or AAA on your cell phone. Every MG should have an AAA card; sign up for one at www.AAA.com. It costs around $68 for the first year (depending on your state) and $48 each additional year. Also program the number into your cell phone (1-800-400-HELP).

Checking and Changing Your Oil

Oil. *Oy.*

Yeah, I know: It sounds so boring. (Couldn't we just talk about olive oil, or even oily skin?). But the fact is, oil is a necessary gear-greaser. If you don't properly maintain the oil in your car, the engine can overheat, give off an awful smell, and even blow up.

Tip 1: See the Light

Don't ignore it when the oil light pops on in your car (it's located on your dash with the word *oil* or a symbol of a little oil can). It's not just there to be cute. Check your oil (see directions below) or take your car to be checked at a gas station or Jiffy Lube (go to www.Jiffylube.com for the location nearest you) as soon as possible.

Tip 2: Think "Three"

You should have your oil checked (or check it yourself) every three months or three thousand miles. Experts say to check your oil level

MG TIP: When you take your car in to have the oil changed, multitask. Ask to have a full check of your car. For example, Jiffy Lube offers the Jiffy Lube Signature Oil Change for about $42.99. The service includes checking and topping off all the fluids in your car—from the transmission to the power steering fluid, replacing your oil filter with a quality filter, and inspecting your air filtration system.

every time you fill up with gas, but let's be real here: No on-the-go MG has the time or energy to do that. Try to check your oil level every fifth time you gas up.

Tip 3: To Check the Oil Yourself:

1. Park your car on level ground, put it in Park or in gear, apply the emergency brake, and turn it off.

2. Pop the hood and prop it up with the prop stick.

3. Grab the dipstick (a long skinny wand) located toward the front of the car, but check your manual if you're having trouble finding it. You'll know you see it if you can spot a ring. Most have a metal ring or handle at the end so you can easily pull it up with your fingers.

4. Pull the dipstick out and wipe it with a rag, paper towel, or even a tissue. Whatever keeps the oil off your hands and clothes.

5. Put the dipstick back in the oil container, and pull it straight back up. There's a line or marker that the oil should come up to that indicates "full." If it doesn't hit the line, it's time to take it to a gas station to have more oil added.

6. Also check your oil for problems like a milky appearance, or a strong smell of gasoline, or a dark, gloppy texture. "Healthy" oil should be amber-colored and have a thin, runny consistency.

Changing Your Oil

Oh please. I'm Jane Bond, not G.I. Jane! Sure, changing your oil is within every Modern Girl's ability, but why would you *want* to when you can just take it to Jiffy Lube instead, and avoid sliding under the bottom of your car to find the oil release valve and drain it into an un-forgiving pan?

Jump-Starting **Your Car**

When you're crazy-busy and in a rush, it's easy to forget to turn things off, whether it's the TV in the morning or the AC before heading out of town. The same goes for my car. I've left my headlights on—twice!—killed the battery, and had to get a "jump."

To understand how the whole process works, think about the sexy docs on *Grey's Anatomy*. Done drooling? Okay, now think about what they do on the show when a patient flatlines. They break out the electric shock pads, and ZZZAP! Alive again. Jump-starting a car isn't all that different. You're using another car's power, via the cables, to bring yours back from the dead. To do it, you'll need:

A Car with a Live Battery
A Modern Girl's gotta work her charm skills and be resourceful when she's caught solo with a dead battery. If you're in a safe place to walk around, seek out a woman or a family who might be able to help. Once you sucker them in, check (either in the manual or on the battery itself) to make sure the other driver's battery is the same voltage as yours.

Jumper Cables
Every MG should have a set of jumper cables in her trunk. When you're armed with your own tools, it's easy to get someone to give you a jump. They should be heavy gauge (four- to eight-gauge), copper, and at least ten feet long. They'll have "pinchers" that look like little hair clips at each end. Two of them are red (positive) and two are black (negative). The cables look like long red and black licorice whips. A set will run you from $20 to $40.

MG TIP: If you don't have jumper cables and can't find any sane-looking person who does, call AAA or a tow truck. Or seek out cabdrivers, cops, and other officials. Most of them carry jumper cables in their cars.

MG TIP: Put those Marlboro Lights away pronto! Smoking near the car battery can fuel an explosion (literally).

MG TIP: I like to offer my jump-starting savior cash for their trouble (chances are, they won't take it). A Modern Girl is just as gracious as she is gutsy.

Getting Ready to Jump

Before you start, protect your eyes and skin from acid that can seep from the battery. Slip on your sunglasses and wear gloves, if you have them. If you don't, use a cloth, towel, or even one of your socks (put your hand inside it) to touch the battery.

1. Have the other car park as close to yours as possible without touching your car. Hood to hood is the ideal position. If not, make an "L" shape.

2. Put the cars in park or first gear if it's a stick shift, and set the emergency brake.

3. Turn off both of your cars, plus the headlights, the flasher lights, the radio, the cigarette burner, and anything else battery-operated.

4. Pop both hoods and locate the batteries. Now it's time for your cars to kiss. Place one red clamp of the jumper cable on the positive post of your dead battery. (Look for a "+" for positive.) Place the other red clamp on the positive post of the "good" battery.

5. Connect one of the black clamps to the minus post (marked with a "-") of the good battery.

6. Hook up the remaining black clamp to the engine or some exposed metal (nonpainted) surface of your car. This is the "ground." Keep it as far away from the battery as possible, and make sure the cables aren't in the way of the engine.

7. Have the other person start their engine and rev it up a little. A minute or so later, start your car, and once it's running, remove the cable clamps. (Don't worry; you won't wind up looking like the Bride of Frankenstein.) Remember to take off the clamps in the *reverse order* that you put 'em on. Or if you forget, remember black-black, red-red, starting with your engine (black), and ending with your battery (red).

8. Cruise in your car for at least a half hour to charge the battery.

How to Stalk Your Ex Online

Some may say it's shameful, some may say it's sinful. I'm just going to say it's a fact of life that now that we have the power of the Internet at our fingertips all the time, it's pretty darn hard to resist the urge to occasionally keep track of one's former flings. So no judgment, but just a friendly tip that if you *are* going to stalk, you should do your best not to get caught. For those Goody-Two-Shoes among you who say you've never done it, consider yourselves morally above the rest of us; for the other 99 percent of you, here are a few tips for at least doing it without getting caught!

- Any single white female knows that Facebook is the mother lode for information, but the "close friends" feature should be called the "stalk-your-ex feature." It allows you to watch every move an FB friend makes once you add a little star next to his name. And he won't even know you've made him a "close friend" to keep an eye on. Of course if he's unfriended you, you can always follow his friends and get some pretty juicy tidbits. And if you're truly desperate, and your ex is, say, a fan of hot blondes, you can always make a fake page and hope he lets you friend him, but just be careful if he starts to flirt!

- Here's a safety tip for stalking via LinkedIn. If you want your ex to think it's some anonymous CEO and not you checking out his recent activity, remember to log out before creeping on his page (or his cute coworker's).

- Spokeo is a great resource. It's kind of like your own private investigator . . . for a small fee (about $4.95 a month plus some add-ons for additional info). You enter your ex's name, up pops all of the people with that name (there are forty-two Jane Buckinghams, by the way), and then you find the right one. It's particularly helpful if you have your ex's e-mail or address. Up will pop his social networks, photos, and pretty much everything he has been doing. And even better yet, your ex will have *no* idea you got the goods on his goings-on.

MG TIP: If you can't help stalking an ex, then make sure you follow a few guidelines:

- *Leave no evidence*: As much as it may be habit to like a picture or post, it will immediately blow your cover and you might find yourself blocked from future missions.

- *Phone a friend*: If you unearth something fishy, make sure you talk to a third party before freaking out. It's easy to overlook the details when emotions are involved, and who knows? The chick in the bikini could be his cousin.

- *Have an exit strategy*: What may have begun as an innocent intelligence-gathering mission can quickly lead to hours of obsessing, and before you know it you will be joining Carrie Mathison in the loony bin.

- Want to see if your ex is embarking on a lot of late-night booty calls? If he's on Twitter you can hopefully see what his typical sleeping hours are by when he's tweeting. (If he's tweeting at 2 A.M., he's probably not getting a lot of booty.)

- If you're feeling like he's taking her to all the places he took you to first, and he happens to be on Foursquare, you can see where he's been, and if he made any notes possibly even who he went with and what he had!

CHAPTER 7

Work It, **Girl**

There are days when I can't stand my job or my boss. The irony is that not only did I create the job, but I *am* the boss! Sure, we all want to find a job we're passionate about and something that truly taps into who we are as people, but even if you lock into your dream career, there are days you'd rather be home watching *Good Morning America*.

Even glamorous jobs can threaten your very sanity. I'll never forget the first time I had a mini–nervous breakdown on the job. I was writing my first magazine article (I started out in journalism), and this was my big chance to prove myself. My assignment was to write an article on a fledgling rock band. After interviewing the members of the group (and, might I add, they were ridiculously wasted the entire time and could barely give me a quote), I realized I had left the Record button on for the rest of the afternoon and taped over half of what they said. No! No! No! The piece was due the next day! Since their publicist wouldn't return my calls, I dug up the name of the hotel they were staying at and stalked them until 2 A.M. in the lobby, only to have them stumble in from some MTV party, deny they knew me, and refuse to talk to me. So I stayed up for the next fourteen hours, downing espresso shots by the triplet, piecing together the few bits of info I still had,

MG TIP: Check out a book called *StandOut* that lets you take a test to define your strengths (okay, the book was written by my husband, but it was a bestseller, so other people liked it too!). Not only should it help you better understand what your talents are, but it might help you better position yourself when talking to prospective employers.

and grabbing every factoid I could find on them online. I handed in my work, bleary-eyed, just before my deadline.

Ten minutes later, I got a call from my boss. "Jane, didn't I tell you? We're not doing a story on the band anymore. We're doing a movie roundup instead. I'm *sure* I told you. Next time I suggest you listen better." She hung up, but I was still holding the receiver. I hadn't slept in two days. I smelled. I had a twitch in my eye from all the caffeine. I wanted to curl up in a little ball and be express-mailed to a small, uninhabited island. The point is, no matter how great your job may seem, there will be times you wish you'd never applied.

And nightmare bosses and panic attacks aren't the only hurdles an MG has to deal with. You have a ton of tricky personalities to handle and pressure to perform (because there's always someone who would *loooove* to steal your plum position out from under you). But if you're smart and know how to work certain people and situations to your advantage, you'll be able to navigate the working girl's sometimes rocky path with panache.

How to Land Your Dream Job

Wouldn't it be nice if we all just stumbled upon our perfect career paths in school and everything fell seamlessly into place? For most of us, it's not that simple. You probably have an idea of the field that you'd like to pursue, but aren't sure in what to specialize. Or perhaps you know exactly what company you want to work for but don't have any contacts. Well, an MG doesn't give up her career hunt just because she hits a few roadblocks.

Network, Network, Network

College contacts can be an easy in to nabbing an interview in your desired field. Lucky for us, most colleges have finally hopped on the digital bandwagon and have launched online directories of contacts ripe for the picking. If your alma mater is a little old-school, contact the alumni office directly via e-mail to get introduced to a recent grad in your field of choice. And if no one is available, ask if there are workshops, lectures, or alumni networking events you could participate in. Another option is to simply start calling and e-mailing everyone you know, asking if they have a contact in the field you're interested in, whether it's PR, television, or graphic design. Who knows? Maybe a friend of a friend of a friend's cousin's husband's sister is in the field and would be willing to give you some pointers and contact numbers—or even set up an interview. Last, don't be afraid to put your feelers out at cocktail parties, yoga classes, and even weddings. You can often make the best contacts in relaxed, nonwork-oriented social settings.

Talk to Headhunters and HR Recruiters

One of the quickest ways to launch your job search is to contact a headhunter in your industry of choice. A headhunter is a placement agent who works with a number of companies in specialized fields; these people have tons of incentive to match you up with the right employer. If you get the job, they get a commission from your employer, not from your pocket. That said, they're also looking for you to do some work as well, so be sure to send them positions you're interested in throughout your search. If you have a particular company in mind that you're dying to work for, go to their website, find the name of their HR recruiter, and send off your résumé and cover letter (more on that later). If you are called in for an interview and you impress the individual who talks to you, he or she will pass your info along to the department heads within the company.

Seek Out Internships

For me, an internship was my in to my profession. Sure, it means low (or often no) pay while you watch other people who are close to your age with more power than you, but if you stick around long enough, have a good attitude, and impress the right people, you may be able to land a full-time job or a freelance position within six months to a year.

MG TIP: Bring your business cards in a sleek case wherever you go. If you're currently unemployed, have a set of personal business cards made up with your name, e-mail address, cell or home phone number, and the general field you're in, such as "writer." It looks more professional and saves the scramble for paper and pen.

MG TIP: Find headhunters on the web at www.selectstaffing.com or www.careerbuilder.com.

MG TIP: Pop a mint a few minutes before your meeting. Bad breath is offensive and so is chewing gum!

MG TIP: Companies are usually flooded with potential interns during the summer, but are often begging for help during the fall, winter, or spring. If you're out of work or your class schedule is light, that's a great time to apply.

Take Classes

MG TIP: There are a number of new sites that allow you to take courses hosted by prestigious colleges and experienced professionals. Check out www.edx.com and www.grovo.com to start.

If you're in your late twenties or thirties and want to switch careers, yet you feel like interning would be a big step backward, consider taking part-time classes online or at a community college. Once you're armed with a few classes or even a new degree under your belt, whether it's in marketing or computer science, it's time to start floating your résumé around. (And you might even meet someone who can help you in your new field.)

Writing a Knockout Cover Letter

Your cover letter is basically a one-page sales pitch, with you as the product. It's not about simply restating what's in your résumé; it's a chance for your future employer to get a taste of your personality and goals.

• *The first paragraph* introduces who you are, what you currently do, and how you heard about the company. If you were referred by someone, you can say, "Jane Doe of Fabulous Inc. suggested I contact you about the position you have open in XYZ."

• *The second paragraph* describes what you have to offer the company, based on your key skills and experience (but keep it punchy; your résumé will spell out exactly what you do).

MG TIP: Always put the ball back in your court for the next step (like a follow-up phone call), so you're not waiting for them.

• *The third paragraph* explains the action you're going to take. For example, you'll say that you intend to follow up with a phone call the following week. Last, you'll thank them for their time and consideration. "Sincerely" or "Best regards" is the best way to close.

Writing a Pro Résumé

Your résumé is basically your brag sheet, where future employers get to see everything you've accomplished. But keep it bold, clean, simple, and honest. Studies show that regardless of how long you spend writing your résumé, an employer will look at it for an average of ten seconds. All the more reason to make it as succinct and snappy as possible.

The Basic Structure

* *Name:* Set in bold or capitalize your name, using letters two to six points larger than the rest of the text. Skip the fancy, funky, and cutesy fonts. Put down the name you wish to be called. Otherwise, you run the risk of taking up the first couple of precious interview minutes explaining why you want to be called Gwyn, not Guinevere.

* *Address and e-mail:* List your home address and personal e-mail. Never use your work e-mail unless you plan on having your boss find out about your job search. Just make sure not to use a cutesy e-mail address, like hotcaliforniagirl@anything.com.

* *Objectives:* Some résumé books approve starting with a statement of your goal—"To get a job"—but skip it. Objectives are usually either too specific or so vague that you look as if you really don't know what you want. The only exception to this rule is if you are applying for a job in a completely different field than what you have experience in on your résumé. This can then be a good place to point out that you're looking to employ the skills learned as an investigative journalist in the fascinating field of criminal research, for example.

* *Work experience:* This section starts with your most recent employment or internships and ends with your least recent employment. Don't be afraid to put down that stint as a hostess if it may be relevant. Many skills are transferable, and it's all in how you spin the experience. For instance, if you're interviewing for a job as a PR assistant, you could say hostessing helped you hone your people skills.

* *Education:* Include your college, degree, graduation year, any awards, and your GPA, if it will help. If you studied abroad, list that too. However, if you simply spent a year gallivanting around

MG TIP: If you're in your first real job and can't ask your current boss for a reference, consider a former professor or teacher or even a friend in a more senior position at a different company.

MG TIP: Triple spell-check—and not just with a computer's spell-check; read it over a few times! Remember, the computer won't catch mistakes like writing "one" instead of "won." Also check the consistency of the type style and punctuation of the various elements. Keep it clean and tight. Often when employers get gazillions of résumés, they'll toss any with typos or minor errors to whittle down the applicant pool.

MG TIP: If the info does not fit, you must omit. Keep your résumé to one page so you don't waste a prospective employer's time. When editing your history to fit the one-page-résumé format, don't squeeze it all into 8-point type. If it isn't essential, drop it.

MG TIP: Lying is simply a bad idea. In the age of Big Brother and Google, chances are you'll get caught.

Europe and didn't actually study at a university over there, you might skip that info. You may come across as spoiled and lacking in work ethic. Leave out your high school info.

- *Salary:* Don't spill your current or desired salary on paper. Not only do you risk having the whole company know what you make (lots of résumés get left on copiers) but you could find yourself boxed in. If you're earning far more than the position is offering, they are unlikely to grant you an interview. If far lower, they might think you're too junior.

- *References:* A simple "references upon request" at the bottom of your résumé is sufficient. You don't need to write a list of names and numbers. If you want to impress your interviewer, though, bring a list of references and letters of recommendation with you.

- *Relevant skills:* Tailor the résumé for the specific position. Most potential employers who post job descriptions will list desirable qualities, such as: "trapeze skills a must," or "knowledge of the history of *The Apprentice* is preferred." Plug these descriptions straight into your résumé (as long as you do have them). Also include what computer programs you're proficient in, along with foreign languages in which you're fluent, if it's relevant.

- *Hobbies/interests:* Many headhunters say not to include hobbies on your résumé. On the other hand, it can show that you actually have a pulse and can display teamwork or other relevant skills—especially in somewhat social fields. And if you're a student, or have little professional experience, listing a couple of your outside interests can give you added dimension. Just don't be too quick to brag about your ventriloquism skills or affinity for shopping.

- *Supplementary résumé:* You can consider supplementing with a newer video résumé or graphic résumé, but best to have a traditional one first!

Acing an Interview

Congratulations! The powers that be are intrigued enough by your cover letter and résumé to give you a call. Now they want to meet you in person to see if you are a good fit for the position you're after. To give an interview that gets you the job, follow these pointers:

Prep Like a Pro
The day before your interview (or even earlier), slip into your interview outfit, sit down in a chair, and have a friend do a practice run with you. Or, better yet, have a career counselor hold a practice interview with you. No matter who is hosting, take out your cell phone and record the session so you can see what you need to work on.

Psyche Yourself Up
For every item on your résumé, try to think of how each one illustrates your strengths or weaknesses. It's perfectly okay to hold a copy of your résumé in your hand if you're worried you'll forget something; just make sure you bring more along for the interviewers to review as well.

Know Thy (Future) Master
No matter how much you rehearse your main points, if you don't know enough about the company, your employer won't be impressed. To start, visit your interviewer's LinkedIn profile, and while you're there check to see if the company has one as well. Often businesses will post recent news there, making your research that much easier. Also, be sure to check out the company's website—a great place to get a grasp of all the different divisions, etc.

Dress Appropriately
Review details later on in this chapter, but don't go low-cut (tops), high-cut (skirts), or clingy (fabrics). This is the time to highlight your best mental features, not your physical ones.

Chill
Get a good night's sleep, eat breakfast, and get some fresh air beforehand.

Give Good Body Language

As soon as you see your interviewer, give him or her a firm handshake without breaking eye contact, and smile. Once you're sitting in a chair, continue giving your interviewer plenty of eye contact as you sit tall with your hands folded in your lap (so you won't fidget).

Ask Questions

Think of an interview like a date: It's no fun if only one person is doing all the questioning. So make up some queries ahead of time to ask during the interview. But stay away from questions that sound petty, like how much vacation time you get, benefits, company perks, and so on. You can ask about these once you *get* the job.

MG TIP: If you meet more than one person during your interview, ask for business cards so that you get everybody's name and title right in your thank-you notes.

Don't Be Afraid of Silence

One interview technique many employers use is the pregnant pause. They use it to see if you are nervous and will thus keep babbling to fill the quiet air. This can easily get you in trouble, as you add things into the conversation that you normally wouldn't. So make your answers complete, but when you're done, don't be afraid to give a smile and simply wait for the next question—as excruciating as that may be.

The Smartest Thing to Do in a Job Interview

If anyone knows how to seal the deal in an interview, it's the person I turn to for advice on everything and truly one of the wisest women I know: Kate White, the former editor in chief of *Cosmopolitan* and the bestselling author of a zillion books, including *I Shouldn't Be Telling You This: How to Ask for the Money, Snag the Promotion, and Create the Career You Deserve*. Here's what she had to say:

Much of the advice people dish out about job interviews involves the first seven-eighths of the appointment, and, of course, a lot goes down during that time and it's extremely important to get it right. For instance, the decision not to hire is often made within the first five to fifteen minutes of the interview, so you want to start strong, with a totally appropriate outfit, self-assured body language, and good eye contact. As the interview progresses, you'll want to speak confidently of your accomplishments and ask at least three or four awesome questions. But then you come to the last eighth of the interview, and it's critical to play this right, too. Don't just let things fizzle out or trail off. When the interviewer draws the session to a close with a comment like, "Do you have any other questions?" say something along the lines of, "No, thank you, your answers were really helpful. But there is something I'd like to say. Everything you've told me about this position is very exciting. I think I could do a terrific job for you here and I'd be honored to be offered the opportunity. I hope you'll seriously consider me."

In sales it's called "asking for the business," and it really works. As a pal of mine in sales says, "In a tie, the one who wants it the most wins."

Thank-You Notes for Ingrates

Following up with your interviewer isn't just important, it's expected. Conveniently enough, e-mail is as acceptable as a written letter (though I recommend sending both). This is your chance to remind your potential boss how fabulous you are and to gloss over anything you might have missed (or flubbed) during your interview. (See chapter 3 for an example.) Be sure to address your letter or e-mail "Ms." or "Mr." no matter how "casual" the person seems. Send it no later than a day after your interview.

How to Score Points with Your Boss

Whether you just landed a new gig or want to boost your standing at the job you currently hold, here are a few key tips:

MG TIP: Write thank-you notes! I know one senior executive who simply won't hire someone who doesn't write a thank-you note. As she says, the note is pretty much the only thing a prospective employee can do to show her interest. For extra points, try to include an article on a relevant subject you discussed. Ideally, it will be work-related subject, but even if she mentioned an upcoming vacation spot or hobby, look for something useful to accompany your note.

MG TIP: Find out what car your boss drives. One time I was running late for an important meeting and, in my haste, rudely cut off a car I felt was moving too slowly. As I screeched into the lot, the offending car pulled in, parked, and out stepped my boss, who snidely suggested I drive more carefully in the future. Ugh.

Mirror Your Manager

Ever heard the saying "Monkey see, monkey do, monkey get promoted"? Well, maybe not the last part, but learning how to mirror your boss plants the seed that you're intellectually in sync. Another smart move is nodding and making eye contact when your boss is speaking to your group. It sounds so simple, but too many people keep their heads down out of embarrassment, or scribble endless notes. By holding the boss's gaze and nodding, you're making an unspoken connection that may make him or her tap you for a project over your just-as-capable coworker who's spacing out at the conference table. Also, make sure you participate in conversations and brainstorms when the head honcho is present. I'll never forget a boss of mine telling me once that she was completely baffled by a few of my former coworkers. Apparently they were complaining about not having enough face time with her, so she called a staff meeting to boost morale and generate ideas. And sure enough, the ones complaining about "no face time" never said a word the entire meeting. The boss took note.

Schmooze Wisely

It's tempting to want to ingratiate yourself with your boss by asking, "So what did you do this weekend?" or, "Have you seen such-and-such movie?" but that kind of small talk doesn't go far. Instead, zero in on what she likes or considers herself an expert at and go from there. If she's a wine buff, ask her for a recommendation for a dinner party you're throwing. You're subtly getting her to open up to you, but she'll still feel like the one in control.

Also steer clear of giving your boss hollow praise, like "Fab outfit!" or "Great speech!" She'll see right through it. The trick to giving a professional compliment is in the details. For example, you might say, "Thanks so much for your insight about Company X. You were absolutely right about the stunts they'd pull on the account, and I was ready for it." It's a win-win compliment: She feels like she's doing her job right, and you look good too.

Have Big-Picture Insights

One of the most attractive qualities to a boss is an employee who can think beyond his or her current position without being asked. Once a month, step back from your specific duties and think about general ways your company could run more efficiently, or trends you see happening in your field that you think your company should hop on. Just make sure to back it up with research or you'll look silly. Be careful; in making suggestions don't step on your boss's toes and criticize his or her job performance. Type everything up in an e-mail, present it, and don't check up on whether it's been read or not (your boss will read it when he or she has time). Don't expect to get tons of praise for your ideas, but don't think they'll go unnoticed. You've essentially told your boss, "Not only can I do my job well—I've got the kind of brain that's primed to *manage* my company well." Just be careful not to sound like you're gunning for your boss's plum position.

Be a Problem Solver, Not a Problem Creator

Don't go to your supervisor with a problem without offering a possible solution. It adds to his or her workload and may make you seem like a dependent whiner. Also, don't bother your supervisor with a low-level question you can ask a peer. Your boss will be annoyed that you wasted his or her time and didn't show good problem-solving skills.

How to Get Promoted

Sometimes, no matter how many brownie points you score, your manager still isn't itching to bump you up the ladder. And don't take it personally—promotions are rarely handed out on silver platters. Truth be told, I've never been "given" a promotion. I've asked for them—four times. And each time, I got it. So if you want the better title, *you* have to take the initiative.

MG TIP: Use counter-offers wisely. If you're going to say another company is interested in you and will promote you, be prepared to walk if your company can't compensate you.

MG TIP: Be careful. No matter how savvy your argument, the company or manager may not be ready to promote you. As with suggesting you have another offer, don't grandstand unless you're prepared to walk away.

Set up a Meeting

The best time to ask for a promotion is at your yearly review. However, if you're midway through the year and truly feel you've made strides in your current position, e-mail your boss saying you'd like to set up a meeting to discuss your progress whenever he or she is available.

Toot That Horn

Come to your meeting prepared with a typed list of ways you've exceeded your position, duties you've fulfilled, and outside projects you've taken on, and how your work has benefited the company. You won't necessarily need to give this list to your boss, but having it in your hands will make for easy reference while you're talking.

Go in for the Kill

After listing your assets, say, "I am very excited about growing with this company, and feel that with my work done on X, Y, Z projects, I have shown that I am ready to move to the next level." Under no circumstances should you ever say, "I was wondering if I could maybe, um, move to the next level at some point?" You'll sound like a wuss. Remember, you're not asking to be upgraded from coach to business class. There are no favors here. You're asking for a promotion you *deserve.*

Make a Timeline

So your boss said you weren't ready to make the leap yet. Don't get huffy. Instead, ask your boss how you specifically need to improve in order to nab that higher position. Then say you are going to work on those goals and would like to meet six months from now to reassess your progress. Remember, tons of promotions (mine included) have come from planting a seed at a meeting and reaping the results six months later.

How to Ask for Mo' Money

It's always wiser to ask for a promotion over more cash because it shows you're invested in growing with your company rather than merely improving your bank account. However, your boss may tell you that a higher position isn't possible—so it pays (literally) to come to your meeting prepared with a plan B . . . as in Benjamins.

Do Your Research

Go to www.payscale.com and www.glassdoor.com to get the inside scoop on top salaries for your position. If you fall under those numbers, it's fair game to mention this to your boss. Say, "I know the competitive rate is X amount, and though I can't be promoted at this time, I feel I should be compensated at the competitive rate."

Don't Compare

Doing a little comparison talk is okay in terms of your field, but not in terms of your office. So even though you may know Rebecca from two cubicles down makes 20K more than you, don't throw this info at your boss, hoping it will shock him or her into paying up. Not only will you be chastised for discussing salaries with your coworkers (a big no-no), you're setting yourself up to be told, "It's not wise to compare yourself to another employee. That's not how it works around here."

MG TIP: If you can't get extra cash out of your employer, ask for other perks. Many companies will compensate their employees with more vacation days, more health-care benefits, or "flex points," which mean you might have a more flexible schedule.

Little Extras That Boost Your Professional Vibe

While these things don't guarantee a promotion or mo' money, they can subliminally put you in better standing among your managers and peers.

MG TIP: Don't ever dress better than your boss. Even if you can afford to and it's acceptable to dress to the nines in your office, you don't want to outshine the boss with your style—it has a subtle way of hinting, "I may be younger, but I'm better than you." It's not the kind of attitude you want to give off come raise time.

MG TIP: Avoid long, brightly painted nails. They might show you'd be afraid to do any work that could chip them. And don't go for a strong scent. No matter how much your boss likes you, he or she might not like the thought of working together in close quarters.

MG TIP: Put out a little dish of chocolates or candy on your desk. Sweets can serve as an easy ice-breaker with coworkers. While they're chomping away on naughty treats, they may also be more inclined to fill you in on the latest office news.

Your Wardrobe

In some work scenarios, jeans and T-shirts are the norm, while in other offices, you can't get away with open-toed shoes or going nylon-less. Figure out what the dress code is by looking at the top dogs in your office and follow suit—even if it's not your first choice. Physically aligning yourself with your bosses subconsciously says, "I respect you and want to be seen as one of you." You want to look pulled-together and stylish, but you never want to stand out too much unless you're working in the fashion industry. Big hair, clunky jewelry, low-cut/sheer blouses, and miniskirts are no-no's. If you don't have that big a wardrobe budget, stick to the classics: thin wool pants, pencil skirts, cashmere sweaters, and crisp white shirts.

Your Office

If you had a date coming over and wanted to impress him, you wouldn't have an unmade bed with clothes and stuffed animals everywhere. Same goes for your work space. An office with piles of papers, books, yellow stickies, and takeout boxes everywhere reflects an unorganized employee. Whether you're in a cubicle or have your own office, you want it to look as clean as possible. To streamline your area, get a few sets of standing files or an accordion filing system. Throw out old magazines and papers you haven't used in the past year. The more papers you have out of sight, the cleaner your office will look. To add a little personality, consider hanging art or framed photos (but don't go nuts and include those crazy pics from Cancun—not professional). Fresh flowers and plants will add a Zen-like vibe.

Your Etiquette

Besides the way you and your office look, the way you act can catapult you above your fellow coworkers.

Introductions

The quickest way to show how professional you are is to give the perfect introduction. The common rule is to introduce the lesser person to the more important person. Always include the more important person's title first, and say their full name. For example, "Ms. Bigcheese, I'd like to introduce you to Ms. Jane Doe. Jane, Ms. Mary Bigcheese is the CEO of my company."

Corporate Functions

For most people, cocktail parties, barbecues, and team sports outings are par for the office course. And along with those outings come a few rules. If you're going to your boss's home, bring a gift. A bottle of wine or flowers are always safe bets—just don't get too personal or your coworkers (and your boss) will think you're a brown-noser. If you're at a public event and don't know how long you should stay, leave only after your manager does.

Office E-mails

A good rule is, never put anything in writing that you'd be too embarrassed to say out loud. Unlike conversations, which won't be documented (unless you're Monica Lewinsky), the words you commit to electronic eternity can come back to haunt you. Or worse, they can be sent to the wrong people (what I like to call the TMI Bite-You-in-the-Ass Boomerang Effect). Let's say you get an e-mail from your coworker about an assignment of yours that's overdue, and there are people "CC'd" on it, like your boss and other staff members. You may be tempted to fire back a defensive e-mail to your coworker (like the fact that your assignment is late because your stupid boss keeps loading the work on and, well, you just got in a major fight with your fiancé and you have this gyno appointment you've been stressing about . . .). When you're frazzled and multitasking, it's very easy to accidentally "Reply All" instead of "Reply" with a slip of the finger.

Outsmarting Nightmare Bosses

While I'd love to say that everyone's boss is laid-back, fabulous, and has zero personal agendas, you may wind up with a hybrid of one of these scary supervisors:

The Micromanager

This boss is super-type A (for Anal). The week you're due to turn in a project, he or she will e-mail you eight times a day for progress reports. When the boss takes a vacation, you get calls on the hour just to make sure his or her bonsai tree is well watered. If you show up to a meeting thirty seconds late, your supervisor's eyebrows rise so high it looks like they'll merge with his or her hairline. Jesus, take a Xanax!

When you have an anal boss, the best solution is to beat your supervisor at his or her own game. Make a point to get into the office fifteen minutes before she does, flood him or her with "update" calls, e-mails, and Xerox copies of memos you've sent, even if they don't directly relate to him or her (your boss will want to see them anyway). Also get in the habit of e-mailing your supervisor weekly "progress reports" on various projects you're working on, and send them in the morning before your boss comes into the office so they're the first thing that pops up on his or her screen. Don't worry if your project is only half done; share your game plan and he or she will feel more in control of the situation (and less likely to hassle you or doubt your ability).

The Mood-Swingy Boss

This boss will be sweet one moment and a PMS mess the next. At first you'll think it's something you're doing wrong. But start noticing his or her piss-off patterns: For example, if you ask the boss anything before he or she has a coffee and muffin in the morning, you get a terse, frosty answer. Or maybe the boss acts irritated whenever you try to discuss anything ten minutes before he or she tries to leave the office every night.

In short, learn your boss's hot buttons and work around them. If you have an important issue to discuss and notice he or she is pre-coffee or winding down the day, steer clear until he or she is in receptive mode again. It will make you snicker when you see that other colleagues haven't figured this out—and why should you tell them? Insight is your edge.

The "Let's Be Best Friends" Boss

This is the trickiest type of nightmare boss to deal with—and let's assume it's a she. (If it was a he, people wouldn't assume you're "friends," if you get my drift.) At first she seems like a dream. From the moment she meets you, she wants you to feel like you can tell her anything. She brings you along to fancy-shmancy business events and even dishes secrets about the company CEO to you. She tells you she wants to take you under her wing.

But blurring the lines of your boss-employee relationship can take on an emotional quality that makes things sticky quickly. When your boss gives you criticism on your projects, you'll find yourself taking it personally ("Gosh, is she coming down hard on me because I ducked out early from that event she invited me to last night?"). You also may get false expectations ("She gets along with me better than coworker X, so why did he get promoted faster than I did?"). Or conversely, you may develop the reputation of an office kiss-ass. To keep things on an even keel, establish boundaries. Involve other coworkers when you attend work-related events, and while she may disclose tons of "friendly info" to you, stay quiet to others about what she's told you. While some jobs have more social components than others, you're judged on the basis of your work, not just how many martinis you can throw back with the head honcho.

When You're the Boss

Once you're a manager you inherit a slew of responsibilities you may not have counted on. But countless books have been devoted to this subject, so with another shameless plug, I refer you to *First Break All the Rules*, a great book on management written by (you guessed it) my hubby.

Can Officemates Make Good Friends?

As we all know, bosses aren't the only work personalities we socially rub up against. Whether you're in a corporate office space of a hundred people or a freelance staff of six, you'll quickly decide that you like some colleagues better than others, and soon think of them as "work friends." With some office buddies, the relationship may consist only of swapping funny "How was your weekend?" stories or picking up lunch together. But with another chosen few colleagues, you may wind up extending invitations to each other's cocktail parties, birthday dinners, and even weddings.

It's completely natural to feel connected to certain coworkers and want to extend the friendship beyond office walls. You form natural alliances that can sometimes exist outside the workplace. But there are a few things to keep in mind when you're socializing:

Blood Is Thicker Than Business Cards

The friends you have outside of work are your family. Your blood buddies. They are the ones you can bitch about your boss to and wear sweatpants and zit cream in front of, and they will not change their opinion of you when they see you at your worst. But work friends *will* (at least at the beginning of your friendship); no matter how close you think you are. One day, when the two of you are up for the same position (honey, it happens), your coworker's going to use those secrets you confided or those less-than-perfect memories she has of you to make you look weaker. And why shouldn't she? For the most part, with office friends, never forget that work comes first, friendship *second*. So don't let even your closest work friends see your weaknesses (you used to have an eating disorder/you're having marital problems) or hear about your insecurities (you can't get promoted/ you're not happy at your company).

Friendships May Change When One of You Is Promoted

The best office friendships are between people on the same level who don't work directly with each other. But if you get bumped up to a higher position in the same field, problems can ensue. The underdog may feel jealous and competitive (it's only natural) and may get resentful. Or, the reverse may happen. She may beg you to put in a good word for her with your boss so she can get promoted too. Tell her you'll try, but don't do it. Though you may feel obligated to look out for her, you'll only look unprofessional in the eyes of your boss.

Don't Advertise Relationships with Old Coworkers

It's certainly smart to stay in touch with old colleagues because you never know when a new job opportunity will pop up. But if the boss and your friend had a falling-out when your coworker left the company, it's best to keep your friendship on the down low. Don't have your friend come to your office to meet for lunches, and don't let anyone hear you talking on the phone. Make plans for coffee over the weekend instead. You don't want your boss hearing that you've been hanging out together because he or she may perceive it as disloyalty to the company.

The Six Toxic Coworkers to Avoid

Though every MG can benefit from having a few key cronies at the office, sometimes people you work directly with are best kept at arm's length if possible. Here's how to deal with their tricky personalities:

The Gossip

A gossip loves to keep you informed about the dirt that's going on in your office—who's on the verge of getting fired, who's sleeping with whom, or new company cutbacks she's heard about through the grapevine. Of course you didn't *ask* her to give you all this taboo info. She simply likes to slip it into conversations . . . especially in the ladies' room.

Sure, a gossip may be valuable to you. Let's say she passes along that your boss was upset with one of your coworkers because they did X or Y, which teaches you not to make that same mistake. But the bad part about getting too close to a gossip is that she gets you to chime in on what *you* think of so-and-so, and then repeats that info to someone else. Remember: If she's gossiping about other people to you, chances are she's gossiped about you to other people.

How to Deal

Play dumb. Say she drops into your office and poses the question, "Gee, did you hear the boss screaming at Bill? I bet he's gonna get canned," or "Can you believe how fat Jennifer's getting? She must be pregnant . . ." Don't nod and agree to anything she says, or you're aligning yourself with her. Take the Swiss route by being perfectly neutral and out of touch. As in, "Huh, I honestly didn't even notice. I have such tunnel vision, guess I'm completely out of the loop!" If you can't give her any new info to gossip about, she can't screw you. But you still benefit from getting new info from her.

The Prozac Case

Anytime there's work to do, she comes into your office and starts bitching about it. Often this will include trash-talking your boss or the company. And it's hard not to chip in a little when you're feeling the pain too. But not only does her whining drag down your morale, she's a total time-suck because you're playing the part of her therapist while she dumps on you about her never-ending life problems.

How to Deal

Try to limit your one-on-one interactions, even if she insists on after-work drinks. When you're helplessly cornered by her in the office, don't indulge her by being too sympathetic and advice-ready. When her stress talk starts getting nutso, cap it off with, "Yeah, I totally know what you mean . . . what time is it? Shoot, I'd love to keep talking but I've gotta get back to the grind. Ugh." Once she senses that you're stressed out too (especially if you put emphasis into rolling your eyes when you say "*Ugh*"), she'll be less likely to see you as the answer to her problems. Then start typing at your keyboard or shuffling through papers—giving her the hint to waddle out of your office already.

The Nosy Parker

The second she meets you, she wants to know everything about you—how long you've been at the company, if you've had any previous promotions, how old you are, which college you graduated from, what your boyfriend or husband does, and where you live. Don't be fooled into thinking it's because she's wants to be fast friends. Constant quizzing is her way of sizing you up, almost in a Darwinian sense, to see if you're competition in the office jungle. And the more info you give her up front, the more likely she'll needle you with stickier questions later on, like asking what your salary is after volunteering hers.

How to Deal

Be as discreet as you can, and don't let her get too close. If she asks you a question, throw it right back at her so she's the one doing the talking. After she answers, switch the subject so she can't go back to it. Should she continue to press you for info, laughingly say, "Wow, are we playing twenty questions or something?!" Or simply be straightforward: "Y'know, I'd love to tell you my salary, but it's the kind of personal info I probably shouldn't give, I'm sure you understand." By being friendly but coolly detached, you'll remain a little mysterious to her. And mystery is key—when she doesn't have you entirely figured out, you stay one step ahead of her.

The Ass-Kisser

Unlike The Rookie (see below) who truly admires you, the ass-kisser only pretends she does. She may come over and give you a big hug for getting a promotion to her level, or compliment your great hair or outfit on a daily basis. She may also tell you things like, "Gosh, you're such a superstar at the company. How do you do it?" Once she feels like she's poured it on thick enough, the favors will come flooding in. For example, she'll ask you to cover for her on her project "because you're so much better than me at this kind of stuff." What she's trying to do is ply you with compliments to manipulate you into thinking she admires you . . . and then saddle you with work.

How to Deal
Throw the BS back in her face (in a friendly way, of course). When she starts overflowing with false flattery, say, "I may be good at X, but you are so great at Y!" When you keep coming back at her with compliments, she'll get sick of giving them—and she'll no longer have an open door to trample you with requests for favors.

The Rookie

She's younger than you and in a position below yours (or is even an intern) but it's clear that she isn't content with being there for long—because she has her eyes on *your* job. She schedules lunches with you so she can "pick your brain." She may turn into a copycat, dressing like you, arranging her office like yours, and imitating your mannerisms in meetings. While we all know that imitation is the best form of flattery, it can get annoying and slap you in the face later on. Of course you want her to succeed, but show her all of your tricks and you may soon be working for *her*.

How to Deal
You can continue to be her "mentor," but establish your authority. Make sure she sees you talking to your superiors in a way that demonstrates that you're more "in" with them than she is. Don't ever let her

see you stressing over a project—it'll only show your weakness. Offer your help on projects to establish that she still has a ways to go before knowing everything you do.

The "Been There, Done That" Cynic

This coworker is older than you (it could be just two or three years) and resentful because she's been at the company longer than you have, yet you're higher on the ladder than she is. She'll be cordial to your face because she doesn't want to look envious or threatened, but behind your back all she can think is, *"She obviously had someone pull some strings for her to make it this far this quickly."* You'll notice her snickering when you can't get the fax machine working or blurt something out in a meeting that gets shot down by the boss. It's her way of taking pleasure in your "sorry, I'm new at this" type of mistake—and reinforcing that *she's* the knowledgeable one who should be in your position.

How to Deal

By no means be an ass-kisser (see above), but give her ego a little stroke. Right now, you're a constant reminder of her "lesser" status—but if you make her feel important it will be harder for her to hate you. Even if you have to delegate things to her, you could ask her the question, "I know you're more of a pro at this than me. How would you suggest we do X, Y, Z?" When she gets the impression that you value her point of view, she'll feel less threatened and be less likely to want to see you do a face-plant in front of the CEO.

How to Deal with Backstabbers

Who, *her*? Screw *you* over? *Naaahh*. Honey, wake up and smell the catty. Sometimes, a toxic coworker can morph into a full-blown backstabber without your realizing it . . . until it's too late. Here's how to do damage control for the following office injustices:

Catty Coworker Crime 1: Someone Starts a Rumor Starring You

One of your work allies pulls you aside and says she needs to tell you that "some things are being said about you, and they're not good." It's all the more frustrating when you can't pinpoint the source of the rumor. You might suspect your loose-lipped gossipy coworker is the culprit, but it could just as easily be that quiet colleague who is jealous of you and let something slip out at the water cooler.

When you aren't sure who started it, it's smarter *not* to try to witch-hunt every possible candidate because they'll simply deny ever spreading it. It's also unwise to send an officewide e-mail stating your innocence; it will only make you look desperate. Instead, think about the most important people the rumor might have made its way to—like your boss and other colleagues who hold you in high esteem—and stop it there. Explain that you've just heard what's been going around and should it make its way to them, you want to be the first to say that it is completely inaccurate. Should anyone ask you about it point-blank, tell them the rumor is untrue and whoever spread it sounds like they have too much time on their hands. Then wash *your* hands of it. When you don't make a big deal out of rumors, they die.

Catty Coworker Crime 2: Someone Bad-Raps You to the Boss

You crept into work fifteen minutes late twice this past week. Or you spent company time surfing for wedding reception venues or catching up on Hollywood gossip. Before you know it, your boss wants to have a little *chat* with you.

After you're reprimanded for your bad behavior (which, in all honesty, you know it was), you can't help wanting to stick your tattletale's head under a Xerox machine. (Which you won't because that would get you into even more trouble.) Since you probably can't prove who tattled on you, let this one go. But just make sure all of your tattletale suspects see you at peak performance from then on. Give them a smug, "I have it all together" smile and they won't get any satisfaction from thinking you got burned by the boss.

Catty Coworker Crime 3: Someone Steals Your Idea

You slaved away on a fabulous new concept, and then it got into the wrong hands. It could be as simple as a coworker reading your notes while you get up to refill your coffee at a meeting (that'll teach you to keep your papers face-down). Or, maybe someone overhears you talking about your idea over the phone. Whatever the case, before you know it, a coworker is presenting *your* idea to your boss at a meeting, right in front of your face. Though you can't yell "thief!" the best way to go is to start asking her specific questions about her plan. Chances are she'll get tongue-tied because she hasn't done all the research you have. Then it's your turn to chime in about how you had a similar idea, but can see a way to troubleshoot around the problems your coworker has posed. Bingo. Smart, sweet revenge.

Are *You* a Backstabber?

While it's often easy to point out who's out to get *you*, it's harder to come to terms with the fact that you may be a backstabber yourself. So be honest: Is there someone in the office you can't help hating? Maybe she's just a little more on her game than you—she's always in the office earlier, dresses better, makes smarter suggestions in meetings, and is a favorite of your boss. And even though you consider yourself a kind person, you'd love to see her mess up, just a little. You might even find yourself gossiping about her to your friends, your significant other, your hairdresser . . .

But stop! Since you're such a smart MG, you know that backstabbing isn't the wisest way to advance your career. So get to the root of your problem: Chances are, you're feeling jealous and threatened by her. The best way to stomp out those feelings is to study her: Take the qualities you're envious of and make them yours.

When It's Necessary to Tell the Boss

While none of us likes to be a tattletale, sometimes a coworker's behavior is so heinous or neglectful that you must say something to a superior. You know what I mean—stealing from the company, stealing someone's ideas big time, lying to a client about the boss. But how do you accomplish this without looking like a snitch or making an enemy? First off, keep in mind that timing is everything. This is not the type of thing that you want to bring up in the middle of a busy day or around busybody coworkers. If possible, try to schedule something off-site, such as coffee or lunch, which will not only give you more privacy, but will look less suspicious than going behind closed office doors. Next, request confidentiality and communicate your concern for maintaining good office relationships. Explain that you seriously considered not saying anything, but felt that it would be in everyone's best interest if you did. Perhaps most important, after explaining the situation, present possible solutions. But don't be too pushy—remain open to your boss's suggestions, as your manager may have a bigger picture understanding of where the problem came from and any steps that are currently being addressed to solve it.

Sex, Lies, and Hopefully Not Videotape

Considering that most of us are spending at least forty hours in the workplace per week, it's no wonder that we're all getting so jiggy at the office. According to a 2013 CareerBuilder survey of more than 4,200 full-time workers, 39 percent of office workers said they had dated a coworker at least once in their working lives, and of those who dated at work, 30 percent said their office romance led to marriage. What was the most common time to start an affair? Twelve percent said happy hour, 12 percent said outside of work, 12 percent said late nights at work, and 11 percent said lunch.

Having an Affair with the Boss

In the CareerBuilder survey, 38 percent of women and 21 percent of men had a romance with a superior. But according to a recent study by the Society for Human Resource Management, employers are taking these relationships more seriously, with 42 percent now reporting relationship policies versus only 20 percent in 2005 and 99 percent forbidding supervisor-subordinate relationships. So these connections are better left for romance novels.

Big, fat no. Not only are you setting yourself up to be gossiped about by your peers, you'll have to deal with the awkwardness of having to answer to this person when you break up. So decide—is it really love? If you can't imagine yourself without your boss, then seek out a new job or a transfer to a different area of your company. Even smarter is putting your lust on ice. Chances are your boss is already married or tangled in a divorce, and you may just be his temporary diversion. You—and your career—deserve better than that.

What happens when people think you're sleeping with the boss and you're not? Even if you just have a cozy rapport with your superior, your coworkers may start to talk.

So how do you deal? As discussed in the section on gossip above, it isn't wise to draft a companywide newsletter stating your innocence. It has a funny way of making you look guilty . . . and paranoid. Instead, make subtle moves that distance you from your boss a bit. Avoid the cute little jokes and compliments you might have shared. If he invites you on a business trip, suggest that another of your colleagues go as well. The shift will be subtle enough that your boss won't notice, yet other people will. Also drop hints about other guys you are seeing. And should someone drunkenly approach you at a company party with the question, "So, I heard you're banging the boss, how is it?" simply say, "Nope, I'm not. But since you're the one who brought up the subject, are *you*?" If it's a guy, he'll be doubly embarrassed.

MG TIP: Avoid dating your assistant. He'll be sleeping with *his* boss and, trust me, it will get awkward. (Getting your coffee will turn into a whole relationship-power discussion.) If your attraction is just too strong, see if he can switch to another department.

What Is Sexual Harassment?

Sometimes flirty office relationships can go one step too far. According to the U.S. Equal Employment Opportunity Commission, sexual harassment is a form of sex discrimination that violates Title VII of the Civil Rights Act of 1964. It's basically any unwelcome sexual advance or conduct on the job that creates an intimidating, hostile, or offensive working environment. It could range from smutty, belittling jokes to on-the-job pornography to blatant sexual assault.

If you feel you've been harassed, experts say the first step is to let the harasser know that the behavior is unwelcome. Confront the

MG TIP: *Before* you make your complaint, experts recommend getting a copy of your employee evaluation to show you're in good standing with the company. If you wait to get your records until after you complain, your employer may retaliate by trying to transfer or fire you, claiming poor job performance (especially if he's the one doing the harassing).

harasser as soon as the behavior occurs, if possible. Say clearly and firmly that the harassment is unwelcome and that you want it to stop at once. Being vague or polite in your communication may not be adequate because the harasser may not realize that his or her behavior was offensive. A clear communication requesting a stop to the behavior may just take care of the problem. In fact, a quarter of men in a 2011 ABC News/*Washington Post* poll said they were worried about being falsely accused of sexual harassment, meaning they might just shape up after a verbal warning.

But if your harasser ignores your verbal requests, or you're too uncomfortable to speak face-to-face, write a terse letter demanding an end to the behavior—and save a copy. If it still doesn't stop, follow the sexual harassment or complaint policy in your employee handbook, or ask someone in the HR/personnel department how to make a sexual harassment complaint. If you are given the runaround, tell a trusted manager and supervisor. And document every offensive piece of evidence you get—letters, photos, e-mails, presents. Though you may not plan to file a lawsuit, if you ever have to prove your case to a company investigator, government agency, or jury, you'll want to have hard evidence.

Making a Smooth Exit

It's pretty much a given that you'll leave your job at some point. You may get lured away by another company, not click with a new boss who was brought in to replace your old one, or simply decide you need a break from nine-to-five-ing and want to start your own business or have a family. Whatever the reason for leaving, it's key to exit on a high note.

Put on Your Hollywood Face

Sure, all you may want to say on your way out is, *"Ha!* I'm off to greener pastures, suckers!"* But put on a smile as you walk out (who cares if it's totally fake?). Remember, this is the last snapshot your coworkers will have of you. And you'll want them to remember you favorably should you call them a year from now to network.

Don't Leave Your Coworkers in the Lurch

Sure, your mind may be on other things, but don't forget that the work isn't the only thing you'll be leaving behind. Your coworkers will be stuck doing whatever it is you didn't. Don't leave your desktop disorganized or piles of papers for them to sort through. They'll resent you forever. The worst is the person who spends her last week getting feted by everyone and leaves that same gang to clean up her mess.

Discourage the Going-Away Party Squad

Unless you're leaving the company to have a baby or start your own company, going-away parties are awkward. Your coworkers may feel resentful that you're going to a presumably better organization that's paying you more cash—or be worried because they have to cover your workload until the boss hires your replacement. Instead of all the fuss and cake, it's better to gather your closest cronies and tell them you'd love to take them all out to lunch on your last day. That way, you won't get any weird surprises.

What to Do If You Are Let Go

You probably want to tell your boss to go to hell. I don't blame you. But you must keep your cool so that your employer can write you a solid recommendation letter. If budget cutbacks or the "last hired/first fired" credo was the reason for your being let go, negotiate a severance package and ask the company to help you with future job placement. If,

MG TIP: Don't let pride keep you from applying for unemployment in between jobs. Go to www.dol.gov to find out information and eligibility for your state.

however, you feel you were wrongfully terminated, you can take legal action to have your reasons for leaving changed from "dismissal" to "resignation," which will look better on your updated résumé.

Maternity Leave: How and When to Break the Big "P" News to Your Boss

So your EPT test just read positive, and you and your significant other are thrilled. But while you may be understandably excited and ready to shout your news to the world, you may want to wait to share the good news with your boss until you get your thoughts together first.

MG TIP: Although doctors say a pregnancy is safest after twelve weeks (translation: you should stay mum until you've successfully hit that three-month mark), you may be anxious to share the news earlier. My advice is to tell only those people whom you talk to regularly and consider good friends (or family). You might need support from them should something go wrong. What you *don't* want to do is tell the world, and months after a problem arises have to relive it with someone you've been out of touch with.

Do Your Research

Once you've given yourself a bit of time to revel in the good news, it's time to do some research and come up with a plan. Through the Family and Medical Leave Act, you are entitled, by law, to up to twelve weeks' leave during a calendar year. Your employer is not required to pay your salary during this time but must give you your same job or a job with equal pay and benefits when you come back. You might be entitled to some disability pay, but it will probably be less than your normal paycheck. Some employers offer paid leave. Check to see what your boss's and company's policies are, check into your particular state's laws, and talk to other employees at work who have been through the process.

If you find that your company policy does not offer paid maternity leave and you can't afford not to work, you'll probably end up using a combination of short-term disability, sick leave, vacation, personal days, and unpaid family leave during your maternity leave. Before you decide how much leave you want to request, weigh the financial consequences. The truth is, it's nearly impossible before actually having your baby to really anticipate how much maternity leave time you'll want to take. So when making your calculations, keep in mind that you'll most likely want—and need—more than you think.

Paid Maternity Leave

If you find that your boss and company offer paid maternity leave and full benefits, count your blessings . . . you are among a lucky few. Just remember that it is being offered with the understanding that you will be returning to work. If you are planning to stop working post-baby, be honest with your boss. If you plan to quit at the end of your leave, don't lie. I know it's painful to think of all that paid maternity leave going to waste, but it's just the right thing to do. You might find that your boss will be willing to compromise by giving you a partial paid leave or allowing you to retain your benefits for a time.

When to Take Your Leave

Deciding when to take your maternity leave is really a question of personal preference. You may want to work right up to your due date so you can spend more time with your new baby. Or you may want to rest up predelivery. Just be flexible with yourself. You may find that at just thirty-six weeks you're feeling exhausted all the time. Give yourself some room to change your mind. Most likely your boss will understand if you ask to redistribute a couple of weeks of your leave time.

Breaking the News to Your Boss

To ensure you'll be covered by the Family Medical Leave Act, you must inform your boss at least thirty days before the date you would like to start your maternity leave. But exactly when you decide to make your announcement before that time is up to you. Before you tell your boss your news, just be sure to have a specific plan mapped out. Don't feel bad if your employer isn't immediately ecstatic at your news. Remember: If you are a valuable employee, the company will be nervous about losing you for three months, let alone for a lifetime. With this in mind, offer to write a detailed plan of how your duties will be delegated in your absence, help find and train a temporary employee, and prepare your coworkers for your absence.

Enjoying Your Time Off

Now that you've done everything to make the transition from the workplace to the maternity ward as easy and worry-free as possible, relax, enjoy, and bask in the anticipation of the arrival of your child. Once the date of your hard-earned maternity leave finally arrives, revel in it. You and your baby deserve it.

When Power Chicks Reenter the Workforce Post-Baby

These days, more and more MGs know they can have it all—a fabulous career and babies to boot. Women make up almost half the nation's workers, with 57 percent of all mothers with children one year old or younger working either full-time or part-time, reports the Bureau of Labor Statistics. But that doesn't mean it's a piece of cake to transition back into the working world after twelve short weeks with your newborn. Here's how to make the process as seamless as possible:

Do a Drive-By

Visit work a week or two before your first day back. Bring baby pictures (it'll help you reconnect with your colleagues). And meet with your boss to discuss your options if you're looking to change your schedule or responsibilities.

Take It Slow

Return to work on a Thursday or Friday; having a short first week makes things easier. Also, for your first couple of weeks, ask your employer if you can work part-time (like three days a week) or work shorter days (leaving at 4 P.M. instead of 6 P.M.).

Discuss Going Part-Time

Sometimes, it's just too much of a transition to go back to a five-day-a-week gig, and frankly, you may not have the desire. If your workplace is flexible, it may be possible to work different hours, only contribute to big projects, or work from home one day per week.

Don't Expect to Operate at Your Peak

You may get frustrated with the fact that you're no longer an on-the-go, wheeling-and-dealing, martinis-with-the-head-honcho type of employee. Your priorities have likely shifted a bit—and even though you want to be at work, you just don't have that same tigress gusto. Relax. The only person who's putting pressure on you is you.

Get Your Man to Stay Home!

Now, a growing number of employers are providing paid paternity leave to fathers, ranging from a few days to a few weeks. Nationally, about 14 percent of companies offer the benefit, according to a 2014 national study of employers by the Families and Work Institute.

Freelancing: Just Too Good to Be True? Will It Take Your Paycheck Away from You?

Some of us just hate working for someone else. I am that kind of person. For whatever reason, I will do *anything* for a client but hate to do something for a boss. I don't know why, and I owe big apologies to the bosses whom I have worked for (yup, you know who you are). And it seems I am not the only one. In the past ten years, the global community of freelancers has grown not only because of the nature of our jobs, but because of our economy and, it seems, preference. But is freelancing right for everyone?

Of course what we all fantasize about when we think about freelancing is working when we want, where we want; taking vacations on

MG TIP: Decide whether you're going to work fewer hours (and reduce your salary) or whether you can truly work from home. Better to reduce your pay (if you can afford to) than to have your boss and coworkers resent your being paid to spend time with your child.

MG TIP: Give yourself a break. Modern mom or not, chances are you expect a lot from yourself. Remember, no one is perfect and you can only do the best you can.

the spur of the moment; not having irritating coworkers; and not having to deal with unwanted confining dress codes or long commutes.

What we forget about are the risks of not having a guaranteed paycheck, having no one to pass work off to, having to do *all* the work—like marketing yourself, accounting, and emptying the trash cans—fixing all the mistakes, and having no paid vacation.

So how should you decide whether the freelance life is for you? And if you want to be a freelancer, how should you go about it? Well . . .

Is Freelancing Right for You?

- Know your personality! Are you self-motivated or do you need someone to keep you going to get the job done? If it's the latter, freelancing may not be for you . . .

- Remember that you will be accountable to your clients . . . and many of them work a typical nine-to-five day! While you may be able to slip out for a movie occasionally, remember that they will want you to be around when they need you. So if you aren't available too often, they may move on to someone who is!

- Know that being freelance doesn't mean that you are suddenly carefree. Chances are, you will probably worry more! I remember showing up late to my own rehearsal dinner because I had to get a report out to a client and there was no one but *me* to do it. And since I was about to head out to my wedding and honeymoon, it had to get done right away. You are responsible to the client and the buck literally stops with you. You may work more nights, weekends, and holidays than you ever have, but at the end of the day, some people like working for themselves more than for someone else. Some people don't. It's neither right nor wrong. It's just different!

But if you still think that freelancing is for you . . . here's what you should do:

SO YOU THINK YOU CAN BE A FREELANCER . . .

- Okay, so you think freelancing is for you . . . well, the most important thing you need to freelance is not a cool business card, great office space, or hip logo. It's clients! So don't quit your day job until you've got a good flow of clients.

- In fact, consider moonlighting as a freelancer at first to see how you like the pace and servicing your clients.

- Set reasonable rates! Try to get a sense of what others are charging in your area of expertise. While it's true that you can always come down in your price and you can never go up (on a project, not in your business overall!), you don't want to drive away your clients off the bat!

- Look at your local paper, Craigslist, or LinkedIn to see what jobs are most wanted. Is your service one of them? If not, make sure you can find a way to market yourself and get your name out there!

- Next, let everyone know what you are doing and offer a referral fee. Often people are more motivated to refer you if there is something in it for them.

- Create a portfolio to show what you do. Consider doing projects for friends or for low or no pay at first to make sure you have some great samples.

- Join professional organizations in your field, both online and in your community.

- Try to have at least six months to a year's worth of savings in the bank before you quit your job.

According to *Forbes*, here are the ten best freelance careers :

Marketing
Marketing coordinator, marketing manager, project manager

Business Project Management
Project manager, process analyst

Web Development
Junior developer, Web application developer, Web content developer

Writing
Content manager, copywriter, editor, technical writer, blog writer

Accounting
Accounting clerk, property accountant, bookkeeper, accountant

Insurance Inspection
Residential insurance inspector, insurance appraiser

Teaching and Tutoring
Subject teacher, instructional designer, education coordinator, consulting teacher

Social Media
Social media coordinator, community manager

Graphic Design
Digital designer, visual designer, communications designer

Administrative Assistance
Executive assistant, personal assistant, administrative assistant

THE PROS AND CONS OF WORKING FROM HOME

More and more companies these days are allowing employees to work from home. And while that may seem like a dream, it's not the right choice for everyone.

PROS	CONS
Flexibility	Isolation
Fewer distractions (coworkers, meetings)	Super distracting/ need to be disciplined (family, mail, organizing the closet)
Being at home! (family, pets)	Being at home (family, obligations, errands)
No commute (less stress)	Overlooked for promotion
More flex time (can shop/do appointments in off hours)	Work never ends (can never turn it off)

Doing Good the Modern Girl Way

While MGs need to find work they're passionate about, more and more we are realizing the importance of doing good, not just doing well in life. I encourage you to find a cause to spend your time, not just your money, on. (Though contributing financially is a good thing too.) Of course, sometimes finding a cause that you want to spend your valuable free time committing to is tricky, so I asked Norah Weinstein, copresident of an incredible group called Baby2Baby, to tell me how she found her way. Baby2Baby donates gently used goods to families in need in Los Angeles. Though they have a prestigious board and team, including Jessica Alba, Nicole Richie, Rachel Zoe, Soleil Moon Frye, and many others, it is the fact that they manage to give out more than a million diapers a year and more that impresses so many. Here's what Norah had to say:

I always wondered how to find the right cause for me— I thought I might have to wait until a horrible disease struck someone I love and then work to combat it . . . but I don't think that's the only way . . .

Of course you have to "connect" to the cause—this might mean something general like children, the elderly, or the arts, or it might mean something very specific, like colon cancer (the disease that did end up striking someone I loved). But not all of us have something like that or feel like that makes sense for us. My mom loves the excitement of volunteering at the emergency room—that sounds scary and awful to me! So make sure you find an organization that works for you!

On the flip side, you should find an organization that wants you! As the copresident of Baby2Baby, I know we pride ourselves on the fact that we need so much help—we need volunteers to sort clothes for low-income children, to make sure their toys have batteries, and to clean up gently used strollers. We need creative people to help plan our events, talented business minds to make recommendations about our investments, and students to intern . . . and then of course we need to raise money. Many organizations, just as deserving in their causes, only need checks! If you are someone who wants to write a check and move on, terrific! If you are looking to get your hands dirty, that is not the right match for you."

CHAPTER 8

Modern Girl Seduction Tricks

It's an MG's birthright to feel sexy and confident, both inside the bedroom and out. But between job stress, weight freak-outs, PMS, and relationship woes, it's no wonder most of us feel more like Bridget Jones than Kate Upton when it comes to seducing men.

Living in the age of *Extreme Makeover* doesn't help either. We're practically shown with a Sharpie where our flaws are and how to fix them with the proper sucking, slicing, and stapling machines. With all that negative input, why bother even taking your clothes off?

In fact, according to a recent survey by Dove Research, only 4 percent of women around the world consider themselves beautiful, with 54 percent noting themselves as their worst critic when it comes to how they look.

But it's not impossible to alter your attitude—you just need to do a little hottie homework. Now, I used to refuse to read any advice on sex and relationships. It seemed that if I read it, it wouldn't be "real" or natural. Yet that's like saying you should be able to prepare every recipe in the world without ever looking at a cookbook. Lately, I've learned to love cookbooks, so you deduce what you want from there. Sex books sell. Not-having-enough-sex books sell. Sure, everyone says they'd rather be smart; but who wouldn't want a little extra erotic appeal?

I remember the first time I "demo-ed" a *Cosmo* move on my man, after resolving to be more open-minded about adding some new sex tricks to my repertoire. As the tip suggested, I set my alarm fifteen minutes early so I could give my husband a particularly pleasurable wake-up call in the morning. (If you're not catching my drift, the move gave whole new meaning to the phrase *"rise* and shine.") Though I won't gross you out with the details, he was so ridiculously ecstatic at what I had just done, he canceled his morning staff meeting due to an "important breakfast meeting with a new client." (You better be catching my drift this time.) And though I wouldn't recommend full-body blindsiding your man to the point that he almost loses his job, shaking up your frisky routine can be a very good, even empowering thing. Whether you're married, dating, or single, every Modern Girl can benefit from a little extra help in the bedroom, the living room, or any other room, for that matter.

How to Feel Sexier in Your Own Skin

Getting rock-solid confidence in the bedroom starts with being completely comfortable with your body. (Because no man will ever say that a chick with body hang-ups makes for a fun sexual partner.) Here are a few techniques that will get you there:

Take Pride in Upkeep

Make good grooming your naughty little secret, no matter how chaotic (or lackluster) life feels at the moment. Sure, you could easily get away with skipping your regular Brazilian bikini waxes and pedicures in the dead of winter or when you're not dating anyone. But I guarantee if you keep up the sexy little rituals even when you haven't been exposed to the sun /a man in months, you're going to walk around feeling more on top of things. And though I can't scientifically prove you'll attract more men knowing you're smoothed, buffed, defuzzed, and polished all over, it often is a fabulous by-product.

Going Brazilian (for Those Afraid to Fly)

Okay, so you want to wax, but it just sounds too painful and too problematic. Well, here are a few tips:

- Never get a bikini wax during, or right before, your period. It will be far more painful (not to mention potentially embarrassing), as your skin is more sensitive then.

- Don't get your legs waxed while wearing a skirt. No matter how good the waxer, your legs will have little red bumps that make it look like you have either hives or chicken pox. The best bet is loose-fitting pants.

- Ditto, don't wax right before a hot date. No matter how hot the evening, no one wants to see anything red and bumpy anywhere.

- Take an Advil forty-five minutes before you start your wax to help keep any inflammation at bay.

- Do be specific. Suffice it to say I once told a waxer to take off what she thought would look good. Well, turns out that was *everything*. While the bare look may appeal to some, it's not what I was going for. Think of her as your hairdresser—while I wouldn't recommend bringing pictures, pointing out your "limits" is appropriate.

- Don't wear nice undies. You're getting a wax, not going on a date. Chances are your waxer will ask you to remove everything (especially if you're going Brazilian), and you may ruin your panties with any residual wax.

- Do ask if they have wax for sensitive skins. Most high-profile salons will have green or purple wax that contains soothing ingredients for a less painful experience.

- Don't feel obliged to chat. If chatting distracts you, great. If you'd rather focus on the pain, just mention how tired you are, close your eyes, and try not to yelp.

- Try to relax and not be embarrassed. Think of your waxer as an aesthetic gynecologist. She's sees what you've got going on ten

MG TIP: Try a product called Tend Skin Liquid (www.tendskin.com) and apply daily to avoid ingrown hairs. I don't know why, but it's the only such product I've found that really works.

times a day. Chances are she's seen many who are hairier/redder/bonier than you are.

Revel in Your Sensual Self

Stop thinking that the only time you need to feel sensual is when you're going out on a date. The truth is, you'll wind up feeling sexier overall if you take time to reward your body in private. So instead of always hopping in for a two-minute shower after the gym, block out time to soak in a bubble bath with vanilla candles all around you. When you step out of the tub, wrap up in thick, fluffy towels and take a generous five minutes to apply scented lotion to your legs. Rub it in slowly and deeply, working your way from the tops of your thighs to the tips of your toes, then give your legs a little squeeze. Instead of getting into sweats or flannel pajamas, slip into something silky so that you can enjoy how deliciously slippery your skin feels.

Get a Guru

There's a reason we pay people to keep our minds and bodies in peak form—it just works. If you think it's frivolous to invest in a personal trainer, Bikram yoga class, or hot stone massage, consider how much money you probably blow going to movies, eating out, and buying yet another pair of jeans—which only makes you feel more guilty when you can't fit into them. I dare you to cut down on those spending outlets for a month and redirect that extra cash toward something purely "you"—even if it's just a weeklong pass for spinning classes at your gym. You'll notice a sexy self-fulfilling prophecy: When you take the steps to treat your body right, you give off the vibe that *you* deserve the best too.

Hush Your Inner Critic

Charlize Theron says she feels sexier when she's carrying around an extra ten pounds. Beyoncé doesn't apologize for her ample tush—she revels in it. Sure, you might be thinking, "Easy for these women to

MG TIP: You're not the only one spending half your paycheck at the salon. According to the YWCA, women in the United States spend a total of $7 billion on cosmetic products each year, which individually adds up to $6,423 every five years. Yikes!

MG TIP: If you're trying to find a trainer, head to your gym and ask for recommendations. Talk to other people this person has trained, and don't commit to a series of sessions until you've seen if you click.

MG TIP: If you'd rather cast a wider net, try www.respond.com, where you can fill out your request and get several trainers "bidding" on you as a client. It works in most major cities.

MG TIP: If you need another reason not to body-bash, a recent survey by the lingerie company Bluebella reported that while most women consider a slender frame with boyish hips the most desirable, men actually want curves.

say; they were born gorgeous!" But that's not the point—they could easily find flaws if they looked hard enough. They're just not wasting their time. So how can you apply this mantra to yourself? Hold your tongue the next time you're tempted to bad-rap your body to others—when you insult a certain part of your body aloud ("my butt looks so big"), it has a funny way of drawing people's attention to it. And stop obsessing about your unattractive traits (bad skin, big thighs) and focus on your best assets. Maybe you have long, thick hair or beautiful arms—play them up by getting lots of deep-conditioning treatments or buying dresses that highlight your upper half instead of your hips.

Buying Lingerie That Looks Classy, Not Trashy

Yes, feeling foxy starts from the inside out, but I'd be lying if I said that a fabulous slip or bra-and-panties set can't work wonders. Splurging on the prettiest underthings is an investment every MG should make. And though you don't always have to spend big bucks for quality, you should remember the basics:

Fit Is Everything

When you're wearing lingerie and it doesn't fit quite right, you're not going to maximize your assets. So when you try your pieces on, be realistic: Are your panties digging even the slightest bit around the waistline, or is your bra making your boobs look like two watermelons about to burst? Screw size. Different sizes will run differently depending on the brand, so if the large fits you better than the medium, buy the large and rip out the tag. You're going to feel foxiest in the size that has the perfect amount of "give" where your body needs it.

HOW TO DETERMINE YOUR BRA SIZE

Sizes do vary by company, so the best way to know if a bra fits is to try it on. It turns out that 70 percent of women are wearing the wrong bra size! So figure out what your basics are before heading out.

To Measure

• While naked (very important), use a tape measure (or a piece of string measured against a ruler) to measure directly under your breasts. Add five inches to that measurement, and that's your bra size. If it works out to an odd number, go to the next even number up.

• Measure around the fullest part of your bustline. The tape should be held horizontally, and your arms should be down. Note that measurement and compare it to the bra size (above).

• To determine your cup size, subtract the first measurement from the second:

  1/2-inch difference = AA cup

  1-inch difference = A cup

  2-inch difference = B cup

  3-inch difference = C cup

  4-inch difference = D cup

  5-inch difference = DD or E cup

MG TIP: Want to leave the fitting to the experts but don't have time to go in person? Check out online retailers like HerRoom, True&Co, and Maidenform, which use digital tools to determine your proper bra fit.

MG TIP: Have four to six great bras that you wear in rotation. *Don't* wear the same bra two days in a row—you want to let it air out a bit; but you don't have to wash your bra after every wearing. You know best, but I can go two to four wearings depending on what I've been doing in said bra.

MG TIP: I hate to say it, but you really should hand-wash your bras. But if that's asking too much (and for me it is), at least get a lingerie bag that will keep them from getting wrapped around the washer, and for the love of support, don't put them in the dryer—the elastic will stretch and break down.

MG TIP: Count your breasts. If you seem to have four, then your cup size is too small.

- Lean forward to let the breasts fall into the cups and fasten the closure on the middle set of the hook-and-eye.

- If the bra has a horizontal seam at the bottom, it should be parallel to the ground. If the seam goes up from horizontal, the straps are too tight. If the seam goes down from horizontal, the straps are too loose.

- Adjust the straps to give firm but comfortable uplift to the bust line. You should be able to run one finger smoothly under the straps to prevent digging into the shoulders.

- With the bra on, make sure the straps are vertical front and back. Straps not lying vertically indicate the wrong bra size or a poorly made bra. This also explains the problem of straps falling off the shoulders.

Quality Checks Are Key

Inspect buttons and beading for loose threads, and check for puckering of seams (give the fabric a tug to ensure that it's tightly woven). Also make sure that all lace and trim lie perfectly flat against your skin—if they bunch up when you try the garment on in the store, they'll certainly bunch up on you at home. And if you're going for underwire, lift your arms and do a few upper-body twists—if you don't feel the wire digging into the outer sides of your boobs, you're good to go.

Neutral Colors Are Classy

Pink, silver, gold, and red may be trendy, but they can border on tacky. Stick to white and black lingerie, or even nude—and steer clear of synthetic fabrics. Even if you're buying at Victoria's Secret, a well-chosen set of lingerie can look like it came from La Perla.

Comfort Is Important, Too

While silk and lace may be perfect for evening, go for microfiber during the day; it's durable and easy to care for, and it looks great. Steer clear of lace, bows, or elaborately stitched cups—the details will show through a simple T-shirt, which isn't sexy.

How to Look Better Naked

Sooner or later you're gonna get naked, and even the most self-confident Modern Gal can feel downright old-fashioned and insecure. Luckily, there are some sneaky secrets to looking better in the buff:

- Try deflecting attention away from parts you don't like to parts you do.

- Keep your shoulders back (it will lift your boobs and make you look taller).

- If lying down, raise your arms over your head. It makes your breasts look firmer and higher. If you're sitting up and want to achieve the same effect, put your hands behind your head as if you're putting your hair in a ponytail.

- Lie on your side and tilt your pelvis forward. It will make your butt look tighter and your stomach flatter.

- Point your toes to make your legs look firmer and longer.

MG TIP: While I'm all for a little fun with your mate and encourage you to feel comfortable naked, for the love of Miley Cyrus, don't ever do a nude photo shoot with a digital (or any other) camera, no matter how much you trust your photographer. And if for some reason you decide to do it anyway, delete the photos from your phone ASAP!

MG TIP: Fake tanner can help you be a lean machine. Apply a coat to areas you wish were slimmer, like your hips or inner thighs, but make sure you blend to ensure a subtle gradation rather than a harsh line.

Giving Your Man a Sensual Spa Massage

Not only can you turn your man to mush with the power of well-chosen words, you can do it with your hot little hands. Even if your guy is the macho type who snickers at the word *Shiatsu*, he'll be begging for your randy at-home therapy from now on. Just follow these tips adapted from Larry Costa, owner of The Parlor, a day spa in New York City, and author of *Massage: Mind and Body*, and Alison Lister, a professional masseuse in Los Angeles:

Massage Move 1: Set the Scene

A great rubdown starts with Zen surroundings:

MG TIP: If your mattress is super-soft, your bed isn't ideal for a massage. Layering blankets over cushions on the floor or using a futon will give him the firm but padded surface he needs.

- *Blissful bed:* Put fresh sheets on your bed and dust them with a little talcum powder so the fabric feels ultra-smooth.

- *Low lighting:* Dim the lights, unplug the phone, and turn any clocks with flashing numbers toward the wall.

- *Seductive scents:* Light scented candles, preferably in vanilla, pumpkin, or lavender. These scents have been scientifically proved to arouse men.

MG TIP: Avoid using those "sensual edible" massage oils. They tend to get sticky (most have corn syrup) and cause a big mess. Also avoid everyday body lotions, which absorb into the skin too quickly.

- *Soothing sounds:* Pick a Spotify or Pandora playlist with a slow, soothing beat and no lyrics.

- *Aromatherapy:* Set a bottle of massage oil on your nightstand. Orange and lavender have calming effects; peppermint, rosemary, and eucalyptus are anti-inflammatory and reduce aches and pains.

- *Warmth:* Body temperature drops during massage, so adjust your thermostat to 70°F or warmer to help his muscles relax. If the room's too drafty, his muscles will tense up. Chances are he'll be naked, or in his boxers. You may want to wear a sexy negligee or his roomy T-shirt.

Massage Move 2: Assume the Position

Your goal is to have as much skin-to-skin contact with your man as possible:

MG TIP: Avoid startling him with cold hands on his back. Try running your hands under warm water before you begin. You can also warm up the oil by running the bottle under hot water for a few minutes.

- *Straddle him:* With your man lying down on his stomach, straddle him, making sure to sit below his tush. Next, place your hands flat on his upper back, hold them there for fifteen seconds, and ask him to inhale deeply. This signals him to slow down his breaths and introduces him to your touch.

- *Start stroking:* Squeeze a few drops of oil into your palms and rub them together to heat up the oil. With your hands next to each other and fingers together, glide your hands down his back, keeping the pressure light, but never taking your hands off his skin. At the end of each stroke, slide your hands back to the start position. Repeat ten times.

Massage Move 3: Show Him You Knead Him

As you do these moves, start slowly and gently, and work your way deeper.

- *Warm up his shoulders:* Using the pads of your fingers and thumbs, gently grip the fleshy part of his shoulders (don't be shy; the more skin you grab, the less it will pinch). With your thumbs leading, push his skin forward and upward with each stroke. If you feel a knot, apply steady pressure to the spot with your thumbs for ten seconds. But don't press too hard. Since your man probably won't say, "Babe, stop! You're using too much pressure!" (it's a macho thing), check to see if his eyes are open or other parts of his body are clenched. If so, use less of an iron grip.

- *Give his lower back and tush TLC:* Move around so you're kneeling at the base of your man's head. Place the heels of your hands at the base of his lower back, right where his buns begin. Keep your fingers raised so all the pressure is in the heels of your hands. Lean forward with your arms straight and apply firm pressure for ten seconds. Next, run your hands down to his butt, and with flat palms, rub his left cheek in large counterclockwise circular motions and clockwise circles on his right cheek.

MG TIP: Be sure to use your whole hand. Even if your hands are small, you can make them feel large by spreading out your fingers and moving your hands together as a unit.

Massage Move 4: De-stress His Legs and Feet

Lucky for your man, he has thousands of nerve endings on each of his feet, just waiting to be pleasured.

- *Knead the backs of his thighs:* Kneeling over your man, make a loose fist and place your hand, knuckles down, at the top of his thigh.

MG TIP: Be careful around his shins—he may be sensitive there from sports injuries.

Apply firm, constant pressure as you push forward, working down to just above the back of the knee. Repeat at least six times. Slide your hands down to his calves and give them a few good squeezes.

- *Ask him to roll over:* You want his feet to be facing upward for maximum results. Grasp his left foot in both hands and position your thumbs next to each other on the fleshy part at the top of his sole. Push your thumbs outward, like you're smoothing wrinkles out of clothing. Starting with the big toe, tug each of his toes and pull up on them a little.

Massage Move 5: Relax His Arms and Hands

Don't skip over his arms and hands; they're some of the most overworked parts of his bod.

- *Give his biceps a simultaneous squeeze:* Slide down to his wrists, and using your thumbs, slide them outward across the tendons and muscle fibers on the tops of his forearms, working your way up to just below his elbow. Repeat twice.

- *Get handy:* Lift his hand, palm side up, and with your thumbs, push forward and out on his palms as if you're flattening a crease out of clothing. Then knead the fleshy part of his palms in a circular motion and give each finger a gentle twist and pull. Ahhh.

MG TIP: Don't be afraid to ask questions. Feedback is a good thing. The answers to questions like "Is this pressure okay?" can be very helpful in gauging his enjoyment.

Massage Move 6: Stimulate His Scalp

Spas often save head rubs for last because they're both relaxing and exhilarating—a perfect ending to a muscle-melting massage.

- *Cradle his head in your lap:* Sit cross-legged at the base of his head, so that his neck is resting on your calves. Gently turn his head to the left, fan your fingers out on the side of his head, and rub in small circular motions. Repeat on the right side, moving your hands closer to his hairline. When you reach his hairline, move your fingers in tighter, firm circles, moving down to each of his temples.

- *Do a light head-scratch:* For the finisher, lightly scratch his scalp (only if you have short nails) for an invigorating rush. You may hear him moaning with pleasure at this point. Prepare to be worshiped for the rest of the evening.

I'm in the Mood for Love, and Not Simply Because I'm Ovulating . . .

Both of you have been holding out for what feels like *ages* and know that full-body contact is right around the corner. When you're out on dates, you look at the menu and read *"sex* frites" instead of "steak frites." Even the most innocuous love scene at the movies makes your neck prickle with sex. Oops, *sweat.* The anticipation of getting him naked is killing you.

What Are the Rules?

Clearly, there are two different camps: the *gung-ho* gals and the *good-girls-don't* gals. So where do you fit in? Well, instead of worrying about what *he'll* think, examine your own motivations. Do you want to sleep with him right away because you're in the mood for a wild romp? If you're only in it for the physical release and have low expectations about turning it into a relationship, go for it without guilt. Who knows? It may turn into something more. But at least you're not going to be diving into Ben & Jerry's and watching reruns of *Antiques Roadshow* if it doesn't. Not that I'm speaking from personal experience, but let's just say Ben, Jerry, and I are on a first-name basis.

Now, if you do find yourself getting emotionally attached (i.e., you're envisioning going on weekend trips together) and are hoping that kicking your intimacy up a notch will make your relationship evolve into something more, put your panties on ice. It certainly doesn't mean you can't indulge in some extended south-of-the-border oral play—he won't get frustrated and you'll feel like you're going at a comfortable pace. Another get-closer move: Take a steamy bath together so you can get acquainted with every slope, curve, and sweet spot on each other's bodies. It may sound a little Khloé Kardashian–esque, but the more time you give your guy to crave you as a whole person, not just a fast fling, the deeper and more meaningful your "merger" will eventually be.

Can I Ask Him About His Exes? How Do I Stack Up?

Though it's tempting as hell to want to know who graced his bed (and how), resist digging for the dirt from his past relationships. Yes, it could give you insight into what he likes in bed and doesn't, but you're better off asking him more vague questions about his sexual preferences in the heat of the moment.

On the flip side, telling him what worked with your ex sexually and what didn't is strictly off limits. You might think it will be helpful, but too much blabbing can backfire. An MG knows that even the most confident man's ego can be fragile—bring up Mike from freshman year biology seminar or François, your summer fling from Europe, and his penis will deflate faster than a kiddie balloon.

I Slept with a Friend . . . Can We Go Back to Being "Just Friends"?

Hey, it happens. Maybe you went on a few dates with a pal of a pal but weren't sure if you were truly attracted. Perhaps he's a guy friend for years who always harbored feelings for you. Or a coworker you've gotten extremely jokey and comfortable with. Whatever the setup, add booze and a little horniness, and what do you have? A one-night stand.

The easiest way to make it clear that you don't want the sexual relationship to go farther is to nip his expectations in the bud as soon as possible. Say something to the effect of, "Last night was incredible . . . but I'm in a place right now where I'm not ready to be in a sexual relationship. Can we still hang out like we did before?" That way, you're being direct but still sparing his ego. Unless he's brokenhearted beyond belief, he'll say of course you can. Whether that winds up being true or not, time will tell. To increase your odds of the friendship surviving, hang out with a group of friends for your next few social outings so you can establish boundaries once again.

What Men Love Most in Bed

Assuming you're with a guy you actually *want* to continue a sexual relationship with, it pays to know what pushes his hot buttons. Ask any guy what he craves most in the sack, and he'll likely answer "*more sex!*" But the truth is, once you peel back a few layers, you'll find that most guys do have a few universal desires that keep popping up again and again. Though every man is different, sex experts and numerous surveys will tell you that the majority of the male species go ga-ga over the following:

A Vocal Partner

Imagine watching your favorite movie with no sound. It would be pretty darn boring—and you wouldn't have much of an idea of what's going on. Same goes for sex. If you stay stone-cold silent throughout the entire frisky feature, not only will your guy feel less engaged, he'll get no feedback about what's turning you on or off. If you feel shy about saying "Honey, just a little to the left," or "Yeah, like that, harder/faster . . ." a little moaning can do the trick. When he's giving you the right touches and the right amount of pressure, a few strategic *oohs* and *ahhs* clue him in to the fact that you want him to keep up steady pressure. If he's not doing something you like, gently use your hands to redirect him where you want him to go. Half of his gratification in bed is knowing he's thoroughly pleasing you.

Speaking of stepping up the lip service, many men dig a little dirty talk. And while you're in no way obligated to indulge his fantasy

MG TIP: Skip the curse words and derogatory terms . . . if he finds that sexy, you may want to trade *him* in.

if it doesn't appeal to you too, you can test the waters by describing exactly what you love about his body, or why you're getting off on what he's doing to you. See how it feels—for some women, being a little verbally experimental is a way of establishing even more intimacy with their partner.

You on Top

Unlike women, who need all their senses to be warmed up for sex, all men need are their eyeballs to get aroused. Which may be why a recent *Esquire* survey reported that girl-on-top is the favorite sexual position for guys—besides seeing you take charge, he gets a full-body view of your breasts, stomach, and down below, in all your bouncing glory. (And hey, the notion that he gets to lay back and relax while you do all the grinding is appealing to him too.) But the bonuses aren't just for him. When you lean forward and rub against his pelvis, you get both clitoral (exterior) and G-spot (interior) stimulation . . . leading to bigger, better orgasms.

MG TIP: Another tip to enhance your pleasure: Grind on top of him in a figure-eight motion; his penis will stimulate all around the inside of your vaginal wall, bringing you more intense sensations.

Spontaneous Sex

No matter how satisfying it is, doing anything in a routine fashion—be it the same workout or the same lunch every day of the week—can get old. This is why guys love it when their partners mix it up on a regular basis. No, this doesn't mean you have to don a latex cat-woman suit and spank him from the ceiling fan. (In fact, I don't recommend it.)

But start expanding your idea of where, when, and how you have sex. For example, if you always head to the mattress when you're doing the dirty, try doing it on the couch, kitchen counter, bathroom sink, or even outside when the urge strikes. Or propose having a quickie ten minutes before you're due at a dinner party or pull him into the bathroom at a cocktail shindig for a little fast love—the flush on his face for the rest of the night will be priceless. And if you always do it with the lights off at night, try surprising him on the weekend by pouncing on him in the middle of the afternoon in broad daylight. You've got nothing to hide, baby.

MG TIP: No matter where or how you get jiggy, remember these rubber rules: A condom keeps for four years after it's made. Always check the date on the box. If you see the letters "M-F-G," that tells you the manufacture date. Some packages are marked "E-X-P," which of course indicates the past-due date. Don't use a condom even one day later . . . and if you have any doubt, throw it out.

How to Be the Best He's Ever Had

Odds are, if your man is panting, sweating, and has a smile plastered to his face post-sex, he thinks you're amazing. But there's always more room for erotic improvement—and these little bedroom boosters will pay off for both of you.

Do Your Kegels

Your vagina is like a muscle; the more you exercise it, the better it will work for you. Kegel exercises will strengthen your vaginal or "PC" (pubococcygeus) muscle in the pelvis, leading to stronger orgasms. Contract as if you're trying to stop yourself from peeing for two to three seconds, and then release. The best part about these exercises is that you can do them at work, while you're driving, or even on a date . . . and no one will ever know.

Lube Up

You heard it here first: Wetter is better. The more lubed up you are, the more easily your man can glide in and out of you during sex—and the more pleasurable sex will be for you. Have your man apply a nickel-sized dollop of lube around your vaginal area (not inside) and prepare for some seriously heightened sensations. From ones that warm to others that are a tasty treat, there are many options when it comes to choosing a lube; just make sure you go with one that is water-based or silicone-based. And once you find the brand for you, have fun with it; there are many uses beyond the one described above.

MG TIP: Avoid all oil-based lubes, like Vaseline and lotion. They can break down the latex in his condom.

Have Solo Sex

So here is the thing. I think even Thomas Jefferson would agree with me that in addition to life, liberty, and the pursuit of happiness, everyone deserves access to mind-blowing sex. And the best part of this amendment is that you can achieve it without the help of anyone else. While a recent survey revealed that 79 percent of female respondents under thirty-five had masturbated, the subject remains taboo. Self-pleasure is a crucial element in every sex life, because the more in touch you get with yourself privately, the more you'll know about what turns you on, and the better you'll be at showing your partner how you like it. For starters, try fantasizing while touching yourself after you've showered and slipped into bed (or under the stream of the showerhead itself). That's when you'll be most relaxed.

Locate Your G-Spot

You may already know how much pleasure your clitoris can give you, but the G-spot is another orgasm-inducing spot on your body that can bring you just as much pleasure. Also practice finding your G-spot. It's a dime-sized erogenous zone located just underneath your front vaginal wall. Find it by inserting your finger inside your vagina and making a "come here" motion with your finger. Once you know where it is, you can maximize your man's chances of hitting it by getting into doggy-style or leaning back in the girl-on-top pose.

Pleasure His Perineum

The P-word is rarely talked about but highly pleasure-inducing for your man. The perineum is the smooth patch of skin located between his testicles and anus, and applying light pressure there with two fingers when he's about to orgasm (whether you're pleasuring him orally or having sex) will give him even greater sensations.

Exercise

Hopping on the StairMaster or going for a quick jog is good for your body, but who knew it could make you more randy? Experts say that exercise stimulates your sympathetic nervous system and increases the amount of endorphins ("feel-good chemicals") pulsing through your body. Hit the gym more often, and you may find yourself hitting the mattress more often—something no guy complains about.

THE LITTLE PERKS OF GETTING LUCKY

If you have to think really hard to remember the last time you got lucky, you may have hit a sexual plateau. Besides the obvious, here are three reasons to have more sex:

• *Booty Bonus 1:* Sex can actually release natural endorphins ("happy drugs") in the body that can relieve stress and depression, and act as a natural pain reliever that nixes cramps, headaches, and PMS.

• *Booty Bonus 2:* Sex three times per week for a year equals 7,500 calories burned.

• *Booty Bonus 3:* Sex increases the levels of oxytocin in your body (aka the "bonding hormone"), which can increase your overall sense of well-being. And when you feel better about yourself, you feel sexier, and that leads to more fabulous sex.

MG TIP: While some foods may help your evening of fun, others may hinder it. Garlic, onions, and beans are pretty obvious, but be careful of dairy. It can cause gas and bloating if you're even a little lactose intolerant. Speaking of gas, beware of carbonated drinks like soda, beer, and even red wine. Whole grains like bran and wheat can make your tummy seem bigger, and anything with fiber can cause cramping and discomfort once you hit the sheets. So avoid veggies (especially broccoli, carrots, and cauliflower).

Feed Each Other Super-Sex Foods

Hot sauce contains capsaicin, which causes a reaction in your body that's similar to sexual arousal. Pumpkin seeds and peanuts have been proved to stimulate arousal in men, and the high concentration of zinc in oysters boosts a man's virility as well. Sprinkling a little nutmeg on your latte won't hurt, either—this spice has long been known to have aphrodisiac properties. Meanwhile, don't OD on wine. One glass can make you randy, but too much will only leave you and your guy feeling sexually sluggish.

Being Kinky-Lite in Bed . . . Should You Really Go There?

Each of us has a different comfort level when it comes to being sexually experimental. But sometimes it pays to push past your natural booty boundaries. Here are common taboo topics that may arise between you and your man . . . and how to know if a little erotic exploration is really right for you.

Taboo Topic 1: Vibrators . . . Why They're Generating Buzz

More than ever, vibrators are gaining in popularity. Even uptight Charlotte from *Sex and the City* realized how many jolts of pleasure a little tool like the Rabbit can bring you. According to a recent study in the *Journal of Sexual Medicine*, one in two women in America uses a vibrator. If you cannot bring yourself to orgasm with your guy or by using your fingers alone, this titillating tool can be your magic key.

No one expects you to walk into a sex shop and buy a batch of vibrators. A more discreet route: Go to www.babeland.com, do some browsing, and make a secure online purchase. If you're not into the idea of a full-fledged vibrator, there are also smaller egg-shaped buzzers that you can use externally to stimulate your clitoris.

Taboo Topic 2: Threesomes . . . Are They a Good Present to Give?

Y Tu Mamá También, *Zoolander*, *Vicky Cristina Barcelona*, *Spring Breakers*. We've entered an age where the two-girls-and-a-guy scenario is being portrayed as deliciously de rigueur on-screen. And according to a recent LELO Global Sex Survey, 20 percent of women have had a threesome. But is bringing another woman into the bedroom right for you? And would she be a complete stranger, or someone you both know well?

Though the prospect of sharing your man with another woman may seem perfectly hot in theory, you may realize that in practice a bunch of other emotions are stirred up that you may not be equipped to deal with. First, you may wonder, "If I'm attracted to this other girl, does this mean I'm gay?" (Probably not, but you still may feel conflicted.) Second, you may suddenly feel "cheated on" when you see

MG TIP: Once you feel comfortable using your vibrator, don't hide it away as your "dirty little secret." Chances are, if your guy truly wants you to feel as much pleasure as possible, he will be happy to use it on you in addition to stimulating you with his own bod.

MG TIP: You should always assume you are being recorded, so make sure you trust your guy before you take things digital. Otherwise keep it PG when on camera (you never know who will be your audience).

him lavishing physical attention on another chick right in front of your face. And last of all, if your man likes your threesome a lot more than you do, going back to just-the-two-of-you sex will bore him. Do you really want to take the chance?

Taboo Topic 3: Face-Time Sex . . . How Do I Have It Without Feeling Stupid?

For long-distance couples, putting your sex life on hold is a fact of life. And if you or your man frequently takes business trips, you have to take similar passion pauses. But having an out-of-sight, out-of-libido approach to love doesn't have to be the only option. Enter visual sex.

The trick to feeling frisky and natural with your man via video is to get yourself in the mood first. Slip between the sheets, turn on some sexy music, play with your newly purchased vibrator, and start fantasizing about your man. Then dial. The quickest way to get him in the mood is to show him what you are wearing (or the lack thereof), hint at what he is missing, and then reveal what you wish he were doing to you at that very moment. If you are going to surprise him with a tantalizing visual opener, make sure he is in possession of his phone and it is not being streamed on the office television. To get him to join in on the fun, ask to see a specific part of his body you are longing for. Once you get a little sexy repartee going, encourage him to pleasure himself while you dip your hands down south. Nope, it's not as good as the real thing, but you're creating an intimate connection that will have you even more excited for a randy reunion.

Taboo Topic 4: Porn . . . Should I Be Grossed Out That My Man Logs On?

The secret's out (and has been for a while)—people watch porn. And it's not just a guy thing. In fact, a recent study published in the *Journal of the American Medical Association* found that 66 percent of men and 41 percent of women in America view pornography at least once a month. But despite high audience participation, Americans don't seem to be getting any more comfortable with the activity: According to one study, only 29 percent of Americans believe watching porn is okay.

Given the varying views on the matter, I get why the topic of porn may leave you morally conflicted. Should you be worried if you catch your guy engaging in a promiscuous viewing party for one? Or should you try to get in on the action, adding a new dirty series to your DVR? Alas, I don't have a concrete answer for this one. Instead, I can only suggest having a discussion with your man about ways to explore the topic together and hopefully reach a happy medium . . . Who knows, it may introduce you to things you didn't even know could turn you on.

Sorry, I can't tell you everything . . . My kids are gonna read this!

Taboo Topic 5: Sexting

A recent *Time* magazine study showed that four out of five college students have sexted. So chances are at some point you're going to find yourself coming up with a catchy way to sound provocative (possibly while also watching your latest obsession on Netflix, but hopefully not). But remember this: If you sext, you will likely have someone other than your intended see your sexts. His buddy, his roommate, his (gulp) mom. As for sexting if you're cheating . . . Well, I'm really not a big fan of cheating, but do yourself and everyone else a big favor and don't sext. It literally adds insult to injury. It's one thing to find out you've been cheated on. It's another thing to read heartbreaking, detailed sexts. No one needs to go through that. It's your business if you want to do the nasty with someone you shouldn't be with, but just don't be so descriptive about it. At least give your partner this courtesy. And if you believe that any service can *really* delete those photos and messages, I should probably also have a talk with you about Santa Claus and the tooth fairy. Also, please think twice—actually, think many times—before you start rapid-firing pictures of your privates, okay?

So assuming you're just doing a little nonadulterous sexting, here are some rules to sext by:

- Delete all your texts after you're finished. Immediately. Like now if you're reading this and you know they are on your phone. Don't save them to read them later. How many times have you lost your phone? Go. Now. What are you waiting for?

- Don't sext something you wouldn't say or do in real life. After all, the person may hold you to it, or want you to repeat it . . . So while you get to take a little literary license, you don't want to find yourself in a rather uncomfortable position when the recipient reminds you that actions speak louder than words.

- Don't sext drunk. Okay, stop laughing. Who sexts sober, right? Well, if you do sext and then realize that you want to recall that particular raunchy rant, consider using a service like Quimby or TigerText that allows you to use the recall feature if you change your mind. Typically they won't work if the person has already read them, and like I said, once something is out there, it's out there, but you can always try.

- Don't use emoticons. They are just not sexy.

- Don't abbreviate. Nothing makes you sound like a teenager more than abbreviations.

- Privates are not always pretty. Even if you're not worried about getting caught, just remember that up close no one's privates look that great.

- Don't be too aggressive at first. And if he doesn't text back, stop.

- Think of some clever words for your special parts . . . It makes it harder for someone else to catch on and it creates a little more of a connection between you.

- If you don't know the person with whom you are sexting, I'm not going to judge, but this is an area where you need to be super extra careful. We've all watched too many episodes of *Law and Order* not to know what can happen if you aren't! Do not give them your full name. Clearly you have decided to do this with someone you don't know for a reason. Hide your face and any distinguishing tattoos. Don't give details about where you live, where you work, or who you are. Just keep it dirty.

CHAPTER 9

Savvy Survival Skills

Okay, sad story. When I was twenty-two, my mother died suddenly.
My brother and I were left to handle her somewhat confused estate, to
keep our home from being foreclosed upon, our family from crum-
bling, and her business from turning into a chaotic circus.

Just to put this in perspective, my biggest concerns up until then
had been dating, shopping, hanging out with roommates, and in-
dulging in post-college discussions along the lines of—"Maybe I'll
just move to Italy and become a famous cafe-owning sculptress" or
"Hey, let's all go road-tripping across the country."

The fact is, I had no idea about all the adult things I'd have to
learn at lightning speed as soon as my mother wasn't there to do it for
me. Things like buying a car on my own seemed like brain surgery.
It was as if I was told to check my fun days at the door and enter this
weird, freaky, serious world I wanted nothing to do with. And while my
brother and I got through it together—learning more than ever about
the value of family, I might add—I realized in a ridiculously huge way
how ill-equipped I was to be considered a real adult.

While I hope your induction into adulthood isn't this dramatic or well, depressing, there are still some savvy survival skills that every Modern Girl is better off knowing sooner rather than later. Because even though topics like investing, mortgages, and home repairs seem tedious and confusing, having an arsenal of tricks up your sleeve will make you a billion times more confident as you enter into a new, more sophisticated stage of your life. Who knows? Five years from now, you might be sharing this wisdom with a younger, more naive MG who'll be so thankful, she'll want to pay you back with multiple lunches and cocktails. My advice? Charge interest.

Modern Girl Personal Finance 101

I know, I know: Most MGs glaze over at the terms 401(k), FICO score, or Roth IRA. And I don't blame them—it's not exactly *fun* to think about. In fact, all kinds of cash talk turns me colder than an ice cream truck.

We've all heard the phrase "Love of money is the root of all evil," but the freedom to indulge in such blissful activities such as a day at the spa, dinner at a hot new restaurant, or a trip to buy a pair of new Manolos comes only from having a little of the evil stuff left over at month's end. And to do that, you've gotta stay on top of your cash flow and employ some tricks to make your savings magically grow.

But the good news is, taking charge of your finances isn't rocket science (if I can do it, so can you). Read on as I shed light on all-important personal finance topics, so that going forward, you'll feel confident and secure that you've made the best choices regarding day-to-day finances, personal credit, major investments, and insurance options.

Best Practices for Online Banking

Some of you may not remember the days of balancing your checkbook, and even if you do, you might have been like me and never did it anyway. So you can only imagine my excitement when we entered the era of online banking and I could kiss my years of financial confusion and overdraft fees good-bye. But the ease of accessing my bank account from virtually any device also has its drawbacks—namely privacy. It goes without saying that every Modern Girl must know how to safeguard her most "valuable" information. After all, you wouldn't want to miss out on those Manolos because you're fighting fraud charges! Follow these tips and you will never miss any shoe sale:

Upgrade Your Passwords

Yes, dogs may be man's best friend, but they do not make good passwords. Nope, middle names and birthdays don't either. I know, I know, with a million accounts it is hard to keep track of them all, let alone come up with a distinct password for each one. Lucky for you, there are sites (like www.strongpasswordgenerator.com) that will do the work for you, creating an endless collection of secure passwords. Now the only issue is what to do when you can't remember your iron-clad password, which means it is time for a password management system like 1Password.

Manage your Smartphone Bells 'n' Whistles

Listen, I am just as much of a sucker for a cool tech feature as the next Modern Girl, but there is no need for Bluetooth in the bedroom or for Candy Crush to be GPS-enabled to get a new high score. The scary truth is the Bluetooth, GPS, and Wi-Fi capabilities on smartphones are three of the most common ways for hackers to get into your device. Keep those settings turned off, unless you are using them.

Go for Two-Factor Authentication

It never hurts to double-check, especially when it comes to keeping your digital information safe. Sites are starting to equip themselves with two-factor authentication, which requires users to enter a second code in addition to their password to successfully log in. Consider it your technology security blanket—just don't forget to turn the setting on!

MG TIP: Mint and Credit Karma are great for MGs who want to get ahold of their spending. These free sites allow you to track your cash flow and credit score as well as help you set financial goals.

MG TIP: Lots of people play a constant switching game, moving balances from cards with high interest to those that offer low interest for a year. And then they do the same thing again. My feeling is that if you have very high interest rates on one or two cards and are only able to make your minimum monthly payment, then transferring balances to lower interest cards will help you to pay them off and lower your debt to credit ratio. But look to transfer balances to cards with a consistent low interest rate, rather than a phenomenal teaser rate that expires in six months, so that you won't have to keep surfing from card to card once the teaser rate expires.

The Art of Getting Kickass Credit

Having a fat checking account is great, but unless you're as rich as J.Lo, many important things in life cost more than you can pay for up front. That's where credit comes in. Credit is essentially a loan from the bank to finance anything from a new dress to a car to purchasing a home, based on the probability that you as the customer will pay the bank back over time.

So, as opposed to dropping $35,000 for a year of grad school up front or $200,000 for your new home, you will pay a manageable fraction of this full amount—say $3,500 for the year of education or a $20,000 down payment for the home. Then, the bank will expect you to pay off the remainder over time through periodic payments, usually monthly. This is referred to as the "principal" portion of your loan.

APR Explained

Now here's the catch: When you pay back those mini-payments every month, the bank tacks on a little extra cash called the "interest" portion of the loan. Usually stated as the "APR" (Annual Percentage Rate); this is the yearly cost to you for borrowing the money. The higher the APR, the more you will pay over and above the amount that was loaned to you. Your APR can drastically affect the cost of borrowing money. Generally speaking, the APR on education loans is the lowest (3 to 5 percent), followed by mortgage loan APRs (4 to 5 percent), auto loan APRs (4 to 5 percent), and credit card loans, which are far and away the most expensive type of loan (13 to 22 percent).

How Can I Get a Low APR?

You may not know that every time you use credit in the form of a credit card, personal loan, auto loan, or student loan to buy clothing, finance your new car, or pay for tuition, your transactions are being monitored by your bank. All of this information is reported to the three national credit bureaus, which each produce what is known as a "FICO" score. FICO stands for "Fair Isaac & Company," the largest provider of consumer credit information. The FICO score basically reflects your relationship with credit and if you're a good borrower who pays back loans on time or if you're often late or miss payments. Based on this score, you will receive either a high or low APR.

Higher APRs are charged to riskier borrowers (by "risky" I mean the bank doesn't trust that you'll pay them back) to compensate the bank for taking greater risk. FICO scores range from 300 to 850 points, with the lower FICO scores being more risky/higher APR and the higher FICOs being less risky/lower APR.

Factors That Make Up Your FICO Score

- Payment history: 35 percent of score
- Current credit usage: 30 percent of score
- Length of credit history: 15 percent of score
- Applications for new credit: 10 percent of score
- Total credit types (mortgage, loans, cars, credit cards, etc.): 10 percent of score

A History of On-Time Payments

This is the biggest ingredient—35 percent of your total score. Lenders want to see that you've paid all of your bills on time—mortgage, utilities, credit cards, loans, and so on—over the past seven years. The more recent the lapse, the more it hurts your score. Not to tell tales on my oh-so-fab hubby, but he used to forget to pay his bills. He figured the companies wouldn't mind waiting an extra week or two while he tended to more pleasant tasks. So while he had the money, his credit rating was suffering. I, after having learned my lesson from having bounced checks, would pay bills so early (the moment I got them), the credit card companies earned interest on money that could have been sitting in *my* bank account. The moral of the story? Stick to a schedule in which you pay bills twice a month—once at the beginning and once in the middle—which will allow you to be on time without being too early.

MG TIP: If you have trouble remembering to pay your credit cards and utility bills on time, sign up for Auto-Pay. To set this up for your cable bill, for example, simply call the customer service number on your monthly bill, give them your credit card info, and be sure to check the statements they send you to make sure they didn't accidentally overcharge you one month. You can also use Auto-Pay to pay off your monthly credit card bills. You need to set this up with your credit card company's customer service division, and provide the company with your checking account number. Each month, the amount you owe will automatically be deducted from your bank account. However, you should always still review your bill to make sure there aren't any erroneous charges.

MG TIP: Don't close unused credit cards as a short-term strategy to raise your score. Don't open a number of new credit cards that you don't need, just to increase your available credit. This approach could backfire and actually lower your score.

MG TIP: If you have been managing credit for a short time, don't open a lot of new accounts too fast. New accounts will lower your average account age, which will damage your score if you don't have a lot of other credit info. Also, rapid account buildup can look risky if you are a new credit user.

MG TIP: To find out your FICO score, go to the consumer website for Fair Isaac (www.myfico.com). It costs $59.85.

How Much Credit You Use Each Month

This makes up 30 percent of your score. For an auto loan, FICO takes the ratio of the original loan amount to the balance you owe on the loan. With credit cards, it's the credit limit on your card versus your current monthly balance. If the amount you owe is close to your credit limit, that is likely to have a negative effect on your score. On the other hand, keeping your balances low or zero and not maxing out your card will make your score higher. Additionally, having large lines of unused available credit makes you look stable in the eyes of creditors and banks. This will give you a better chance to get a lower APR when you're applying for a mortgage or auto loan.

Length of Credit History

This accounts for 15 percent of your FICO score. Generally, FICO scores consider the length of your credit track record. The longer you've been a reliable credit user, the higher your score will be. If you are just coming out of college, with only one year of credit history, this may be one of the weaker components of your FICO score. But that can be offset by other factors, such as timely payments and low balances.

Recent Credit Checks

Have you applied for new credit recently? Many scoring models consider whether you have applied for credit recently by looking at "inquiries" on your credit report when you apply for credit. If you have applied for too many new accounts recently, that may negatively affect your score. Also beware of offers from stores that give you 10 percent off a purchase if you sign up for a card that day. Turns out, it's rarely worth the 10 percent savings. Why? Because every time you sign up, the employee will run a credit report to approve you for the card, which will lower your FICO score. Save this offer for the big stuff, like $200 saved on a $2,000 couch, not $5 on the $50 sweater at the mall. Also, the number of credit inquiries from lenders in recent months is 10 percent of your score, and too many will lower it. This will hurt you when you're seeking a mortgage or auto loan. However, not all inquiries are counted. Inquiries by creditors who are monitoring your account or looking at credit reports to make "pre-screened" credit offers are not counted.

Paying Off Different Kinds of Debt

The final 10 percent of your score comes from how well you're able to put a dent in your debt, whether it's for credit cards, car loans, or college loans. Most of us have $8,000 of credit card debt. And the biggest mistake a MG can make is not to pay it off ASAP because the interest rates are highest on credit cards.

How to Build Your Nest Egg (Even if Your Egg's Smaller Than Sevruga Caviar)

Do you want a guaranteed 20 percent return on your money? Well, pay off your credit card debt. Because that is what it is costing you in monthly APR (interest rates) on the outstanding balance for each month. There are very few investments out there today that return 20 percent, so it wouldn't make much sense to invest $1,000 at an 8 percent return while you have a $1,000 credit card balance charging you a 20 percent APR. This would lead to an annual loss of $120! So focus on paying off all of that high-interest-rate credit card debt so you can move on. Now it's time to think about porking up your piggy bank. By 2017, the government will be paying out more in Social Security than it takes in, so the time to start saving is *now*. If you're smart about socking away your money into the right investments, you'll be livin' the good life in your later years.

Sure, you may say, "Why bother saving for when I'm sixty? I'm only in my twenties!" But the beauty of saving now is that you'll be compounding your cash over time, explains financial whiz Suze Orman. Let's say you're twenty-five years old and put $100 each month into a good mutual fund within your retirement account. By the time you're sixty-five with normal market returns, guess how much you'll have? One million dollars! But if you wait until age thirty-five to start saving, you'll have only $300,000. If you wait until you're forty-five, you'll only have $97,000. Saving early is everything!

MG TIP: Get in the habit of checking your credit report every six months from each of the three national bureaus to make sure there are no random credit cards opened in your name or suspicious inquiries on your account. With identity theft at an all-time high, monitoring your credit report is about the only safeguard you have. If a credit card has been stolen, your wallet has been misplaced, or you suspect you're the victim of identity theft, call the national bureaus below to ensure the theft or suspicious activity is not a strike against you and that your credit profile is kept healthy.

- Equifax 800–525–6285

- Experian 800–301–7195

- TransUnion 800–680–7289

- The Social Security Administration also has a fraud line at 1–800–269–0271.

Nest Egg Builder 1: Your 401(k)

Contributing to your 401(k) each year is basically your way of getting free retirement money from your employer (what a brilliant idea!). Financial planners recommend you save at least 10 percent of your income if possible. Here are the bonuses for doing so:

401-Fabulous Perk: It Makes Your Company Pay Up

For example, many companies will match the amount of money you put into your 401(k) at fifty cents on the dollar, or dollar for dollar. That means if you put in $3,000 this year, you could wind up getting $6,000 total. Of course, there's a limit to how much a particular company will contribute, as well as the amount the federal government will allow you to contribute before and after taxes (meaning you are not charged income tax on a certain portion of your contributions). The pretax limit rose to $17,500 in 2013, and will remain the same in 2014. But if you want to save more than that, you can contribute on an after-tax basis as well, up to $52,000 combined (pre- and post-tax) a year.

MG TIP: To get the full benefits, put in at least as much cash as your company will match.

401-Fabulous Perk: Reduce Your Taxable Income

The first $17,500 of your 401(k) contributions comes out of your pay *before* taxes are withheld. So, if like me, you cried when you got your first paycheck because you realized how much the government gouges out of your monthly check, you'll realize how fabulous this pretax feature is.

401-Fabulous Perk: Tax-Deferred Growth

With a 401(k) plan, you're not taxed until you hit retirement, which lets your money compound more quickly than it would if it were taxed yearly.

Choosing Your 401(k) Investments

Your 401(k) is made up of a mix of stocks and bonds. You're limited to the investments your employer chooses for your 401(k) plan, but contact your company's employee benefits rep to discuss how much flexibility you have within those constraints. If investing makes your skin crawl, go with what's called "a broad-based index fund," which is a secure, conservative portfolio that's professionally managed for you. That way you're not putting all your nest eggs in one basket.

Rolling Over Your 401(K)

When you change jobs, you have some options: Leave your 401(k) cashola where it is, roll it into an IRA (more on that below) or another 401(k), or cash out. Cashing out is the worst option—you just wind up losing money that could've been growing (see below).

Taking Money Out of a 401(k) Before It's Ripe

The catch of a 401(k) is that you can't touch the cash until you've hit retirement at sixty (well, fifty-nine and a half, technically). If you withdraw money before then, you'll have to pay income taxes plus a 10 percent penalty fee.

Nest Egg Builder 2: Your IRA (Individual Retirement Account)

An IRA is your personal account, based on investments you make via a financial institution such as Fidelity or Charles Schwab. You can easily set one up at your bank for low or no fees. If you have extra money that can't be contributed to your 401(k), you aren't currently employed, or your employer doesn't offer a 401(k) plan, opening up an IRA is a smart choice. And it's still wise to open an IRA if you already have a 401(k) going and have contributed to the max. What you're doing is giving yourself another cushion for retirement in case you wind up quitting your job for good.

Opening an IRA

To open an IRA, most financial institutions require you to put in a minimum of $2,000 (with a maximum of $5,500 until you're fifty and $6,500 after fifty). It's based on after-tax dollars, meaning it won't compound as fast as your 401(k), but it will compound. When interest is compounded, you earn interest on the principal and also earn interest on the interest. To demonstrate, assume you have $1,000 that earns 5 percent *compounded* per year. After the first year, your account will be worth $1,000 × 1.05 = $1,050. However, in year two, you will again earn 5 percent on your $1,000 but you will also earn 5 percent on the $50 interest paid in the first year. This means that after the second year your account will be worth $1,050 × 1.05 × 1.05 = $1,102.50. With compound interest, the *total account value* is multiplied by 1.05 every year rather than just the initial $1,000 principal amount.

To demonstrate how an IRA investment works, say you start out investing the $2,000 minimum per year at 5 percent in your IRA at twenty-five and you aim to pull it out at sixty. By the time you're sixty, you'll have over $180,000. Max out your IRA investment each year and you'll see a return of over $270,000.

Your IRA will be a mix of stocks and bonds. (We'll get into stocks and bond specifics later in this chapter.) As a rule of thumb, to figure out what proportion of your investments should be in stocks, subtract your age from one hundred. So for example, if you're twenty-five years old, 75 percent of your money should be in stocks. If you're forty, 60 percent of your money should be in stocks. Stocks tend to be riskier as investments than bonds, which have slower growth but are more stable. Over time, however, stocks tend to earn more.

The Bonus of a Roth IRA

There are two types of IRAs: traditional and Roth. You may only make Roth contributions if you are a single taxpayer earning less than $114,000 annually. If you're married, your combined income must be less than $181,000 for you to contribute to a Roth.

With a Roth IRA, you won't be penalized for taking money (contributions, not gains) out of your account before you hit age fifty-nine and a half. However, in a traditional IRA, you do get penalized (just as you do in your 401(k) plan).

Another bonus of the Roth IRA is you pay taxes when you put your money into the account instead of when you take your money out for retirement. That means when you're older (and hopefully earning wads more than you do now) you won't get taxed in your higher bracket. You already paid the taxes when you put your money in.

MG TIP: If you can't quite swing the full $5,500 to add to your IRA per year, sock away as much as you can (even $200) and then set up an auto-pay plan with your IRA holder so they'll take a teeny amount from you every month. It adds up, and you won't really notice it being taken out if it's done automatically.

MG TIP: Don't buy into the "grass is greener" myth by thinking that people with higher salaries are necessarily "richer" than you are. Sure, someone may have a bigger cash flow than you, but the question is, are they accumulating more or spending it? Even if you're not a high-wage earner, systematically putting money into a savings account or investment or mutual fund can ultimately make you richer than those who earn more.

Stocks and Bonds: The Bulls and Bears of the Money Jungle

When most people think of "investing," they think of the stock market. After all, stocks are sexy. You buy, you sell. You "own" cool companies. Some people win big. Some people lose big. But it's not all about stocks.

Bonds don't have the same sex appeal as stocks, but they can be great investments. During raging bull markets (an up stock market), bonds offer a seemingly piddly return compared to stocks. However, all it takes is a bear market (a down stock market) to give investors a reality check on how safe and stable a bond can be. But hey, it's not easy to simplify a business that takes years to master, so I highly recommend reading a book called *Shoo, Jimmy Choo!* by Catey Hill. Finally someone who can translate finances into a language I understand: designer shoes.

Stock Basics: What Are Stocks?

A stock is a share in the ownership of a company. It is essentially a claim on the company's assets and earnings. As you acquire more stock, your ownership stake in the company becomes greater. Whether you say shares, equity, or stock, it all means the same thing.

Being an Owner

Holding a company's stock means that you are one of the many owners (shareholders) of a company. So basically you have a tiny piece of the company—every deal that they make that brings in money, every investment they make that earns money, every trademark. But being a shareholder of a public company doesn't mean you have anything to do with daily details of the business.

What you are entitled to is your share of the company's earnings, and there are voting rights attached to the stock. At annual meetings, shareholders have one vote per share to elect the board of directors. So basically, you have a say in who's running the company, and can help make changes if your current director isn't performing well.

Now, here's the bad news: Any stock may go bankrupt, which means you lose your entire investment (think: Enron, WorldCom, Global Crossing). But the good news is, public companies are limited-liability companies, which means you won't be on the hook for any outstanding debts or legal proceedings the company may have. You'll only lose the amount you put in.

Although the risk might sound all negative, there is a bright side. Taking on greater risk can mean a greater return on your investment. This is why stocks have historically outperformed other investments such as bonds or savings accounts. Over the long term, stock investments have historically had an average annual return of around 10 to 12 percent.

Mutual Funds: Letting People Invest for You

I don't know about you, but I've got better things to do with my day than anxiously watch the Dow rise and fall. This is where a stock mutual fund comes in. Basically, you have your money manager (you can go through institutions such as Charles Schwab) invest in an array of stocks for you. It could be ten different stocks out of a hundred choices. He or she will move your stocks around depending on how they perform. Now, here's the thing: Other people are also investing in the same funds as you are (hence, the "mutual"). And there's power in numbers. The more people who invest, the more growth the fund typically gets. When a fund does well, you should reap the rewards. And the best news is you only need $1,000 to start investing with most funds. Each month, you'll get a statement from your money manager charting the gains and losses you've made.

The great thing about mutual funds is diversity. You're not putting all your eggs in one basket (it's like dating a few guys at once so you don't put all your energy into just one dude and get crushed). You may not win big because you're not super invested in any one company; but you're also protecting yourself from losing big with one company that takes a nosedive.

Bond Basics: What Are Bonds?

Think about times when you've borrowed money from a friend, or even from a bank for a down payment on your car. You were given a loan. Basically, bonds are loans but *you're* the lender. Just as people need money, so do companies and governments, often more than the average bank can provide. Their solution is to raise money by issuing bonds to the public (i.e., you). The organization that sells a bond is known as the issuer. You can think of it as an IOU given by a borrower (the issuer) to a lender (the investor).

MG'S MONEY GLOSSARY

- *Stocks*: A stock is a share in the ownership of a company. The more shares you earn, the more say you have in a company—and the more opportunity to make money off it.

- *Bonds*: Loans you agree to give to various companies/ governments. In return they pay you interest for your loans.

- *Mutual funds*: An equity or bond fund that pools the money of many individual investors. The advantage of the fund is that it offers professional management and diversification of investments for a fee. Some funds, called "no-load," don't even require a fee.

- *The stock market*: All the stocks that are available to buy in the United States.

- *NASDAQ* (National Association of Securities Dealers Automated Quotation system): It's not a place, per se; it's an automated system accessible via telephone and computer.

- *NYSE (New York Stock Exchange)*: A physical space in the heart of the city's financial center where stock trades take place. There are other exchanges in cities like L.A., Chicago, San Francisco, Boston, London, and Tokyo.

- *Dow Jones Industrial Average*: The most well-known index in the stock market, it lists the average stock prices of the thirty biggest industrial companies in the United States.

Now you may be thinking, "Hold up. Why the heck would I lend a company *my* hard-earned money?" Here's the answer: because you earn interest. Your bond issuer has to pay you a little something extra for the privilege of using your dough. The interest rate with bonds is often referred to as the "coupon." The date on which the issuer has to repay the amount borrowed, known as "face value," is called the "maturity date."

If stocks are like exciting, noncommittal lovers, bonds are like steady boyfriends. They're known as "fixed-income securities" because you know the exact amount of cash you'll get back, provided you hold the security until maturity. Pretend you buy a bond with a face value of $1,000, a coupon of 6 percent, and a maturity of ten years. This means you'll receive a total of $60 ($1,000 times 6 percent) of interest per year for the next ten years. When the bond matures after a decade you'll get your $1,000 back.

The perk of having bonds is that if the company goes bankrupt, you as the bondholder will get paid before a shareholder does. The downside of being a bondholder is that you get zero profits if the company does well—all you take home is your principal plus interest. There's less risk in owning bonds compared to owning stocks, but bonds can be your safe haven while the equity markets are super volatile.

And Just Because a Modern Girl Loves Finding a Little Free Cash . . .

Think about how great it feels to discover an old $20 bill in your pocket. Well, there's actually a website that can give you the same kind of perks on a bigger scale. It's called www.foundmoney.com, and it has access to over thirty million unclaimed accounts and continues to add more daily. The website was started in 1995 by Edward Palonek after his parents died and he realized how hard it was to track down their assets. Now anyone can run a free search on his site to see if there's money out there just waiting to be claimed.

Here's how it works: Simply type in your name or the name of a deceased relative, and it searches for stocks, bonds, and property that you or they may own but haven't claimed—plus the contact info for the financial institution holding the money. If you or a relative comes up in a free search, you'll have to pay a fee to get more info. But think of it as a little money well spent to retrieve a potentially large cash stash.

Does an MG Need an Accountant?

I'll admit, all of this money talk is dizzying . . . but what's even more complicated is filling out your income tax forms correctly. Sure, we're all intelligent enough to do the math, but plunking down at your kitchen counter with your tax forms, a calculator, and a Number 2 pencil isn't the smartest route. Not only are you prone to make careless errors, you may not realize that you're eligible for additional deductions (which means more money for you). You've got two great options here:

Hiring a CPA

For a few hundred bucks and a couple of hours, you can hire a CPA (Certified Public Accountant) to do your taxes for you. I personally feel more comfortable relying on a live human to do my taxes for me and point out where I can save money—it's worth the $200 or $300 bucks each year. If you're going to go this route, ask for referrals from people you trust, especially ones in your same line of work. Accountants who specialize in certain industries—whether it be media, medical, or real estate—are more familiar with the typical deductions for people in these fields. When you sit down with him or her, ask tons of questions so that you get your money's worth. If your finances are relatively simple (no mortgages, new business ventures, divorces, and so on), you may feel confident enough to try your hand at doing your own taxes the following year. Here are some questions you may want to ask:

- Is he or she a Certified Public Accountant (CPA) or an Enrolled Agent (EA)? CPAs focus mainly on broad-based tax issues, but

MG TIP: Be up front. When you first meet with your accountant, ask for an estimate of how much your tax return will cost. Trust me, this isn't poor etiquette. Tax preparation fees vary depending on how complex or easy your tax return is. Do you have mortgages? Your own small business? Investments? Have a number of cash inflows from different places? These factors may make your fee spike. So try to take everything into "account" first, because you don't want to be shocked at a bill that's double or triple what you anticipated.

some may specialize in other areas. EAs are licensed by the federal government and specialize in tax issues. If you're concerned about being audited, keep in mind that only attorneys, CPAs, and EAs are allowed to represent you before the IRS. Research has shown that CPAs, EAs, and tax attorneys have the lowest error rate on prepared tax returns. Unenrolled tax preparers can prepare and sign your return, but they are not tested by the IRS or the state. Because they may or may not have had any formal training, it's smart to steer clear of them. If you're looking for an accountant to give you complicated financial advice or manage the financial affairs of your business, you may want to ask if they are a Chartered Certified Accountant. After five years of professional practice, an accountant can establish further credibility by attaining Chartered Certified Accountant status through a series of exams. This just means that they may have more experience and expertise than a regular CPA, and will perhaps be more qualified to manage the financial systems of a business, give financial advice to colleagues and clients, and undertake audits and evaluations of business systems.

- How long have they been in the business? Try to find someone with over three years' experience.

- What is their experience? What is their specialty? If you freelance as a musician, for example, look for a tax pro who is very familiar with your specific field. An EA who spends most of his time dealing with audits may not be right for you. A CPA who handles returns for large businesses isn't likely to be the best choice if you have a small start-up company with just a few employees. While both of these tax pros could be more than qualified to prepare your returns, it's better and more cost effective, to go with someone whose clients have similar needs to your own.

- Will they be dealing with your finances directly or will they be sharing the load with an employee or coworker?

- How much do they charge for their services? Is it an hourly or per return rate? For a straightforward tax return (i.e., you don't have tons of properties, deductions, different jobs and sources that bring in your cash flow) you can expect to pay anywhere from $200 to $400. For clients whose tax situations are more complicated and whose returns might take ten to twenty hours to complete (including time spent meeting with you), a CPA might charge $1,000 plus. Also keep in mind that accountants who work for big firms are likely to charge more than those who are self-employed.

- Do they have insurance? Make sure you hire an accountant who carries liability or errors and omissions insurance. This will compensate you for damages if your accountant makes a mistake.

- Ask for references. Have each accountant provide you with a few names and numbers of their clients and contact each reference.

H&R Block: Good or Bad Idea?

If you don't have a good reference from friends, family, or coworkers for a good accountant, you can also look to your local H&R Block for competent and affordable tax return help. Though your fee will depend on the complexity of your financial situation, they tend to be low. The average cost of a client's 2013 return was $198. That included a basic federal return, a state return, and possibly one attached schedule, all prepared in-office. You can either go to an office or file with their tax pros online if you're too busy to go to their office. H&R Block also guarantees to provide the maximum refund you are entitled to. So if you spot a slipup in their tax preparation, then your tax prep is done free. The downside is, those slipups could occur more often because they're working with so many customers. Additionally, it's going to feel more impersonal than working with a private accountant who will likely stick with you through the years and offer you other pieces of smart financial advice.

Using Your Computer

If you're a computer whiz who likes the idea of filing online and wants to save some dough, spring for software like Turbo Tax ($40) that will do your taxes for you online, as well as point out deductions where necessary. If you're still a little shaky on whether you've done everything right online, take your tax forms to an accountant to have it reviewed. There's no shame in getting a second opinion when it comes to your health—or even on how your butt looks in a particular pair of jeans—and it's no different with your taxes.

When a Modern Girl Makes a Major Purchase

Once you have a steady stream of cash coming in and have a firm hold on your finances, you may be ready to drop a fair share of ducats on your first hefty "Big Girl" purchase. The trick to making big buys is to be calculated and well informed—not to get caught up in the heat of the moola moment. (Translation: You can't have the same "Omigosh! I've gotta have this now!" attitude you do when you impulse-buy a sweater.)

Whether you're in the market for a set of wheels, your first house, or even a pricey piece of art or jewelry, you've got to make some savvy decisions and avoid some easy-to-make missteps. Here are all the smart-buying tips your seller's not likely to tell you:

How to Buy a Car—Without Getting Taken for a Ride

We all know the stereotype of a car dealer: slick, sneaky, and full of BS. And whether that's actually true or not, you can't walk onto a car lot ready to be a victim. The more you know, the less likely you'll get a raw deal.

Get to Know Kelley and Edmunds Before You Meet Joe Dealer

Go to websites such as www.edmunds.com or Kelley Blue Book (www.kbb.com) so you can get a sense of what your dream car is really worth. Make sure to note the MSRP (Manufacturer's Suggested Retail Price). This is basically the "wholesale" price the dealership paid for the car, before they mark it up and try to sell it to you.

Buy "Out of Season"

Think about it—you always get a better deal on bikinis when you buy last season's in the winter, rather than shelling out for one of summer's new styles before Memorial Day. Let's say you're going for a 2014 convertible. If you buy right before summer, the value (and thus the price) will be higher than if you wait until the fall. Another bonus of waiting: When the 2015 convertibles come on the lot in the fall, they'll want to get rid of the 2014s and will have no choice but to lower the prices big-time.

Don't Get Sucked In by Extras

I'll admit I'm the type of gal who will wind up buying three compacts of blush at a department store counter if it means they'll throw in a free lipstick too. But you can't get lured in by the "free gift monster" when you're shopping for a car. You don't want to end up with a lemon because the dealer offered to throw in heated seats—especially if you live in San Diego. Strip away all the shiny accessories (or even rebates and financing deals) your dealer is throwing at you. Is the car still as appealing to you? If not, keep looking.

MG TIP: Shop toward the end of the year. Fall is when new cars come out and dealers want to unload last year's cars. Also head in at the end of the day. After a full day of no sales, your sales guy might be more willing to cut you a break.

Negotiate After Incentives

One of the biggest "free gifts" dealers dangle in your face is extra money, like an extra $2,000 to $3,000 incentive if you buy the car. But keep this in mind: The reason dealers can do this is that the car is already marked up beyond its true value. That means you're not getting a cash break at all. So first negotiate the price without incentives tacked on, and try to get it as close to the MSRP (what the dealer paid for the car originally) as possible. Then ask them, "So what else can you give me?" Don't be shy.

MG TIP: Lowball. If your goal price is $20,000, keep that to yourself. If they come back with $22,000, offer $18,000. You'll have somewhere to go. Also, don't let dealers tell you if you don't buy today, you lose the car. You're in control. They have to sell cars to get paid.

Financing Your Car

If you aren't able to pay the entire sticker price of your car all at once, make a down payment and finance the rest. And even if you *can* afford to buy the car, financing can be a good option because of the low interest rates. But if you plan to take out a longer-term loan, beware. Although it cuts your monthly payments, it sharply increases your total interest costs.

Above all, make sure to walk onto the car lot with *your own* financing plan at the ready. All you need to do is go to your bank or credit union and get preapproved for a loan and ask for the lowest interest rate they can offer. Why go to the trouble? Because otherwise, you may get ripped off. So be smart and get the lowest rate possible from your bank. Then, when the dealership offers you a rate through *their* financing institution, tell them the lower rate your bank's offered you. The dealership will likely try to beat or match it.

If they do match it, it seems convenient to do it through the dealership because it's one-stop shopping and the dealer will do all the paperwork and submit it to the bank for you. It seems like minimal hassle. But you should still be wary, because the fine print may have hidden traps. Your dealer may have struck a deal with the dealership's financing partner where they make a profit off you. For example, you may be offered 0 percent financing for your car or a $2,500 rebate. If you already have a low interest rate through your bank, you should take the rebate and go with your bank's rate. Once you lower your principal by a few thousand dollars and multiply it by the rate, you'll wind up saving more than if you did 0 percent financing on a more expensive car.

Leasing Your Car

Also consider leasing a car, which doesn't require you to even leave a down payment. The basic difference between a car lease and a car loan is that a lease finances the use of a vehicle that you don't own, and a loan finances the purchase of a vehicle you do own.

If having a new car every two or three years is important to you, leasing is a smart option. Plus, you only have to put down a few hundred dollars per month, as opposed to a hefty down payment for buying a car. However, since you don't own a leased car, you can't alter it, slap on a new coat of paint, or even install a new stereo system. Additionally, there are mileage limits to leasing automobiles and putting more miles on the car than the lease allows can cost you big money, since you'll pay so much per mile for every mile driven over the allowance. Another point to consider is that you won't own the car at the end of your lease, but you'll wind up paying more for the same amount of car because your monthly payments were higher than if you'd bought it. But the good news is, with many car dealerships, you can lease with the option to buy your car later, with the price adjusted in proportion to how much it has depreciated in value.

MG TIP: Knowledge is power when it comes to purchasing wheels. To know where you stand (and what interest rates you should be offered) go to www.myfico.com for an approximate credit rating. It will tell you the kinds of financing deals you'll get on a new car. For example, a person with a score of 720 or more can get a rate of 4.9 percent, while someone with a rating of 520 could get slapped with a rate of 18.5 percent.

Consider a Used or Certified Pre-Owned Car

It's been said that the moment a new car is purchased and driven off the lot it loses between 20 to 40 percent of its value—and you can take advantage of this fact by going for a used car. You can still get a great car but for up to half the price.

To make sure you get the most car for the least cash, walk onto the lot at the right time. Experts say the best time to buy a used car is at the end of the month, in lousy weather, and between late December to early January—they're said to be cheapest at that time.

MG TIP: Read the fine print of your proposed lease and make sure you understand all the terms. Sign only closed-end leases, which means that if at the end of the lease, the car is worth less than the leasing company estimated when you signed your lease, they're responsible for paying up, not you.

Here are some other tips when going for used:

- Look for low mileage, an extended warranty option, and certainly the physical and mechanical condition.

- Tell them you want to have your mechanic check out the car before the deal is finalized, and go to a mechanic you trust. You may be required to leave a credit card or deposit as collateral against the vehicle when you bring it to be looked at.

MG TIP: About 95 percent of all Certified Pre-Owned vehicles sold in America come with a vehicle history report so that buyers can really understand how many people owned it, where it's been, and its mileage history.

- Ask for referrals on dealerships if you decide to go the used route. Some used-car dealerships are notoriously sketchy. Stick to those in your town that have been in business for some time.

- Make sure to check out the car in broad daylight. Dark or wet conditions will easily hide a car's faults. Take a friend or relative as a second opinion (two pairs of eyes are better than one).

- Make sure to order a vehicle history report from either CarFax or Car Detective—they keep a national database of car damage and repairs. All you need is the VIN, or Vehicle Identification Number. This is the best protection against buying a used car with costly hidden problems. The report costs $30 but could save you quite a bit more.

- Make sure all the documentation you would expect to find is available. This will normally include the Registration Document or log book, service and insurance records, and receipts for repairs, maintenance, etc.—as well as the receipt or invoice that shows the seller owns the car.

- Definitely reference the blue book to see the car's value versus what they're asking for it.

- And most important, take your time. Don't fall in love with a shiny paint job or model you never thought you could afford. If it seems too good to be true, it probably is!

Certified Pre-Owned Cars

If you're not sure you want to put up so much moolah for a new car (and watch it dive in value) or you're a little sketched out about buying a used car and praying it doesn't turn into a lemon, buying a Certified Pre-Owned car is a smart middle ground. If a car is "Factory Certified" it means it was a used car that was offered for sale by your local dealer and is maintained by the vehicle's manufacturer. That means getting perks. For example, the original manufacturer of the vehicle is using their dealer network to inspect the car, determine if it is worth certifying, then guaranteeing to cover your warranty protection for a period of time after your original warranty expires.

Trade in Your Old Car

Whether you're buying new or used, you'll likely want to get rid of your old clunker. The best route is to trade in the car at the same dealership where you're buying the new one. The benefit is that you can knock down the price of your new car by subtracting the amount you got for your old one. Working from a lower principle for your new wheels will make your overall interest payments lower. Go to www.edmunds.com for your trade-in's value.

Car Apps

Now that you've got your car, here are two apps to download immediately!

RepairPal: Given how much time we spend in our car, it turns out that statistically, we are most likely to have an emergency *in* our car. So you better be prepared. RepairPal offers immediate roadside assistance, lists the warranty services/manufacturer help lines for every car company, lets you make calls from right inside the app, gives you car repair estimates (both for fixing problems and routine maintenance), and locates the nearest repair shops. And unlike most other things related to your car, it's *free*.

MG TIP: Negotiate your trade-in *before* you decide what new car you want to buy. If you do the trade-in last, you'll be more likely to want to get rid of it, and could wind up throwing away money because you didn't fight hard enough for your trade-in.

MG TIP: Know exactly what you want to be paid for your car and don't go under that. When the dealer starts haggling with you, make like a broken record and keep repeating what you want. They'll get annoyed at first, but eventually they'll find a way to appease you.

iWrecked: I hope you don't get in an accident, ever, but if you do, this is a great app to have. It tells you everything you need to do and includes space to write a detailed accident log/report, a place to store your car and insurance information and emergency numbers, and a taxi/tow locator. (You may also want to check with your insurance provider as they may have an app that offers the same on their own forms.) And it's free.

How to Buy Art

You may not be in the market to start building up a major collection, but you can still buy quality art that you love (and that may have the potential to appreciate in value). Here are some wise art buying tips from art expert Alan Bamberger, author of *The Art of Buying Art*:

Do Your Research

Just as you wouldn't buy a car or apartment without looking into all the details first, you shouldn't stroll into a gallery and drop a bundle for art you haven't become adequately familiar with. Sure, falling in love with a painting is about passion, but you need to be smart if you're spending, say, a thousand bucks or more on something.

Get the Dirt on the Artist

Once you spot a painting you love, don't clam up and "yes" the dealer just because you aren't an art pro. Pick his or her brain as much as possible. What else has the artist done? How long has the artist been showing paintings? Has the artist won any awards or been featured in books or articles? What are the recent sales for this artist's other similar works? Your dealer will have this info on record. If you notice the dealer being standoffish about answering, be on guard. He or she may be hiding something.

Find Out How "Original" It Is

A key question is to ask your dealer if the art is original or a reproduction. What you might hear is that the work is a "limited edition print." Well, don't get swept up by the fancy title. A limited edition print has a set number of copies, usually fewer then two hundred, which are numbered and signed by the artist. But here's the catch: Many limited edition prints are actually digital/photographic knockoffs made by a publishing company, not the artist.

Cover Your Butt as a Buyer

Before you plunk down your credit card, make sure to get as much documentation about the painting as possible—especially the authenticity of the work. Also ask the dealer to make out a receipt that details the condition of the art when you bought it and has a clause that says you'll get your money back for the painting if you find out that the art you just bought was not represented accurately by the gallery.

Should You Buy Art Online?

The great thing about the Internet is that it obviously gives you a bigger gallery (literally) to choose from. If you know the artist or type of artwork you are looking for, then shopping online might be a great way to go, as you can search for the artist, piece, or style you want. However, if you are an art-buying newbie, you may find the Internet overwhelming. Also, don't think that because it's on the Internet you're getting a great deal. Artists usually have their price and may be unlikely to move from it, plus you may have greater shipping prices depending upon where the piece is coming from. Here are a few things to keep in mind:

- Be sure there is a return policy. Especially with expensive art. You are taking a leap of faith and you need to know you don't have to keep it if you don't like it.

- Try to view images of the artwork at as high a resolution as possible. Expand the thumbnails, and if you can't get a larger image, ask the artist or gallery to send you actual photos.

- Remember that oftentimes monitors display different colors than what the actual artwork may be.

- Read the description carefully! Check the size, whether it's an original or reproduction, a papier-mâché sculpture or made of cement!

- Ask about framing and shipping costs. It will cost more to ship something framed, but the seller may be able to cut you a break on the framing. But if you don't like what they have planned or are particular about framing styles . . . skip it!

- And most important, look for a reputable site. Some of my favorites are:

  - Paddle8
  - Saatchi Art
  - Eyestorm
  - Artspace
  - Artsy

Have It Appraised by a Third Party

Until you find dealers, galleries, and resources you can trust, it's good to have some idea of what the art should be selling for before you buy. Experts say you don't necessarily need to have it appraised, but you can comparison-shop from gallery to gallery, check to see whether the artist has ever sold at auction, and ask the seller to provide information on the artist's recent sales history. That way you have a better chance of getting a good deal.

However, once you buy, it's wise to get your art appraised by another dealer or appraiser in the business. Sure, the last thing on your mind is selling it right now, but you'll want to know that you have the option to sell it down the road if your tastes or circumstances change. You don't want to ask the dealer who just sold it to you because he or she will give you an inflated value (after all, they want it to seem like everything hanging in their gallery is worth top dollar).

Is Art Really a Good Investment?

Here's the cold, hard truth: Art isn't considered the safest investment—unless you're buying blue-chip art from a high-profile auction and/or gallery and are positive of its resale/appreciation value. In fact, investing in art is no less risky than investing in the stock market. The Mei/Moses index, calculated by two economists from New York University, shows a long-term annual return of 8.2 percent for art investments (at best), compared with 9.8 percent for the S&P 500 Index average.

Choosing Modern Versus Old School

While acquiring an early painting from an older, well-respected artist is probably your smartest investment (early works tend to be more valuable), you may be immediately entranced by a piece of modern art or sculpture by an up-and-coming artist that you spot at an art fair or gallery opening. By all means invest in the latter, as long as you have done your research on the artist and can see that he or she will produce a more impressive body of work in the future. Who knows? Your contemporary piece may have significant cultural importance that will make it appreciate in value over time, and the artist may hit it big in the next fifteen years. But then again, you might be left with a big Rothko-esque canvas on your wall that doesn't sell for over $100. The experts say the bottom line is to buy something because you love it and can't live without it on your wall, not because you want to make an investment. Sure, maybe a true collector will be making money off their art, but the only returns an MG should expect are compliments like, "Ooh, where did you find that spectacular painting in your foyer?!" at cocktail parties. Still, in this day and age where everyone's place looks like a Pottery Barn catalog, that kind of praise is priceless.

How to Buy Your First "Real" Piece of Bling

Sometimes the best art investment is the kind you wear on your body: jewelry. Just as Destiny's Child sang in "Independent Women," "I buy my own diamonds, and I buy my own rings," there's no reason you should wait for a guy to give you rocks. But if you're a jewelry-buying virgin, you can easily get taken advantage of. Here's how to shop smart:

Set Your Spending Range

Experts advise dropping at least $3,000 for a piece of collectible jewelry, as it takes that much to get something really "significant." If you aren't sure what you want when you walk into a store, tell them your price range and see what it can buy. Just make sure that the jewelry seller you're dealing with isn't trying to sell you a piece by virtue of how cheap it is. Nobody gives jewelry away free.

Know the Four C's

Diamonds are a girl's best friend . . . and a very popular jewelry buy for first-timers. The basics you need to know are:

Cut
It's easy to think that "cut" means shape, but the cut of a diamond is really the angles and finish that make light pass through the diamond, giving it brilliance and shimmer. A diamond's cut is graded according to the following: Ideal Cut (the most brilliant), Premium, Very Good, Good, Fair, and Poor. Often you can get away with buying a Premium or Very Good cut and have it look nearly as flashy as the Ideal.

Clarity
The fewer "inclusions" (blemishes, scratches, or mineral material) a diamond has inside it or on its surface, the better quality it is. An F-IF (Flawless or Internally Flawless) or VVS1-VVS2 (Very Very Slightly Included) graded diamond is *very* pricey (think Kim

Kardashian's Lorraine Schwartz engagement ring from Kanye West). Diamonds graded VS are still fabulous, and SI1 and SI2 grades are more practical buys. An "I" grade means you can see the diamond's flaws with your naked eye. Don't buy "I" if you can avoid it.

Color

A colorless diamond is the most coveted because it lets the most light pass through it. A "D" grade diamond is the most colorless (and most pricey); while a "Z" grade is the worst (with a brownish tint . . . yuck). The exceptions to this rule are the now trendy "colored" diamonds, like the pink one Mariah Carey scored from Nick Cannon.

Carats

A carat is the weight (and size) of a diamond—and is the most obvious feature of a ring, bracelet, necklace, or set of earrings.

Shop for Certified Diamonds

No matter what the size of your stone, your diamond should be certified before you purchase it. Well-known laboratories are GIA (www.gia.edu) and EGL (www.egl.usa.com). If purchasing a diamond from a store that doesn't offer GIA or EGL certified diamonds, always be sure to request the credentials of the certifying lab.

Have It Appraised by a Third Party

In addition to having your diamond certified, you should also have it appraised before you buy. "Appraisal" means "independent replacement value." The jewelry store will offer an appraisal, but experts say it's smarter to go to another source. You can find one in the phone book, but make sure the appraiser belongs to the proper organizations for appraisal. You may also be able to purchase a diamond that already comes with a third-party appraisal. Just make sure to check the appraisal papers to ensure they're from a legit company.

MG TIP: A diamond is a "colored" diamond if it has more color than a Z diamond, and then the value begins a gradual increase. Other colors are evaluated according to their saturation and hue, not described with the letter or number grades. They are extremely rare and are therefore valued individually.

MG TIP: Go to www.thediamondbuying guide.com for more detailed info.

MG TIP: Look for a "CGA-Certified Gemologist Appraiser." According to the American Gem Society (www.americangemsociety .org) the title of CGA is the highest awarded by the American Gem Society and is given only to those who have proved their expertise and professionalism.

MG TIP: Rarity and demand drive diamond prices.

MG TIP: Baubles are just like boobs—if you employ a few smart tricks they can instantly look bigger. Ask your jeweler about ways to make your stone look bigger, like by putting it in an elevated prong setting. Also, adding smaller diamonds around a solitaire can double the appearance of its size— without doubling the price tag.

Laser Your Girdle

The girdle of your ring is the widest part of the stone, and some diamonds such as Forevermark diamonds (www.forevermarkdiamond.com/us) will come with an inscribed type of ID number that can be seen only through a magnifying glass. So when you take your diamond to be repaired or cleaned, you can check to make sure a cheaper stone isn't swapped for your precious gem. If you're purchasing a diamond that isn't already inscribed, you can request that your local retailer send it to the GIA Gem Trade Laboratory for inscription services.

Ask About Upgrade Plans

They say diamonds are forever, but a good jeweler will have a trade-in policy so that you can upgrade to a larger or higher-quality stone in the future. (Just hold on to your receipt—that is the only proof-of-purchase you'll have when you trade it in). But don't look for appreciation in value. Although historically diamonds have increased in value, like a car they can decrease in value after purchase. But a diamond you inherited from your grandmother is probably worth more today.

Remember Resale Value

Besides beauty, quality, and rarity, experts say desirability is what gives a stone its lasting value. Will a jeweler want to buy it from you? Will it sell quickly on eBay? Do your research beforehand. Another tip to max your investment: Always buy smaller and buy better, especially with stones. That way you know you're making a good investment. But if size matters more to you than resale value, go for a slightly less perfect stone that's got a little more heft.

Read the Fine Print on Your Receipt

Before you buy from any dealer, be sure you know the return policy.

Consider Going "Estate"

Estate jewelry simply means it's been pre-owned. And if you're looking for a deal on a diamond or a strand of pearls, why not give someone else's gorgeous gems a repeat performance? You can wind up with an elegant piece that is truly one of a kind.

- You can look for estate jewelry at antique shows, flea markets, and jewelry stores. But at flea markets, be on guard—you can easily get taken for a ride.

- One way to tell if the jewelry is fake is to look at the backside of the stone. If it's a bogus bauble, it'll be covered with metal or foil to create faux shine.

- It's impossible as a newbie to know exactly what you're looking at, so make sure you stick to your budget and buy only things that you love (in case they're worthless). For more expensive purchases, deal only with a reputable jeweler.

MG TIP: Know the difference between antique and vintage. Anything "antique" has to be a hundred years old or more. "Vintage" just has to be something that's made in the past—it could be ten, twenty, or thirty years old. And the interesting thing about estate jewelry is that it could actually be made in 2013. As long as it's resold, it's considered estate.

How to Buy Your First Home or Apartment

The biggest investment a Modern Girl can make is buying her own pad. Just think—no more flushing your rent down the toilet and dealing with cramped spaces. But before you start fantasizing about relaxing in that elusive backyard, Poggenpohl kitchen, or steam shower you're dying to call your own, you need to follow a few steps. They're not a cakewalk, that's for sure. But the more knowledgeable you are, the faster you'll be picking out a new welcome mat and thinking, "Yeah, girl, I *own* this joint."

If you're single and putting off buying a home because it seems more like a "man thing," get this: Pew Research Center reported in 2013 that a record 40 percent of all households with children under the age of eighteen have female breadwinners who are either the sole or the primary source of income for the family. Something to be proud of! In fact, sometimes you can spend almost exactly what you're paying in rent but have it be toward something you truly own. The rule of thumb is that you should spend no more than 30 percent of your income on rent or mortgage, but if you've got a shoe addiction like mine, you might want to keep that number closer to 25 percent.

Dream Home Hint 1: Get Preapproved for a Mortgage

Before you can even start looking at homes, you need to get the green light to buy your pad. That means getting prequalified and then preapproved (a two-step process) for a mortgage from your lender.

In case things are getting fuzzy, a mortgage is a home loan that you pay off over a number of years. Let's say you want to buy a condo for $500,000. You'll need to put down around 10 percent as a down payment ($50,000) and can pay the remainder ($450,000) over the next fifteen to thirty years (depending on your contract), plus interest.

So who needs to approve you for a mortgage? Your lender could be your bank, such as Chase or Wells Fargo, or it could be a separate mortgage agency. The best bet is to comparison-shop for the lowest rates possible so you know you're getting the best deal. This is a good reason to go to a mortgage broker or lender because he or she closely monitors which banks are giving the best deals, taking the guesswork away for you. Another popular source for mortgage rate comparison shopping is www.lendingtree.com.

To preapprove you, your lender has to look at your income, your tax returns over the past few years, pay stubs, a credit report, and your bank statements. They'll also want to know how much debt you have—but since you're a savvy MG, we know you've kept that to a minimum.

Don't freak if this whole process sounds foreign to you. The more dialogue you have with your lending officer, the less anxious you'll feel.

Although there isn't a single or simple answer to what *type* of mortgage is right for you, locking in a good rate depends on the following factors:

MG TIP: For more info check out: www.mortgage101.com. The site is operated by Lion Inc. (www.lioninc.com), an online service that connects mortgage brokers to lenders and consumers.

- Your current financial picture
- How you expect your finances to change
- How long you intend to keep your house
- How comfortable you are with your mortgage payment changing

For example, a fifteen-year fixed-rate mortgage can save you lots of interest payments over the life of the loan, but your monthly payments will be higher than those with a thirty-year mortgage. An adjustable-rate mortgage may begin with a lower monthly payment than a fixed-rate mortgage—but your payments could get higher when the interest rate changes.

Bottom line: The best way to pick a mortgage is to discuss your plans, financial prospects, and preferences with a mortgage professional.

Dream Home Hint 2: Find a Fabulous Real Estate Agent

Once you get preapproved for a mortgage (yes, you will), your lender will inform you, based on your individual data, how expensive a home you can feasibly make an offer on. But beware: Often the number they give you is the maximum amount. This is not necessarily what you want to spend unless you plan on eating Chef Boyardee for the next five years and furnishing your home with a futon. Figure out what the monthly payments work out to be and see if you're comfortable with that figure before you proceed.

Now it's time to take that information to a real estate agent so he or she can find homes for you in your price range. To locate a quality agent, get references from friends and family or look online for reputable agencies who will provide an agent for your area (just make sure they are licensed).

MG TIP: Whatever you do, don't go with the realtor who's trying to sell the house you're looking to buy! She's not going to keep your needs paramount and may wind up trying to muscle you into the deal.

MG TIP: Never look at a home while the sellers are there—you don't want them to know how interested you are. And if you're shopping for a home with your hubby, don't say anything out loud in front of your realtor until the two of you have had a chance to talk privately. Should your husband exclaim, "Oh, this place is great!" in front of anyone, pretend you just saw a mouse. Acting unimpressed with the place (even if you're jumping up and down inside) will keep you from looking desperate.

Dream Home Hint 3: Location! Location! Location!

Once your realtor starts showing you places, you need to make some decisions. Investmentwise, it's smarter to buy a smaller home in a great or up-and-coming area than a palace in a run-down neighborhood. Sure, you may love the idea of finding a great place in the middle of nowhere and hoping the neighborhood cleans up and gets better schools, restaurants, and shopping malls, but that doesn't always happen overnight. The best way to know if you're making a smart investment is to ask your realtor. Also, do a little research online at www.homevaluehunt.com. Just plug in your information and you will be e-mailed the most recent fifteen records in your neighborhood by proximity to the house you are interested in.

Also, make a list of what's most important to you: Are you planning on having a baby in the next five to ten years? You'd be better off taking a place with adequate space, child-friendly amenities, and a good school district, even if it means sacrificing charm.

Dream Home Hint 4: Start Negotiating

Once you find your dream abode, you need to make an offer on it. Sure, the sellers have already told you *their* number, but you can (and often should) make a lower bid. Ask your realtor for a fact sheet on comparable sales in the area so that you can get a sense of what is a fair offer. Also take note of certain renovations you'll have to do—let's say the kitchen needs to be totally remodeled—and factor those in as well. But also keep in mind how hot the market is at the time in that neighborhood. If everything in the area tends to be selling for *over* the asking price and you're really in love with the house, you may want to consider coming in at the asking price to assure a quick sale.

Once you make your bid, I wish I could tell you things won't get ugly. But chances are, they'll be stressful at the very least. Not only may your sellers try to bluff you into thinking you've bid way too low but you may wind up getting into a "bidding war." That's what happens when there's more than one person/couple who's making an offer on the house. Make sure you have a realtor who will do the majority of the haggling for you.

Dream Home Hint 5: Make It Legal!

When the seller accepts your offer (and that pushy couple who also wanted the house runs away with their tails between their legs), it's time to pat yourself on the back! You're almost there—except for some paperwork and inspections ahead of you. For starters, you'll fill out a sales contract and a loan application from the bank who preapproved you. You'll also need to have your home inspected by a licensed professional engineer (P.E.). Do not skip this step, no matter how good shape you think the place is in. The P.E. will need to state in writing that your home is structurally sound (i.e., no termites, no radon, a working septic system, and no contaminated water). If there's a big repair you would like to have made, such as plumbing, you can stipulate that you want to have the fix repaired before closing. Or, you can renegotiate your offer and say you'll pay for the fixes yourself.

Next, the seller's attorney will draw up a conditional contract of sale, which will have an agreed down payment (typically 10 percent) that will be held in an escrow account by the seller's attorney until your closing date. When you get your mortgage approved, the contract becomes unconditional (which means you typically can't pull out of the deal). All that's left is a final "walk through" with your agent to make sure the home is the way it was promised to you in the contract, and going to "the closing table," which means all parties sit down with a "closing attorney" to close the deal. You will provide the remainder of your cash down payment, along with your mortgage, to equal the selling price. You'll also give them a certified check for closing costs and show them any legal documents regarding your loan, insurance, etc. If everything goes as planned, the deed passes to you. Get ready to throw your first housewarming shindig.

MG TIP: Keep in mind that the "cost" of your house isn't all that you'll pay. In addition to the price, you're likely to have to pay for a lawyer, escrow fees, real estate taxes, and insurance, just to name a few. Tally these up as best you can ahead of time and consider *that* your price for your place. Otherwise you may not realize how much cash you're going to lay out. To learn more about these "hidden" costs and the many other variables you should be aware of when buying a home, I recommend *Nolo's Essential Guide to Buying Your First Home,* by Ilona Bray, Alayna Schroeder, and Marcia Stewart.

Home Improvements: When Do You Need Help?

Once you own your own home you'll want to make sure you can avoid mini-disasters that can cost you lots of moolah. And even if you're renting, sometimes it's nice *not* to have to pay an expensive handyman to twist a screw, pull a plug, and solve your problem for a hundred bucks! Case in point: A few months ago I dropped my wedding ring down the sink. And freaked. I just stood there, paralyzed, wondering which sewer my diamond was swimming through and too horrified to tell my husband what I'd done. Luckily, I had found Barbara K, female tool 'n fixit guru, who walked me through the recovery.

How to Fish Your Ring Out of the Drain

MG TIP: Don't do what I did and turn on the faucet to rinse the pipe unless you've got a big bucket. Duh! There was no pipe to keep the water from dripping onto the floor, and while I got my ring back, I had a whole new mess to clean up.

Like I said, I freaked when my bling went bye-bye. But it turns out all you may need is a great, female-friendly tool kit like the one you can find on www.projecthome.us. It comes with a lighted screwdriver that has a magnetic tip and a telescopic magnetic lens. Put a little duct tape on the tip and stick it down the drain so the ring can adhere to it.

But if this method fails to work, turn off the water immediately—first the faucet, and then the water supply, which is located under the sink. Slip on some rubber gloves. Locate the "sink trap" (the curved or U-shaped pipe) under your sink. Slip a bucket underneath the pipe. Loosen the nut on each side of the curved piece of pipe with groove joint pliers. But if your trap is made of plastic, you should be able to loosen the nuts by hand. Slide the nuts out of the way and pull the curved piece off. Once you've removed the trap, chances are there will be some water, hair (yuck), slime (double yuck), and hopefully your lost treasure nestled within. Empty the contents into the bucket, using a toothbrush if necessary to coax out any hair, debris, and hopefully, jewelry, that has collected in the trap, recover your ring, and simply reattach the pipe.

How to Fix a Leaky Faucet

Another situation in which you don't need handyman help is when you have a leak—even if it's big. Here's how to take charge and solve your own domestic problems. The following are instructions for basic compression faucet repairs, but there are other types of faucets, such as cartridge, ball-type, and ceramic disk.

Suss Out the Source

To get started, simply figure out whether the leak is coming from the hot or cold faucet, and where it's dripping. If the water is leaking from the tap, you'll have to replace a washer but if the leak is coming from the sink handle, you'll need to replace something called the "O-ring."

Make Dupes

You'll need to take the old parts to the hardware store and get exact replicas. First, turn off the water at the shutoff valve underneath the sink; it looks like a small lever. Take off the decorative cap on top of the faucet handle and use a wrench to unscrew the exposed screw. Now you can easily take off the handle.

MG TIP: I recommend picking up an easy-to-follow book on plumbing, like *Complete Plumbing* published by Stanley Books (an imprint of Meredith Books).

Replace the O-ring

Use an adjustable wrench to loosen and remove the stem nut, then grab the stem with a pair of pliers and pull it out. Roll or cut the old O-ring from the stem. Rub plumber's grease on the new O-ring and slide it into place. Then press the stem nut back over the stem.

Replace the Washer

Follow the above instructions for removing the stem. Remove the washer screw from the stem, press the new washer into the bottom of the stem, and tighten the washer screw into place. Coat the washer and stem thread with heatproof plumber's grease.

Put It All Together

Reinstall the stem. Next, add the stem nut and attach the faucet handle, then screw it down. Replace the decorative cap. Finally, turn on the water at the shutoff valve. Voilà!

What Happens When Your Toilet Overflows

I can't tell you how many times I got a little more wet-and-wild than I wanted to in my first apartment—and not in the biblical sense. In fact, once I came home to find my living room floor flooded with—yep, you guessed it—toilet water.

Toilet Tip 1: Check to See if the Toilet Bowl Is Not Draining Properly

If it's not, don't flush the toilet until it begins to drain. Remove the tank lid and check the guide rod or chain on the tank stopper to see if it's been eroded or twisted, in which case you should just untwist it or replace the chain. If the chain is too long, you can easily adjust and reconnect it so that it has less slack.

Toilet Tip 2: Check the Floating Ball

Lift the float ball up. If this stops the water from running, then try to bend the arm down so the float ball is buoyant. The float ball should be replaced if it is not floating on top of the water. Just unscrew it and replace it with a new one from the hardware store.

Toilet Tip 3: Check for Erosion

Listen and look: Is your toilet still running? There may be sediment buildup that won't let the stopper (flapper) seal shut completely. Shut off the water and flush, then clean the flush valve seat (the rubber-covered hole at the bottom of the tank that allows water to seep in and out) with a nonmetallic scrubbing pad. If you're still having toilet trouble, check the flapper (the thing that closes over the flush valve seat) to make sure it is centered in the seat; if not raising and twisting the flapper may solve the problem. If this doesn't help, you'll need to install a new one. Replacing an old flapper is simple and easy; replacement flappers and even replacement flapper kits are available for almost every toilet. Some flapper kits will even include a new flush valve seat that can be sealed tightly over an existing seat, perfect for those instances when you're having trouble getting a flapper to seal. Be sure to bring the old flapper to a hardware store so that you can find the right replacement. If after all this your toilet is still running or overflowing, it's probably time to call the super or a plumber.

Springing for a Handyman . . . and Not Getting Ripped Off

I'll admit it—sometimes you just can't pull off home repairs alone. That's where the professionals come in. When you're having a major plumbing, electrical, or heating problem in your home, it's not safe to tackle it by yourself.

Here's the problem with handymen, though: Many of them aren't as competent as they let on. They may say they're legit and work directly for a contracting company. They'll brag that they're charging you a lower fee than a plumber or electrician would.

But in reality, you may risk doing yourself a disservice by entrusting these people to take care of your home. Many handymen don't actually have a company address or shop—they just pick up all their parts at a hardware store. This may not seem like such a bum deal as long as they do their job right. But the fact is, if they make an error rewiring something in your home—say an electrical line in your basement—you're putting your family in danger. And the risk becomes twofold: With no insurance policy to back them up if they make a misstep, you're not going to be covered. Their mistakes will come out of *your* pocket.

Handyman Hint 1

For a properly licensed, bonded, and insured handyman in your area, check with your county or city contractors' licensing department or your local Better Business Bureau. You want to make sure the handyman is reputable and has insurance to cover any damage he may incur while working at your home.

Handyman Hint 2

Don't let a handyman bully you into paying in full up front. Have him estimate both the cost of the necessary parts he may need to buy plus the cost of labor. Then put your deal in writing and both of you sign it. Pay him only for the parts he buys and 10 percent of his labor cost in the beginning, and the total when he has completed the project.

Handyman Hint 3

Stipulate that you need to see all receipts for new parts he purchases. Without the receipts, you won't reimburse him. It's that simple.

The Getaway!
How to Travel Savvy—and Safely

MG TIP: Get a confirmation number in case the hotel "can't find" your reservation. Ditto if you cancel a reservation. I had booked a pricey weekend getaway and then canceled when the romance faded fast. Problem was, the hotel claimed I hadn't called it off. I was out one boyfriend and two hundred bucks!

Since I spend so much time running around like a madwoman at home, all I want to do when I take a vacation is relax to the max. I used to be more of a carefree, youth-hostel-happy traveler, but now that I'm a little older, I've realized that accommodations can make or break any getaway. And too often, we're disappointed when service isn't what's been promised. So unless you're willing to rough it, according to the experts at the swanky and Modern Girl–friendly W Hotels Worldwide, there are some important questions you need to ask before booking your getaway:

Are There Any Extra Costs?

It may sound like a good deal, but hidden costs like taxes, surcharges, and hefty overnight parking fees can add up quickly. Make sure to find out what hidden costs are waiting for you.

What's the Cancellation Policy?

Some hotels keep a portion of your deposit no matter when you cancel. Others give a full refund if you cancel within a specified amount of time. And if you're arriving late, how long will they hold your reservation? Be sure to ask.

Can You Be Penalized for Leaving Early?

What happens if your retreat gets rained out, or if you come down with the flu? Find out if they'll let you leave a day early without a pocketbook penalty.

Will There Be Any Renovations Taking Place?

One weekend Marcus and I took a well-deserved break to a local hotel. We had visions of lying by the pool, drinking margaritas, and sleeping till noon. Turns out the pool was under renovation (with the jackhammering starting at 7 A.M.), and our weekend was a big bust. Do yourself a favor and ask in advance.

What Does Your Room Look Like?

Ask for a picture and even square footage of the room you're reserving. Be leery of hotels with brochures and websites that show only sweeping views of the scenery or the front of the hotel. It may be that the rooms themselves are more Motel 6 than Mar-a-Lago.

MG TIP: Ask if your room has a hair dryer and what amenities the hotel provides. With all the room you save not packing a hair dryer and full bottles of shampoo and conditioner, you can squeeze in those strappy sandals you really don't "need" to bring.

MG TIP: Sometimes you can get a lower rate when you book online if you book for a longer stay. Just make sure you won't get penalized if you cancel early.

Safeguarding Your Home Before Your Getaway

Not only do *you* want to feel secure when you're traveling, you want your home to be safe, too. The best way to cover all the bases is to start "closing house" a few days before you're due to leave. Don't get caught in that all-too-familiar trap of dashing around frantically for the five minutes before you go on a trip, then forgetting your plane tickets are back on the kitchen counter. Just follow these simple steps:

Go Incommunicado

A few days before your trip, temporarily suspend your mail and newspaper delivery. Contact the post office (www.usps.com) to hold your mail and packages, or have a trusty neighbor do it for you. Be sure to bring her back a little token from your trip to show your thanks.

Let There Be (Fake) Light

Install plug-in timers (find 'em cheap at Home Depot) on light fixtures in a few chosen rooms. Rig them so they turn on and off at different times. You can do the same timer trick with radios and TVs.

Turn off Water, Gas, and Electrics

We're talking pilot light, washing machine and dryer, TV, toaster, as well as the water supply to your house (to prevent floods). Not only will you save energy, you'll keep damaging power surges at bay.

Move Your Plants

Get those greenies out of direct sun (they'll drink up less water), soak them a few hours before you're out the door, and add a little extra fertilizer.

Find a Pet Sitter

If you have pets, obviously you'll need to find someone to care for them while you are away. I prefer finding a responsible friend or family member to look after my pets; it makes me feel less guilty (which means I'll be able to enjoy my mai tai more) if I leave them in the care of someone they know.

But if you just can't bear the thought of asking your best friend, with the three kids and a full-time job, to pet-sit one more time, you'll have to board your pet or hire a pet sitter. Just be sure to get references from a friend, a veterinarian, or a local shelter when selecting a boarding kennel. To find a pet sitter you can get referrals from "pet people" you trust, but you can also contact the National Association of Professional Pet Sitters (www.petsitters.org) or Pet Sitters International (www.petsit.com) for a referral. Both organizations offer pet sitter accreditation to qualified sitters with a certain amount of professional experience and training.

Leave Your Shades Partially Open

A few hours before you jet off, twist your shades a touch so they show light through them. That way, your lights will be visible through windows at night, and the half-open vibe will give the impression that people are actually living in the house.

Lock All Your Windows and Doors

Duh, I know . . . but it's so easy to forget! This includes your garage if it can be locked.

Staying Comfy and Safe in Transit

Planning a trip and locking up your house can be tough enough, but if you have to fly to get where you're going, things get a lot more compli-

MG TIP: If you're stuck in your seat because the seat belt sign is on or serving carts are clogging up the aisle, do this in-seat stretch: Rest your right ankle on top of your left knee. Lean your whole body forward so you feel the stretch in your right hip. Switch and repeat.

MG TIP: *Always* get a seat assigned at the earliest opportunity when you book your tickets, even if it's an undesirable one. When it comes to overbooked flights, there is a big difference between having a specified seat and being told they'll have to assign one at the gate. When overbooked, most airlines will have to ask you to give up your seat and reward you with something in return—like a free ticket. Also, you then have the power to choose whether you feel like spending that extra day on vacation, or desperately need to get back for an important meeting. If you have no seat assigned, then airlines are less likely to give you any remuneration.

cated. From battling in-flight bloat to keeping your muscles from stiffening up, try these easy tricks to find some much-needed cabin comfort.

Beat the Bloat

Isn't it weird how your fingers, ankles, and joints swell to piggy proportions whenever you fly? The reason: Low pressure in the cabin causes the nitrogen gas in your body to expand. To outsmart any body stretching that takes place, wear loose-fitting clothing (think drawstring pants and cotton tops) plus shoes with removable insoles so your feet will be comfy even if they've swelled a size.

Take Stretch Breaks

It's scary to think about, but sitting on a five-hour-plus flight without standing up and stretching can contribute to blood clots in your legs. Make a deal with yourself that every half hour when the seat belt sign is off, you'll take a little walk. A great stretch: Grab your ankle and pull it straight back so your heel hits your butt, as if you were a flamingo. (But do keep a hand on a seat back so that you don't kick into someone's lap.) Switch legs and repeat.

Carbo-Load

Carbs are easier to digest than proteins in low-oxygen environments like airplanes, so nosh on pretzels, fruit, and bagels.

Keep Your Rx's at the Ready

Never put prescription meds in your luggage—if it gets lost you're screwed. It's smarter to keep them in your carry-on at all times, in their original containers even if they're big bulky bottles. It will help people who may need to know exactly what you're taking should there be any kind of emergency situation, and the bottles are designed to protect the medicine.

What to Do When You're Bumped Off a Flight

Grrr. There's absolutely nothing more annoying than having your perfect travel plans all mapped out . . . and then being told when you check into your gate that they're "terribly sorry . . . we're over-booked." Why you? Why?

Although most airlines only remunerate volunteers, no MG will just stand there meekly and say, "Okay! No problem!" But she won't throw a princess fit either. Instead, be a little more industrious and work those sugar lips. Explain how you are a loyal customer to said airline and you are disappointed. This delay is going to disrupt your schedule for the day—and you had important business where you're headed. Then say, in a sweet but firm voice, "I know you understand the inconvenience I'm being put through; I think it's more than rea-sonable for me to either get a complimentary domestic ticket or at least be bumped up to first class on the next available flight." By throwing out the more demanding request for the free ticket first (which the agent will likely refuse), the second request won't seem all that difficult to grant.

Prepare to recline a full 150 degrees in a plush leather seat and be served warm chocolate chip cookies and champagne. And don't you dare feel guilty about requesting an upgrade.

What Kind of Insurance Does an MG Really Need?

Your home, your car, your loved ones. Logic tells us that the more you safeguard them, the better off you'll be. But that's not necessarily true for your insurance. While being uninsured or underinsured could leave you facing huge bills or leave you unprotected from a nasty lawsuit, being overinsured means you're throwing money away. In other words, when it comes to finding a policy, bigger isn't always better. Here are the bare essentials you'll need:

MG TIP: Many airlines won't assign seats within forty-eight hours of flight time, so be sure to get one when you book, or as far in advance as possible. However, you can often get exit row and unas-signed seats if you arrive at the airport early enough.

MG TIP: Twelve of the fifty states (FL, HI, KS, KY, MA, MI, MN, NJ, NY, ND, PA, and UT . . . as well as Washington, DC) have some form of no-fault law. No-fault insurance requires both drivers to carry insurance for their own protection *and* places limitations on their ability to sue other drivers for damages. Your insurance company pays for your damages, and other drivers involved are covered by *their* insurance company no matter who was at fault. The downside is that no-fault insurance can be pricey, so be sure to shop around. Keep in mind that no state is purely no-fault. Most states use a combination of the no-fault system and the standard liability system, by allowing you to sue for noneconomic damages if the amount of these damages exceeds a specified threshold. A great reference for more in-depth information on no-fault laws is www.auto insuranceindepth.com.

Auto Insurance

People get into accidents faster than you can say, "Hey, watch it!" Each state has different requirements when it comes to insuring your car, but the bottom line is, you don't want to skimp on it. Shop around for insurance policies, and get quotes from at least three agencies. Also, ask for discounts. Some companies will give you a lower rate if you have airbags, antilock brakes, and automatic seat belts. Some will even lower your rate if you have a spotless driving record.

When you're buying insurance start with liability coverage. It pays for injuries, property damage, and legal bills if you're at fault in an accident. This type of coverage is mandatory in all but a handful of states. But those few states that don't require liability insurance still require that you prove you can pay specified amounts if you cause bodily or property injury while driving. Since it's impossible to predict just how much damage you might do in an accident, this is one place where it can pay in the long run to buy more coverage now.

Collision insurance will pay to repair your car in the event of an accident, but it's normally the most expensive component of your policy. A standard collision insurance policy will pay for any repairs up to the fair market value of your car. Keep in mind that this value can be significantly lower than the actual cost of replacing your car (or your loan balance). If your car is financed or leased, you will need to get gap insurance to reimburse you for the difference between what you owe and what the car is worth. You can estimate your car's value using www.edmunds.com or Kelley Blue Book at www.kbb.com. To lower your premium, choose a higher deductible (the amount you pay before the insurance kicks in) on your collision insurance (say, $500 or $1,000).

Homeowner's Insurance

You may be thinking, "Hey, I live in a safe area and try not to set my home on fire as much as possible," but skimping on homeowner's insurance (it can also be called hazard insurance) isn't an option. If you own a home, your mortgage company requires you to have it.

A typical policy usually covers up to half the value of your house, but experts say you should buy a policy that covers at least an additional 20 to 25 percent of your home. Also, if your possessions are worth more than 50 percent of the value of your home, you should have personal property coverage (and probably an alarm system!). In this day and age, it's also smart to elect for broader coverage in case of disasters like fire, flood, lightning, or wind damage.

So, the big question is, how much will you have to pay up? It's not a set rate—your policy depends on a number of factors:

- *What your home is made of:* For example, brick costs less to insure than wood-frame homes.

- *Where your home is located:* If you're in a heavy "fire" area, you may have to pay up, and the same typically goes for heavy flood and hurricane areas. But if your home is near a fire station, you'll likely pay less.

- *Security measures you've taken:* If you've installed a high-tech burglar and fire alarm, your premium will go down.

- *Your plumbing/electrical/heating systems.* The newer they are, the less you'll have to pay.

Renter's Insurance

The apartment may belong to your landlord, but all that stuff inside it—like the TV, DVD player, and computer—is all yours.

Renter's insurance will cover theft as well as fire and water damage that ruin your personal possessions. It will also cover you if any lawsuit-ripe mishaps happen under your roof—say, if a guest at one of your sangria-drenched shindigs walked into a sliding door. Liability coverage pays both the cost of defending you and any damage that the court rules you must pay. A typical policy costs between $150 and $300 per year, and normally gets you $30,000 or $35,000 for personal items and from $100,000 to $300,000 in liability coverage.

MG TIP: The best policies have a "guaranteed replacement" clause that will cover extras that are damaged in your home, such as moldings and wallpaper. Some insurance agencies call them HO-3s, but your agency may have a different term for this type of policy, so be sure to consult with your agent.

MG TIP: Remember that the "best" policies are not always the most expensive. For instance, you could live in a low-risk area and be needlessly paying more for an extensive policy, while someone else who lives in a high-risk area could be paying less for a standard policy (when really they should invest in a more extensive policy). The best policy will be one that suits your needs and gives you the most bang for your buck. Seek the advice of an insurance agent you trust to find the "best" policy for you.

MG TIP: Update your policy every time you make a home improvement.

MG TIP: As with auto insurance you can also lower the premium of your homeowner's insurance by upping your deductible. Most homeowner's deductibles are $250, but boost it to $500 and you can lower your premium by more than 10 percent.

MG TIP: Shop around for a company that sells homeowner's, car, and liability coverage—they'll often shave 5 to 15 percent off your premium if you piggyback and purchase two or more policies from them. Getting one big "umbrella" policy also allows you to have higher deductibles on some things because they're covered by other sections of the policy, which saves you money in the long run.

MG TIP: Extras extras extras. Often you can insure that bling and the new art that you've purchased under your homeowner's policy—but sometimes they are extra line items, so double-check that you're covered. The same goes for covering things like lost luggage while you're traveling or personal effects that are stolen from a hotel room. If you travel a lot, these are worth adding to your policy.

There are two types of renter's insurance you can purchase: replacement and actual cash value. Replacement value replaces the item with a new item of the same quality. Try to get this policy if you can. If you go with the other, "cash value" policy, if your three-year-old TV is stolen, you will only be covered for whatever it is worth *right now*, not for the cost of a brand-new boob tube.

Umbrella Policies for Liability Insurance

We've been talking about "liability insurance" in terms of homeowner's, renter's, and auto insurance. But sometimes those types of liability insurance don't cover you enough. That's why getting an umbrella policy is so important—it expands where your normal policies leave off (picture an umbrella shielding you from tons of raindrops called lawsuits). Let's say your car skids out of control, runs into your neighbor's prizewinning Great Dane, their parked car on the sidewalk, and into the side of their house. If you don't have enough to cover you (home and auto coverage is usually limited to between $100,000 and $300,000), you're looking at a big fat lawsuit from your friendly neighbors. But an umbrella policy will kick in after your other insurance runs dry (and can cover you for up to one million bucks). You should inquire with your current homeowner's insurance agency about upgrading to an umbrella policy, as most agencies will require that you receive your homeowner's and auto insurance from them before they will allow you to apply for an umbrella policy.

The other reason you want to have an umbrella policy is to protect you in court. Let's say you got into a minor fender bender, or a friend of a friend steps on broken glass in your house during a pool party. Sure, most people would be honest and only ask for medical coverage if necessary, but if the other party knows you've got bucks to spare, they'll come up with any excuse to make you to fork over as much as possible for damage and suffering ("My foot was so damaged I had to quit my job for a year."). And sometimes you are accused of doing something you're innocent of. Doesn't matter. You're going to have to pay for a lawyer to prove your innocence. Liability insurance will cover your legal expenses and court judgments (up to a predetermined amount). Usually, your insurance company will find a lawyer to defend you. Trust me, shelling out a few hundred more bucks per year will save you from having to pay thousands—even tens of thousands—in the event of an accident for which you might be liable.

Life Insurance

The biggest insurance policy a Modern Girl can get is one for her life—especially if she has dependents (a husband and/or a child). Basically, it's a policy that works like all the rest: You pay a certain amount each month or year (depending on the policy) and in return, those closest to you will be covered financially in the event of your death.

Some experts advise going for "term" life insurance rather than permanent life insurance. "Term" provides death benefits for a specified period—usually five, ten, or twenty years. For instance, you could purchase a term policy that would give your family a percentage of your income until your kids are out of college or your spouse is eligible for retirement. Meanwhile, permanent insurance stays in force as long as you live, pays a death benefit, and even accumulates a cash value. The catch: "permanent" can be more expensive. But it can pay off in the long run, depending on your age and state of health. Check out the Web life calculator at www.life-line.org to help you tabulate what kind and how much insurance you need.

Willing Yourself to Write a Will

I know you haven't been, uh, dying to try your hand at writing your will. In fact, 55 percent of us haven't. But as soon as you have more assets than you had in college (like a house, for example) finance experts recommend it. Why? Because if you die *sans* will, your home state divvies up your assets in a way that can lead to ugly lawsuits, confusion for your relatives, and the allocation of assets to people in your

MG TIP: Take an inventory of all your belongings when you first move into an apartment. For more general household and wardrobe items, just keep a general record of what you have, so that you can guestimate a value for them. For your more valuable items (furniture, electronics, art, expensive shoes, clothing, etc.), take photos and keep the photos in a place other than your apartment. Or better yet, narrate a video with descriptions and prices of items (keep a copy at a friend or relative's pad, too). Update your inventory annually to include new purchases. Also, save receipts on big-ticket items.

MG TIP: If you have some VIP items, such as jewelry or an expensive computer, you might want to get special riders to cover them. Your basic renter's insurance will have a limit on how much it will cover.

MG TIP: To contact the insurance department in your state, go to the Insurance Information Institute, (www.iii.org). The site will also give you detailed info on what insurance to have if you're twenty-something or a college student.

MG TIP: No matter what type of coverage you're shopping for—from life insurance to auto insurance—check out your carrier's rating. All reputable insurance companies are rated by independent financial rating services. You can access these ratings at most libraries or directly from the rating companies themselves, who may charge for their services. Standard and Poor's (877-772-5436; www.standardandpoors .com) and Moody's Investors Service (212-553-1653; www.moodys.com) are two of the best. Look for a rating of A or higher.

MG TIP: Although you may not need life insurance now, getting it early can often lock you into a better rate than when you're applying for it a decade or two later, when you are older.

family who may be ill-equipped to handle them. And the worst-case scenario: If there is no living dependent to pass your money on to, the government can pocket it all.

If you have small kids or plan to soon, a will is an absolute must. Not only will you be safeguarding their financial future, the will also allows you to spell out who their guardian will be, appoint a financial guardian (such as a bank), and indicate at what age your kids will inherit your assets. Without a will, your spouse will get custody of your children—but if both of you die at once and there is no will, the courts will decide who'll take care of them. A basic will should cost you less than $500 to set up, with or without a lawyer.

"Will Do" 1

Just signing your name on a piece of paper doesn't make a legal will. So make sure you take the time to cross the t's. When you're filling out the form, you'll want to have two witnesses who are recognized by a notary public.

"Will Do" 2

Allocate your assets by percentages rather than in dollars because the dollar value of your estate will fluctuate.

"Will Do" 3

Make sure to include a financial power of attorney and a medical power of attorney in your will. They let you delegate someone (your husband, your sister, your parents, and so on) to have the final say about your money or your health based on your wishes, should you become incapacitated (like how long to keep you on life support if you're in a coma). Depending on your state, this will involve signing a form called a Declaration of Preneed Guardian, as well as a Health Care Advance Directive. Make sure your doctor, lawyer, and close family member have copies. For more information go to www.uslivingwill registry.com.

"Will Do" 4

Think about creating a Revocable Living Trust as your will. A living trust is an arrangement in which you transfer ownership of your assets from yourself to the trust. It is called a living trust because it is created during the settlor's lifetime. The person who manages the trust is called the trustee (you can appoint yourself, a lawyer, or a trusted family member). That means you have complete control over your assets. And whereas most trusts are irrevocable (meaning that once you give your assets away, you can rarely get them back), a living trust lets you make changes whenever and however you want, should circumstances change in your family or your health. Besides giving you flexibility, it safeguards you from getting whipped by taxes. Let's say you're leaving your home to your child and are afraid of the estate taxes they will have to pay. You can state in your trust that you want to terminate your trust if the taxes mount to a point at which it isn't in your child's best interest to take on the inheritance. Another bonus: Assets are transferred to your beneficiary immediately after your death (with a regular will, it can take up to two years or longer). Also, because the trust is in your name, you won't be subject to legal fees from attorneys and court costs because they have no control over the living trust. Last, because your trust is guaranteed to be private, you are safeguarded from family members contesting the ways you've allocated assets (with a will, it's easy).

MG TIP: For more advice and the necessary forms, check out www.legalzoom.com or www.buildawill.com.

"Will Do" 5

Consider tax-free "gifting." While you're still alive, you're allowed to give away up to $14,000 per year to as many people as you like without paying a gift tax on it. Married couples can "gift split" and give up to $28,000 per year to each person they please. You're also able to give away up to $5.43 million to your spouse during your lifetime or after you pass away—without paying any federal gift or estate tax on it.

How to Save Someone's Life

It's not just about legally protecting the lives of the people you love—it's about keeping them safe, too. Of course it's a no-brainer to dial 911 when someone is in trouble. But seconds count when someone loses consciousness, so you have to act quickly—sometimes before help arrives. Brain damage can occur in as little time as four minutes without oxygen. What I recommend is to take a CPR (Cardiopulmonary Resuscitation) class at your local Red Cross chapter (find your local chapter at www.redcross.org/where/where.html) so that you have a basic knowledge of life-saving techniques.

If you feel hesitant to use the CPR techniques you learn in class on someone in need, remember this: There is a Good Samaritan law in effect to protect people who help in an emergency.

To get you acquainted with what you'll be learning in CPR class, here are some basic guidelines from the American Red Cross:

Check for Consciousness

If you can tell that the person is not injured, lightly tap the victim on the arm and yell, "Are you okay?" If you don't hear a response, call 911.

Think A-B-C: Airway, Breathing, Circulation

Here's how it breaks down:

- *Open the airway.* Kneel next to the victim, place one hand on the victim's forehead and gently tilt it back. At the same time, place the index and middle fingers of your other hand under the chin and lift to pull it forward.

- *Check for breathing.* As you're keeping the airway open, put your cheek near the victim's mouth and look, listen, and feel for breathing. Look at his or her chest to see if it's rising or falling, and listen and feel for breath against your cheek. If none of this happens it's time to do rescue breathing.

• *Rescue breathe.* Pinch the victim's nostrils shut with your thumb and forefinger. With your other hand, continue tilting up the chin to keep the airway open. Take a deep breath and place your mouth over the victim's, forming a tight seal. Give two full breaths, then check for signs of circulation such as normal breathing, coughing, or movement in response to the rescue breaths. If signs of circulation are there, continue to give rescue breaths until help arrives or the victim starts breathing on his or her own.

MG TIP: Do two breaths every fifteen seconds for an eight-year-old or older.

MG TIP: Remember this equation in your head: 4 x (15 chest compressions + 2 breaths).

• *Do chest compressions* If there are no signs of circulation, begin chest compressions. For adults, kneel next to the victim with your knees perpendicular to their rib cage and trace your fingers up the ribs to where they meet at the bottom of the breastbone (aka the sternum). If you are kneeling on the right side of the victim, place two fingers from your left hand on the tip of the breastbone and the heel of your right hand directly above your fingers. Now slip the two fingers away, and place your left hand on top of your right. Don't allow your fingers to touch the chest—they could damage the ribs. Straighten your arms, lock your elbows, and center your shoulders above your hands. Press down in a steady rhythm, using your body weight and keeping your elbows locked. The force from each thrust should go straight down onto the breastbone, pushing down 1.5 to 2 inches. It may help to count "one and two and three and four . . ." up to fifteen compressions. Give one downward thrust each time you say a number. Lift your weight (but not your hands) from the victim's chest each time you say "and." After fifteen compressions, open the airway with the head tilt and chin lift, and give two full, slow breaths, taking one breath in between. Repeat the fifteen compressions and two-breath cycle four times. Check for breathing and pulse again. If there's a pulse but no breathing, just do rescue breathing. If there is no breathing and no pulse, go back to your fifteen compression/two-breath cycle until help arrives.

Choking Versus Heart Attack

It's a beyond-scary thing to see someone (whether it's a loved one or a stranger) start to uncontrollably cough or gasp from chest pains. How do you know whether people are having a heart attack or if they swallowed something down the wrong pipe and need to have the Heimlich maneuver performed on them? They're probably having a heart attack and you should call 911 immediately if:

- They feel pressure, intense burning, tightness, aching, and a squeezing-crushing sensation in their chest

- They have pain radiating to their back/arms/shoulders/wrists/neck/jaw/teeth

- Other symptoms are: sweating, shortness of breath, nausea, vomiting, dizziness, total weakness, fainting, rapid or irregular heartbeat

- Their pain has lasted longer than three to five minutes or goes away and returns

The Heimlich Maneuver

MG TIP: If the victim loses consciousness, gently lower the person to the ground and call 911.

If you are certain the person is not having a heart attack but is choking on food or another object, call 911. In the meantime, there are measures you can take. Stand behind the victim and wrap your arms around his or her waist. If the person is standing, place one of your feet between the victim's feet so you can support the individual's body if he or she loses consciousness.

Step 1
Make a fist with one hand. Place the thumb side of your fist against the victim's abdomen, just above the navel but well below the sternum.

Step 2
Grasp your fist with the other hand. Give quick inward and upward thrusts. This may cause the object to pop out.

How to Save Your Own Life

Sometimes it's not other people who need saving—it's you. Sure, MGs are fearless and don't like anything getting in the way of doing what we've got to do, like driving or walking where we want, at whatever hour we want. But there's a difference between being fearless and not being safe. Keep these safety tips in mind the next time you're walking or driving alone:

MG TIP: If you are taking a car service like Uber (which I love) but are ever feeling nervous, take a picture of your driver as you get in and say your boyfriend always makes you text him, because he's overprotective. If for whatever reason he was thinking something sketchy, this might be a good deterrent.

Ladies, Prepare Your Weapons . . .

When you're in an unfamiliar situation, go ahead and take out your keys and hold them daggerlike between your fingers, or carry pepper spray. But what's more important to understand is that the keys have to be out and ready when you're walking to your car. Spend one second fiddling to get them out and your attacker will have the upper hand.

Don't Glue Your Cell to Your Ear

While opening up your cell phone and pretending to call your boyfriend can deter a potential attacker, blindly babbling to your friend isn't wise when you're walking alone. Why? When you're gabbing away on your phone, your defenses are down because you're distracted in conversation. Not only are you not looking at what's around you, you're not able to listen as clearly. If you absolutely must make a call, stay alert as to who's around you in a 360-degree radius.

Get Physical

When in doubt, go for the groin. Think about kicking your attacker all the way to his throat, via his groin. Another technique if your attacker has you in a headlock: Gouge his eyes in any way you can. Don't get caught up in feeling like he's the bad guy and you're the victim. You have to transform your mind-set in a split second from being the prey to being the predator. Your mantra should be, "You're attacking me? No, no, no, I'm attacking you."

LIFE SAVING APPS

Though apps come and go as quickly as my hair shades, there are some apps you should download for when the unexpected happens. And while I like to spend my life believing people and things are mostly good, Modern Girls should always be prepared.

1. **Guardly:** This app lets you instantly connect with friends and family in emergencies. With a few taps, you can dial for help or send out an alert, and triggering an alert enables real-time location tracking. On the app's map, you can see which friends and family members are close by. And one of my favorite features is that you can easily sound off a blaring siren to "deter would-be attackers" and "signal for help." Cost: Free with some in-app purchases.

2. **Circle of 6:** Though originally designed for college students, this app is great for any circle of friends. In an uncomfortable situation, you can discreetly send a group distress call. If you tap the phone icon, you'll send out a message that says, "Call and pretend you need me. I need an interruption." If you press the car button, you send out a text complete with your current GPS location. Your group gets your message to pick you up. For big emergencies, you can call 911 from within the app. There's also a chat icon with links to information online about sexual assault, relationships, and other issues. Cost: Free.

3. **MyForce:** If you live or work somewhere sketchy, or just get nervous when you're out alone, you might want to try MyForce. This subscription-based app is like having a personal body guard in your pocket. If you are sensing danger you tap the button and trigger a silent alarm, which connects you to an operator. Your call begins being recorded and your location begins to be tracked. If the monitoring operator determines it is an emergency she will contact 911 and your emergency contacts. Cost: $11.99 to $14.99 per month.

continued

4. **Smart-ICE4family:** Though I'd recommend this for everyone, it's particularly helpful if you have a complicated medical history. This app allows you to record your medical information, which will immediately play upon the opening of the app, so that no time is wasted. EMS and other medical professionals are trained to look for ICE on your phone (it stands for "In Case of Emergency"), and the app will also store who should be contacted as well as your family's information and your insurance information. It also has a "my location" button that quickly finds your current location to give to EMS dispatchers. Cost: $2.99.

5. **iTriage:** First, I always recommend calling 911 over DIY when it comes to any emergency, but if for some reason you can't (I watch a lot of bad TV, so I assume at some point I will deliver a baby and have to perform a tracheotomy) and you or your loved ones are hurt, sick, or injured, iTriage may help. It can also help you find a doctor, and you can store your medical history in the app. Cost: Free.

6. **SAS Survival Guide:** One of my very favorite books of all time is *The Survivors Club* by Ben Sherwood; it basically explains how to survive all kinds of disasters. It became my bible. I read it so many times you would have thought I was about to write *The Modern Girl's Guide to Everyday Disasters*. So let's just say that I like to be prepared. And since Sherwood didn't do an app, I had to dig around to find another great one; luckily I came upon SAS Survival Guide. While it won't help you with broken nails or sexting, like I do, it will help you be prepared for disasters such as a plane crash, car accident, tornado, or earthquake—even nuclear blasts are covered. Cost: $5.99.

The Emergency Kit Every MG Needs in Her Home

Being an adult is about being prepared for life's little catastrophes—whether it's being accosted on the street or dealing with one of Mother Nature's disasters. And I'm beyond embarrassed to admit this, but when my husband and I were in New York City (aptly during the August 2003 gigantic blackout), we were anything but prepared. In fact, I think we'd win the award for Dumbest Couple in a Disaster. Thankfully, our kids were safely ensconced with grandparents in well-powered Los Angeles.

Instead of worrying about the fact that we had no water, candles, or food for who knows how long, we popped open the one bottle of Veuve Clicquot in our fridge (hey, it was going to go flat, right?) and got blitzed. Then we took a long shower together (don't worry . . . I'm getting to my point). Well, an hour later the water shut off in my building. As in, can't-flush-the-toilet-or-brush-your-teeth-or-wash-your-hands shut off. And it stayed like that for two days, until the power came back on in our neighborhood. If only we had been a little better prepared, we wouldn't have been stinky, grimy, dehydrated, hungry, and flashlight-less. And here's the kicker: I found out later that you're supposed to fill your bathtub with water whenever there's a blackout, because you can use it for toilet flushing by pouring a bucket of water down the toilet to create a gravity flush. Well, there's always next time . . .

Here's a Modern Girl Emergency Kit that I should have had that fateful day—stock up yourself so you don't get caught unprepared like me. Store these supplies in a waterproof container:

- A flashlight and extra batteries
- Bottled water and canned/nonperishable food (and a can opener)
- A first aid kit
- A utility knife

- Candles with waterproof matches
- A garbage bag
- Moist towelettes
- Band-Aids
- Tampons
- Work gloves
- A heavy wool blanket
- Extra clothing
- A raincoat
- At least $200 cash
- Vital prescriptions (make sure you stay up to date)
- Emergency phone numbers
- Your insurance policy

Whew. Now that you're armed with all this info—from plumping up your anorexic bank account to tapping into your inner Katniss Everdeen in *The Hunger Games* when disaster strikes—I hope you're feeling pretty badass and prepared to take on the world. Don't worry if you screw up and forget half of what you've just read in these many pages. (Goodness knows I've had my blank-brained moments where I feel absolutely clueless . . . and I *wrote* the book.) But that's the beauty of having all this info at your fingertips. The real secret of being a Modern Girl isn't pretending to be a holier-than-thou super-woman who knows absolutely everything—it's about looking for those key strategies to make your life easier, richer, more workable for you. And I hope throughout these pages, I've paved the way for you to get there, whether that means being a domestic goddess, perfect hostess, stick-shift master, star CEO, stiletto survivor, legendary lover, golf pro, financial guru, lifesaver, or all of the above. Because with a few savvy shortcuts and a little help from her friends, a Modern Girl *can* have it all.

Bibliography

No gal knows everything, so I would like to thank the many friends, family, and experts who lent me their wisdom while I was researching this book. I would also like to extend thanks to the following books, authors, and websites for additional research:

Aslett, Don. *Don Aslett's Stainbuster's Bible: The Complete Guide to Spot Removal.* New York: Plume, 1990.

Bader, Dr. Myles H. *4001 Food Facts and Chef's Secrets.* Auburn: Mylin Enterprises, 1992.

Bamberger, Alan. *The Art of Buying Art.* Phoenix: Gordon's Art Reference, 2002.

Costa, Larry. *Massage Mind and Body.* New York: DK Publishing Inc., 2003.

Mendelson, Cheryl. *Home Comforts: The Art and Science of Keeping House.* New York: Scribner's, 1999.

Sidey, Ken, ed. *Complete Plumbing.* New York: Stanley Books, 2003.

Siler, Brooke. *The Pilates Body.* New York: Broadway Books, 2000.

Tuckerman, N., and Dunnan, N. *The Amy Vanderbilt Complete Book of Etiquette.* New York: Doubleday, 1995.

www.AAA.com The American Automotive website.

www.about.com A compendium of articles and links for everything under the sun.

www.ags.com The American Gem Society's official website.

www.answerbag.com A user-generated website with answers to all kinds of questions under the sun.

www.apple.com The official website for Apple Computers, iPods, etc.

www.askmen.com A men's lifestyle and sexuality online magazine.

www.autoinsuranceindepth.com   Everything you need to know about auto insurance.

www.babycenter.com   An online resource for new and expectant parents.

www.bankrate.com   Info on mortgage rates, credit cards, auto loans, and personal financial advice.

www.barbarak.com   Fix-it tools for women and how to use them.

www.baseballtips.com   Information on baseball and slang terms used in baseball.

www.broadartfoundation.org   An educational and lending resource for contemporary art.

www.choice.com   Australian Consumer Association website.

www.Cosmopolitan.com   The online home of *Cosmopolitan* magazine, the best-selling women's magazine worldwide.

www.cnnmoney.com   A comprehensive finance-oriented site by the editors of CNN and *Money* magazine.

www.consumerreports.com   Features ratings and recommendations on practically everything.

www.Dewars.com   The website of Dewar's scotch.

www.thediamondbuyinguide.com   An online guide to purchasing diamonds.

www.diynet.com   The do-it-yourself network, with tips on crafts, home improvements, and more.

www.dol.gov   The official site of the U.S. Department of Labor.

www.edmunds.com   New car prices, used car pricing, and Edmund's online car buying guide.

www.eeoc.gov   The official website of the U.S. Equal Opportunities Commission.

www.epicurious.com   The world's greatest recipe collection.

www.fanstop.com   Complete NFL, NBL, NHL, NBA, NCAA, and NASCAR sports coverage.

www.gia.org   The Gemological Institute of America.

www.hgtv.com   The online guide for the Home and Garden television channel.

www.howstuffworks.com   Practical info on everything from electronics to science to money to health.

www.hrblock.com   The website of H&R Block tax preparation services.

www.hsus.org   The Humane Society of the United States website.

www.intelihealth.com   Comprehensive health website featuring Harvard Medical School's consumer health information.

www.investorguide.com   The leading online guide to investing.

www.ivillage.com   Women's health, relationships, pregnancy/parenting tips, beauty, and more.

www.Jiffylube.com   The Jiffy Lube website with car maintenance tips.

www.kiplinger.com   Personal finance advice.

www.leaseguide.com   A consumer's guide to smart car leasing.

www.mannersmith.com   A website with fabulous etiquette tips.

www.meetmark.com   A beauty website.

www.mlb.com   The official site of Major League Baseball.

www.mochasofa.com   The website of the following magazines: styleathome.com, canadianliving.com, and homemakers.com.

www.moma.org   The official website of the Museum of Modern Art.

www.mortgage101.com   Everything you need to know about financing your dream home.

www.moveout.com   Tips on moving out plus moving supplies.

www.MSNBC.com   The MSNBC news website.

www.myfico.com   A division of Fair Issac with everything you need to know about your Fico score.

www.nba.com   The official website of the National Basketball Association.

www.nfl.com   The official website of the National Football League.

www.paint.org   The National Paint and Coatings Association website.

www.redcross.org   The official website of the American Red Cross.

www.scotchwhisky.com   A comprehensive online guide to scotch whisky and its history.

www.soyouwanna.com   A comprehensive site with easy-to-understand how-to tips on virtually everything.

www.techsoup.org   Technical website that offers great how-to tips and products.

www.toiletology.com   Everything you wanted to know about toilet care and repair but were afraid to ask.

www.usda.gov   The United States Department of Agriculture website.

www.usga.org   The official website of the United States Golf Association.

www.thevault.com   Infinite career information website, from résumé writing to interviewing tips.

www.webmd.com   Resource that provides services that help physicians, consumers, providers, and health plans navigate the complexity of the healthcare system.

www.winespectator.com   Website for the savvy wine magazine offering tips and information about wine and the magazine.

www.womanmotorist.com   Online consumer automotive magazine for women with information on buying, selling, and leasing cars, safety tips, and more.

Index